Census Substitutes
& State Census Records

Census Substitutes & State Census Records

An Annotated Bibliography of Published Name Lists for all 50 U.S. States and State Censuses for 37 States

by

William Dollarhide

Volume 1 – Eastern States

Family Roots Publishing Company
Bountiful, Utah

On the cover: The image on the computer screen comes from Ancestry.com's Kansas State Census Collection 1855-1915, and illustrates an 1875 enumeration page of families in Drywood Township, Bourbon County, Kansas. The various books and documents shown are the property of the publisher.

Published by Family Roots Publishing Co.
PO Box 830
Bountiful, UT 84011
www.familyrootspublishing.com

Library of Congress Control Number 2007939391
ISBN-13: 978-1-933194-37-0
ISBN-10: 1-933194-37-5

Printed in the United States of America

Books by William Dollarhide

Published by Genealogical Publishing Co., Inc., Baltimore, MD:
- *Map Guide to the U.S. Federal Censuses, 1790-1920*
  (with William Thorndale) (1987)
- *Managing a Genealogical Project* (1988)
- *Genealogy Starter Kit* (1993);
  also published with the title, *Getting Started in Genealogy* (2001)
- *Getting Started in Genealogy ONLINE* (2006)
- *New York State Censuses & Substitutes* (2006)

Published by Heritage Quest, North Salt Lake, UT:
- *Seven Steps to a Family Tree* (1995)
- *Map Guide to American Migration Routes, 1735-1815* (1997)
- *British Origins of American Colonists, 1629-1775* (1997)
- *America's Best Genealogy Resource Centers*
  (with Ronald A. Bremer) (1998)
- *The Census Book: A Genealogist's Guide to Federal Census Facts, Schedules, and Indexes* (1999)
- *Grow a Family Tree!* (2001)

Published by Family Roots Publishing Co., Bountiful, UT:
- *Census Substitutes & State Census Records* (2008)

Contents – Volumes 1 & 2

Contents – Continued:

State Finder – Volumes 1 & 2:

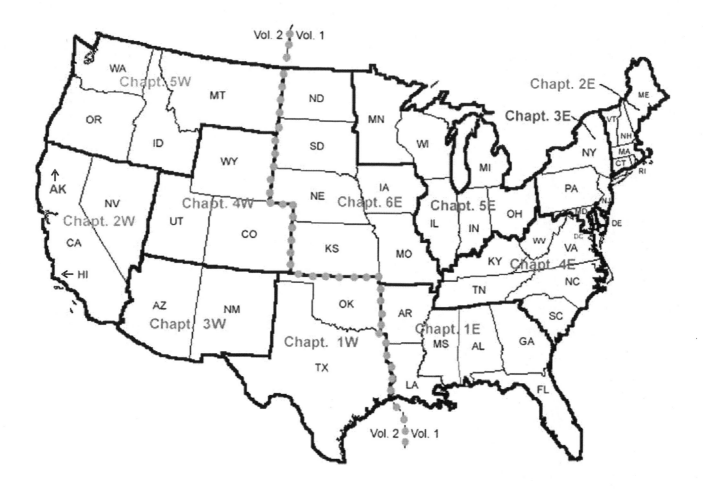

Foreword

by Leland K. Meitzler

In late 2003 Bill Dollarhide came by my office and asked if I had any ideas for *Genealogy Bulletin* articles. As it turned out, I had just finished organizing materials for a lecture on state and territorial census records and had a file folder full of data I had collected over the years on my desk. I suggested he put something together on that subject and gave him the file to review. After looking through my file, Bill decided that we needed to identify the many substitutes to censuses (statewide tax lists, voter registration lists, and such), as he quickly noted that a number of states didn't take any state or territorial censuses at all. Bill began compiling a bibliography of not only extant state and territorial censuses, but substitute lists as well.

Researched and compiled by region, he added timelines of historical references to show the jurisdictions in place at the time of each census. Compiling the material by region was a stroke of genius on Bill's part, as we quickly realized that in most cases, it would have been very difficult to write about one state without writing about those surrounding it. So you might note that this book starts with Alabama, does not move on alphabetically to Alaska, but deals with Arkansas instead!

Much of the data found herein was initially published in serial form in *Genealogy Bulletin*. That said, the District of Columbia, for which there are many excellent sources, was never published. However, it is included in this volume. Numerous online sources have been added, reflecting the ongoing efforts of both public and private companies to digitize genealogically relevant records. Name lists have been added. Bill also spent countless hours

compiling three charts that may be worth the cost of this book all by themselves. The first, found on page 5, is a chart for the non-state census states. There happens to be 14 of them (including the District of Columbia). This chart lists the states and the years covered by census substitutes recommended in this book, and its companion volume (covering the western states). The second chart, found on page 6, lists the 37 states that have extant colonial, pre-statehood, territorial, and state censuses, complete with the census year, as well as an indication if the census is available online as of the date of publication. The third chart, found on page 7, shows in graphic form the states that had censuses taken in common years – "on the fives." Census dates for some states are within a range, e.g., within 3 years of 1825, and indicated in the 1825 column. Another good example is the 1892 New York State census, indicated in the 1895 column.

You might note that the title of this volume is **Census Substitutes & State Census Records, Volume 1 – Eastern States.** This reflects the fact that the book is really a list of census substitutes, with state censuses turning out to be in the minority. Substitutes outnumber censuses by a factor of ten to one! However, the state censuses identified in this book, and its companion, **Census Substitutes & State Census Records, Volume 2 – Western States** are by far the most complete lists of Colonial, Territorial, and State Censuses published to date. The *Western States* book includes extensive never-before-published information on the Northwestern states of Oregon, Washington, Idaho, and Montana. It might also be noted that Bill did not use the Mississippi River as the line dividing Eastern and

Western states. He decided to include the Central Plains states of Iowa, Kansas, Missouri, Nebraska and the Dakotas in this volume. While it may seem logical to include this area in the *Western States* book, historic ties as well as page count dictated where the line dividing the volumes would be.

State and Territorial Censuses have long fascinated me. Many were taken in order to get congress to allow statehood. Some territories would take censuses on a nearly annual basis, in the attempt to show that they had the population base necessary to justify statehood.

Other states, like New York, had authorization of non-federal censuses written into their state constitutions. New York was one of the most prolific when it came to state censuses, as it produced numerous schedules, most falling on the ubiquitous "fives" as noted above. Today we have extant New York censuses for 1825, 1835, 1845, 1855, 1865, 1875, 1892, 1905, 1915, and 1925. Some of the early years are not complete, but what is available is certainly useful. The 1925 New York census was taken as well as any other, and the population returns are largely legible and complete. However, the census was wrought with scandal, leaving New Yorkers with a taste of bitterness for such things. To make a long story short, it seems that the New York Secretary of State, a former Dean of Home Economics at Syracuse University, Florence Elizabeth Smith Knapp, took nepotism to a whole new level. As the state official in charge of the 1925 census, she put family and friends on the payroll, and while this wasn't illegal, most of these folks did little or nothing to earn their salaries. Even her 74-year old mother, Ella Smith, enjoyed a non-working stint as an assistant supervisor. Florence's step-daughter, Clara Blanche Knapp, a professor at Middlebury College in Vermont, was on the payroll for over $5,000 in income, while never leaving the state of Vermont. Moreover, checks written to both Ella and Blanche seemed to have been endorsed into Florence E.S. Knapp's bank

account. Numerous other family members and friends were paid substantial sums for non-work. In 1928, Mrs. Knapp finally went on trial for her misdeeds, and found guilty of first-degree grand larceny for misappropriation of state funds. She served 30 days in the Albany Jail. She could have gotten 10 years. So ended the brief political career of the first woman ever to be elected to state-wide office in New York. So also ended the state censuses of New York State.

Iowa, Kansas, Rhode Island, Florida and North Dakota, South Dakota also took censuses up through 1925. South Dakota and Florida even took censuses in 1935 and 1945! The real value of state censuses is found in the numerous schedules enumerated in the mid-nineteenth century. Thirty-seven states took non-federal censuses that are still extant today.

And then there are the substitutes. They are of prime importance, since 13 states, as well as the District of Columbia, took no state censuses at all. And even if your ancestors lived in a state where censuses were taken "on the fives," census substitutes are helpful, especially if the family was on the move.

Although Mr. Dollarhide has used all kinds of substitutes throughout this volume, more attention has been given to tax lists, voter registration rolls, vital records, directories, statewide probate indexes, land records, and even military censuses, than most others. These records are often easily accessible and using this guide, you will be able to quickly find them for your own use. You are in for a treat, so sit back and look up the states of your ancestors. You will find information on records you never knew existed. Then... go get the records, and happy hunting!

Leland K. Meitzler
Publisher

Introduction

Census Substitutes & State Census Records

Census Substitutes are those name lists derived from tax lists, directories, military lists, land ownership lists, voter registrations, and other compilations of names of residents for an entire state, one or more counties of a state, or one or more towns of a county. A census substitute can be used to determine the names of residents in a given area when a federal or state census is missing. Moreover, a census substitute can be used as an alternative name list; confirming, contradicting, or adding to information found in a federal or state census.

This book identifies at least ten times the number of Census Substitute titles than any previous work ever published. All states are represented with significant alternative name lists – name lists that stop time for a certain year and place, and name the residents of a certain place. Since all of these name lists are specific to a certain year, they are listed for each state in chronological order. Incorporated into the lists are any **State Census** titles – a reference to a state census taken for a specific year.

Federal vs. State Censuses

Federal Censuses have their origins in the constitutional provision for apportionment of the U.S. House of Representatives. The first federal census was taken in 1790, and beginning about the same time, state censuses were conducted for the same reason, that is, apportionment of the various state legislatures.

Although the primary purpose of all censuses was to simply count the population, beginning with the first federal census of 1790, more information than a simple tally was added. This included the name and age of a person and progressively more details about a household for each subsequent census year. State censuses followed this same pattern.

State censuses usually add even more information than the federal censuses, and as a result, they are premier genealogical resources. Except in cases where a federal census is lost, state census records are not substitutes for the federal censuses – state censuses were almost always taken between federal census years, and usually add unique information and details about a household not found in a federal census. If a state census exists between federal census years, it may add marginally to the knowledge one gains about a family. But, more often, it will add critical information, such as more exact dates of birth, marriages, deaths; plus additional children, different residences, other relatives living with a family; and more.

Non-State Census States

Fourteen (14) states (including DC) have never conducted a state-sponsored census. For these **Non-State Census States**, this review attempts to identify as many census substitutes as possible. In some cases, the census substitutes are for a single county within a state, and by listing multiple county name lists for about the same time period, regional coverage is achieved.

For an overview of the Non-State Census States, see **Table 1** (page 5) showing the years for which census substitutes exist. More detail for each census substitute year indicated on the table is covered in the bibliographic sections.

State Census States

Thirty-seven (37) states have conducted censuses separate from the federal censuses. The number of censuses taken by each of the **State Census States** ranges from one (1) census year, e.g., the 1852 California; to twenty-four (24) census years, e.g., the 1792-1866 Mississippi territorial/state censuses. For this review, all of the state-sponsored censuses are identified, plus, to a lesser degree than the non-state census states, any census substitutes available. See **Table 2** (page 6) for an overview of the State Census States, the year for each surviving census for a state; and an indication of which specific years are now available online as digitized databases.

Locating the Extant State Census Records

Generally, state censuses were conducted from the time of territorial status or early statehood up until about 1905, but a few continued until 1925, 1935, or 1945. The last state censuses taken by any of the states was in 1945 (Florida and South Dakota). Due to budget restraints, the Depression Era of the 1930s was a contributing factor to states ending their census-taking endeavors. Eventually, all states of the Union stopped using the population figures from state censuses, and began using the federal census figures for apportionment of their state legislatures.

While the surviving federal census manuscripts are all located mostly in one repository (the National Archives), state census manuscripts are spread across the country in the

various state archives or local repositories. The accessibility of state censuses may be just as good as federal censuses – but one needs to know where they are located first.

Beginning in 1941, the U.S. Bureau of the Census issued a bibliographic report identifying all known state censuses, those undertaken by the various states separate from the federal censuses since 1790.[1] Prepared by Henry J. Dubester of the Library of Congress, the report was the first known attempt to research all of the state constitutions and subsequent laws related to state censuses for all of the states. The Dubester report sought, first, to identify what state censuses had ever been authorized by a state constitution or legislature; and second, to identify what census manuscripts still survive. The identification of extant state censuses was very incomplete, due to the war and under-funding of the project.

However, Dubester's review of each state's constitutional provisions for taking state censuses still stands as the best overview of what state censuses were ever authorized. The report cites the specific articles of the state constitutions or the actual state laws relating to censuses for all states.

Unfortunately, the fact that a state legislature authorized a state census does not mean one was actually taken. For example, the State Constitution of California of 1849 authorized a census in the years 1852 and 1855 and each ten years thereafter, all for the purpose of apportionment of its state legislature. Yet, only one was ever taken, that for 1852. Later, the California Constitution of 1879 provided that the decennial national census serve as the basis for legislative apportionment.[2]

This was fairly typical of all states. Even in those states for which several decades of state censuses now survive, they eventually got out of the census business, turning to the federal decennial censuses to determine apportionment. For example, New York took state censuses from 1825 and every ten years thereafter until 1925, yet, in 1938, New York decided to use the federal decennial censuses thereafter.[3]

Since the Dubester report, there have been several attempts to list all known state censuses, where they are located, and the contents of the census name lists. All of these attempts differ dramatically, because some of the lists rely on the Dubester report, which may have been accurate in identifying which state censuses were ever authorized, but was not nearly complete in identifying the extant manuscripts of state census records. For example, Table 4-8 of *The Source*,[4] seems to use the census years cited in the Dubester report for "authorized state censuses" rather than those actually extant. There are lists of state censuses for each state in *The Red Book*,[5] but are only a slight improvement over those found in *The Source*. And, several Internet sites offer lists of state censuses, all of which seem to take data previously published in the *Source* or *The Red Book*, and similar publications.

Based on survey results from all states, the Family History Library prepared a two-volume publication, *U.S. State and Special Census Register: A Listing of Family History Library Microfilm Numbers,* compiled by G. Eileen Buckway and Fred Adams, a revised edition published by the FHL in 1992 (FHL book 973 X2 v. 1 & 2, and fiche #6104851 (vol. 1) and #6104852 (vol. 2). This is a very good guide to military censuses, school censuses, and special censuses of American Indian tribes. As a guide to state censuses, however, the list is incomplete. Since the results of the surveys from each of the states were only partially successful, there are many omissions.

Clearly, the best list of state censuses to date is Ann S. Lainhart, *State Census Records,* published by Genealogical Publishing Co., Inc., Baltimore, in 1992. The book identifies state censuses in 43 states, including 6 states without

state censuses (but have major state-wide census substitutes available). For the 37 state census states, the lists generally do not include colonial or pre-territorial censuses. With a few exceptions, census substitutes such as those compiled from tax lists, voter registration lists, military lists, or other name sources, are also not included. Still, Lainhart's book stands as the most complete list ever done.

At the time when most of the previous state census lists were put together, there were some research tools unavailable to the authors. Today, the Internet as a resource for finding place-specific records is overwhelming – there are more ways to creatively seek keywords, subjects, places, etc., than most of us have thought of yet. And, special tools such as the Periodical Source Index (PERSI)[6] which indexes articles in over 6,500 different genealogical periodicals (by subject, place, and surname) gives a big boost to the task of finding references to relevant articles using keywords such as "state census," "territorial census," or "tax list." In addition, the State Archives and/or State Libraries where obscure census originals and substitute name lists reside often have a website with an online searchable catalog.

For any genealogical research project, it helps to be close to the Family History Library (FHL) in Salt Lake City. But from any place where a researcher has access to the Internet, the Family Search™ online catalog as a genealogical research tool has no equal. Searching for state censuses and census substitutes in the FHL catalog will not bring up every extant resource, but it is estimated that at least 90% of everything published is there.

Expanding the scope to include census substitutes of tax lists, voter registration lists, military lists, etc., the number of name lists increases by a factor of at least ten.

For this nationwide review, we decided to start with the areas of the United States that had the earliest census/name list records. That meant moving from the East Coast to the West Coast. The first chapter is for Census Substitutes and State Censuses available for the states of Alabama, Arkansas, Florida, Georgia, Louisiana, and Mississippi. This area could be called "The Old Southwest," and since the settlements beginning in St. Augustine, Mobile, Pensacola, Natchez, and New Orleans were the earliest in North America, this region is where the earliest census/name lists were created. The Old Southwest has gone through several jurisdiction changes under control of the Spanish, French, English, and Americans. To reflect these changes, a timeline for the region was prepared to put the area into historical perspective. This grouping of states and a common timeline for each group was continued for all eleven chapters.

As a bibliography of census substitutes and state censuses, references to the location of schedules and indexes to the federal censuses, 1790-1930, are generally not included. The exceptions are those lists of state and federal censuses using a combined index, such as those found at **www.ancestry.com**, **www.census finder.com/** or **www.census-online.com**. Federal censuses may also be mentioned in the chronological timelines or bibliographic lists, to assist in locating census substitutes for a missing federal census year. For several of the western states, federal censuses are included to fill in the lack of state censuses and substitutes. In the case of lost federal censuses which have been reconstructed for a state or part of a state, any book titles or articles that could be found are included.

For those who want to review the federal censuses in more detail along with these substitutes and state census lists, refer to *The Census Book*[7] to see population figures, maps of the U.S. for each census year, and a review of published federal census indexes.

The maps of the changing county boundaries for all of the states shown in *Map Guide to the U.S. Federal Census, 1790-1920*[8] should also be helpful for reviewing substitute or state census years between federal census years.

Notes:

1. *State Censuses: An Annotated Bibliography of Censuses of Population Taken After the Year 1790 by States and Territories of the United States*, prepared by Henry J. Dubester, Chief, Census Library Project, Library of Congress, published Washington, DC, by United States Department of Commerce, Bureau of the Census, 1941, rev. 1948.

2. Dubester, *State Censuses*, p. 3.

3. Dubester, *State Censuses*, p. 50.

4. *The Source: A Guidebook of American Genealogy*, first edition, edited by Arlene Eakle and Johni Cerny, published by Ancestry, Inc., Salt Lake City, 1984.

5. *The Red Book: American State, County & Town Sources*, edited by Alice Eichholz, rev. ed., published by Ancestry, Inc., Salt Lake City, UT, 1992.

6. Allen County Public Library, *Periodical Source Index*, updated semi-annually. [database online] Provo, UT: Ancestry.com, 1998- . Original data: Allen County Public Library. Periodical Source Index, Fort Wayne, IN: Allen County Public Library Foundation, 1985- .

7. *The Census Book: A Genealogist's Guide to Federal Census Facts, Schedules and Indexes*, by William Dollarhide, published by Heritage Quest, North Salt Lake, UT, 2000. A PDF file of the entire book is available for downloading at the Heritage Quest website at **www.heritagequestonline.com/ prod/genealogy/html/help/census_book.html**

8. *Map Guide to the U.S. Federal Censuses, 1790-1920*, by William Thorndale and William Dollarhide, published by Genealogical Publishing Co., Inc., Baltimore, 1987-2005.

Table 1 – Non-State Census States • 5

Table 1 – Non-State Census States. The following 14 states (including DC) have never conducted a state-sponsored census (or no state census survives). Census Substitutes for each state are shown for a range of years. Refer to the bibliographic listings for details about each.

State	Terr.	State	Years for which Census Substitutes are Available
Alaska	1912	1959	1870, 1873, 1878, 1885, 1887, 1890-1895, 1902-1912, 1905, 1908-1914, 1910- 1929, 1913-1916, 1917-1918, 1947, 1950, 1959-1986, and 1960-1985.
Connecticut	—	1788	1636-1670, 1688-1709, 1710-1711, 1756-1774, 1790-1850, 1799- 1838, 1845-1853, 1862-1866, 1883-1886, 1905-1929, 1913-1928, and 1917-1980.
Delaware	—	1787	1609-1888, 1646-1679, 1680-1934, 1682-1759, 1684-1693, 1726, 1755, 1759, 1779, 1782, 1785, 1790, 1800, 1807, 1850-1860, and 1862-1872.
District of Columbia	—	1791	1803, 1807, 1818, 1867, 1878, 1885, 1888, 1894, 1897, 1905-1909, 1912-1913, 1915, 1917, 1919, and 1925.
Idaho	1863	1890	1863, 1865-1874, 1871-1881, 1880, 1890, 1911-1937, 1911-1950, and 1930.
Kentucky	—	1792	1773-1780, 1774-1796, 1780-1909, 1781-1839, 1782-1787, 1782-1875, 1787, 1787-1811, 1787-1875, 1788-1875, 1789-1882, 1792-1830, 1792-1913, 1792-1796, 1793-1836, 1794-1805, 1794-1817, 1795, 1796-1808, 1797-1866, 1800, 1820-1900, 1851-1900, 1859-1860, 1860-1936, 1861-1865, 1862-1866, and 1895- 1896.
Montana	1864	1889	1860, 1856-1993, 1864-1872, 1868-1869, 1868-1929, 1870, 1880, 1870-1957, 1872- 1900, 1879-1880, 1881-1928, 1881-2000, 1891-1929, 1894, 1913, 1906- 1917, 1909- 1910, 1917-1918, 1921, and 1930-1975.
New Hampshire	—	1788	1648, 1709. 1723, 1736, 1740, 1763, 1767, 1775, 1776, 1779, 1789, 1795-1816, 1797, 1802, 1803, 1821, 1826, 1833, 1836, 1838, 1849, 1855 & 1865 MA, 1860, 1862-1866, 1903, and 1902-1921
Ohio	1787	1803	1787-1840, 1787-1871, 1788-1799, 1788-1820, 1790, 1800-1803, 1801-1814, 1801-1824, 1802, 1803-1827, 1804, 1807, 1810, 1812, 1816-1838, 1816-1838, 1825, 1827, 1832-1850, 1833-1994, 1835, 1846-1880, 1851-1900, 1851-1907, and 1907.
Pennsylvania	—	1787	1682-1950, 1759, 1680-1938, 1680s-1900s, 1760s-1790s, 1700s, 1780, 1798, 1740- 1900, 1887-1893, and 1870.
Texas	—	1845	1736-1838, 1700s-1800s, 1756-1830s, 1782-1836, 1809-1836, 1814-1909, 1821-1846, 1826, 1826-1835, 1820s-1846, 1820-1829, 1826-1836, 1829-1836, 1830-1839, 1835, 1835-1846, 1836, 1836-1935, 1837-1859, 1840-1849, 1840, 1846, 1837-1910, 1851-1900, 1858, 1861-1865, 1863, 1865-1866, 1867, 1874, 1882-1895, 1884, 1889-1894, 1890, 1914, 1917-1918, 1896-1948, and 1964-1968.
Vermont	—	1791	1770s-1780s, 1700s-1800s, 1654-1800, 1710-1753, 1721-1800, 1770-1832, 1771, 1782, 1788, 1793, 1796-1959, 1800s-1870, 1807, 1813, 1815, 1816, 1827-1833, 1828, 1832, 1843, 1852-1959, 1855-1860, 1861-1866, 1865, 1869, 1871-1908, 1874, 1880-1881, 1881-1882, 1882-1883, 1883-1884, 1884, 1887-1888, 1888, 1889, and 1895-1924.
Virginia	—	1788	1600s-1700s, 1600s, 1619-1930, 1623-1990, 1623-1800, 1632-1800, 1654-1800, 1704-1705, 1720, 1736-1820, 1740, 1744-1890, 1760, 1769-1800, 1779, 1779-1978, 1779-1860, 1782-1785, 1785, 1787, 1809-1848, 1810, 1815, 1828-1938, 1835, 1835-1941, 1840, 1861, 1861-1865, 1852, 1853-1896, and 1889-1890.
West Virginia	—	1863	1600s-1900s, 1777-1850, 1787, 1782-1907, 1782-1850, 1782-1860, 1782, 1783-1900, 1783-1850, 1785-1850, 1787,1850, 1789-1850, 1792-1850, 1797-1899, 1797-1851, 1799-1850, 1800, 1801-1850, 1810, 1811-1850, 1862-1866, 1863-1900, and 1899-1900.

From *Census Substitutes & State Census Records* by William Dollarhide, published by Family Roots Publishing Co., Bountiful, UT

Table 2 – State Census States. The following 37 states have extant censuses available, including colonial, pre-statehood, territorial, and state censuses.

State	Year a Terr.	Year a State	Years for which State Censuses are available (underlined years, [e.g., 1814] indicates an online database is available)	Notes
Alabama	1817	1819	Colonial: 1706-1796. Terr.: 1816*, 1818; State: 1820**, 1821, 1823, 1832, 1838, 1844, 1850**, 1855, 1866	* as part of MS Terr. ** separate from federal.
Arizona	1863	1912	1864, 1866. County voter registrations are good substitutes.	
Arkansas	1819	1836	French/Spanish Colonial: 1686-1791; Territory: 1814*, 1823, 1827, 1829, 1833, 1835; State: 1838, 1854, 1865	* as part of MO Terr.
California	—	1850	Spanish: 1790. State: 1852 only. Countywide Great Registers are good substitutes.	
Colorado	1861	1876	1861, 1866*, 1885	* 2 counties only
Florida	1822	1845	1825, 1840*, 1855, 1875, 1885, 1895, 1925, 1935, 1945.	* Military census
Georgia	—	1788	1800 federal*, Partial lists for 1827, 1838, 1845, 1852, 1859, 1879, 1890 federal**, 1890 (statewide, reconstructed).	* Oglethorpe Co only ** Washington Co only
Hawaii	1900	1959	Kingdom of Hawaii: 1840-1866, 1878, 1890, 1896	
Illinois	1809	1818	1810, 1818, 1820*, 1825, 1830*, 1835, 1840*, 1845, 1855, 1865.	* separate from federal
Indiana	1800	1816	1807. A few townships only:* 1857, 1871, 1877, 1883, 1889, 1901, 1913, 1919, 1931.	* IN State Library only
Iowa	1838	1846	1836*, 1838, 1847, 1849, 1854, 1856, 1859, 1873, 1875, 1885, 1895, 1905, 1915, 1925	* as part of WI Terr.
Kansas	1854	1861	1855, 1856, 1857, 1858, 1859, 1865, 1875, 1885, 1895, 1905, 1915, 1925	
Louisiana	1809	1812	1804, 1833, 1837, 1890 federal*	* Ascension Parish only
Maine	—	1820	1837 only. Published Town records are good substitutes.	
Maryland	—	1788	1776, 1778, 1783 (tax list)	
Massachusetts	—	1788	1855, 1865	
Michigan	1805	1837	1836, 1837, 1845, 1854, 1864, 1874, 1884, 1894	
Minnesota	1849	1858	1849, 1853, 1855, 1857*, 1865, 1875, 1885, 1895, 1905.	* federal census.
Mississippi	1798	1817	1792, 1801, 1805, 1809, 1810, 1813, 1815-1817, 1816, 1818, 1820*, 1822, 1823, 1824, 1825, 1830*, 1837, 1840*, 1841, 1845, 1850*, 1853, 1857, 1866	* separate from federal
Missouri	1805	1821	1844, 1845, 1846, 1852, 1856, 1864, 1868, 1876	
Nebraska	1854	1867	1854, 1855, 1856, 1865, 1869, 1874, 1875, 1876, 1877, 1878, 1879, 1882, 1883, 1884.	
Nevada	1861	1864	1861, 1862, 1863, 1864, 1875, 1870-1920* (full extraction//index, all federal censuses).	* NV State Archives
New Jersey	—	1787	1855, 1865, 1875*, 1885, 1895, 1905, 1915.	* a few townships only
New Mexico	1850	1912	Spanish: 1600. Terr/State: 1885 only. County voter registrations are good substitutes.	
New York	—	1788	1825, 1835, 1845, 1855, 1865, 1875, 1892, 1905, 1915, 1925.	
North Carolina	—	1789	1784-1787. County tax lists are good substitutes.	
North Dakota	1861*	1889	1885*, 1905 (statistics only), 1915, 1925.	* Dakota Territory
Oklahoma	1890	1907	1890*, 1907 federal (Seminole Co. only)	* separate from federal
Oregon	1848	1859	OR Prov. Terr.: 1842, 1843, 1844, 1846; OR Terr.:1849, 1853, 1854, 1855, 1856, 1857, 1858, 1859. OR State: 1865*, 1875*, 1885*, 1895*, 1905	* indexes for a few counties only
Rhode Island	—	1790	1865, 1875, 1885, 1905, 1915, 1925, 1935.	
South Carolina	—	1788	1829, 1839, 1869, 1875.	
South Dakota	1861*	1889	1885*, 1895, 1905, 1915, 1925, 1935, 1945.	* Dakota Territory
Tennessee	1790	1796	1790 reconstructed, 1891 males over 21 (partial)	
Utah	1850	1896	1856 only. LDS member censuses, 1914-1960, are good substitutes.	
Washington	1853	1889	1851*, 1856, 1857, 1858, 1859, 1861, 1871, 1879, 1881, 1883, 1885, 1887, 1889, 1892, 1894.	* As part of OR Terr.
Wisconsin	1836	1848	1836, 1838, 1842, 1846, 1847, 1855, 1865, 1875, 1885, 1895, 1905	
Wyoming	1868	1890	1869 only. Statewide directories are good substitutes.	

From *Census Substitutes & State Census Records* by William Dollarhide, published by Family Roots Publishing Co., Bountiful, UT

Table 3 – State Censuses Taken in Common Years   • 7

Table 3 – State Censuses Taken in Common Years. As a means of comparing state censuses taken by the 37 state census states, this table shows the common years for which many states conducted a state census. Many were done in years ending in "5." Census dates for some states are within a range, e.g., within 3 years of 1825, are indicated in the 1825 column.

	1815	1825	1835	1845	1855	1865	1875	1885	1895	1905	1915	1925	1935	1945
Alabama	•	•	•	•	•	•								
Arizona						•								
Arkansas	•	•	•		•	•								
California					•									
Colorado							•	•						
Florida		•			•		•	•	•			•	•	•
Georgia		•	•	•	•		•							
Hawaii					•		•	•	•					
Illinois		•	•	•	•									
Indiana														
Iowa				•	•	•	•	•	•	•	•	•		
Kansas					•	•	•	•	•	•	•	•		
Louisiana			•											
Maine			•											
Maryland														
Massachusetts					•	•								
Michigan			•	•	•	•	•	•	•					
Minnesota					•	•	•	•	•	•	•			
Mississippi	•	•	•	•	•	•								
Missouri					•	•	•	•						
Nebraska					•	•	•	•						
Nevada						•	•							
New Jersey					•	•	•	•	•	•	•			
New Mexico								•						
New York		•	•	•	•	•	•		•	•	•	•		
No. Carolina														
No. Dakota								•			•	•	•	
Oklahoma										•	•			
Oregon				•	•	•	•	•	•	•				
Rhode Island						•	•	•	•	•	•	•	•	
So. Carolina		•	•			•	•							
So. Dakota								•	•	•	•	•	•	•
Tennessee									•					
Utah					•									
Washington					•	•	•	•	•					
Wisconsin			•			•	•	•	•	•	•			
Wyoming						•								
No. of States:	3	8	12	11	20	20	17	15	15	11	7	7	3	2

From *Census Substitutes & State Census Records* by William Dollarhide, published by Family Roots Publishing Co., Bountiful, UT

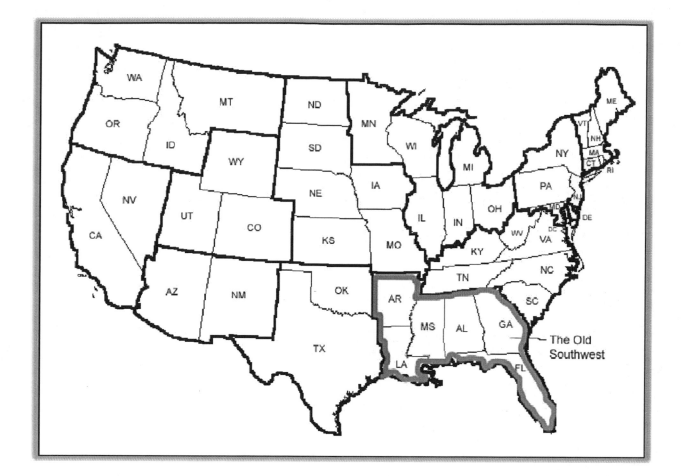

The Old Southwest

Chapter 1E – The Old Southwest

Alabama, Arkansas, Florida, Georgia, Louisiana, and Mississippi

Timeline of Census Jurisdictions

For an understanding of censuses, when they may have been taken, and who was in charge, here is a timeline of historic jurisdictions prior to statehood relating to the states of **Alabama, Arkansas, Florida, Georgia, Louisiana**, and **Mississippi**.

1513 Florida. Spaniard Ponce de Leon explores and names Florida (Pascua Florida, after the Feast of Flowers). The fountain of youth he was looking for did not happen until Disney World arrived 458 years later.

1526 Georgia. Possibly the first colony on mainland America was established by Spaniard Lucas Vazques de Ayllon, believed to be on Georgia's Sapelo Island. This piece of history is in all of Georgia's high school history books, but not Florida's.

1539 Florida. Spaniard Hernando De Soto, who thought he had discovered the Pacific Ocean, landed on Florida's West Coast, near Cape Coral, traveled inland towards Tampa Bay and then further north to present-day Tallahassee. Looking for gold, he left Florida disappointed.

1565 Florida. First colony founded at St. Augustine Bay founded by the Spanish. Although sacked, burned, pillaged, and generally not treated very well by the French or English, St. Augustine is still considered the first permanent settlement in America.

1586 Florida. British seafarer, Sir Francis Drake, raids and burns St. Augustine, but the fort is rebuilt again by the Spanish soon after, along with several more missions in Florida over the next century.

1682 Louisiana. French explorers Cavalier and LaSalle erected a cross near the confluence of the Mississippi River and the Gulf of Mexico, after floating down the river from the Great Lakes. They claimed the entire Mississippi basin for Louis XIV of France, for whom Louisiana was named.

1686 Arkansas. A son of an expatriated Italian, French soldier/trader Henri deTonti founded Arkansas Post, near the point where the Arkansas River joins the Mississippi. Arkansas Post was the first white settlement in the Lower Mississippi River Valley. DeTonti, who accompanied LaSalle in several explorations of the Mississippi Valley, was to later build a fort on the Yazoo River, now Mississippi, and was known to have explored Texas, all before 1700. deTonti spoke Texan, but with a heavy French accent.

1698 Florida. Pensacola founded by the Spanish. It did not become the name of a TV show for several years.

1699 Mississippi. The French established the first settlement on Biloxi Bay at Old Biloxi (now Ocean Springs). New Biloxi, founded in 1719,

was the capital of French Louisiana until 1722, when New Orleans replaced it.

1702 Alabama. Mobile founded by the French. Since then, Mobile's six flags were French, Spanish, English, U.S., Confederate, and U.S. again.

1716 Mississippi. Natchez, founded by the French, is the oldest city on the Mississippi River.

1718 Louisiana. New Orleans founded by the French. Jazz came a few years later.

1719 Florida Panhandle. The French capture Pensacola and about the same time occupy all of the gulf ports west to New Orleans, but as a result of an alliance with Spain against England, the French soon return Pensacola to Spain.

1733 Georgia. Although earlier grants were made for the area of Georgia, in 1732, Englishman James Oglelthorpe and his associates received a Royal Charter from George II. In January 1733 Oglethorpe transported the first English settlers to Georgia and Savannah. Like other colonies on the Atlantic coast, the language of the Royal Charter included all land "sea to sea," which meant that Georgia claimed land from Savannah to San Diego. Georgia was the 13th British colony from which the United States was formed, 126 years after the Jamestown colony of Virginia of 1607.

1755 Louisiana. Resulting from the war between France and England, France ceded to Britain its claim to that portion of Louisiana east of the Mississippi, except for New Orleans.

1763 Treaty of Paris. Until this year, many cross-claims to territory in the New World existed between the French, English and Spanish, and it took a war to settle the issue of land ownership in North America. In Europe it was called the Seven Years War, but in North America it was called the French and Indian War. France was the loser, and at the 1763 Treaty of Paris ending the war, the English gained undisputed title to Nova Scotia, Upper and Lower Canada, the thirteen America colonies, and all other lands east of the Mississippi River. Spanish lands were recognized as those west of the Mississippi. France was divested of its large North American claims, including New Orleans and Mobile, but continued to support a few settlements along the St. Lawrence River. Before 1763, the British had grandiose western claims based on Royal Charters of its Atlantic colonies using the words "sea to sea." In the Treaty of 1763, the British modified their western claims to end at the Mississippi River. At this time, the British claims included the area of present-day Georgia, Alabama, Mississippi, and Louisiana east of the Mississippi, all based on Georgia's 1732 Royal Charter.

1763 Florida. By separate treaty, the Spanish ransomed Florida to the British in exchange for Cuba. The British immediately divided the territory into East Florida and West Florida with the Chattahoochee River as the dividing line.

1780-1783 Florida. During the Revolutionary War, the British hold on East and West Florida came to an end. With the Spanish as allies of the French, the British lost West Florida to Spanish forces, who captured Mobile in 1780 and Pensacola in 1781. The British then returned East Florida to Spain in 1783, causing many American loyalists who had fled the Revolutionary War to St. Augustine to flee again, this time heading for the Bahamas or West Indies.

1783 United States of America. The treaty of Paris of 1783 first recognized the United States as an independent nation. Its borders were described generally from the Atlantic Ocean to the Mississippi River, and from Maine to Georgia. However, the northern third of Maine was not included; nor was East Florida or West

Florida south of Latitude 31º.

1783 Florida, Alabama, Mississippi. Spain successfully continued its claim to East and West Florida after the 1783 Treaty of Paris between the U.S. and Britain. Spain also claimed the area south of Latitude 32º 30' of present-day Mississippi and Alabama, which was left out of the U.S. and remained in dispute.

1788 Georgia. On 2 January 1788, Georgia delegates formally adopted the Constitution of the United States, becoming the 4th state.

1790 Federal Census. The present-day area of Alabama and Mississippi was part of Georgia, part of the disputed area, and part of Spanish West Florida at the time of the 1790 federal census. Although there were American settlements at Nachez and north of Mobile, no federal census was taken there. Georgia's 1790 federal census was lost.

1797 Alabama, Mississippi. The U.S. resolved the Spanish-U.S. disputed area by purchasing the area from Spain. The lands above West Florida (Latitude 31º up to 32º30'), became U.S. territory. The purchase did not include East Florida or West Florida.

1798 Mississippi Territory. Congress created Mississippi Territory within the purchased lands. This area is now in both Alabama and Mississippi, from Latitude 31º to Latitude 32º30'.

1800 Federal Census. Georgia's 1800 federal census jurisdiction included Indian lands in present-day Alabama and Mississippi, but no whites were enumerated there. The entire GA 1800 census was lost. Washington County, Mississippi Territory was enumerated in the 1800 census, but that census was also lost.

1802 Georgia Land Cession. In this year, the portion of present-day Alabama and Mississippi above Latitude 32° 30′ was ceded by Georgia to the U.S. federal government's "public domain." Georgia's land area has not changed since.

1802 Louisiana. Napoleon defeats the Spanish in battle and gains title to Louisiana after trading them a couple of duchies in Italy. However, Napoleon finds that his troops in the Caribbean are under siege and unable to provide much help in establishing a French government in Louisiana. About a year later, when a couple of American emissaries show up trying to buy New Orleans from him, he decides to unload the entire tract to the Americans (to help finance a trip to Russia he had in mind).

1803 Louisiana. Surprised and delighted that Napoleon was willing to sell the entire tract called Louisiana, President Thomas Jefferson urges Congress to vote in favor, and the U.S. purchased the huge tract from France, doubling the size of the United States. The purchase of Louisiana immediately created a dispute about ownership of lands east of the Mississippi River, since the legal description of the Louisiana Purchase was the "drainage of the Mississippi and Missouri Rivers." The Spanish did not agree that it included lands east of the Mississippi and maintained their claim to West Florida.

1804 Louisiana and Orleans Territory. Congress divided the Louisiana Purchase into two jurisdictions: Louisiana District and Orleans Territory. The latter had north and south bounds the same as the present state of Louisiana, but did not include land east of the Mississippi River, and its northwestern corner extended on an indefinite line west into Spanish Texas.

1804 Arkansas. The Arkansas settlements were part of Louisiana District (which later would become Missouri Territory), contained within the sub-districts of New Madrid and Arkansas.

1804 Georgia, Mississippi. Congress officially added the 1802 Georgia land cession to Mississippi Territory, doubling its size, from Latitude 31° to Latitude 35°.

1805 Louisiana. Louisiana District became Louisiana Territory. All sub-districts became counties.

1806 Louisiana-Texas Line. The Louisiana Purchase caused a border dispute between the U.S. and Spain over the Louisiana-Texas boundary. Spain claimed east to the Red River; the U.S. claimed west to the Sabine River. They made a compromise in 1806 with the so-called Neutral Ground, where neither exercised jurisdiction. From 1806 to 1822, the Neutral Ground became a haven for outlaws, fugitives and pirates. (The French pirate, Jean Lafitte, was a frequent visitor to the Neutral Ground, in and around the Lake Charles and Calcasieu regions). Yet, in the 1810 census for Orleans Territory, a few hundred settlers were actually enumerated in the Neutral Ground.

1810 Federal Census taken in Georgia, Mississippi Territory, Louisiana Territory, and Orleans Territory, but only the manuscripts from Orleans survive.

1810 Florida. By treaty with Spain, the U.S. purchased part of West Florida, those areas west of the Perdido River.

1812 Florida, Mississippi and Orleans Territory. The portion of the West Florida Purchase from the Perdido River to the Pearl River was added to Mississippi Territory, and the portion from the Pearl River to the Mississippi River was added to Orleans Territory.

1812 Louisiana. Orleans Territory became the state of Louisiana on 30 April 1812, the 18th State.

1812. Louisiana Territory renamed Missouri Territory.

1817. Alabama Territory was created on 3 Mar 1817 with nearly the same boundaries as the current state bounds.

1817. Mississippi became the 20th state on 10 December 1817, with nearly the same boundaries as today.

1819. Alabama became the 22nd state on 14 December 1819, with nearly the same boundaries as today.

1819. Arkansas Territory was created with the capital at Arkansas Post. The area included most of present-day Oklahoma and all of Arkansas.

1819 Arkansas Territory. A treaty between the U.S. and Spain set the international boundary as the line of the Sabine River north to Latitude 32°, then due north to the Red River. Arkansas Territory misinterpreted the new boundary, thinking their southern line on Latitude 33° extended west at that point.

1820 Federal Census taken in Arkansas Territory and the states of Georgia, Alabama, Mississippi, and Louisiana. The original manuscripts are lost for Arkansas Territory and Alabama.

1821 Florida. In 1819 the United States acquired Florida from Spain by treaty and cash, but the treaty was not ratified by Congress until 1821. Florida's population was not enumerated in the 1820 federal census.

1822. Florida Territory created by Congress.

1828 Arkansas. Congress establishes the boundary separating Arkansas from territory to the west, setting the Arkansas-Oklahoma boundary as it is today with the exception of old Miller County, where the boundaries were still misunderstood. Miller County lay entirely within Mexican Texas.

1836. Arkansas became the 25th state on 15 June 1836.

ALABAMA

Censuses and Substitutes, 1706-1927

Alabama's several constitutions and acts of the General Assembly authorized several heads of household censuses, beginning with the year 1818 (Territory of Alabama), to be conducted by county tax assessors. No record of the 1818 name lists seems to exist. The legislature authorized state censuses to be taken in 1820, 1821, 1823, 1832, 1838, 1844, 1850, 1855, and 1866, all of which were known to be taken, but less than half of them survive. Only portions from the 1820, 1850, 1855, and 1866 state censuses are extant.

An 1875 Alabama State Census was authorized but never taken. The 1875 Constitution of Alabama determined that beginning with the 1880 federal census, apportionment of representatives would be determined by federal census population figures rather than state censuses. As a result, it appears that the 1866 state census was the last statewide census taken by the state of Alabama.

Surviving non-federal censuses have all been published and those on microfilm are available on interlibrary loan, mostly located at the Alabama Department of Archives and History (ADAH) in Montgomery or the Family History Library (FHL) in Salt Lake City.

Other locations and/or publications where Alabama's colonial, territorial, state, and census substitutes may be seen are indicated below, beginning with the oldest known lists, and continuing in chronological order to align with the timeline for census jurisdictions. If you have an Alabama ancestor, start with the time period you know he/she was living there to see what census lists exist within a region or county.

■ **1706 Colonial French Census** of settlements in or near Mobile. Name list published in "Census at Fort Louis de la Louisianne," *Deep South Genealogical Quarterly*, Vol. 1, No. 1 (Aug 1963), p. 30.

■ **1721 Colonial French Census** of settlements in or near Mobile. Name list published in *Deep South Genealogical Quarterly*, Vol. 1, No. 2 (Mar 1964), pp. 136-139; and "Fort Louis, Mobile," in *New Orleans Genesis*, Vol. 27, No. 107 (Jul 1988).

■ **1725 Colonial French Census** of settlements in or near Mobile. Name list published in *Deep South Genealogical Quarterly*, Vol. 1, No.2 (Dec 1963), p. 86.

■ **1764 Colonial English Census**, "Mobile residents who took the oath of allegiance," in *Deep South Genealogical Quarterly*, Vol. 13, No. 2 (May 1976).

■ **1785 Colonial Spanish Census** of the town of Tensas, east of Mobile. Published in DeVille, Winston, "Some Anglo-Americans in the Deep South, 1785," in *Genealogical Helper*. (Sept-Oct. 1982): pp5-6. There are 46 men listed, which can be seen at an online database at **www.geocities.com/BourbonStreet/Square/2320/ provincial.html.**

■ **1786 Colonial Spanish Census, Mobile**, in *Deep South Genealogical Quarterly*, Vol. 19, No. 1 (Feb 1982).

■ **1781, 1785, 1786, 1791** and **1795 Colonial Spanish Census** records available in Feldman, Lawrence H., *Anglo-Americans in Spanish Archives: Lists of Anglo-American Settlers in the Spanish Colonies of America; A Finding Aid.*

Baltimore, Md.: Genealogical Publishing, 1991. Included in this book are lists of heads of household for Mobile and Tombecbe now St. Stephens, Washington County. See FHL book 973 X2.

■ **1790 Mississippi Territory Federal Census.** The U.S. disputed Spain's control over the Tombigbee settlements in present-day southwestern Alabama north of 31° but took no census there.

■ **1786, 1787, 1789** and **1805 Colonial Spanish Censuses** were published in Andrews, Johnnie, Jr., and William David Higgins, *Spanish Census Reports at Mobile*, Bienville Historical Society, 1973.

■ **1796 Colonial Spanish Census**, Mobile Families, in *Everton's Genealogical Helper*, Vol. 37, No. 6 (Nov 1983).

■ **1800 Mississippi Territory Federal Census.** The federal census was taken for Washington County, north of Mobile, but the census was lost.

■ **1801, 1808, and 1810 Mississippi Territory Censuses** can be found in: "Washington County (now) Alabama 1801, 1808 and 1810 Census," in *The Alabama Genealogical Register*, Vol. 9, No. 3 (September 1967), pp 123-26.

■ **1809 Mississippi Territory Census.** Includes present-day Alabama area. A name list was published as part of *The Territorial Papers of the United States*, compiled and edited by Clarence Edwin Carter, United States Department of State. See FHL film #42234.

■ **1809 Mississippi Territory Census.** Madison County (now AL) census published in: "Madison County, Alabama 1809 Census." in *The Alabama Genealogical Register*, Vol. 10, no.4 (December 1968): pp175-82.

■ **1810 Mississippi Territory Censuses.** The federal census was taken for Washington and Baldwin counties, (now Alabama), but both were lost. But Mississippi Territory took its own census in 1810 in addition to the federal census. Washington County survives in the territorial census. See "Washington County (now) Alabama 1801, 1808 and 1810 Census," in *The Alabama Genealogical Register*, Vol. 9, No. 3 (September 1967), pp 123-26.

■ *1811-1819 Decennary Census Index*, by Ronald Vern Jackson, (Accelerated Indexing, SLC, Utah, 1983). FHL book 976.1 X22j 1811-1819. Although the title has impossible dates for Alabama, it appears that the name lists were extracted from areas of present-day Alabama (Mississippi Territory, 1811-1816; Alabama Territory, 1817-18; and the state of Alabama, 1819.

■ **1816 Mississippi Territory Census.** Census name list published in the *Alabama Historical Quarterly*, Vol. 24, No. 1 (Spring 1962). Pell City, (now AL) census published in *Inhabitants of Alabama in 1816, Pell City, Ala.*: Broken Arrow Chapter, DAR, 1955; Clarke County (now AL) name list published in *American Monthly Magazine*, Vol. 83, No. 5 (May 1949). Monroe County (now AL) name list published in *American Monthly Magazine*, Vol. 83, No. 4 (April 1949) and in *Roots & Branches*, Vol. 19, No. 2 (April 1998), and in *Clarke County Historical Society Quarterly*, Vol. 10, No. 1 (Summer 1985).

■ **1818 Alabama Territory Census.** Montgomery County name list published in *Alabama Historical Quarterly*, Vol. 18, No. 1 (Spring 1956).

■ **1820** Alabama Federal Census lost for all counties, but Alabama took a state census in 1820 and several county lists survive.

■ **1820 Alabama State Census** (taken separately from 1820 federal census). Originals/microfilm at ADAH. Eight counties only: Baldwin, Conecuh, Dallas, Franklin, Limestone, St. Clair, Shelby,

Wilcox. Includes name of head of household; free white males and females in age categories; number of slaves and free persons of color in age categories. The name list was published in *Alabama Census Returns 1820 and An Abstract of Federal Census of Alabama 1830*, by Marie Bankhead Owen, published by Genealogical Publishing Co., Inc., 1967. See FHL book 976.1 X2o. In addition, an 1820 Dallas County, Alabama name list was published in *American Monthly Magazine*, Vol. 78, No. 3 (March 1944).

■ **1821-1829 Alabama State Censuses.** Extracts of names in *Alabama, 1821-1829 Decennary Census Index*, by Ronald Vern Jackson (Accelerated Indexing, SLC, UT, FHL book 976.1 X22j 1821-1829).

■ **1831-1839 Alabama State Censuses.** Extracts of names in, *1831-1839 Decennary Census Index*, by Ronald Vern Jackson (Accelerated Indexing, SLC, UT, FHL book 976.1 X22j 1821-1829).

■ **1834-1861 Voters Lists, Sumter County, Alabama,** compiled by James T. Dawson, published by the Lauderdale County Department of Archives and History, Inc., Meridian, MS, 1988. 2 volumes. See FHL books 976.141 N4d (vol. 1) and 976.141 N4d (vol. 2).

■ **1850 Alabama State Census.** Separately taken from the 1850 federal census. Originals at ADAH, but little information about the extent of the surviving schedules is provided by the ADAH, except the following: "no index, includes name of head of household; free white males and females in age categories; number of slaves and free persons of color in age categories."

■ *Alabama 1850 Agricultural and Manufacturing Census*, transcribed by Linda L. Green, published Woodbridge, VA, 1999, 2 vols. Includes surname index for each volume. Contents: v. 1. Dale, Dallas, De Kalb, Fayette, Franklin, Greene,

Hancock and Henry counties -- v. 2. Jackson, Jefferson, Lawrence, Limestone, Lowndes, Macon, Madison and Marengo counties. FHL book 976.1 X2g v.1-2.

■ *Alabama Records*, compiled by Kathleen Paul Jones and Pauline Jones Gandrud, published by Huntsville Democrat, Huntsville, AL, 1939-, 235 vols. At least one volume for each Alabama county, this major compilation includes probate, vital (births, deaths, marriages), cemetery, Bible, census lists, (including AL 1850 state census), military, land, and court records. Also includes extracts from newspapers, family history information, and other miscellaneous materials of genealogical value. Filmed by the Genealogical Society of Utah, 1939-1983, 43 rolls, FHL film #840512-844391. (Additional filming was done in 1972).

■ **1852 California State Census (Alabama People)**, see "Alabama People Listed in 1852 CA State Census," in *Alabama Family History and Genealogy News*, Vol. 18, No. 3 (Jul 1997).

■ **1855 Alabama State Census.** Indexed. 14 counties extant: Autauga, Baldwin, Blount, Coffee, Franklin, Henry, Lowndes, Macon, Mobile, Montgomery (on film, but not included in the index), Pickens, Sumter (not on microfilm and not included in the Index), Tallapoosa, Tuscaloosa. Includes name of head of household; number of free white males and females in age categories; number of slaves and free persons of color in age categories. Originals at ADAH. Microfilm at ADAH and FHL. Indexed in *Alabama 1855 Census Index* by Ronald Vern Jackson, et al, Accelerated Indexing, SLC, UT. See FHL book 976.1 X2j 1855. In addition, Franklin County was extracted in *Valley Leaves*, Vol. 11, No. 2 (Dec 1972) through Vol. 22, No. 4 (Jun 1988).

■ **1866 Alabama State Census.** Originals at ADAH, microfilm at ADAH and FHL. No index.

46 counties extant. Lists the heads of households, regardless of color, and gives the number of persons in the various age ranges. It also indicates the number of deceased or disabled Confederate soldiers who were members of that family. See also "Mobile Head of Households," in *Deep South Genealogical Society*, Vol. 27, No. 3 (Aug 1990); Vol. 27, No. 4 (Nov 1990); Vol. 28, No. 1 Feb 1991); Vol. 28, No. 2 (May 1991); and Vol. 28, No. 3 (Aug 1991). A few indexes to countywide lists can be found on the Internet. Use your browser to locate them with the key words "1866 Alabama State Census."

■ **1866 Voter Registration Lists**. Available on microfilm at ADAH. This series was created in accordance with an act passed by Congress on March 2, 1867, "to provide for a more efficient government of the rebel States," and particularly to extend suffrage to the millions of freedmen across the south. All adult black and white males who had sworn an oath of loyalty to the United States were eligible to register to vote. Included is the person's name, race, length of residence in the state, county and precinct, the book and page where his oath is recorded, naturalization information, and reasons for rejecting some registrants. Arranged alphabetically by county, then chronologically by date of registration.

■ **1876 Registration Book of Voters, Barbour County, Alabama.** Originals housed in the Barbour County Courthouse in Clayton, Alabama. Microfilmed by the Genealogical Society of Utah, 1988. See FHL film #2317867 Item 2.

■ **1890 Federal Census.** Alabama was one of eight states that had fragments survive from the fire and water damaged census schedules. Surviving the 1890 census were these fragments in Alabama: Perry County (Perryville Beat No. 11 and Severe Beat No. 8). An index to the 6,160 names from all surviving fragments was published by the Family History Library and others. See FHL book 973 X2.

■ **1890 Tax List of Crenshaw County, Alabama**, compiled by Betty Holley and Wayne Rogers, Crenshaw County Historical Society, Luverne, AL, 1993, 23 pages. Includes index. See FHL book 976.136 R48h.

■ **1889-1895 Reconstructed Census of Marshall County, Alabama,** compiled by Margene Hemrick Black and Betty Jean Taylor, Past and Present Publications, Guntersville, AL, 1995?, 80 pages. See FHL book 976.194 X2bm 1889-1895.

■ **1894 Voter Census, Autauga County, Alabama**, compiled by MariLee Beatty Hageness, published by MLH Research, Anniston, AL, 2000, 76 pages. See FHL book 976.1463 N4h.

■ **1901-1914 Voters, Lawrence County Alabama**, compiled by MariLee Beatty Hageness, published by MLH Research, Anniston, AL, 2000. See FHL book 976.192 N4h.

■ **1906-1930 Register of Voters (Male), Calhoun County, Alabama.** Originals housed in Calhoun Probate Court in Anniston, Alabama. Microfilmed by the Genealogical Society of Utah, 1992. See FHL film #1845117 Item 2; and **1920-1942 Register of Voters (Females), Calhoun County, Alabama**. Originals housed in Calhoun Probate Court in Anniston, Alabama. Microfilmed by the Genealogical Society of Utah, 1992. See FHL film #1845117 Item 3.

■ **1901-1932 Voters List, Washington County, Alabama**, originals housed in the Washington County courthouse, Chatom, Alabama. Microfilmed by the Genealogical Society of Utah, 1991, 1995. See FHL film #1987691 Item 1 (1901) and #1752977 Item 2 (1902-1932).

■ **1902-1934 Voter Lists, Butler County, Alabama**, registered voters from probate court

originals housed in the Butler County Courthouse in Greenville, Alabama. Microfilmed by the Genealogical Society of Utah, 1989. Names are listed alphabetically. See FHL film #1630451.

■ *1907 Alabama Census of Confederate Soldiers*. Originals and microfilm at ADAH. Abstracts published in five volumes by Gregath, Cullman, AL, 1982. The volumes are alphabetical by county. This census gives the soldier's name, full birth date, city and state of birth, when and where enlisted, unit, and mustering-out date. See FHL book 976.1 X22c 1907. An index was prepared in a separate volume: *Master Index to 1907 Census of Alabama Confederate Soldie,* compiled by the ADAH, published by Gregath, Cullman, AL, 1982, 100+ pages. See FHL book 976.1 X22c 1907 index.

■ **1907 Census of Confederate soldiers,** in *Alabama Genealogical Society Magazine*, Vol. 6, No. 2 (Apr 1972) to Vol. 8, No. 3 (Jul 1974).

■ **1907-1927 Alabama Confederate Soldiers**. Originals and microfilm at ADAH. Filmed by the Genealogical Society of Utah, 1988, on 10 FHL films beginning with #1533727. The films for 1907 are first, followed by 1921 and 1927. The 1907 census includes each person's name, place of residence, date and place of birth, rank, date of entry into military service, date and place of discharge or separation, and name of military unit. The 1921 census provides each veteran's name, place and date of birth, place of residence, length of Alabama residence, occupation, wife's age and place of birth, marriage date and place, names of living children, occupation, and post office box. The forms also contain the veteran's rank, company, regiment, captain and colonel's name, battles, wounds, captures, imprisonments, and transfers. The 1927 census contains the veteran's name, his widow's name, her age and birth date, and their marriage date. The records are arranged by county, then alphabetically by the name of the soldier or widow. This series is not complete. Some of the returns are found in the Confederate Pension Applications.

■ **1908-1926 Voter Lists, Elmore County, Alabama**, in *Alphabetical Registration of Voters in Elmore County, Alabama*. Microfilm of originals in the Elmore County courthouse in Wetumpka, Alabama, filmed by the Genealogical Society of Utah, 1991. See FHL film #1750445.

■ **1908-1926 Voter Lists, Monroe County, Alabama**. Originals in the Monroe County courthouse in Monroeville, Alabama. Some years are missing. Microfilmed by the Genealogical Society of Utah, 1988. See FHL film #1547983.

■ **1910-1912 Registration Book of Voters, Barbour County, Alabama**. Originals at the Barbour County Courthouse in Clayton, Alabama. Microfilmed by the Genealogical Society of Utah, 2002. See FHL film #1547514 Item 1 (1910-1911) and #1547514 Item 2 (1912).

■ **1910-1923 Voter Lists, Bullock County, Alabama**, registration book of voters,. Microfilm of originals in the Bullock County courthouse in Union Springs, Alabama, filmed by the Genealogical Society of Utah, 1991. See FHL film #1536091.

■ **1912 Voter List, Chambers County, Alabama**, voter register, originals housed in the Chambers County Courthouse in LaFayette, Alabama, filmed by the Genealogical Society of Utah, 1992. See FHL film #1854807.

■ **Alabama Civil War Service Database**. Available at the ADAH website: **www.archives.state.al.us/civilwar/**. This alphabetical name list of Alabama Civil War veterans has over 106,000 individual cards of the estimated 250,000 on file. Currently all entries under the letters A-K are available (Jan 2004).

Alabama Censuses & Substitutes Online

■ **1810-1890 Alabama Censuses**. Originally compiled by Ronald V. Jackson, Accelerated Indexing, Salt Lake City, UT. Electronic files were acquired by Ancestry, Inc. which has these Alabama lists indexed at their website, **www.ancestry.com**. Combined index includes:
- 1810 Census Index
- 1810-1819 Tax Lists Index
- 1820 Federal Census Index
- 1830 Federal Census Index
- 1830-1839 Early Records
- 1840 Federal Census Index
- 1840 Pensioners Index
- 1850 Federal Census Index
- 1855 State Census Index
- 1860 Federal Census Index
- 1860 Mortality Schedules
- 1860 Slave Schedules
- 1870 Federal Census Index
- 1890 Pensioners Index
- Alabama Early Census, Vol. 1 & Vol. 2.

■ **1810-1890 Alabama Census Records Online** (CensusFinder.com). Several Alabama census lists are available at various sites on the Internet. One place to access them is through the **www.censusfinder.com/alabama.htm** site, where you can find links to the following sites for Alabama:
- 1810-1890 Alabama Census Records Database Search
- 1835 Federal Pension List - Statewide
- 1880 Federal Census
- 1880 Federal Census Search at Family Search
- 1883 Pensioners on the Roll - Statewide

■ **Links to Online Census Records**. (Census-Online.com). This is an Internet website featuring links to census records online. Go to **www.census-online.com/links/AL/** to review Alabama census records published online. An example of what is available for one Alabama County is shown below:

Washington County, Alabama

Federal Censuses
- 1810 Federal Census
- Index to 1830 Federal Census
- Index to 1840 Federal Census
- Index to 1850 Federal Census
- Index to 1850 Federal Census - Slave Schedule
- Index to 1860 Federal Census
- 1860 Federal Census - Mortality Schedule
- 1870 Federal Census
- 1920 Federal Census - Healing Springs Partial

State Censuses
- 1866 State Census - Colored Population

Tax Lists
- 1803 Personal Tax Roll

Military Rosters
- 1883 Pensioners

Miscellaneous
- 1797 Census - District of San Esteban De Tombecbe

ARKANSAS

Censuses and Substitutes, 1686-1926

A few lists of inhabitants of the Arkansas area were identified in early French and Spanish censuses, 1686-1791. Missouri Territory's Arkansas County had at least one county-wide tax list taken in 1814, which was the first American census substitute for the populated area that became Arkansas Territory in 1819. Several censuses were authorized by the territorial legislature, and a few surviving name lists exist for 1823, 1827, 1829, and 1835. Upon statehood in 1836, the Arkansas Constitution provided for enumerations of the inhabitants of the state each four years commencing in 1838 for the purpose of legislative apportionment. The General Assembly directed that a census be taken on January 1, 1842, and every four years thereafter. As was done in the territorial censuses, the Sheriffs of the various counties were to be in charge of conducting the state censuses. Although authorized, it can not be confirmed if all of them were actually taken. Only the state censuses of 1838, 1854, and 1865 have any extant manuscripts that can be found. Other locations and/or publications where Arkansas's colonial, territorial, state, and census substitutes may be seen are indicated below, beginning with the oldest known lists, and continuing in chronological order to align with the timeline for census jurisdictions.

■ **1686-1804 Arkansas Colonials: A Collection of French and Spanish Records Listing Early Europeans in the Arkansas Area.** Includes a number of censuses, militia lists and other records, by Morris S. Arnold and Dorothy Jones Core. FHL book 976.7 H2a.

■ **1723 Colonial French Census** of Louisiana, Arkansas Colonists. Names listed in *Louisiana Genealogical Register*, Vol. 8, No. 2 (Jun 1961).

■ **1749 Colonial French Census** of Louisiana, Arkansas Colonists. Names listed in *White County Heritage*, Vol. 2, No. 3 (Jul 1964); and in *Genealogical and Historical Magazine of the South*, Vol. 3, No. 3 (Aug 1986).

■ **1791 Colonial Spanish Census, Inhabitants of Arkansas Post**. Name list in *Genealogical and Historical Magazine of the South*, Vol. 3, No. 2 (May 1986).

■ **1814 Missouri Territory, Arkansas County Tax Lists.** Originals at Missouri State Archives. An online extract of the name list accessible at **www.censusfinder.com/arkansas.htm.**

■ The **1820** Arkansas Territory Federal Census was lost. A reconstruction was compiled from tax lists, voter lists, and other sources, by Bobbie Jones McLane in 1965, and again as *1820 Census of the Territory of Arkansas (Reconstructed)* by James Logan Morgan, published by Arkansas Research, Conway, AR, 1992, 108 pages. FHL book 976.7 X2.

■ *Arkansas Territory 1820 Census Index,* Ronald Vern Jackson, editor, Accelerated Indexing, Salt Lake City, 1982, 57 pages. Since the 1820 AR Territory census was lost, and Mr. Jackson does not indicate where the names came from, it is assumed that he got the names from Bobbie Jones McLane's 1965 work. The Accelerated Indexing book is FHL book 976.7 X22a.

■ **1820 Arkansas Territory Census, Clark County (Reconstructed)**. A name list can be found on the Internet at **www.rootsweb.com/~arpcahs/davidkelley/CEN20CLK.HTM**.

■ **1820 Arkansas Territory Census, Hempstead County (Reconstructed)**. A name list can be found on the Internet at **www.rootsweb.com/~arpcahs/davidkelley/CEN20HMP.HTM**.

■ **1823 Arkansas Territory Census, Arkansas County**. See *Arkansas County Sheriff's Census,* a typescript of the name list, 3 pages. See FHL book 976.786 X2p.

■ **1823** and **1829 Territory Censuses** (More often called "Sheriff's Censuses" because the legislature dictated that the county sheriffs would be in charge). See *Arkansas Sheriff's Censuses, 1823 & 1829* by Ronald Vern Jackson, et al, Accelerated Indexing, Salt Lake City, UT. FHL book 976.7 X2s 1823, 1829.

■ **1827 Arkansas Territory Census, Phillips County**. Name list published in *Tri-County Genealogy,* Vol. 9, No. 3 (Fall 1994).

■ **1829 Arkansas Territory Census. Lawrence County**. See *Lawrence County, Arkansas 1829 Sheriff's Census,* transcribed by Marion Stark Craig, 1994, 30 pages. Includes photocopy of original records along with transcription and full-name index. See FHL book 976.725 X2c.

■ *1833 Reconstructed Census of Scott County, Arkansas,* researched and compiled by John Paul O'Nale, Scott County Historical & Genealogical Society, Waldron, AR, 19??, 20 pages, 2 maps. Census and land records were among the records

used to reconstruct the census. Includes index. See FHL book 976.744 X2o 1833.

■ **1835 Arkansas Territory Census**. Names listed in *Tracks and Traces,* Vol. 18, No. 2 (Nov 1996).

■ **1838 Arkansas State Census, Madison County**. Some names published in *Madison County Musings,* Vol. 1, No. 2 (Summer 1982).

■ **1854 Arkansas State Census, Madison County**. Name list published in *Madison County Musings,* Vol. 2, No. 1 (Spring 1983).

■ **1865 Arkansas State Census, Washington County**. For the only county with extant records from the 1865 state census, see *Washington County, Arkansas, Sheriff's Census for 1865,* by Nancy Maxwell, published by Heritage Books, Bowie, MD, 1993, 74 pages. Includes surname index. FHL book 976.714 X2m.

■ **1868 & 1872 Arkansas County Voter Lists**. The originals were microfilmed by the Genealogical Society of Utah, 1975. See FHL film #978533.

■ *1890 Census of Clark County, Arkansas,* by William L. Newberry, Clark County Historical Association, Arkadelphia, Arkansas. The 1890 Federal census was completely destroyed for all of Arkansas. This book reconstructs the name lists from the Clark County Tax Receipt Book for 1890. FHL book 976.749 R48n.

■ *1890 Census Reconstruction, Garland and Montgomery Counties, Arkansas,* reconstructed from 1890 tax receipt books, compiled by Inez Halsell Cline, Bobbie Jones McLane, Wendy Bradley Richter, Typescript, 132 pages, map. Arranged in alphabetical order by surname. See FHL book 976.74 X2c 1890.

■ *1890 Reconstructed Census of Grant County, Arkansas,* compiled and published by Joan G. Threet, 72 pages. This reconstructed census was compiled by using personal property tax records, court minutes, marriage records & personal data from the compiler's husband's family. Also includes: list of post offices; Pine Grove (at Grapevine, Ark.) & Dogwood school photos (3 altogether); data on Threet & Moore families (1 page). Includes full-name index. Also includes index to 1890 marriages. See FHL book 976.771 X2t 1890.

■ *1890 Reconstructed Census of Greene County, Arkansas*, by the Greene County Historical and Genealogical Society, Paragould, AR, 1989, 50 pages. Includes surname index. Includes a 1930 map of school districts. This Greene County "census" was reconstructed through the use of tax records. See FHL book 976.7993 R4r.

■ **1890 Census of Howard County, Arkansas,** by Lucilee Westbrook,. This "census" was compiled from tax assessment records. The names are in alphabetical order by school district. FHL book 976.7483 R4w

■ *1890 Tax Book (Reconstructed 1890 Census) Logan County, Arkansas,* compiled by Bill Hanks, Arkansas Ancestors, 1987, 118 pages. According to the transcriber, for the most part tax records are being used to reconstruct the 1890 census in Logan County, Arkansas. Names are listed in alphabetical order. See FHL book 976.737 X22h .

■ *20 Years in Miller County, Arkansas: 1875-1890: Tax & Census Record Index,* by the Texarkana U.S.A. Genealogical Society, 200+ pages. Contains 1875 Miller County personal property tax assessment index, 1880 Miller County federal census index, 1885 Miller County personal property tax assessment index, 1890 Miller County personal property tax assessment index. See FHL book 976.756 R42.

■ *1890 Reconstructed Census of Mississippi County, Arkansas,* compiled and published by Joan G. Threet, 132 pages. This "census" was reconstructed from court records, marriage records, newspapers and family records. Names are in alphabetical order. See FHL book 976.795 X2t 1890.

■ *1890 Phillips County, Arkansas "Census" From Real Estate Tax Records,* compiled by Carrie Davison and Rose Craig White of the Tri-County Genealogical Society, 1989, 84 pages, published by Ole English Press, Clarendon, AR. Includes surname index. See FHL book 976.788 X2.

■ *1890 Census of Pike County, Arkansas,* by Russell Pierce Baker. This "census" is a reconstruction of the destroyed-by-fire federal census of 1890 from the 1893 Pike County tax receipt book. FHL book 976.7485 X2b 1890.

■ *1890 Census, Polk County, Arkansas,* compiled by Wanda Tilley; typed and printed by Gypsie Cannon, Mena, AR, 198?, 21 pages. From preface: "Compiled from the 1888 real estate tax book; 1890 marriage records; and book of delinquent sales, 1878-1898, list of delinquent land sold on 10th day of June, 1890." Arranged in alphabetical order by surname. See FHL book 976.745 X2.

■ *Prairie County, Arkansas 1890 Census Reconstruction: A Sesquicentennial Project,* compiled by Margaret Harrison Hubbard, Hot Springs, AR, 1986, 105 pages, maps. This is a reconstruction made by using tax records and other records for that time period. Includes index. See FHL book 976.777 X2p 1890.

■ *1890 Census of Randolph County, Arkansas as Constructed from the Personal Property Tax List,* by Burton Ray Knotts. FHL book 976.724 R4k.

■ *1892-1898 Voters Lists, Polk County, Arkansas,* compiled, typed, and printed by Shirley "Gypsie" Cannon, Mena, AR, 198?, 65 pages. Arranged in alphabetical order by surname. See FHL book 976.745 N48.

■ *1890 Saline County, Arkansas Taxpayers: A Substitute for the Missing 1890 Census, with Full Name Index*, compiled by Carolyn J. Billingsley, published by C. J. Billingsley, Alexander, AR, 1986, 103 pages. From preface: "This book was compiled from the 1889 Saline County tax book, the 1889 Saline County (paid) tax book, and the 1889 Saline County tax receipt book." Includes index. The names are arranged by school districts as they are on the tax books. See FHL book 976.772 R4b.

■ *1833 Reconstructed Census of Scott County, Arkansas*, researched and compiled by John Paul O'Nale, Scott County Historical & Genealogical Society, Waldron, AR, 19??, 20 pages, 2 maps. Census and land records were among the records used to reconstruct the census. Includes full-name index. See FHL book 976.744 X2o 1833.

■ *1890 Census (Reconstruction) of Sebastian County, Arkansas*, compiled by members of the Frontier Researchers (Genealogical Society) of Fort Smith, AR,198?, 223 pages. Includes indexed names from the following books: (1) Lower District Real Estate Tax Record Book; (2) Lower District Personal Property Tax Record Book; (3) Upper District Real Estate Tax Record Book; (4) Upper District Voter Registration for 1892; (5) Fort Smith City Directory; (6) Fort Smith Marriages for 1890; (7) Birnie Brothers Funeral Home Records for 1890, Fort Smith; (8) First Lutheran Church Records, Fort Smith. See FHL book 976.736 X22c 1890.

■ *Sevier County, Arkansas, 1890 Census Reconstructed From Tax Records: Sesquicentennial Project of State History Commission*, compiled by Vinita Lovell Long, Martha Johnson, Mary McCrory, 1978, Arkansas, 83 pages. Includes index. See FHL 976.747 X28L 1890.

■ *1890 White County, Arkansas "Census," Reconstructed From the 1890 Personal Property Tax Book*, compiled by Wensil Marsh Clark,

Arkansas Genealogical Society, Hot Springs, AR, published by W. M. Clark, Little Rock, AR, 1986, 98 pages, map. Includes surname index. See FHL book 976.776 R48c.

■ **1911 Census of Confederate Veterans**. Complete for 44 counties. Includes the name of the veteran, address, date of birth, place of birth, where enlisted, names and birthplaces of the soldier's parents and grandparents, maiden name of wife, date and place of marriage, names of her parents, and names of children. An extract was compiled by Bobbie Lee Jones McLane and Capitola Glazner as *1911 Census of Confederate Veterans*, published by Arkansas Ancestors, Hot Springs, AR, 1981, 3 vols., FHL book 976.7 X2m v.1-3. Indexed separately by Bobbie Lee Jones McLane. FHL book 976.7 X2m index.

● *1926 Official List of Legal Voters of Howard County, Arkansas*, published by Madigan's books, Charleston, IL, 198?. See FHL book 976.7 A1 no. 137.

Arkansas Censuses & Substitutes Online

■ **Arkansas Censuses 1819-1870**. Indexes originally compiled by Ronald V. Jackson, Accelerated Indexing, Salt Lake City, UT. These databases were acquired by Ancestry, Inc. which has these Arkansas lists indexed at their website, **www.ancestry.com**. The combined online index includes:
- 1819-1829 Tax Lists Index
- 1820 Federal Census (Reconstructed) Index
- 1823 Sheriff's Census Index
- 1829 Sheriff's Census Index
- 1830 Federal Census Index
- 1830-1839 Tax Lists Index
- 1840 Federal Census Index
- 1840 Pensioners Index
- 1850 Federal Census Index
- 1850 Slave Schedule
- 1860 Federal Census Index
- 1870 Federal Census Index.

■ **Arkansas Census Records Online**. Several Arkansas census lists are available at various sites on the Internet. Use the Census Finder site at **www.censusfindercom/arkansas.htm** to link to the following sites:

- 1814 Arkansas Territory (sic) Tax List
- 1816 Arkansas Territory (sic) Tax List
- 1819-1870 Arkansas Census Records Search at Ancestry
- Pre-1830 Arkansas Territory Tax List
- 1835 Federal Pension List - Statewide
- 1860 Federal Census Index of Indian Lands now located in Oklahoma. (The name list of non-Indians living in the Indian Territory was attached to the end of the Arkansas 1860 federal census).

■ **Links to Online Census Records**. (CensusOnline.com). This site features links to census records online. Go to **www.census-online.com/links/AR/** to review Arkansas census records and substitutes. An example of what is available for one Arkansas county is shown below:

Miller County, Arkansas
Federal Census
- 1830 Federal Census. Includes people in NE Texas and SE Oklahoma.
- 1880 Federal Census Images
- 1880 Federal Census - Sulphur Twp.
- Index to 1830 Federal Census Surnames

Miscellaneous
- 1821 Hempstead / Miller Index
- 1825 Petition
- 1828 Petition
- Index to 1825 Petition
- Index to 1828 Petition

FLORIDA

Censuses and Substitutes, 1783-1885

Censuses of the territory and state of Florida were taken in 1825, 1838, 1845, 1855, 1865, 1875, 1885, 1895. 1905. 1915, 1925, 1935, and 1945. Only fragments of the early records have been preserved. No manuscripts of the 1865, 1905, 1915, and 1925 censuses have been located. Other locations and/or publications where Florida's colonial, territorial, state, and census substitutes may be seen are indicated below, beginning with the oldest known lists, and continuing in chronological order to align with the timeline for census jurisdictions.

■ **1759 Colonial French Census, Fort Mose** (now St. Johns County). Name list published in *Ancient City Genealogist*, Vol. 4, No. 4 (Dec 1993).

■ **1781, 1785, 1786, 1791** and **1795 Colonial Spanish Census** records available in Feldman, Lawrence H., *Anglo-Americans in Spanish Archives: Lists of Anglo-American Settlers in the Spanish Colonies of America; A Finding Aid*. Baltimore, Md.: Genealogical Publishing, 1991. Included in this book are lists of heads of household from early settlements in Florida. See FHL book 973 X2.

■ **1780-1819 Spanish Land Grants in Florida**. The Florida State Archives website has an online index to names of persons granted land by the Spanish, go to **www.floridamemory.com/Collections/SpanishLandGrants/**.

■ **1776 Colonial British Census, East Florida**. See "Inhabitants, 1776, East Florida," in *Jacksonville Genealogical Society Quarterly*, Vol./No. not cited. Publ. 1990.

■ **1779 Colonial British Census, Pensacola**. Names published in "Inhabitants of English Pensacola," in *West Florida Footprints*, Vol. ?, No. 1. (Spring 1984).

■ **1783-1793 Colonial Spanish Censuses**. See *Early American Series*, vol. 2, 1783-1793, also known as "Early Florida Census," Ronald Vern Jackson, editor, Accelerated Indexing, 1984. See FHL book 973 D2jef.

■ **1783-1796 Colonial Spanish Censuses**. Excerpts of the 1783 and 1793 Spanish Censuses of Florida, Father Hassett's Census of St. Augustine and Vicinity, 1786, and censuses of the Mosquito Territory including San Pablo Beach, Talbot, Shell and Amelia Islands, Tiger Isle, St. Mary's River, St. John's River, Nassau River, and Fernandina with index. Originals microfilmed by FHL (film #1014120).

■ **1783-1793 Colonial Spanish Censuses**. See *Early American Series*, vol. 2, 1783-1793, also known as "Early Florida Census," Ronald Vern Jackson, editor, Accelerated Indexing, 1984. See FHL book 973 D2jef.

■ **1783-1793 Colonial Spanish Censuses**, published in "Spanish Census Listing, 1784-85," in *Southern Genealogists Exchange Quarterly*, Vol. 11, No. 55 (Fall 1970).

■ **1783 Colonial Spanish Census**, published in "Spanish census of 1783," *Georgia Genealogical Magazine*, No. 39-42. (1971).

■ **1784 Colonial Spanish/British Census**, in *The Last Days of British Saint Augustine, 1784-1785: a Spanish Census of the English Colony of East Florida*, by Lawrence H. Feldman. (Genealogical Publishing Co., Inc., Baltimore, 1998). Lists the English residents of East Florida in 1784 when it changed from British to Spanish rule. Includes index. See FHL book 975.918/S1 X2f.

■ **Florida's First Families: Translated Abstracts of Pre-1821 Spanish Censuses**, compiled by Donna Rachal Mills, published by Mills Historical Press, Tuscaloosa, AL, 1992, 201 pages. Includes index. FHL book 975.9 X2f.

■ **1820 Census to Louisiana's Florida Parishes.** The "Florida Parishes" were those East of the Mississippi River and formerly part of West Florida .The area was transferred to Louisiana in 1812, and at the time of the 1820 census the area

had five parishes: St. Tammany, Washington, St. Helena, Feliciana, and East Baton Rouge. See *An index to the 1820 Census of Louisiana's Florida Parishes and 1812 St. Tammany Parish Tax List*, compiled and published by Mary Elizabeth Sanders, Lafayette, LA, 1972, 47 pages. See FHL book 976.3 A1 no. 10.

■ **1820 Florida**. "Florida Territory 1820 Census Index," Ronald Vern Jackson, editor, Accelerated Indexing, Salt Lake City, 1982, 68 pages. Florida did not become a territory until 1822, and its population was not included in the 1820 federal census. The Ancestry, Inc. site refers to the "1820 Census Index, Pensacola and Escambia River," which is probably what Jackson's reconstructed name list contains. See FHL book 975.9X22j.

■ **1821 Florida Panhandle**. A selected name list from various sources, published in "West Florida's Citizens, 1821, (Selected)," *Pensacola History Illustrated*, Vol. 5, No. 3 (Summer 1999).

■ **1825 Florida State Census, Jackson County**, name list published in the *Florida Genealogist*, Vol. 16, No. 2 (Spring 1993); and in the *Huxford Genealogical Society Magazine*, Vol. 5, No. 1 (Mar 1978).

■ **1825 Florida State Census, Leon County**. Name list published in the *Southern Genealogists Exchange Quarterly*, Vol. 14, No. 68 (Winter 1973); and in the *A.I.S.I. Journal of Genealogy*, Vol. 1, No. 3 (Jul 1988); *Keystone Kin*, Vol. 2, No. 4 (Oct 1988); and *Florida Genealogist*, Vol. 24, No. 2 (Summer 2000)

■ **Florida Territorial and State Election Records, 1826-1865**, by Florida Division of Elections. Originals and microfilm located at state archives, Tallahassee, Florida. Election records arranged alphabetically by county, then chronologically (by date of election) within each county. Includes returns of elections for county, state and national offices, amnesty oaths, poll books, lists of registered voters, original ballots, etc. Filmed by the Genealogical Society of Utah, 1990. See FHL film #1673224-1673232.

■ **1838 Florida State Census, Jackson County,** name list published in the *Florida Genealogist,* Vol. 16, No. 3 (Summer 1993).

■ **Tax Rolls of Florida Counties, 1839-1891,** Florida Tax Commission. Originals at the Florida State Archives, filmed by the Genealogical Society of Utah, 1956. Includes name lists of Florida residents for all counties. Some missing records. See FHL film #688 Thru 6937 (66 rolls).

■ **1855 Florida State Census, Marion County.** Name list published in the *Florida Genealogist,* Vol. 11, No. 4 (Summer 1988).

■ **1855 Florida State Census, Orange County.** Name list published in *Buried Treasures,* Vol. 30, No.3 (July 1998).

■ **1855 Florida State Census, Putnam County.** Name list and index in *Putnam County Genealogical Society Quarterly Journal,* Vol. 3, No. 4 (Winter 1986).

■ **1864 Florida Military Census.** See *Department for the South, November 1864, for Jacksonville, Fernandina and St. Augustine, Florida, Ordered by the Department of the South, Hilton Head, South Carolina,* Florida State Genealogical Society, Tallahassee, FL, published by Heritage Books, Bowie, MD, 2002, 280 pages. Includes index. From the forward: "One of the forgotten legacies... was a special census of eastern Florida conducted on the orders of Federal military authorities. Its motivation is to this day unclear, but it seems likely to have been part of the work done to help register voters under Lincoln's "10%" reconstruction plan. African-Americans living in the region were also enumerated despite the fact that they did not yet have the legal right to vote." Includes name, height, color

of eyes, complexion, age, where born or contraband [slave], last residence, where registered for draft or name of owner, date moved into the south, oath of allegiance, and remarks. See FHL book 975.91 X2f.

■ **1864 Florida Military Census, Fernandina County.** Name list published serially in the *Nassau County Genealogist,* Vol. 1, No. 1 (Winter 1994), thru Vol. 2, No. 1 (Fall 1994).

■ **1845 Florida Statehood Election Returns,** originals by Florida Division of Elections. Originals and microfilm of records located at state archives, Tallahassee, Florida. From the introduction: "Includes lists of electors or voters from Alachua, Baker, Benton, Calhoun, Columbia, Dade, Duval, Escambia, Franklin, Gadsden, Hamilton, Hillsborough, Jackson, Jefferson, Leon, Madison, Marion, Monroe, Mosquito, Nassau, St. Johns, St. Lucia, Santa Rosa, Wakulla, Walton, Washington counties." Filmed by the Genealogical Society of Utah, 1990. See FHL film #1672587 Item.

■ **Florida Voters in Their First Statewide Election, May 26, 1845.** This is a printed extraction and index to the "Florida Statehood Election Returns" shown above. Voter name lists by county, compiled by Brian Michaels, published in Tallahassee by Florida State Genealogical Society, 1987, 128 pages. See FHL book 975.9 N4.

■ **1867-68 Florida Voter Registration Lists,** compiled by members of the Tallahassee Genealogical Society, Published Tallahassee, FL, 1992, 400 pages. Compiled from original documents at the Florida State Archives. Includes index. Includes county voter lists of Hernando, Leon, Levy, Liberty, Madison, Marion, Nassau, Orange, Polk, Putnam, St. Johns, Santa Rosa, Sumter, Suwannee, Taylor, Volusia, Wakulla, Walton, and Washington counties. Includes voter's name, race, length of residence in the state, where born and date of registration, as provided by the voter himself. From forward: "A qualified voter had to be at least twenty-one years old, a resident of his county... For the first time in southern history, race was not a qualifying factor in registering to vote. See FHL book 975.9.

■ **1867 Florida Voter Registration List, Madison County,** compiled by the Tallahassee Genealogical Society, published serially in *Tallahassee Genealogical Society Newsletter*, beginning with Vol. 15, No. 3 (Spring 1996).

■ **1867-1905 Florida Voter Registration Rolls,** Florida Secretary of State. Microfilm of records at Bureau of Archives and Records Management, Tallahassee, Florida, filmed by the Genealogical Society of Utah, 1990. From the introduction: "Congress passed an act on March 23, 1867 calling for a registration of qualified voters. These voters would then elect delegates to a convention for the purpose of establishing a constitution and civil government. A qualified voter had to be male, twenty-one years of age, a resident of the county, and had to take an oath of allegiance to the United States government. A Board of Registration composed of three loyal officers or persons was set up to make, complete, and witness the registration. This was the first time that Blacks were allowed to register to vote." "Most volumes list voter's name, race, time of residence in county and state, native (of what state), naturalization (where, when, and how) and date of registration." See FHL film #1672578 and 1672579.

■ **1875 Florida State Census.** See *State Census Book for 1875 Alachua County, Florida*, Florida Secretary of State. Original records microfilmed at the State Capitol, Tallahassee, Florida, by the Genealogical Society of Utah, 1956. See FHL film #6962.

■ **1884-1885 Florida State Censuses (Substitutes).** See *Census of Apalachicola, Franklin Co., Florida, 1884-1885,* compiled by Rose Marie Lovett, privately published book filmed by Genealogical Society of Utah, 1976. Includes index. Patrick J. Lovett (marshal of Apalachicola, Florida) took this census, 1 January 1884-31 May 1885. The census was taken on blank pages in an account ledger; it does not appear to be part of the 1885 state census. See FHL film #988192 , Item 3.

■ **1885 Florida State Census,** (taken with federal assistance). This special census required that Florida supply a copy of the schedules to the federal government, which they did soon after it was completed. The Florida State Archives has no record of the state's copy, and presumably, their own copy was lost, unless it is buried in some unknown Florida repository. The National Archives microfilmed their copy as series M845, 14 rolls. Missing from the federal copy of the 1885 Florida state census are Alachua, Clay, Columbia, and Nassau counties. A name index to the 1885 Florida census was compiled by William T. Martin and Patricia Martin of Miami, FL in 1991, but there is no copy of this index at the Family History Library (check Florida libraries first). FHL film numbers for the original 1885 Florida census schedules: #888962 thru #888974. Countywide extractions of the 1885 Florida Census are available for the following counties:

- **Dade County**. 1885 name list published in "Census, 1885, Dade County, Florida," in *Southern Genealogists Exchange Quarterly*, Vol. 21, No. 96 (Winter 1980): and in, *Heritage*, Vol. 17, No. 3 (Jul 1990).
- **Duval County**. 1885 name list published in "Census, 1885, Duval County, Florida," in *Southern Genealogists Exchange Quarterly*, Vol. 22, No. 97 (Spring 1981).
- **Jackson County**. 1885 name list serially published in *Southern Genealogists Exchange Quarterly*, beginning with Vol. 18, No. 83 (Fall 1977).

- **Liberty County**. 1885 name list published in *Southern Genealogists Exchange Quarterly*, Vol. 25, No. 109 (March 1984).
- **Orange County**. 1885 name list published in *Buried Treasures*, beginning with Vol. 31, No. 2 (Apr 1992) through Vol. 29, No. 2 (April 1997).
- **Putnam County**. 1885 name list published in *Putnam County Genealogical Society Quarterly Journal*, beginning with No. 20 (Apr 1994).
- **Wakulla County**. 1885 name list in *Southern Genealogists Exchange Quarterly*, Vol. 21, No. 94 (Summer 1980).
- **Washington County**. 1885 name list in *Florida Genealogist*, Vol. 16, No. 4 (Fall 1993).

■ **1895 Florida State Census.** See *1895 State Census, Nassau County, Florida,* compiled by the Jacksonville Genealogical Society, 1976, 236 pages. Includes index. See FHL book 975.911 X2j.

■ **1935 and 1945 Florida State Censuses,** original records at the State Library & Archives of Florida, Tallahassee. The FL state archives website refers to the "1885, 1935, and 1945 Florida State Censuses which, with a few exceptions, are complete enumerations of the state's residents." The current online catalog does not reveal a single reference to the 1935 or 1945 censuses, and, apparently, no further information from the archives about these state census records is available. However, from other sources, it can be determined that there is no microfilm, no index, and that the organization of the census schedules is first by county, then election precinct. The name lists are fairly thorough, with name, age, nativity, relationship to head of household, and several more items of interest. While the 1885 census is available on microfilm at the FHL, the 1935 and 1945 FL state censuses must be accessed by special request of the archives research services. (which is limited to 30 minutes in indexed materials only, thus, they are not accessible at all). The archives recommends that you contact them for a list of professional researchers to research these state censuses. Go to **http://dlis.dos.state.fl.us/archives/research.cfm**.

Florida Censuses & Substitutes Online

■ **Florida Censuses 1820-1890.** Originally compiled by Ronald V. Jackson, Accelerated Indexing, Salt Lake City, UT. Electronic files were acquired by Ancestry, Inc. which has these Florida lists indexed at their website, **www.ancestry.com**. The combined index contains the following:
- 1820 Census (sic) Index, Pensacola and Escambia River
- 1825 Leon County Census Index
- 1830 Federal Census Index
- 1840 Federal Census Index
- 1840 Pensioners List
- 1850 Federal Census Index
- 1850 Slave Schedule
- 1860 Federal Census Index
- 1860 Slave Schedule
- 1870 Federal Census Index
- 1890 Veterans Schedule
- 1890 Naval Veterans Schedule

■ **1783-1883 Florida Census Records Online.** (CensusFinder.com). Several Florida census lists are available at various sites on the Internet. Access the lists through **www.censusfinder.com/florida.htm** for links to the following sites:
- 1783 Spanish Census of East Florida
- 1820-1890 Florida Census at Ancestry
- 1835 Federal Pension List - Statewide
- 1840 Florida Military Census
- 1880 Federal Census
- 1880 Federal Census Search at Family Search
- 1883 Pensioners on the Roll - Statewide

■ **Links to Online Census Records.** (CensusOnline.com). This is an Internet website featuring links to census records online. Go to **www.census-online.com/links/FL/** to review Florida census records published online. An example of what is available for one Florida county is shown below:

Hillsborough County, Florida
Federal Census
- 1850 Federal Census - Slave Schedule
- 1860 Federal Census - Agricultural Schedule
- Index to 1850 Federal Census

State Census
- 1885 State Census
- 1935 State Census - Muggin Memorial Home

Military Roster
- 1917 - 1918 Civilian Draft Registration (by alpha)

Miscellaneous
- 1890 Registered Voters - Tampa

GEORGIA

Censuses and Substitutes, 1733-1901

For the purpose of apportionment of the state legislature, Georgia's Constitution of 1798 provided that a state census be taken in 1810 and every seven years thereafter. Accordingly, the state legislature authorized censuses to be taken in the years 1810, 1817, 1824, 1831, 1838, 1845, 1852, and 1859. Legislative journals confirm that all of these censuses were actually taken through reference to resolutions for compensation of enumerators, reports from governors, etc., yet in 1941, the Public Archives of Georgia had only one package containing fragments from the censuses of 1824 and 1831. Since then, a few partial lists were found in various Georgia county courthouses for the 1800, 1827, 1834, 1838, 1845, 1852, and 1859 state censuses, but still represent just a fraction of the totals taken for those years. The census of 1859 was probably the last state census taken in Georgia. No census legislation has been seen subsequent to the act of 1858, and the Constitution of 1877 provided that reapportionment be based on the results of the decennial national census. Other locations and/or publications where Georgia's colonial and state census substitutes may be seen are indicated below, beginning with the oldest known lists,

and continuing in chronological order to align with the timeline for census jurisdictions.

■ **Surviving Georgia State Censuses**. Scattered original state census returns for the following years and counties are available at the Georgia Department of Archives and History (GDAH) in Morrow, GA.
- **1827** Taliaferro County.
- **1838** Laurens, Lumpkin, Newton, Tattnall
- **1845** Chatham, Dooly, Forsyth, and Warren
- **1852** Jasper, Chatham County, and the City of Augusta
- **1859** Terrell and Columbia Counties

■ **1838-1879 Georgia State Census Records**. Under this title, some of the above listed state censuses were filmed by the Genealogical Society of Utah, 1957, 1961, including:
- 1838 Laurens County, Film 7010 Item 4;
- 1838 Newton County, Film 7010 Item 5;
- 1838 Tattnall County, Film 7010 Item 6;
- 1845 Chatham County, Film 7010 Items 1-2;
- 1845 Forsyth County, Film 7010 Item 3;
- 1845 Warren County, Film 7010 Items 7-8;
- 1845 Dooly County, Film 7010 Item 9;
- 1852 Jasper County, Film 7010 Item 10; and
- 1859 & 1879 Columbia County, Film 234619.

■ See *Indexes to Seven State Census Reports for Counties in Georgia 1838-1845*. Atlanta, GA: R.J. Taylor Foundation, 1975, 152 pages. FHL book 975.8 X2.

■ *1733-1819, Early Georgia*, Ronald Vern Jackson, editor, Accelerated Indexing, Bountiful, UT, 1981, 561 pages. Extracted from registers of vital records from several Georgia counties. Not a census, tax, or voter list, but for this period may help locate people in Georgia. FHL book 973 D2.

■ *1780 Tax List, Greene Co., Georgia*, compiled by MariLee Beatty Hageness, Anniston, AL, MLH Research, 1998, 13 pages. Tax list is abstracted in alphabetical order by name of tax payer. FHL book 975.8 A1 no. 147.

■ *1789 Tax List, Greene County, Georgia*, compiled by MariLee Beatty Hageness, Anniston, AL,MLH Research, 1998, 13 pages. FHL book 975.8612 R4.

■ **1790-1810 Federal Census Substitutes:** Except for 1800 Oglethorpe County, the first three federal census name lists for all of Georgia were lost. (The GDAH website explains that the earliest censuses were probably lost when the British burned Washington during the War of 1812 – but no census originals from any state were ever sent to Washington until an 1830 federal law asked for them – so the early Georgia census losses should probably be blamed on the Clerk of the U.S. District Court in Georgia, not the British Army). Statewide tax lists and indexes to the early Georgia Land Lotteries for a few years can be used as substitutes to the lost 1790-1810 censuses. Refer to the following publications:

■ *An Index to Georgia Tax Digests, 1789-1817*. 5 vols., published for the R. J. Taylor Foundation; Spartanburg, SC: Reprint Co., 1986. FHL book 975.8 R42i.

■ *Some Early Tax Digests of Georgia, 1790-1818*, edited by Ruth Blair, State Historian, 2 vols., 174 pages. (Atlanta: Georgia Archives, 1926). FHL book 975.8 R4.

■ *Substitute for Georgia's Lost 1790 Census*, Albany, Ga.: Delwyn Associates, 1975). Wills, deeds, tax digests, court minutes, voter lists, and newspapers were searched to compile this list. FHL book 975.8 X2L

■ *Index to Some Early Tax Digests of Georgia*, compiled by Earldene Rice, 68 pages, 1971. FHL book 975.8 R4g.

■ *1805 Georgia Land Lottery*, name list of lottery ticket holders transcribed and indexed by Virginia S. Wood and Ralph V. Woods, published by Greenwood Press, Cambridge, 1964, 414 pages. FHL book 975.8 R2wv 1805. For information about Georgia's land lotteries 1805-1832, visit the following website: **http://ngeorgia.com/history/lotteries.html.**

■ **Index to 1807 Land Lottery of Georgia**, Originals at Surveyor General's Office. Typescript index filmed by the Genealogical Society of Utah, 1957. Lists name of lottery participant, county, military district, county in which the person drew land. Lottery participants are listed alphabetically by surname. FHL film 159018. See also *The Second or 1807 land lottery of Georgia*, compiled by Silas Emmett Lucas, published by Southern Historical Press, Easley, SC, 1986, 168 pages, map, index. FHL book 975.8 R2Ls. For information about Georgia's land lotteries 1805-1832, visit the following website: **http://ngeorgia.com/history/lotteries.html.**

■ *1796 Tax List, Oglethorpe County, Georgia: With Statistical Information Added*, name list compiled by Joseph T. Maddox, 1980, 40 pages. FHL book 975.8175 R4m. See also *Oglethorpe County, Georgia Tax List for the Year 1796 in the Office of the Clerk of the Superior Court*, compiled by Mrs. Edgar Lamar Smith, 1958. FHL book 975.8175 R4s.

■ *1799 Tax List of Oglethorpe County, Georgia*, compiled by MariLee Beatty Hageness, Anniston, AL, 1995, 26 pages. FHL book 975.8175 R4h.

■ *1800 (Federal) Census of Oglethorpe County, Georgia: the Only Extant Census of 1800 for the State of Georgia*, transcribed from the originals at the GDAH and indexed by Mary Bondurant Warren, Athens, GA, 1965, 53 pages. Includes index. FHL book 975.8175 X2p 1800.

■ *1797-1802 Tax Digest, Jackson County, Georgia*, compiled by Belinda E. Savadge. Published by B.E. Savadge, Jefferson, GA, 2000, 369 pages. Includes index. See FHL book 975.8145 R4s.

■ *1798-1839. Franklin County, Georgia Tax Digests*, compiled by Martha Walters Acker. Birmingham, AL, 1980, 4 vols., Each volume includes three indexes. Contents: vol. 1: 1798-1807; vol. 2: 1808-1818; vol.. 3: 1819-1823" vol. 4: 1825-1839. FHL book 975.8135 R4f v.1-4.

■ *Lincoln County, Georgia Tax Digests: 1799-1806, 1839*, original name lists filmed by Heritage Papers, Danielsville, GA, 198?. See FHL film 1276564.

■ *Franklin County, Georgia Tax Book, 1800, and Tax Digest, 1810*, filmed by Heritage Papers, Danielsville, GA, 198?. FHL film #1276565 Item 2.

■ *Jones County, Georgia Tax Digest, 1811-1819*, copied by the Georgia State College and James B. Deireaux. Typescript at the GDAH, filmed by the Genealogical Society of Utah, 1946. Includes index. FHL film 7139.

■ *Baldwin County, Georgia, 1813 Tax List*, compiled by Frances Ingmire, Signal Mountain, TN, Mountain Press, 1999, 20 pages. FHL book 975.8573 R4if.

■ **Index to 1820 Land Lottery of Georgia**, originals from Georgia Surveyor General's Office. Contains list of participants in the 1820 land lottery. Contents: v. 1. A-M -- v. 2. M-Z. See FHL book 975.8 R2iL 1820 v.1 and 975.8 R2iL 1820 v.2. See also *The Third or 1820 Land Lottery of Georgia*, compiled by the Rev. Silas Emmett Lucas, Jr., published by Southern Historical Press, 1986, 374 pages, map, index. FHL book 975.8 R2La. For information about Georgia's land lotteries 1805-1832, see the following website: **http://ngeorgia.com/history/lotteries.html**.

■ 1820 Census, Rabun Co, Georgia **(reconstructed)**. One of the lost counties in the 1820 census for Georgia, a reconstructed name list can be found on the Internet at **www.usgennet.org/usa/region/southeast/garabun/1820/1820.html**.

■ **Index to 1821 Land Lottery of Georgia**, typescript at the state archives, filmed by the Genealogical Society of Utah, 1957. See FHL film 159020. For information about Georgia's land lotteries 1805-1832, see the following website: **http://ngeorgia.com/history/lotteries.html**.

■ *First Tax Digests of Fayette County, Georgia, 1823-1834*, published by Ancestors Unlimited, Jonesboro, GA, 1988, 246 pages. Includes tax digest for the years 1823, 1824, 1827, 1829, 1831, 1832, 1833, and 1834. Includes index. FHL book 975.8426 R4f.

■ *Washington County, Georgia, 1825 Tax Digest*, edited by Elizabeth Pritchard Newsom, Sandersville, GA, 1968, 168 pages, includes index. See FHL book 975.867 R4n.

■ *Reprint of Official Register of Land Lottery of Georgia, 1827*, compiled and published by Martha Lou Houston, 1929, Walton-Forbes, Columbus, GA, original printed in 1927 by Grantland & Orme, Milledgeville, GA, 298 pages, map, index. See FHL book 975.8 R2h.

■ *Washington County, Georgia, Index to 1828 Tax Digest, Index to 1836 Tax Digest, With Genealogical Gleanings*, compiled by William R. Henry for the Central Georgia Genealogical Society, Warner Robins, GA, 1987, 55 pages. FHL book 975.8672 R4h index.

■ *State of Georgia, Sixth or 1832 Land Lottery: Lists of Persons Eligible to Draw*, compiled by Joel Dixon Wells ; indexed by Mrs. Fred H. Hodges, Armchair Publications, Hamption, GA, 1983, 62 pages, index. See FHL book 975.86 R2w.

■ **1834 Georgia State Census**. Countywide extractions available for the following counties:
• **Cass County.** 1834 name list in *Georgia Genealogical Magazine*, No. 90 (Fall 1983).
• **Cobb County.** 1834 name lists published in *Alabama-Georgia Queries*, Vol. 5, No. 3 (May 1996); *Georgia Genealogical Magazine*, No. 89 (Summer 1983); and *Family Tree Newsletter*, No. 62 (Jul 1984).

- **Forsyth County**. 1834 name list published in *Georgia Genealogical Magazine*, No. 86 (Fall 1982).
- **Lumpkin County**. See *1834 Census of Lumpkin County, Georgia*, compiled by Frances T. Ingmire, St. Louis, MO, 198?, 8 pages. An alphabetical listing of all heads of household from 1834 Lumpkin County, Georgia State Census. FHL book 975.8 A1 no. 80.
- **Lumpkin County**. 1834 name list published in *Georgia Genealogical Magazine*, No. 87 (Winter 1983); and in *Georgia Genealogist*, No. 31 (Summer 1977).
- **Cass/Bartow County**. See *1834 State census, Cass/Bartow Counties, Georgia*, name list compiled by MariLee Beatty Hageness, Anniston, AL, MLH Research, 1994. Bartow County was called Cass County from 1831-1961. See FHL book 975.8365 X2.
- **Cherokee County**. See *1834 State Census, Cherokee County, Georgia*, name list compiled by MariLee Beatty Hageness, Anniston, AL, MLH Research, 1995, 6 pages. FHL book 975.8253 X2h 1834.
- **Cass, Cherokee, Cobb, Forsyth, Gilmer, Lumpkin, Murray**, and **Union** county-wide 1834 name lists published in *Northwest Georgia Historical and Genealogical Society Quarterly*, Vol. 12, No. 2 - 4.

■ *1838 Tax Digest for Macon County, Georgia*, by Davine V. Campbell, published by McDowell Publications for the Central Georgia Genealogical Society, Warner Robins, GA, 1993, 51 pages. Includes index. FHL book 975.8513 R4c.

■ **1838 State Census of Lumpkin County, Georgia**, name list published in *Armchair Researcher*, Vol. 4, No. 1 (Summer 1983); and in *Georgia Genealogist*, No. 31 (Summer 1977), and No. 32 (Fall 1977).

■ **1838 Georgia State Census, Paulding County**, name list published in *Northwest Georgia Historical and Genealogical Society Quarterly*, Vol. 12, No. 4; and in *Georgia Genealogical Magazine*, No. 86 (Fall 1982).

■ **1838 Georgia State Census, Murray County**, name list published in *Georgia Genealogical Magazine*, No. 91 (Winter 1984).

■ **Tax Digest, 1840-1845, 1858, Crawford County, Georgia**, originals at the Court of Ordinary, filmed by the Genealogical Society of Utah, 1965. FHL film 415203.

■ *1852 Tax Digest for Macon County, Georgia*, by Davine V. Campbell, published by McDowell Publications for the Central Georgia Genealogical Society, Warner Robins, GA, 1989, 55 pages. Includes index. FHL book 975.8513 R4c.

■ **1852 California State Census (Georgia People)**. See *Georgia Residents in the 1852 California State Census*, compiled by MariLee Beatty Hageness, Anniston, AL, MLH Research, 1998, 63 pages. See FHL book 975.8 X2h 1852.

■ **1859 State Census, Heads of household, Columbia County, Georgia**, compiled by the Gwinnett Historical Society, Lawrenceville, GA, published by MariLee Beatty Hageness, 1995, 127 pages. FHL book 975.8635 X2h.

■ **1859 State Census of Columbia County, Georgia**. Name list published in *Georgia Genealogical Society Quarterly*, Vol. 13, No. 4 (Winter 1977).

■ *1864 Census For Re-Organizing the Georgia Militia*, compiled by Nancy J. Cornell, published by Genealogical Publishing Co. Inc., Baltimore, 2000, 843 pages. From preface: "From originals at GDAH, this is an extraction and index of a special statewide census during the Civil War of all white males between the ages of 16 and 60 who were not at the time in the service of the Confederate States of America, it is a list of some 42,000 men; name, age, occupation, place of birth, and reason (if any) for his exemption from service. See FHL book 975.8 X22.

■ *Berrien County, Georgia, 1867 Tax Digest*, compiled by Myrtie Lou Griffin, et al, published by the Huxford Genealogical Society, Homerville, GA, 19??. FHL book 975.8862 R4b.

■ *Tax Digest of Dodge County, Georgia, 1871-1880*, originals at the Court of Ordinary filmed by the Genealogical Society of Utah, 1966. FHL film 470171.

■ *Berrien County, Georgia, 1885 Tax Digest*, publication information unknown, 150 pages. FHL book 975.8862 R49b.

■ *Clinch County, Georgia, Tax Digest, 1889-1897*, published by the Huxford Genealogical Society, Homerville, GA, 19??, 3 vols. Contents: Vol. 1. Wild land or unimproved land -- v. 2. Real estate and personal estate – v. 3. Real estate and personal estate. FHL book 975.8812 R4c v.1-3.

■ *Gwinnett County, Georgia 1890 Tax Digest with Land Lots: Substitute For Lost 1890 Federal Census*, compiled by Terry Edward Pyatt Manning, published by the Gwinnett Historical Society, Lawrenceville, GA, 127 pages. FHL book 975.8223 .

■ *1890 Tax Digest of Coweta County, Georgia: A Partial 1890 Census Substitute*, compiled by Mrs. Artie May Jones Storey and Elizabeth Faith Storey for Coweta County Genealogical Society, Inc., Newnan, Ga., 1992. Includes index. 141 pages. FHL book 975.8423 R4.

■ **1890 Federal Census, Washington County, Georgia,** one of only two counties in the U.S. with a county copy of the 1890 name lists (local officials copied the name lists into their Court of Ordinary records). See *1890 Federal Census, Court of Ordinary, Washington County, Georgia: Population Schedule,* compiled by William R. Henry, published by the Central Georgia Genealogical Society, Warner Robins, GA, 1994, 262 pages. FHL

book 975.8672 X28h. The originals are on 3 rolls of microfilm, FHL film #295947-295949.

■ *Berrien County, Georgia, 1901 Tax Digest*, published by the Huxford Genealogical Society, Homerville, GA, 19??, 104 pages. FHL book 975.8862 R4b 1901.

■ *1905 Tax List Catoosa County, Georgia*, compiled by MariLee Beatty Hageness, Anniston, AOL, MLH Research, 2001, 52 pages. FHL book 975.8326 R4h.

Georgia Censuses & Substitutes Online

■ **Georgia Censuses** (Including Federal, State, and Substitutes). Indexes originally edited by Ronald V. Jackson, Accelerated Indexing, Salt Lake City, UT. Electronic files were acquired by Ancestry, Inc. which has these Georgia lists indexed at their website, **www.ancestry.com**. Combined index contains the following:
- 1790 Tax Substitute Index
- 1792-1819 Tax Lists Index
- 1800 Oglethorpe County Census Index (from county copy of federal census)
- 1820-1930 Federal Census Index
- 1838 State Census
- 1840 Pensioners List
- 1845 State Census Index
- 1850 Slave Schedules
- 1850-1880 Mortality Schedules & Index
- 1860 Slave Schedule
- 1885-1940 Indian Census Schedules
- 1890 Veterans Schedule
- 1890 Reconstructed Census - Index
- 1900 Federal Census, Irwin County
- 1920 Federal Census, Worth County

■ **Georgia Census Records Online.** (CensusFinder.com). Several Georgia census lists are available at various sites on the Internet. Go to **www.censusfindercom/georgia.htm** to link to the following databases:
- 1790-1890 Georgia Census Search Engine at Ancestry
- 1835 Federal Pension List - Statewide
- 1880 Federal Census
- 1880 Federal Census Search at Family Search

■ **Links to Online Census Records**. (CensusOnline.com). This is an Internet website featuring links to census records online. Go to **www.census-online.com/links/GA/** to review Georgia census records published online. An example of what is available for one Georgia county is shown below:

Burke County, Georgia
  Federal Census
  • 1850 Federal Census
  • 1860 Federal Census - Slave Schedule
  • 1860 Federal Census - Slave Schedule Surname Matches with 1870 Census
  • 1880 Federal Census - Mortality Schedule
  • Index to 1850 Federal Census (alpha)
  Military Roster
  • Co. D - 48th GA Volunteers Infantry
  • Co. F - Cobb's Legion Cavalry

LOUISIANA

Censuses and Substitutes, 1696-1940

In its first legislative session of 1806, Orleans Territory authorized a census for that year. Although statistical returns were transmitted to the federal government, there appears to be no name list associated with the census. Louisiana's constitution of 1812 provided for state censuses to be taken every four years commencing in 1813. Only the statistical reports of the 1853 and 1858 enumerations have been found, neither with name lists. In 1898, Louisiana adopted the decennial censuses as the means of apportionment of state legislative districts. It appears that no statewide census name lists survive for Louisiana. Only a few isolated parish-wide lists have been found in local courthouses. The Louisiana State Archives in Baton Rouge has 1791 and 1804 censuses of New Orleans and 1849-1864 New Orleans registers of free persons of color. Other locations and/or publications where Louisiana's colonial, territorial, state, and census substitutes may be seen are indicated below, beginning with the oldest known lists, and continuing in chronological order to align with the timeline for census jurisdictions. If you have an Louisiana ancestor, start with the time period you know he/she was living there to see what census lists exist within a region or county.

■ *Early Louisiana Settlers, 1600s-1800s.* CD-ROM publication No. 525, produced for Family Tree Maker (Broderbund) archives in collaboration with Genealogical Publishing Co., Inc., Baltimore, 2000. Contents: *The Canary Islands Migration to Louisiana, 1778-1783: the History and Passenger Lists of the Islenos Volunteer Recruits and their Families,* compiled and written by Sidney Louis Villeré; *The Settlement of the German Coast of Louisiana and the Creoles of German Descent,* by J. Hanno Deiler; *The Census Tables for the French Colony of Louisiana from 1699 through 1732,* compiled and translated by Charles R. Maduell; *Louisiana Census Records, 1810 & 1820;* compiled by Robert Bruce L. Ardoin (vols. I-II); *Gulf Coast Colonials: A Compendium of French Families in early Eighteenth Century Louisiana,* by Winston De Ville: *The New Orleans French, 1720-1733: A Collection of Marriage Records Relating to the First Colonists of the Louisiana Province,* by Winston De Ville; *Old Families of Louisiana,* by Stanley Clisby Arthur, editor and compiler, George Campbell Huchet de Kernion, collaborator and historian; *Louisiana Troops, 1720-1770,* by Winston De Ville; *Louisiana Colonials: Soldiers and Vagabonds,* translated and compiled by Winston De Ville; and *Louisiana Soldiers in the War of 1812;* by Marion John Bennett Pierson.

■ **1696-1781 Colonial French Censuses**. Originals by the Governor-Generals of Louisiana, located at Archives Nationales, Paris. Includes correspondence, passenger lists, censuses, and land grants during the French administration of Louisiana. Filmed by the Genealogical Society of Utah, 1974. See FHL Film #1080001-1080002.

■ **1699-1732 Colonial French Louisiana Censuses.** Census lists for this period identified in **The Census Tables for the French Colony of Louisiana from 1699 through 1732**, compiled by Charles R. Maduell, first published 1916, reprinted by Genealogical Publishing Co., Inc., Baltimore, 1965, 190 pages. FHL book 976.3. (Included in 1723-1791 Louisiana: Mississippi Valley Mélange).

■ **1722-1803 Natchitoches Colonials: Censuses, Military Rolls, and Tax Lists**, Vol. 5 of Cane River Creole Series, by Elizabeth Shown Mills published by Adams Press, Chicago, 1981, 161 pages. This is a very complete listing of colonial censuses for the areas of Louisiana north and west of New Orleans. See FHL book 976.365 X2.

■ **1723-1791 Louisiana.** See *Mississippi Valley Mélange: a Collection of Notes and Documents for the Genealogy and History of the Province of Louisiana and the Territory of Orleans*, compiled by Winston De Ville, 3 vols., publ. Ville Platte, LA, 1996. Includes indexes. **Vol. 1** includes: *Illinois church records, 1723-1724; the French fort in the Tombigbee, 1729; on the founding of Pointe Coupée Post, 1729-1732; French troops of Illinois in 1752; Fuselier de la Claire and the lands of Attakapas and Opelousas in 1770; the census of Opelousas Post, 1774; Joachin de Ortega on the Texas Frontier--the Galvez correspondence of 1779; building Fort Miró in the Ouachita Valley of Spanish Louisiana, 1790-1791; slave owners of Pointe Coupée & False River in 1795; Metairie, Louisiana census of 1796; Bayou Sarah settlers in 1797; a Rapides Post petition of 1797 with 38 transcribed signatures; Southwest Louisiana ranchers, a ca. 1810 tax list.* **Vol. 2** includes: *knighthood in colonial Louisiana; Juchereau de St. Denys and the Order of St. Louis; Louisiana officers in 1740—the Bienville recommendations; French troops in New Orleans, 1745; land owners below New Orleans in 1751; Acadians in Philadelphia; a pro- spective first militia of Attakapas Post—the roll of 1773; the D'Hauterive land grant of 1775—aristocratic perquisite in south-*west Louisiana; Galvez rosters of 1779—soldier selection at the German and Acadian coasts during the American Revolution; southwest Louisiana militianmen during the American Revolution—the rosters of Attakapas and Opelousas posts in 1780; Louisiana loyalists in 1781; of clavinette and violin in colonial Louisiana—questions on Acadian music in 1785; Attakapas Post petitioners of 1791—an Acadian and Creole defense of a commandant; the greening of New Orleans in 1792—Governor Carondelet as environmentalist; lost in the Latin South—a petition of some Anglo-Americans, ca. 1792; turmoil in Spanish Louisiana—a public notice of 1793.* **Vol. 3** includes: *The Bermudez Manuscript of 1612; Louisiana officers in 1714; Military deserters of Louisiana in 1716; Constructing a future cathedral, 1724; A Natchitoches narrative of 1732; Four letters of 1734; on the family Fontenette; Anglo-Americans in British West Florida; The loyalist military in colonial Mississippi, 1779; Terre aux Boeufs militia men in 1779; Anglo-Americans in early Mobile, 1780; Public balls of New Orleans in 1792; the Ursuline convent in 1795;* and *Militia officers of Orleans Territory in 1808.* FHL book 976.3 D2de v.1-3.

■ **1724 Louisiana Censuses.** See *German Ancestors and Patriots of Louisiana, 1722-1803*, by Leroy E. Willie. Includes 1724 census & other name lists. FHL book 976.3 D2w.

■ **1749 Louisiana.** See "German coast of LA, 1749: Reconstructed Families," in *Louisiana Genealogical Register*, Vol. 29, No. 4 (Dec 1982).

■ **1758-1796 Louisiana.** See *Some Late Eighteenth Century Louisianians, 1758-1796,* by Jacqueline K. Voorhies, publ. Lafayette, LA, 1973. (Book not at FHL, check New Orleans Public, LSU, or LA state archives). Note: The name lists in this book, combined with the lists in Elizabeth Shown Mill's *1722-1808 Natchitoches Colonials* are more complete than those identified elsewhere.

■ **1759-1812 Spanish / French / American Censuses, Louisiana Jurisdictions**, originals at the Louisiana State Archives, microfilmed as a ten-roll series TXU7, Natchez Trace Provincial and Territorial Records (Louisiana Jurisdictions):

- 1759-1812 Pointe Coupe
- 1764, 1791, 1796, 1798 Natchitoches
- 1767-1794 New Orleans
- 1768 German Coast (Allemant)
- 1772 Natchez
- 1772-1810 Iberville
- 1784 -1787 The Missouri
- 1793-1796 Rapides
- 1793-1812 Feliciana/West Feliciana
- 1794-1812 New Orleans
- 1777-1811 Opelousas
- 1777 Attakapas
- 1783-1812 Natchez
- 1783-1806 Avoyelles
- 1798-1812 Baton Rouge/East Baton Rouge
- 1803-1812 Concordia
- 1804-1812 St. Helena
- 1807, 1811 West Florida
- 1810 Lafourche
- 1812 Acadia

■ **1766, 1769, 1777 Acadian Coast Census Indexes**, see *Louisiana's Acadian Coast Census Index, 1766, 1769, 1777: With Annotations*, by Phoebe Chauvin Morrison. CD-ROM Publication, published Houma, LA, 2001. Index indicates both husbands and wives by family numbers, with annotated census records citing the sources of location: Fam. No., Name, Born, Married, Spouse, Parents, & Notes. See FHL CD-ROM no. 684.

■ **1770-1789 Colonial Spanish Louisiana Censuses**. See *Louisiana Census and Militia Lists, 1770-1789, Volume I : German Coast, New Orleans, below New Orleans and Lafourche*, compiled, translated and edited by Albert J. Robichaux, Jr., original published: Harvey, LA,1973, 170 pages. Census records acquired from the Papeles Procedentes de Cuba deposited in the General Archives de Indies in Seville, Spain. Includes: 1770 militia lists of New Orleans; 1777 general census of the city of New Orleans; 1770 militia of the German Coast; 1784 general census of the second German Coast; 1785 militia list of St. Charles Parish; 1770 general census below New Orleans; 1789 general census of Lafourche. Includes index. Filmed by the Genealogical Society of Utah, 1991. See FHL film 6088510.

■ **1779 Colonial Spanish Census**. See *The Acadian Coast in 1779: Settlers of Cabanocey and La Fourche in the Spanish Province of Louisiana During the American Revolution,* by Winston De Ville, pub. 1993, Ville Platte, LA. Includes index. FHL book 976.3 X29d.

■ **1781-1797 Colonial Spanish Louisiana Censuses**. See *Anglo-Americans in Spanish archives: lists of Anglo-American settlers in the Spanish colonies of America; a finding aid,* by Lawrence H. Feldman. Published by Genealogical Publishing Co., Inc., 1991, 349 pages. Abstracted from original census documents, includes genealogical data about individuals and families who settled in the French territories of Louisiana and the Floridas after they came under Spanish rule in 1766. Includes an index of personal names. FHL book 973 X2fe.

■ **1781 Attakapas Tax List**, see "Census and Tax List for Church at Attakapas, 1781," in *Attakapas Gazette*, Vol. 20, No. 1 (Spring 1985).

■ **1782, 1786 & 1793 Censuses, Louisiana's Florida Parishes**. See *Baton Rouge & New Feliciana: Census Reports for Louisiana's Florida Parishes in 1782, 1786, & 1793,* by Albert J. Tate and Winston De Ville, publ. by Provincial Press, Lafayette, LA, 2000, 90 pages. Louisiana's "Florida Parishes" include the following parishes of today: East Baton Rouge, West Feliciana, East Feliciana, St. Helena, Livingston, Tangipahoa, Washington and St. Tammany. See FHL book 976.3 X2t.

■ **1784 Colonial Spanish Census, Valenzuela**. See *Valenzuela in the Province of Louisiana: A*

Census of 1784, by Winston De Ville, publ. 1987, LA?. The settlers were natives of the Canary Islands who arrived between 1778 and 1783. Includes surname index. FHL book 976.3 A1 no. 56.

■ **1790-1791 Colonial Spanish Census Substitute**. See *The Natchez Ledgers, 1790-1791: A Finding-Aid for Anglo-Americans in Pre-Territorial Mississippi,* compiled by Winston De Ville, publ. Ville Platte, LA, 1994, 89 pages. FHL book 976.2 R49d.

■ **1791 Colonial Spanish Census of New Orleans**. An English translation, made by the City Archives Department, is filed under call number AA840, New Orleans Public Library. The census is indexed in *New Orleans Genesis,* vol. 1; the original index to the census is housed at the Louisiana State Museum. This census, dated November 6, 1791, is arranged by street of residence of the enumerated individuals, apparently the heads of households. In addition to the named individuals, each entry also records the numbers of other members of the household by category as follows: white men, white women, free men of mixed blood, free women of mixed blood, free negro men, free negro women, male slaves of mixed blood, female slaves of mixed blood, negro male slaves, and negro female slaves.

■ **1793 Colonial Spanish Census, New Feliciana**. See *New Feliciana in the Province of Louisiana: A Guide to the Census of 1793,* by Winston De Ville, publ. 1987, 32 pages. Includes surname index. See FHL book 976.3 A1 no. 57.

■ *1795 Chimney Tax of New Orleans: A Guide to the Census of Proprietors and Residents of the Vieux Carré,* compiled by Winton De Ville, publ. Ville Platte, LA, 1995, 31 pages. FHL book 976.335/N1 R4d.

■ **1795 Louisiana Tax List**, see "Tax on Slave Owners, 1795," in *Raconteur,* Vol. 13, No. 1 (Apr 1993) and Vol. 2, No. 12 (Aug 1992) and Vol. 3-4 (Dec 1992).

■ **1804 Census, City of New Orleans**, originals filmed as *Mayor's Office, Census of the City of New Orleans, 1804.* Microfilm at New Orleans Public Library, filed under call number TK840 1804. Contains a record in English and French, giving names of male residents and their wives or other adult women living in the household, the profession and employment of the male, the age of males and females, the number of boys and girls living in the household, and, usually, their ages. The number of male and female adult and juvenile slaves in each household is also tallied; no names are recorded for slaves. A final column, labeled "Observations," indicates the head of household's military status, listing the company in which he served. Also available at FHL as film 1309932 Item 1.

■ *Southwest Louisiana in 1807: The Land and Slave Tax of St. Landry Parish in the Territory of Orleans,* by Winston De Ville, publ. Ville Platte, LA, 1993, 51 pages. FHL book 976.346 R4d.

■ **1808 Tax List**, see "Taxpayers, 1808," in *Louisiana Genealogical Register,* Vol. 11, No. 4 (Dec 1964).

■ **1813 Louisiana State Census, St. Landry Parish**. See "Census of 1813--Territory of Louis Carriere", in *Louisiana Genealogical Register,* Vol. IV, No. 2 (Jun 1967). Names listed at **http://ftp.rootsweb.com/pub/usgenweb/la/stlandry/ census/cen1813.txt**.

■ **1817, 1818 Louisiana Land Holders, St. Landry Parish**. See *Land Holders of Southwest Louisiana: Tax Lists for St. Landry Parish, 1817 and 1818,* compiled by Ramona A. Smith, publ. Ville Platte, LA, 1990, 70 pages. FHL book 976.346 R2s.

■ **1833 Louisiana State Census, St. Tammany Parish**. Name list available at: **ftp://ftp.rootsweb.com/pub/usgenweb/la/sttamman/census/cens1833.txt**.

■ *1835 Tax List and 1840 Census, St. Helena Parish, Louisiana*, compiled by Donald W. Johnson and Inez B. Tate. Includes 1835 tax information in a case of miscellaneous papers in the office of the clerk of court, St. Helena Parish, Louisiana, published by the St. Helena Historical Association, Greensburg, Louisiana, 2000. Includes surname index.

■ **1837 Louisiana State Census, St. Tammany Parish**. Name list available at **ftp://ftp.rootsweb.com/pub/usgenweb/la/sttamman/census/cens1837.txt**.

■ **1837 New Orleans Census.** Originals at Orleans Parish Courthouse, filmed by the Genealogical Society of Utah, 1972 as *Assessment of Property and Census of Slaves and their Owners, 1837.* See FHL film 906708 Item 3.

■ **1844-1846 Census of Licensed Merchants, City of Lafayette. Commissary of Police.** The City of Lafayette, covering the area now known as the Garden District and the Irish Channel, was incorporated as part of Jefferson Parish in 1833. In 1852, it was annexed to the City of New Orleans as the Fourth Municipal District. Its original boundaries were the River, Toledano Street, St. Charles Avenue, and Felicity Street. This census, arranged by type of business (e.g., coffee houses or taverns; dry goods merchants), gives the name and location of businesses, the date the license was issued, the term of the license, and its expiration date. Original records at the New Orleans Public Library, filed under call number II LM430 1841-1849.

■ **1845 Pointe Coupee Census.** Extract of names available online at **www.geocities.com/Heartland/Acres/5571/pc1745cen.htm**.

■ **1850-1890 Germans of New Orleans.** See *Zur Geschichte der Deutschen Kirchengemeinden im Staate Louisiana*, by J. Hanno Deiler, publ. New Orleans, 1894. The story of the German church in Louisiana and a history of the Germans of the lower Mississippi with a census of New Orleans German schools and foreign inhabitants, 1850-1890. Includes index. Filmed by the Genealogical Society of Utah, 1981. See FHL film #1305374 Item 4.

■ **1854-1857 Census, City of Carrollton.** The City of Carrollton was incorporated in 1845 as part of Jefferson Parish and, in 1874, was annexed to the City of New Orleans. The boundaries of Carrollton were the River, the present Jefferson Parish line, the shore of Lake Pontchartrain, and Lowerline Street (and its projected extension to the Lake). This census gives the name and occupation of householders in the City of Carrollton and tallies the number of males and females in each household, and the number of children in general age groups. The names are grouped alphabetically by first letter of the name only. Original records at the New Orleans Public Library, Volume 1 (1854-1855) is not filmed. Volume 2 is filed under call number IV TK840 1854-1857.

■ *1855-1856 New Orleans Census of Merchants and Persons Following Professions Requiring Licenses*, 3 vols., original records at the New Orleans Public Library, filed under call number LC840. These volumes give name, residence or place of business, callings or professions, number of license, amount paid, and remarks; individuals are listed together by square of property occupied; related forms are also included at the front of each volume. Volume one (1855) is for the Second Ward; volume two (1855) covers the Third Ward; and volume three (1856) is for the Third Municipal District. Indexed.

■ **1863-1866 Internal Revenue Assessment Lists for Louisiana,** Bureau of Internal Revenue, microfilm of originals at the National Archives, Central Plains Region, 1985, 10 rolls. National Archives series M0769. **District 1 contains** Ascension, Jefferson, Lafourche, Livingston, Orleans, Plaquemines, St. Bernard, St. Charles, St.

Helena, St. James, St. John the Baptist, St. Tammany, Terrebonne, Washington parishes. **District 2 contains** Assumption, Avoyelles, Calcasieu, East Baton Rouge, East Feliciana, Iberville, Lafayette, Natchitoches, Pointe Coupee, Rapides, Sabine, St. Landry, St. Martin, St. Mary, Vermilion, West Baton Rouge, West Felilciana parishes. **District 3 contains** Bienville, Bossier, Caddo, Caldwell, Carroll, Catahoula, Claiborne, Concordia, De Soto, Franklin, Jackson, Madison, Morehouse, Ouachita, Tensas, Union, Winn parishes. Microfilm also located at FHL, see film #1578469-1578478.

■ **1864 Tax List, Ascension Parish**, see "Direct tax, 1864," in *Ascension Roots*, Vol. 10, No. 1 (Mar 1990).

■ **1865 Louisiana Tax List**. See *The Civil War Tax in Louisiana, 1865: Based on Direct Tax Assessments of Louisianians,* original printed 1892 with the title, *List of Names of Citizens of Louisiana From Whom the United States Direct Tax was Collected in 1865, Together with the Amounts Paid by Each.* Reprinted 1975 by Polyantos, Inc., New Orleans, 363 pages. See FHL book 976.3 R4c.

■ **1860s Louisiana Tax Lists**. Over 100 references to published parish-wide tax lists for this time period can be found in genealogical periodicals. Find them using the PERSI search engine at Ancestry's website: **www.ancestry.com/search/ rectype/periodicals/persi/main.htm**. Use "PERSI's U.S. Locality Section," select "Louisiana" for the locality and for the Record Type, use "Tax." Four samples of the results from this specific search are shown below:
- **1865 Tax List, Bienville**, see "Assessment Roll, 1865," in *Claiborne Parish Trails*, Vol. 12, No. 1 (Feb 1997).
- **1865 Tax List, Caddo**, see "Assessment rolls, 1865," in *Friends of Genealogy Journal*, Vol. 3, No. 1 (1991).
- **1865 Tax List, Baton Rouge**, see "Assessment list, 1865, 2nd District," in *Baton Rouge*, Vol. 20, No. 2 (Summer 2000).
- **1865 Louisiana Civil War Tax Lists**, see "Civil War Tax lists, 1865." In *Living Tree News*, Vol. 23, No. 1-4 (Winter 1998).

■ *1869-1870 Orleans Parish Poll Tax Rolls*, compiled by Judy Riffel, et al., publ. Baton Rouge, LA, 1996, 258 pages. An index to the original tax records for the city of New Orleans, Louisiana. The original microfilm reels are located at the Louisiana State Archives (accession numbers: P1978-170 for 1869; P1978-172 for 1870). Index book only at FHL, book 976.335/N1 R42r.

■ **1879, 1881, 1885, 1890 Louisiana Tax Rolls, Madison Parish**. See *Tax Rolls, Madison Parish, Louisiana Tax Rolls*, compiled by Richard P. Sevier, published Midland, TX, 1998, 2 vols. Names are in alphabetical order. For each person/year: name; ward; plantation or property name and/or location; property description; number of acres; assessed value of land; line number. See FHL book 976.381 R4m v.1 (1879 & 1881) & 976.381 R4 v.2.(1885 & 1890).

■ **1887 Winn Parish Tax List**, see "Tax roll, 1887," in *Legacies & Legends of Winn Parish*, Vol. 4, No. 3 (Oct 2000).

■ *Ascension Parish, Louisiana, 1890 U. S. Census,* compiled and edited by Rita Babin Butler, published by Oracle Press, Baton Rouge, LA, 1983, 256 pages. One of only two counties/parishes in the U.S. for which a county copy of the 1890 name lists exist. The 8 wards of Ascension Parish are included. See FHL book 976.319 X2b.

■ *1890 Louisiana Census Index: Special Schedule of the Eleventh Census (1890) Enumerating Union Veterans and Widows of Union veterans of the Civil War*, Ronald Vern Jackson, editor, Accelerated Indexing, Salt Lake City, 198?, 126 pages. FHL book 976.3 X22L. See also *1890 Louisiana Census Index of Civil War Veterans or their Widows*, Bryan Lee Dilts, editor, publ. 1984, Salt Lake City, 68 pages. FHL book 976.3 X2d.

■ **1892-1898 Registers of Direct Tax Payers**, microfilm copy of original records located at the State Archives and Records Service, Baton Rouge, Louisiana. Does not include Acadia, Calcasieu, Cameron, Grant, Iberia, Lincoln, Red River, Richland, Tangipahoa, Union, Vermilion, Vernon, or Webster parishes. Filmed by the Genealogical Society of Utah, 1985. 5 rolls, FHL film 1412744-1412748.

■ *1899 Census of Vernon Parish, Louisiana Children Between the ages of 6 and 18 years,* compiled by Karl R. & Doris H. Mayo, publ. Leesville, LA, 1990, 70 pages. Includes children's ages, sex, and race in alphabetical order by ward. See FHL book 976.361.

■ **1911 Enumeration of Confederate Soldiers and Widows of Deceased Soldiers of Louisiana**, microfilm of original records located at the State Archives and Records Service, Baton Rouge, Louisiana. Filmed by the Genealogical Society of Utah, 1985. Indexed as *Enumeration of ex-Confederate soldiers and widows of deceased soldiers of Louisiana, made in 1911*, by Houston C. Jenks, FHL book 976.3 M22j.

■ **1920-1940 New Orleans Voter Registration Cards**, New Orleans Registrar of Voters. Microfilm copy of original records located at the New Orleans Public Library, New Orleans, Louisiana. Contains names, birthplace, age, date of birth, sex, race, and political persuasion. Filmed by the New Orleans Public Library, Louisiana Division, 1983, 11 rolls. Also available at the FHL as *Voter registration cards, 1920-1940, second series*, FHL film #1412334-1412343, and 1689670.

Louisiana Censuses & Substitutes Online

■ **Louisiana Censuses 1810-1930**. Originally compiled by Ronald V. Jackson, Accelerated Indexing, Salt Lake City, UT. Electronic files were acquired by Ancestry, Inc. which has these Louisiana lists indexed at their website, **www.ancestry.com**. The combined index contains the following:
- 1699-1722 French Colony Census Tables
- 1810 & 1820 Census Records, Avoyelles and St. Landry, Iberville, Natchitoches, Pointe Coupee, and Rapides Parishes.
- 1810 Orleans Territory Federal Census
- 1820 Federal Census
- 1830 Federal Census
- 1840 Federal Census
- 1850 Federal Census
- 1850 Slave Schedules
- 1850-1880 Mortality Schedules & Index

- 1860 Federal Census
- 1860 Slave Schedules
- 1870 Federal Census
- 1880 Federal Census
- 1885-1940 Indian Census Schedules
- 1890 Veterans Schedules
- 1900 Federal Census
- 1910 Federal Census
- 1920 Federal Census
- 1930 Federal Census

■ **1810-1880 Louisiana Census Records Online.** (CensusFinder.com). Several Louisiana census lists are available at various sites on the Internet. Access through **www.censusfinder.com/ louisiana.htm** to link to the following sites:
- 1810-1890 Louisiana Census Records
- 1835 Federal Pension List - Statewide
- 1867-1868 Louisiana State Seminary, Students/Faculty
- 1867-1868 Louisiana State Seminary, Military Academy
- 1880 Federal Census
- 1880 Federal Census Search at Family Search

■ **Links to Online Census Records.** (CensusOnline.com). This is an Internet website featuring links to census records online. Go to **www.census-online.com/links/LA/** to review Louisiana census records published online. An example of what is available for one Louisiana parish is shown below:
St. Tammany Parish, Louisiana
  Federal Census
- 1830 Federal Census

  Tax List
- 1851 Non-Resident Taxpayers
- 1852 Delinquent Taxpayers
- 1872 Tax List

  Miscellaneous
- 1833 Census
- 1833 Voters Census
- 1837 Census
- 1838 Voters List
- 1864 Civil War Tax List
- 1868 Voter Registration
- Voter Registration 1868-1870

MISSISSIPPI

Censuses and Substitutes, 1776-1886

Census lists were created in the earliest settlements on the Gulf Coast, including those in present-day Mississippi by the French, Spanish, and Americans. References to territorial censuses in Mississippi archives describe those taken in 1801, 1805, 1808, 1810, and 1816. Territorial legislation in 1803 called for censuses to be taken by captains of the militia, showing free white males and females, slaves, and free persons of color. Only the head of a household was named in these early censuses. The MS Department of History and Archives (MDHA) has original state censuses relating to all Mississippi counties, and all have been microfilmed. Those from 1792-1866 are shown below (microfilm recently digitized and made available online at **www.ancestry.com**). Other locations and/or publications where Mississippi's colonial, territorial, state, and census substitutes may be seen are indicated below, beginning with the oldest known lists, and continuing in chronological order to align with the timeline for census jurisdictions. If you have a Mississippi ancestor, start with the time period you know he/she was living there to see what census lists exist within a region or county.

- **1776-1816 Natchez District Censuses**. See *Early Inhabitants of the Natchez District*, by Norman Gillis, published by the author, Baton Rouge, LA, 1963, 152 pages, FHL book 976.2 X2p.

- **1781-1797 Colonial Spanish Censuses**. See *Anglo-Americans in Spanish Archives: Lists of Anglo-American Settlers in the Spanish Colonies of America; a finding Aid*, by Lawrence H. Feldman, published by Genealogical Publishing Co., Inc., Baltimore, 1991, 349 pages. Includes original census documents and genealogical data about individuals and families who settled in the French territories of Louisiana and the Floridas after they came under Spanish rule in 1766 (the areas settled correspond to the present-day states of Florida, Alabama, Mississippi, Louisiana, and Missouri. Includes an index of personal names. See FHL book 973 X2fe.

- **1790 Federal Census.** The U.S. in 1790 objected to Spain's control over the Natchez area in present-day southwestern Mississippi north of Latitude 31^0, but took no 1790 census there.

- **1790-1791 Colonial Spanish Census Substitute**. See *The Natchez Ledgers, 1790-1791: A Finding-Aid for Anglo-Americans in Pre-Territorial Mississippi*, compiled by Winston De Ville, publ. Ville Platte, LA, 1994, 89 pages. FHL book 976.2 R49d.

- **1792-1866 Mississippi State Census Records**. Originals located at the MDAH, Jackson, MS. Microfilm at MDAH and FHL in Salt Lake City, under the title, *State Census Records, 1792-1866*, Mississippi Secretary of State. This series of 3 rolls of microfilm begins with abstracts of census statistics, 1801-1845; plus the Spanish census of 1792 for Natchez District, beginning on FHL film #899868; followed by territory and state census records by county and year, for Adams - Holmes Counties, 1810-1866; Issaquena - Simpson Counties 1805-1866; Smith - Yazoo Counties 1805-1866. (Census dates indicated below with an asterisk (*) are copies of census statistics only, and do not include a name list).

Roll 1, FHL film #899868
- Natchez District, Spanish Census of 1792
- Adams County 1816, 1818, 1823*, 1830 (Natchez only), 1841 & 1853
- Amite County: 1810, 1816, 1820, 1824*, 1833*, 1845 & 1853
- Attala County: 1841
- Bainbridge County: 1823
- Baldwin County: (now Alabama) 1810 & 1816
- Bolivar County: 1841, 1866
- Chickasaw County: 1837 & 1841
- Choctaw County: 1837, 1840*, 1860, & 1837
- Claiborne County: 1810, 1816, 1822*, 1823* & 1825
- Clarke County: 1816, 1841* & 1853
- Coahoma County: 1841

- Copiah County: 1822*, 1824*, 1825*, 1841 & 1853
- Covington County: 1825* & 1841
- DeSoto County: 1841*
- Franklin County: 1810, 1816, 1820, 1833* & 1841
- Greene County: 1816, 1825*, 1841* & 1853
- Hancock County: 1823*, 1825*, 1830*, 1840 & 1853.
- Hinds County: 1824* & 1850
- Holmes County: 1866

Roll 2, FHL film #899869
- Issaquena County: 1866
- Itawamba County: 1837, 1841, 1853 & 1860
- Jackson County: 1825 & 1841*
- Jasper County: 1866
- Jefferson County: 1805, 1808, 1810, 1816, 1823*, 1825*, 1841*, 1853 & 1866
- Jones County: 1837, 1841 &1853
- Kemper County: 1837 & 1841*
- Lauderdale County: 1841* & 1853
- Lawrence County: 1818, 1823, 1824*, 1824*, 1825*, 1830*, 1841 & Census, date unknown.
- Leake County: 1841, 1853 & 1866.
- Lowndes County: 1837.
- Madison County: 1841, ca. 1830-1840.
- Marion County: 1816, 1820, 1823*, 1824*, 1825*, 1841, 1866.
- Marshall County: 1841
- Monroe County: 1815-1817, 1841, 1845, ca. 1841-45
- Noxubee County: 1841*, 1845 & 1853
- Oktibbeha County: 1837, 1841 & 1845
- Panola County: 1837, 1841, 1845 & 1853
- Perry County: 1822-3*, 1825*, 1841*, 1845 & 1853
- Pike County: 1816, 1820, 1825*, 1830*, 1841* & 1845*
- Pontotoc County: 1837 & 1845
- Rankin County: 1845 & 1853.
- Scott County: 1841& 1845.
- Simpson County: 1824*, 1825*, 1837, 1841, 1845* & 1866

Roll 3, FHL film #899870
- Smith County: 1841, 1845, 1866
- Sunflower County: 1845
- Tallahatchie County: 1841, 1845*
- Tippah County: 1841 & 1845
- Tishomingo County: 1837, 1841* & 1845
- Tunica County: 1841 & 1845*
- Warren County: 1816, 1825* & 1845
- Washington County: (now Alabama) 1808 & 1810
- Washington County: (created 1827) 1841 & 1845*
- Wayne County: 1816, 1820, 1841, 1845, 1853 & 1866
- Wilkinson County: 1805, 1813, 1816, 1820, 1822*, 1823*, 1825 & 1845
- Winston County: 1837, 1845* 1853
- Yalobusha County: 1845
- Yazoo County: 1824*, 1825*, 1841 & 1845

■ **1797-1817 Mississippi Territory.** See *Residents of Mississippi Territory,* by Jean Strickland and Patricia N. Edwards, published Moss Point, MS, 1995, 3 vols. Contains miscellaneous records such as court records, land and property, census, maps, passports, tax rolls, etc. FHL book 976.2 X2s v1-3.

■ **1797-1817 Mississippi Territory.** See *Residents of the Southeastern Mississippi Territory,* by Jean Strickland and Patricia N. Edwards, published Moss Point, MS, 1995-96, 7 vols. Includes censuses, tax rolls and petitions; James Leander Cathart journal; Journey from Georgia to Louisiana, 1812; John Landreth Journal; Washington and Baldwin Counties, Alabama Wills, Deeds and Superior Court minutes; Records of Spanish West Florida, 1782-1806; and Records of Spanish West Florida, 1806+. FHL book 976.21 H29s v.1-7.

■ **1800** Mississippi Territory Federal Census. The federal census was taken for Washington County, which lay mostly in Alabama, but with parts into present-day Mississippi. Unfortunately, that census was lost.

■ *Washington County, Mississippi Territory 1803-1816 Tax Rolls,* compiled by Ben and Jean Strickland, publ. Milton, FL, 1980, 117 pages. Washington County, Mississippi Territory later became Wayne, Greene, Jones, Perry, George and Jackson Counties, Mississippi and Washington, Baldwin, Monroe, Clarke and Mobile Counties, Alabama. Includes index. FHL book 976 R4s.

■ **1801 Mississippi Territory Census, Jefferson County.** Name list published in Vicksburg Genealogical Society Newsletter, Vol. 5, No. 1 (Sep 1988).

■ **1801 Mississippi Territory Census, Washington County.** Name list in Mississippi Records, Vol. 2, No. 3 (Jul 1990).

■ **1805 Mississippi State Census, Wilkinson County.** Name list published in Journal of Mississippi History, Vol. 11, No. 2 (Apr 1949).

■ **1809 Mississippi Territory Census.** Includes present-day Mississippi and Alabama areas. A name list of heads of households was published as part of *The Territorial Papers of the United States*, compiled and edited by Clarence Edwin Carter, United States Department of State. See FHL film #42234.

■ *1809 Squatters Census, Mississippi Territory*, a census of "Squatters" listing head of household in alphabetical order. Author/publisher unknown, 1995?. A squatter was someone who moved into and settled an area of the U.S. Public Domain land before the land was surveyed and available for sale by the Federal Government. Congress passed several acts relating to "preemption," where squatters were given an opportunity to prove title to their land based on their early occupation – but only if they could show that they actually lived on the property and crops had been planted. See FHL 976.2 X28s.

■ **1800, 1810, 1816 Mississippi Territory Censuses (Western Part).** Name lists published in *Alabama Historical Quarterly*, Vol. 24, No. 1 (Spring 1962).

■ **1810 Mississippi Territory Census.** The federal census was taken for Washington and Baldwin counties and both were lost. But, Mississippi Territory took its own census in 1810 in addition to the federal census. A portion of old Washington County was in the present-day area of Mississippi, and a county name list survives for the territorial census. See "Washington County (now) Alabama 1801, 1808 and 1810 Census," in *The Alabama Genealogical Register*, Vol. 9, No. 3 (September 1967), pp 123-26.

■ **1815 Mississippi State Census** (sic), **Monroe County**, "State census, 1815," in *Northeast*

Mississippi Historical & Genealogical Society Quarterly, Vol. 6, No. 3 (Spring 1986). Title probably refers to an 1815 name list taken during the territorial period. MS became a state in 1817.

■ **1816 Mississippi Territory Census.** Statewide name list published serially in *Alabama Family History and Genealogy News*, Vol. 1, No. 1 (Jan 1980) thru Vol. 1, No. 3 (Jul 1980).

■ **1816 Mississippi Territory Census.** Countywide extractions published in periodicals for the following counties:
- **Adams County**. 1816 name list published serially in *National Genealogical Society Quarterly*, Vol. 37, No. 4 (Dec 1949) thru Vol. 38, No. 3 (Sep 1950).
- **Amite County**. 1816 name list published serially in *National Genealogical Society Quarterly*, Vol. 33, No. 4 (Dec 1945) thru Vol. 34, No. 2 (Jun 1946).
- **Clarke County**. 1816 name list published in *Deep South Genealogical Quarterly*, Vol. 16, No. 1 (Feb 1979); and Mississippi Memories, Vol. 10, No. 1 (2000).
- **Greene County**. 1816 name list published in *Success*, Vol. 7, No. 3 (Jul 1977); and in *American Monthly Magazine*, Vol. 83, No. 3 (Mar 1949); and also in *Deep South Genealogical Quarterly*, Vol. 14, No. 4 (Nov 1977).
- **Jefferson County**. 1816 heads of households listed in *Mississippi Memories*, Vol. 6, No. 1 (1996).

■ **1820-1825 Mississippi Censuses**, indexed in *Mississippi, 1820-1825: Covering 1820, 1822, 1823, 1824 &1825*, edited by Ronald Vern Jackson, et al, Accelerated Indexing, North Salt Lake, UT, 1986, 119 pages. FHL book 976.2 X22j.

■ **1825 Mississippi State Census, Jackson County**, see "State census, 1825," in *Jackson County Genealogical Society Journal*, Vol. 2, No. 2 (Spring 1985) and again in Vol. 17, No. 1-4 (Dec 2000).

■ **1825 Mississippi State Census, Wilkinson County**, name list in *Mississippi Genealogical Exchange*, Vol. 32, No. 4 (Winter 1986).

■ **1827-1840s:** *Early Mississippi Records, Issaquena County & Washington County,* compiled by Katherine Branton & Alice Wade, published by Pioneer, Carrollton, MS, 1983-2000. Earlier title: *Early Mississippi records, Washington County, Mississippi.* It should be noted that Washington County, Mississippi Territory (now Alabama) was created in 1800. The current Washington County, Mississippi was created in 1827; Issaquena was formed from Washington in 1844. Both lie adjoining the Mississippi River. These extracted county records include court documents, will and probate records, cemetery records, census records, deaths, marriage records, patents, packet gleanings, medical licenses, and an index to apprentice records. See FHL book 976.24P28v.1-4.

■ **1830-1837 Mississippi Censuses.** Indexed in *Mississippi 1830/1837,* edited by Ronald Vern Jackson, et al, Accelerated Indexing Systems, North Salt Lake, UT, 1986, 63 pages. FHL book 976.2 X2jac.

■ **1833 Mississippi State Census, Simpson County.** Name list published in *Frameworks,* No. 2 (Summer 2000).

■ **1835 Federal Pension List, Mississippi.** Report from the Secretary of War in Relation to the Pension Establishment of the United States. There are a few names online at **http://members.tripod.com/~rosters/index-45.html.**

■ **1837 Mississippi State Census.** Countywide extractions published in periodicals for the following counties:
- **Chickasaw County,** see "State census, 1837," in *Northeast Mississippi Historical & Genealogical Society Quarterly,* Vol. 7, No. 1 (Fall 1986); and in *Chickasaw Times Past,* Vol. 9, No. 4 (Jan 1991).
- **Jones County,** see "State census, 1837," in *Mississippi Genealogical Exchange,* Vol. 16, No. 2 (Summer 1970) and Vol. 16, No. 3 (Fall 1970).
- **Kemper County,** State census, 1837," in *Mississippi Genealogical Exchange,* Vol. 18, No. 1 (Spring 1972); Vol. 18, No. 2 (Summer 1972), and

Vol. 18, No. 4 (Winter 1972).
- **Itawamba County.** 1837 and 1841 name lists published in *Northeast Mississippi Historical & Genealogical Society Quarterly,* Vol. 6, No. 4 (1986).
- **Panola County.** 1837 name list published serially in *Mississippi Genealogical Exchange,* Vol. 19, No. 1 (Spring 1973) thru Vol. 19, No. 3 (Fall 1973).
- **Pontotoc County.** 1837 name list published in *Mississippi Records,* Vol. 1, No. 4 (Oct 1989); and in *Mississippi Genealogical Exchange,* Vol. 25, No. 1 (Spring 1979); and also in *Northeast Mississippi Historical & Genealogical Society Quarterly,* Vol. 6, No. 4 (1986).
- **Simpson County.** 1837 name list published in *Mississippi Records,* Vol. 2, No. 1 (Jan 1990).
- **Tishomingo County.** 1837 name list published in *Cross City Connections,* Vol. 8, No. 2 (Dec 1999); and in *Mississippi Genealogical Exchange,* Vol. 17, No. 1 (Spring 1971) thru Vol. 17, No. 2 (Summer 1971).

■ **1840/1841 Mississippi Censuses,** indexed in *Mississippi 1840/41* edited by Ronald Vern Jackson, et al, Accelerated Indexing, North Salt Lake, UT, 1986. FHL book 976.X22mi.

■ **1841 Mississippi State Census.** Countywide extractions published in periodicals for the following counties:
- **Attala County,** see "State census, 1841," in *Mississippi Records,* Vol. 1, No. 1 (Jan 1989).
- **Chickasaw County.** 1837-1841 name lists published in *Chickasaw Times Past,* Vol. 9, No. 4 (Jan 1991); and 1841 in *Mississippi Memories,* Vol. 6, No. 3 (1996).
- **Itawamba County.** 1837 and 1841 name lists published in *Northeast Mississippi Historical & Genealogical Society Quarterly,* Vol. 6, No. 4 (1986).
- **Madison County.** 1841 list abstracted in *Mississippi Records,* Vol. 3, No. 1 (Jan 1991).
- **Newton County.** 1841 name list published in *Mississippi Records,* Vol. 1, No. 3 (Jul 1989).
- **Scott County.** 1841 name list published in *Mississippi Records,* Vol. 3, No. 3 (Jul 1991).
- **Tippah County.** 1841 name list published in Northeast *Mississippi Historical & Genealogical Society Quarterly,* Vol. 6, No. 4 (1986) and Vol. 7, No. 1 (Fall 1986).
- **Tunica County.** Name list published in *Mississippi Genealogical Exchange,* Vol. 16, No. 1 (Spring 1970); and *Tate Trails,* Vol. 6, No. 2 (Jun 1982).

■ **1845 Mississippi State Census.** Statewide index in *Mississippi, 1845,* edited by Ronald Vern Jackson , et al, Accelerated Indexing, North Salt Lake, UT, 1986, 169 pages. FHL book 976.2 X2j.

■ **1845 Mississippi State Census,** Countywide extractions published in periodicals for the following counties:
- **Attala County,** see "State Census, 1845," in *Frameworks,* Vol. 9, No. 1 (Spring 2000).
- **Newton County, see** "State census, 1845," in Mississippi Genealogical Exchange, Vol. 26, No. 1 (Spring 1980) and in *Mississippi Records,* Vol. 2, No. 4 (Oct 1990).
- **Noxubee County,** see "State Census, 1845," in *Mississippi Records,* Vol. 1, No. 2 (Apr 1989).
- **Pontotoc County,** see "State Census, 1845," in *Northeast Mississippi Historical & Genealogical Society Quarterly,* Vol. 20, No. 3 (March 2000).
- **Sunflower County,** see "State Census, 1845," in *Mississippi Memories,* Vol. 2, No. 3 (1992).; and in Mississippi Genealogical Exchange, Vol. 24, NO. 2 (Summer 1978).
- **Tishomingo County,** see "State Census, 1845," in *Northeast Mississippi Historical & Genealogical Society Quarterly,* Vol. 7, No. 2 (Dec 1986).

■ **1853 Mississippi State Census,** statewide list indexed in *Mississippi 1853 State Census Index,* edited by Ronald Vern Jackson, et al, Accelerated Indexing Systems, North Salt Lake, UT 1988, 251 pages. FHL Book 976.2 X2jr.

■ **1853 Mississippi State Census, Hancock County.** Names for 1840 and 1853 censuses listed in *Florida Parishes Genealogical Newsletter,* Vol. 16, No. 2 (May 1994).

■ **1865-1866 Internal Revenue Lists for Mississippi,** U.S. Bureau of Internal Revenue. Microfilm of originals in the National Archives, Washington, D.C, filmed 1988. Name lists for all of Mississippi, organized by districts. 3 rolls, FHL film #1578481-1578483.

■ **1866 Mississippi State Census,** statewide name index in *Mississippi 1866 State Census Index,* edited by Ronald Vern Jackson, et al,

Accelerated Indexing Systems, North Salt Lake, UT, 1988, 158 pages. FHL book 976.2 X22m.

■ **1866 Mississippi State Census, Tippah County.** Name list published serially in *News and Journal,* Vol. 8, No. 3 (1982) thru Vol. 12, No. 2 (Summer 1986).

■ **1886 Natchez, Mississippi** – See *City of Natchez, Mississippi, August, 1886 Census of Inhabitants, Buildings, Churches and Schools, Orphan Asylums and Hospitals and Manufactures.* Name list available online at: **www.natchezbelle.org/adams-ind/cs_1886.htm**.

■ **Mississippi Countywide Tax Lists.** Over 325 references to published Mississippi tax lists for the 1800s time period can be found in genealogical periodicals. Find them using the PERSI search engine at Ancestry's website: **www.ancestry.com/search/rectype/ periodicals/persi/main.htm**.

Use "PERSI's U.S. Locality Section," select "Mississippi" for the locality and for the Record Type, use "Tax." Five samples of the results from this specific search are shown below:
- **1800 Tax List, Adams County, Mississippi,** in *Southern Genealogists Exchange Quarterly,* Vol. 14, No. 66 (Summer 1973).
- **Pre 1820 Mississippi Tax rolls,** in *Deep South Genealogical Quarterly,* Vol. 29, No. 2 (May 1992)
- **1834 Tax list, Carroll County, Mississippi,** in *Mississippi Genealogy And Local History ,* Vol. 5, No. 2 (Jun 1976).
- **1855 Tax list, Bolivar County, Mississippi,** in *Mississippi Genealogy And Local History,* Vol. 5, No. 2 (Jun 1976).
- **1890 Tax List, Alcorn County, Mississippi,** in *Northeast Mississippi Historical & Genealogical Society Quarterly,* Vol. 3, No. 2 (Dec 1982).

Mississippi Censuses & Substitutes Online

■ **Mississippi Censuses 1810-1930.** Originally compiled by Ronald V. Jackson, Accelerated Indexing Systems, Salt Lake City, UT. Electronic files were acquired by Ancestry, Inc. which has these Mississippi lists indexed at their website, **www.ancestry.com**.

- 1699-1722 French Colony Census Tables
- **1792-1866 Territorial/State Census Collection:** 1792, 1805, 1808, 1810, 1813, 1815-1817, 1816, 1818, 1820, 1822, 1822-1823, 1823, 1824, 1825, 1830, 1837, 1840, 1841, 1845, 1850, 1853, 1860, and 1866.
- 1805 Jefferson and Wilkinson Counties
- 1810 Territorial Census Index
- 1818 State Census Index
- 1820 Federal Census
- 1820 State Census Index
- 1822 State Census Index
- 1823 State Census Index
- 1824 State Census Index
- 1825 State Census Index
- 1830 State Census Index
- 1837 State Census Index
- 1840 Federal Census Index;
- 1840 State Census Index
- 1840 Pensioners List
- 1841 State Census Index
- 1845 State Census Index
- 1850 Federal Census Index
- 1850 Slave Schedules
- 1850-1880 Mortality Schedules & Index
- 1853 State Census Index
- 1860 Federal Census Index
- 1860 Slave Schedule
- 1866 State Census Index
- 1870 Federal Census Index
- 1880 Federal Census
- 1885-1940 Indian Census Schedules
- 1890 Veterans Schedules
- 1900 Federal Census
- 1910 Federal Census
- 1920 Federal Census
- 1930 Federal Census

■ **1792-1917 Mississippi Census Records Online**. (CensusFinder.com). Direct links to Internet websites where census name lists have been published. Go to **www.censusfinder.com/ mississippi.htm**. Censuses arranged by county, each with similar listings as shown below:

Adams County, Mississippi (formed 1799 from Natchez District)

- 1792 Spanish Census of Natchez District – Mississippi Territory
- 1820 Federal Census Surname Index, SK pub.

- 1830 Federal Census Surname Index by SK Publications
- 1840 Federal Census Surname Index by SK Publications
- 1850 Federal Census Surname Index by SK Publications
- 1886 Census of City of Natchez
- 1729 Massacre at Fort Rosalie with death list
- 1798-1906 Naturalizations Index
- 1818 Tax Rolls
- 1892 City Directory Images of Natchez
- WWI Draft Registrations - Files arranged alphabetically
- 1910-1921 Births
- 1910-1921 Deaths
- 1921 High School Year Book

■ **1790s-1930s Links to Online Census Records**. (CensusOnline.com). This is another website featuring links to census records online. Go to **www.census-online.com/links/MS/** to review Mississippi census records online. An example of what is available for one Mississippi county is shown below:

Itawamba County, Mississippi
Federal Census
- 1850 Federal Census - Mortality Schedule
- 1880 Federal Census Images
- Index to 1840 Federal Census
- Index to 1840 Federal Census Surnames
- Index to 1850 Federal Census Surnames
- Index to 1880 Federal Census
- Index to 1900 Federal Census

State Census
- 1841 State Census

Tax List
- 1836 Tax List
- 1838 Tax List
- 1839 Tax List
- 1866 State Tax List

Military Roster
- 1898 Confederate Pensioners
- 1910 Civil War Veterans
- 1925 Confederate Pensioners

Miscellaneous
- 1838 Jury List

Chapter 2E – New England

Connecticut, Maine, Massachusetts, New Hampshire, Rhode Island, and Vermont

Timeline of Historical Events, New England Jurisdictions

1492 Spanish Discovery. Christopher Columbus, an Italian sailing for Spain, starts a trend of using cruise ships to visit the Caribbean.

1497 English Discovery. English seafarer John Cabot sailed to the Grand Banks off of Newfoundland and recorded an abundance of codfish he found there, but not one word about Maine's lobsters.

1524 French Discovery. Italian Giovanni da Verrazzano explored the coast of New York and New England in 1524, and wrote of his travels to his sponsor, King Francis I of France. While he encountered very friendly natives near Rhode Island, Maine's natives were less welcoming. They greeted Verrazzano's men from the height of a cliff, refused to approach the shore, and would only trade by lowering items on a rope. When they were finished trading, Verrazzano wrote that they "showed their buttocks and laughed immoderately." For this, Verrazzano named the area, *terra onde la mala gente,* or "the land of the bad people."

1558. Elizabeth I becomes Queen of England. All of the great explorations of North America take place during her 45-year reign, including the earliest attempts at colonization.

1559 Norumbega. Englishman David Ingram was one of New England's early real estate promoters. He claimed to have traveled the length of the Atlantic seaboard from Florida to Maine, and on his return to England, he told stories of what he saw on that journey. In an area that is thought to be near present-day Bangor, Maine, Ingram said he had visited the wealthy city of Norumbega, where the streets were "far broader than any street in London," the men were bedecked with gold and silver bracelets, and the women with gold plates and pearls as big as thumbs. He told of houses with pillars of gold, silver, and crystal, and spoke of how he could grab fist-sized nuggets of gold from the streams. Though Ingram may have exaggerated a bit, he did spark an interest in the New England region, and other explorers followed in his footsteps, in search of this mythical land of Norumbega.

1603 England.   James I (James VI of Scotland since 1566), becomes King of England, the first monarch to rule both England and Scotland. During his reign, the first permanent British colonies of North America were established in Virginia and New England.   James I is most remembered   for   commissioning   a   Bible translation.   He was the first English King to publicly assert that he was blessed with "the divine right of Kings," meaning he was the voice of God on earth, at least in England and Scotland.   James I was in power when England acquired title to Northern Ireland, and was responsible for the transportation of thousands of clan people living along the Scottish-English border to Ulster Province. After about 120 years in Ireland, many of these "Scots-Irish" were to migrate to the interior of Massachusetts.

1604 Maine.   Frenchman Samuel de Champlain charts the Maine coast and tries to establish a permanent settlement on St. Croix Island.   The natives objected.

1607 Popham Colony.   George Popham and Raleigh Gilbert try to establish an English settlement, known as the Popham Colony, at the mouth of the Kennebec River. Popham died a year later, and Gilbert returned to England. The abandoned colony soon disappeared.

1609 New York/Vermont. Frenchman Samuel de Champlain discovers Lake Champlain, which by coincidence, had the same name.

1610.   The Jamestown Colony begins sending fishing vessels to the Gulf of Maine, and lobsters and codfish are first harvested there. The Jamestown leader, Captain John Smith, a known lover of seafood, decides to investigate the area closer.

1614 Massachusetts and Maine. English Captain John Smith (of the Jamestown Colony) visits Massachusetts and Maine, then writes his *Description of New England,* which encourages Englishmen to settle there.   Smith is credited with first calling the area New England, which had previously been known as Norumbega. Back in England, Christopher Jones was one seafarer who was known to have read Smith's description of New England, and later remarked that he would like to go there. He got his wish as the master of the *Mayflower* in 1620.

1614 Connecticut. Dutchman Adriaen Block sails up the Connecticut River. He claimed Connecticut as part of the New Netherland colony. The Dutch were famous for trading a few beads and baubles for large tracts of land from the natives.

1620 Plymouth Colony. The *Mayflower* drops anchor off Cape Cod, and soon after Plymouth Colony was founded by a small group of Pilgrims/Separatists, who had fled England for Holland a year earlier. Unlike the Puritans, the Pilgrims did not want to purify the Church of England, they just wanted to get away from the church's Prayer Book.

1622 Maine and New Hampshire. James I grants the region between the Salem and Merrimac rivers, under the name of Mariana to John Mason and Sir Ferdinando Gorges. And the same year, the king grants the region between the Merimac and Kennebec rivers under the name of the Province of Maine, to David Thomson and associates. The first New Hampshire settlement of Piscataqua was founded by Thomson later that year, but was short-lived.

1623 New Hampshire. Dover, the first permanent settlement in New Hampshire is founded.

1625 England. Charles I becomes King of England, Scotland, and Ireland. Charles believed in the same principles his father, James I had espoused, i.e., that as King, he was the infallible interpreter of God's will on earth. Soon after taking office, Charles began to note a large number of non-conformists among his subjects. Along with his Archbishop, William Laud, the King began a campaign to purge his church of the largest group of non-conformists, the so-called "Puritans," a militant Calvinist religious group attempting to purify the Church of England. Unfortunately, Charles I took on a job

that led to civil war in England as well as the loss of his head. But, his campaign can be credited as the cause for the founding of English settlements in New England.

1629.   The Great Migration to New England Begins. As a result of the Charles I campaign to purge non-conformists from the Church of England, 1629-1640, large groups of people were disenfranchised. Charles I disbanded Parliament and ruled England alone for eleven years. The Puritans referred to this era as "the eleven years of tyranny." It was during these eleven years that 80,000 Puritans felt compelled to leave England. About a fourth of them moved to Holland; another fourth of them to Ireland; a fourth to the West Indies, particularly the islands of Barbados, Nevis, and St. Kitts; and the final group, some 21,000 Puritan immigrants, were to establish the Massachusetts Bay Colony of North America.

1629 New Hampshire. John Mason receives a grant of that portion of the Province of Maine which lay between the Merrimac and the Piscataqua River, under the name of New Hampshire.

1633 Connecticut. The British founded a settlement in Windsor, the first permanent settlement in Connecticut. In the same year, the Dutch built a fort on the present site of Hartford, but the Dutch were asked to leave by the British in only a couple of years.

1636 Connecticut Colony. The British settlements of Hartford, Wethersfield, and Windsor are formed into the Connecticut Colony.

1636 Rhode Island.   Not all the English emigrants adhere to the Puritan lifestyle. Rhode Island is settled by a young minister, Roger Williams, who is banished from Massachusetts for his objection to the colony's seizure of Indian lands. In this year, Williams purchases land from the Narragansett Indians in the area around

Providence. At the same time, other areas are settled along the Maine and New Hampshire coasts and the Connecticut River valley, mostly by Massachusetts people not thrilled with the Puritan ethic.

1638. New Haven Colony was formed as an independent colony, separate from Connecticut Colony.

1641 Massachusetts Bay. The "Great Migration" to New England ends. It is also the beginning of the Civil War in England, and by 1649, Charles I and William Laud lose their heads; Oliver Cromwell, a Puritan, becomes Lord Protectorate, ruling England for the next decade. The group of Royalists who supported Charles I are now out of power, the Puritans are in control (and there is no need to send any more Puritans to New England, in fact many of the "purged" Puritans return to England). Instead of Puritans to New England, another English migration begins, this time to Virginia by the opponents of the Puritans, who become known as Cavaliers.

1641 New Hampshire. The Massachusetts Colony gains control of the New Hampshire settlements.

1643 Massachusetts. County government established, with the first three counties of Essex, Middlesex, and Suffolk. It was no coincidence that these three counties had the same names as the East Anglia counties where the majority of the Puritans had lived back in England.

1643 New Haven Colony. The coastal settlements of Branford, Guilford, Milford, Stamford, plus Southold (on Long Island), all joined the New Haven Colony.

1660 England. Charles II is restored to the throne as King of England, Scotland, and Ireland. He had lived in exile after the execution of his father, King Charles I. In 1649, the Scots had proclaimed

Charles the king of Scotland. But the Puritan leader Oliver Cromwell defeated his army in 1651, and Charles fled to France. After Cromwell died in 1658, the English people became increasingly dissatisfied with the government that Cromwell had established. In 1660, Parliament invited Charles to return and declared him king. He ruled until his death in 1685, and during his 25-year reign, the British colonies forced out the remaining pockets of Atlantic settlements made earlier by the Dutch, Swedes, Danes and French. Charles II saw the colonies as a source of trade and commerce, supported development, and granting several more charters for settlement (including one to William Penn in 1681). All of the British colonies thrived as a result. He was the first monarch to recognize the potential for the North American colonies to become a contiguous, viable commonwealth. He encouraged the development of post roads, and a regular communication between the Governors. Charles II was responsible for setting the tone of self-government, religious tolerance, and individual freedoms in the British colonies that was to become an American institution.

1663 Rhode Island. Charles II grants a Royal Charter to the "Rhode Island & Providence Plantations."

1665 Connecticut. New Haven Colony and Connecticut Colony merged into one chartered colony, retaining the name Connecticut.

1674. The English ask the Dutch to leave New York and Connecticut. Outnumbered, the Dutch comply.

1679 New Hampshire. England forms New Hampshire as a separate royal colony.

1691 Massachusetts. A new charter merges the old Plymouth Colony into the Massachusetts Bay Colony.

1724 Vermont. Fort Dummer, built by the English near the site of Brattleboro, is considered the first permanent settlement in what is now Vermont.

1741 New Hampshire/New York. When Benning Wentworth became royal governor of New Hampshire, according to his commission, New Hampshire extended west across the Merrimack River until it met "with our other Governments." Since the English crown had never publicly proclaimed the eastern limits of the colony of New York, this vague description bred considerable confusion.

1749 Vermont Area. New Hampshire's Governor Wentworth, assuming that New York's modified boundary with Connecticut and Massachusetts (20 miles east of the Hudson River) would be extended even farther north, made the first of the New Hampshire Grants (Bennington) to a group that included his relatives and friends. However, New York claimed that its boundary extended as far east as the Connecticut River, and Gov. George Clinton of New York promptly informed Governor Wentworth that he had no authority to make such a grant. Wentworth thereupon suggested that the dispute between New York and New Hampshire over control of Vermont be referred to the crown. The outbreak of the last of the French and Indian Wars in 1754 briefly suspended interest in the area, but after the British captured Ticonderoga and Crown Point in 1759, Wentworth resumed granting land in the area of present Vermont.

1754. French and Indian War begins. France and Britain fight for seven years over the territory of Canada, the Great Lakes, and the Mississippi River Valley down to New Orleans. In Europe it is called the Seven Years War.

1763. Treaty of Paris is signed by France, Spain, and Britain, ending the French and Indian War. France is the loser. England now owns all the territory east of the Mississippi River. Spain takes everything west of the Mississippi. The British area becomes known officially as "British North America."

1764 Vermont Area. British authorities uphold New York's territorial claim to Vermont. New York immediately tries to assert its jurisdiction— Wentworth's grants were declared void, and new grants (for the same lands) were issued by the New York authorities. For the next 25 years, Vermont fights for recognition and independence from New York and New Hampshire.

1775 Revolutionary War. Ethan Allen, who organized Vermont's Green Mountain Boys, directed most of his violence towards New York, breaking up courts and generally creating havoc over the issue of Vermont's independence. But as soon as the Revolutionary War broke out, the Green Mountain Boys took on the British threat to split the colonies at the Hudson River. Fights between New Hampshire, New York, and Vermont are put on hold while they fight a common enemy – the British.

1777. Vermont declares itself an independent republic, and it is the first time the name is used. Both New York and New Hampshire still claim the area, however. Vermont's independence is basically ignored by the other colonies, and Vermont does its share to help in fighting the British. But Ethan Allen, who was working both sides, almost succeeds in getting Vermont annexed to Canada.

1788. Connecticut Statehood, 9 January, the 5th state.

1788. Massachusetts Statehood, 6 February, the 6th state.

1788. New Hampshire Statehood, 21 June, the 9th state.

1790. Rhode Island Statehood, 29 May, the 13th state.

1791. Vermont Statehood, 4 March, the 14th state. After many delays and misunderstandings the dispute with New York was finally adjusted in 1790.

1820. Maine Statehood, 15 March, the 23rd state.

Important New England Name Indexes

■ *The Great Migration Begins: Immigrants to New England, 1620-1633*, by Robert Charles Anderson, F.A.S.G., 3 vols., (New England Historic Genealogical Society, Boston, 1995); and the current series, *The Great Migration Begins: Immigrants to New England, 1634-1635*, 3 Vols. (NEHGS, 1999-). This classic anthology features comprehensive biographical sketches of the earliest New Englanders. It has become a census substitute without equal. The project continues, with the goal of providing authoritative and detailed biographical sketches of the approximately 21,000 original immigrants to New England from 1620 to 1641. Each immigrant is identified with details concerning parents, spouse(s), and children. For information about the status of the project, visit the NEHGS's Great Migration Web site at **www.nehgs.org/research/database/great_migration/**.

■ **Early New England Settlers, 1600s-1800s**. CD-ROM publication by Broderbund in collaboration with Genealogical Publishing Co., Inc. (FHL CD-ROM No. 9 pt. 504). This is a library compilation of 21 books related to the early settlers of New England. This series qualifies as a census substitute for all six states, as the names of the founders of New England are identified and indexed. Book titles include:

1. *Chronicles of the First Planters of the Colony of Massachusetts Bay from 1623 to 1636*, by Alexander Young.
2. *Peirce's Colonial Lists: Civil, Military, and Professional Lists of Plymouth and Rhode Island Colonies*, by Ebenezer W. Peirce.
3. *The Colonial Clergy and Colonial Churches of New England*, by Frederick Lewis Weis.
4 *Directory of the Ancestral Heads of New England families, 1620-1700*, compiled by Frank R. Holmes.
5. *Genealogical Guide to the Early Settlers of America: With a Brief History of Those of the First Generation*, by Henry Whittemore.
6. *Genealogical Notes, or, Contributions to the Family History of Some of the First Settlers of Connecticut and Massachusetts*, by Nathaniel Goodwin.
7 *Genealogical Notes on the Founding of New England: My Ancestor's Part in that Undertaking*, by Ernest Flagg.
8. *Genealogical Notes of New York and New England Families*, compiled by S.V. Talcott.
9. *A Genealogical register of the First Settlers of New England*, by John Farmer.
10. *The History of New England from 1630 to 1649*, by John Winthrop (vols. I-II);
11. *Immigrants to New England, 1700-1775*, compiled by Ethel Stanwood Bolton.
12. *Marriage notices, 1785-1794 for the Whole United States, Copied from the Massachusetts Centinel and the Colombian Centinel*, by Charles Knowles Bolton.
13. *One hundred and Sixty Allied Families*, by John Osborne Austin.
14. *The Real founders of New England: Stories of Their Life Along the Coast, 1602-1628*, by Charles Knowles Bolton;
15. *Result of Some Researches Among the British Archives for Information Relative to the Founders of New England: Made in the Years 1858, 1859 and 1860*, by Samuel G. Drake.
16. *Soldiers in King Phillips War: Being a Critical Account of That War With a Concise History of the Indian Wars of New England from 1620-1677;* by George Madison Bodge.

17. *The Pioneers of Maine and New Hampshire: A Descriptive List Drawn From Records of the Colonies, Towns, Churches, Courts, and Other Contemporary Sources,* by Charles Henry Pope.

18. *The English Ancestry and Homes of the Pilgrim Fathers: Who Came to Plymouth on the 'Mayflower' in 1620, the 'Fortune' in 1621, and the 'Anne' and 'Little James' in 1623,* by Charles Edward Banks.

19. *The Planters of the Commonwealth: A Study of the Emigrants and Emigration in Colonial times, 1620-164,* by Charles Edward Banks.

20. *Topographical dictionary of 2,885 English Emigrants to New England, 1620-1650,* by Charles Edward Banks.

21. *The Winthrop Fleet of 1630: An Account of the Vessels, the Voyage, the Passengers and their English Homes, from Original Authorities;* by Charles Edward Banks.

■ **1791-1906 New England Naturalization Petitions**. Index to New England Naturalization Petitions by the United States Immigration and Naturalization Service. Microfilm of original records in the National Archives, Washington, D.C. This is an index to naturalization documents in courts in Connecticut, Maine, Massachusetts, New Hampshire, Rhode Island and Vermont, from 1791 to 1906. Index cards are organized by state and then by name of petitioner, arranged according to the Soundex system. Index gives name and location of the court that granted the naturalization, date of naturalization, and volume and page (or certificate) number of the naturalization record. NARA series M1299, 117 rolls, FHL film begins with film #14296761.

■ **Online Index,** New England Historic Genealogical Society, Boston, MA. A website at **www.newenglandancestors.org/** has a "Search for Your Ancestors," feature, where non-members may search for a name online. Results come from Census lists, Tax Lists, *Great Migration* series, Genealogies & Biographies, Military, the NEHGS *Register*, Newspapers, and much more.

CONNECTICUT

Censuses and Substitutes, 1636-1980

There were no known state censuses taken by Connecticut before or after statehood. A "lost census" of the entire colony for 1762 was found, published in 1979, but it is probably a list of names from tax lists or other sources. There are several colony-wide and state-wide name lists that have been compiled which may serve as substitutes. Connecticut's state census substitutes are indicated below, beginning with the oldest known lists, and continuing in chronological order to align with the timeline for New England census jurisdictions.

■ **1636 Hartford,** See "Original Proprietors of Hartford, 1636," in *McHenry County Illinois Connection Quarterly*, Vol. 7, No. 4 (Oct 1989).

■ **1600s Connecticut**. See "Divisions of Land, Valuations & Taxes, 1600s," in *Windsor Historical Society Annual Reports*, Vol. 29 (1950).

■ **1656-1700 Norwalk Register of Voters**, in "Register of Voters, 1656-1700, Norwalk," in *Car-Del Scribe*, Vol. 12, No. 4 (Jul 1975).

■ **1669-1670 Middletown, Windsor, Hartford, and Wethersfield**. Name lists of inhabitants in "The Wyllys papers: Correspondence and Documents Chiefly of Descendants of Gov. George Wyllys of Connecticut, 1590-1796," by Lemuel A. Welles, in *Collections of the Connecticut Historical Society*, v. 21, 1870. FHL book 974.B4.

■ *1670 Connecticut Census: A Reconstructed Listing found in Household, Estate, Tax, Landowner, Church and Freeman Lists Between 1660 and 1673* compiled by Jay Mack Holbrook (Oxford, MA, Holbrook Research Institute, 1977), 74 pages. FHL book 974.6 X2h.

■ **1688-1709 East Haddam Proprietors**. See "Proprietors, 1688-1709, East Haddam," in *New England Historical and Genealogical Register*, Vol. 13, No. 1 (Jan 1859).

■ **1688 Saybrook Tax List.** See "Tax List, Saybrook, 1688," in *Hear-Save*, Vol. 2, No. 1 (Dec 1987).

■ **1710-1711 Military Roll**. Names listed in *Roll and Journal of Connecticut Service in Queen Anne's War, 1710-1711,* Morehouse & Taylor Press, 1916, 62 pages. See FHL film #6019415.

■ **1740 Connecticut Voter List**. Name list in "Election of 1740 in CT," *Connecticut History*, No. 22 (Jan 1981).

■ **1741 Lebanon.** See "Rate Bill, 1741, Lebanon," in *New England Historical and Genealogical Register*, Vol. 20, No. 1 (Jan 1866).

■ **1744 Kent**. See "Tax List, 1744, Kent," in *American Genealogist*, Vol. 11, No. 1 (Jul 1934).

■ **1746-1760 Salisbury**. See "Taxpayers, 1746, 1756, 1760, Salisbury," in *National Genealogical Society Quarterly*, Vol. 71, No. 2 (Jun 1983).

■ **1750 Brookfield**. See "Tax List, circa 1750, Brookfield," in *New England Historical and Genealogical Register*, Vol. 20, No. 2 (Apr 1866).

■ **1756-1774 Connecticut Town Populations**. "1756-74 Town Populations," in *Historical Footnotes*, Vol. 11, No. 4 (Aug 1974).

■ **1762 Colonial Connecticut Census**. See "Lost Census of 1762 Found," in *Notes and News*, Vol. 3, No. 3 (Jan 1978); and "Census, 1762, Found at New Haven," in *Connecticut Historical Society Bulletin*, Vol. 44, No. 2 (Apr 1979).

■ **1776 Newington Census.** See *A Census of Newington, Connecticut,* Compiled by Frederic

B. Hartranft, published Hartford, 1909. Includes name of every person in a household, plus place of birth, and remarks. See FHL book 974.62/N2 X2p.

■ **1776-1783 Connecticut Loyalists**. See "Connecticut Loyalists List, Revolution," in *Generations*, Vol. 20 (Jun 1984).

■ **1780-1788 Brookfield**. See "Tax List, circa 1780-88, Brookfield," in *New England Historical and Genealogical Register*, Vol. 28, No. 1 (Jan 1874).

■ **1790-1850 Index of Connecticut Census Records** (federal censuses). This is a special card index created by the Connecticut State Library in Hartford, Connecticut. The residents of cities beginning with the letters A to New Haven are alphabetically indexed by name. The residents of the remaining cities are indexed alphabetically by city. Some surname variations are alphabetized together. Example: Buckley, Bulkley, Bulckley are all found under Buckley. Filmed by the Genealogical Society of Utah, 1950, 95 rolls of microfilm, beginning with FHL film #3434.

■ **1799 New Britain**. See "Taxpayers, New Britain, 1799," in *Genealogy*, Vol. 1, No. 14 (Apr 1912).

■ **1800 New Haven Voter List**. Names listed in "East Guilford Voters, 1800 & CT Property Test," *Connecticut Historical Society Bulletin*, Vo. 19, No. 4 (Oct 1954).

■ **1817 Branford, Connecticut**. See "Tax List, 1817, Branford," in *Connecticut Nutmegger*, Vol. 26, No. 3 (Dec 1993).

■ **1838 New Canaan Town**, Connecticut Tax List. See "New Canaan Town Tax, 1838," in *New Canaan Historical Society Annual*, Vol. 3, No. 3 (Jun 1953).

■ **1845 Hamonsette, Connecticut**. See "Tax Records, 1845, Hamonsette," in *Connecticut Nutmegger*, Vol. 27, No. 3 (Dec 1994).

■ **1845 New London, Connecticut**. See "Borough Tax Rolls, 1845, New London," in *Historical Footnotes*, Vol. 25, No. 2 (May 1988).

■ **1853 Tax List, Redding**. See "Tax, Redding, 1853," in *Connecticut Nutmegger*, Vol. 17, No. 3 (Dec 1984).

■ **1855, 1865 & 1875 New York State Censuses (Connecticut People)**. See "Connecticut Born, NY State Census, 1855, 1865, 1875," in *Stamford Genealogical Society Bulletin*, Vol. 10, NO. 1 (Sep 1967).

■ **1855-1924 The New London City Directories**, microfilmed by Research Publications, Woodbridge, CT, 1980-1984. Copies at Family History Library.

■ **1862-1866 Internal Revenue Assessment Lists for Connecticut**, microfilm of original records at the National Archives, Washington, DC. District 1 contains Hartford and Tolland counties; District 2: Middlesex and New Haven counties; District 3: New London and Windham counties; and District 4: Fairfield and Litchfield counties. Filmed by the National Archives, series M758, 1968, 23 rolls, beginning with FHL film #1534625.

■ **1883-1886 Directories of Tolland County Towns and Villages**, including Rockville, Tolland, Vernon, Coventry, Ellington, Stafford Springs, Somers, Willington, Bolton, and Manchester. Microfilm by Research Publications, New Haven. See FHL catalog for copies and film numbers.

■ **1905-1929 Hartford Directories**. Microfilm by Research Publications, Woodbridge, CT. FHL copies and areas include:
• **1905-1906:** Hartford suburban directory for Bloomfield, Glastonbury, Newington, West Hartford, Wethersfield, East Windsor, South Windsor, Windsor and Windsor Locks, Conn. Film #2308491 Item 1.
• **1911-1912:** Hartford suburban directory for Bloomfield, East Windsor, Farmington, Glastonbury, Newington, South Windsor, West Hartford, Wethersfield, Windsor, and Windsor Locks, film #2308491, Item 2.
• **1913:** Hartford, Connecticut little suburban directory for the towns of Canton, Granby, Rocky Hill and Simsbury Film #2308491, Item 3.
• **1913-1914:** Hartford suburban directory for Bloomfield, East Windsor, Farmington, Glastonbury, Newington, South Windsor, West Hartford, Wethersfield, Windsor and Windsor Locks, film #2308492, Item 1.
• **1915:** Hartford, Connecticut, little suburban directory for the towns of Avon, Canton, East Granby, Granby and Simsbury, film #2308492, Item 2.
• **1915-1916:** Hartford suburban directory for Bloomfield, East Windsor, Farmington, Glastonbury, Newington, South Windsor, West Hartford, Wethersfield, Windsor and Windsor Locks, film #2308492, Item 3.
• **1918-1919:** Hartford suburban directory for Bloomfield, East Windsor, Farmington, Glastonbury, Newington, South Glastonbury, South Windsor, Unionville, Wethersfield and Windsor, film # 2308492, Item 4.
• **1927:** Hartford suburban (Connecticut) directory for Avon, Bloomfield, Farmington, Glastonbury, Newington, South Windsor, Wethersfield, film #2308493, Item 1.
• **1929:** Manning's Hartford suburban (Connecticut) directory for Bloomfield, Farmington, Glastonbury, Newington, South Windsor, Wethersfield, film #2308493, Item 2.

■ **1913-1928 Directories for Windham County Towns and Villages**, including Danielson, Attawaugan, Brooklyn, Connecticut Mills, East Brooklyn, Center, Balouville, Dayville, Killingly, East Killingly, Elmville, Pineville, River View. Filmed by Research Publications, New Haven.

■ **1917 Connecticut Military Census**. See "1917 Connecticut State Military Census," in *Stamford Genealogical Society Bulletin*, Vol. 22, No. 3 (Feb 1980); and "1917 Military Census, World War I - Connecticut," in *Connecticut Maple Leaf*, Vol. 8, No. 2 (Winter 1997).

■ **1917-1918 Civilian Draft Registrations, Connecticut**. Original draft registration cards are located at the National Archives in East Point, Georgia, microfilmed by the National Archives, copies at FHL. The draft cards are arranged alphabetically by state, then alphabetically by county or city, and then alphabetically by surname of the registrants. Includes name of registrant, address, date of birth, age, race, citizenship status, birthplace, occupation, place of employment, dependent relative, marital status, father's birthplace, name and address of nearest relative. Cards are in rough alphabetical order. FHL has 68 rolls of film, beginning with FHL film #1561876.

■ **1920 Voters List, Eastford**. Names listed in "Eastford, Admission of Electors, Roll, 1920," in *Eastford Historical Society Quarterly*, Vol. 17, No. 3 (Sep 1995).

■ **1913-1928 Directories, Connecticut River Valley:** Microfilm of city directories by DeWitt White Co., Publishers, and others. Includes the following years and areas:
• **1913-14:** The Connecticut River Valley (south of Middletown) directory, containing Centerbrook, Chester, Clinton, Cobalt, Deep River, East Haddam, East Hampton, East River, Essex, Guilford, Haddam, Higganum, Ivoryton, Lyme, Madison, Middlefield, Middle Haddam, Moodus, Niantic, Saybrook, Shailerville, Westbrook. Film #2308483 Item 2.
• **1918-1919:** Connecticut River Valley and Shore Line Directory, containing Centerbrook, Chester, Clinton, Cobalt, Deep River, Durham, East Haddam, East Hampton, East River, Essex, Flanders, Guilford, Haddam, Higganum, Ivoryton, Lyme, Madison, Middlefield, Middle Haddam, Moodus, Niantic, Saybrook, Shailerville, Westbrook Union Publishing Co., publishers. Film #2308483 Item 3.
• **1924:** Connecticut River Valley and Shore Line directory, containing Centerbrook, Chester, Clinton, Cobalt, Deep River, Durham, East Haddam, East Hampton, East River, Essex, Flanders, Guilford, Haddam, Higganum, Ivoryton, Lyme, Madison, Middlefield, Middle Haddam, Moodus, Niantic, Saybrook, Shailerville, Westbrook ... Frank P. Morse, publisher. FHL Film #2308483 Item 4.
• **1928:** Dunham's Southern Connecticut Valley and Shore Line directory, covering the towns of Chester, Clinton, Durham, East Haddam, East Hampton, East Lyme, Essex, Guilford, Haddam, Killingworth, Lyme, Madison, Middlefield, Old Lyme, Old Saybrook, Saybrook, and Westbrook, Conn., including villages of Centerbrook, Cobalt, Deep River, East River, Flanders, Higganum, Ivoryton, Middle Haddam, Moodus, Niantic, Shailerville, and Tylerville, compiled and published by Charles H. Dunham. FHL film #2308483 Item 5.

■ **1915-1926 Estate Record Card Index**, Microfilm of original records in the Connecticut State Archives, Hartford. Records are arranged alphabetically by name of deceased, with coverage for all towns of Connecticut. Contains name of deceased, residence, date of death, probate district, value of estate, tax information, etc. Filmed by the Genealogical Society of Utah, 1989. 19 rolls, starting with film #1503783 (Aaronson, A – Barrows, M.).

■ **1930 & 1940. The Greater Hartford Directory**: Including Hartford, East Hartford, West Hartford, Wethersfield, Windsor, Bloomfield, and Newington, Hartford Printing Co., FHL books cataloged as 974.62 E4ph.

■ **1931-1972 Manchester Directories**. Published New Haven, Price & Lee. FHL has 1931, 1970, & 1972. FHL books cataloged as 974.62/M1 E4p.

■ **1931-1979 Directories:** Torrington, Winsted, Litchfield, Norfolk, Goshen Directory: Combining Five Distinct Directories: Governmental Directory, Buyers' Directory, Alphabetical Directory, Numerical Directory, Classified Directory, 1931, 1967, 1973, 1976, and 1979. Originally published New Haven: Price & Lee, 1931. Filmed by the Genealogical Society of Utah, 1985. FHL film #1425529 & 1425513.

■ **1931- 1979 Directories:** Middletown, Portland Directory, New Haven, Price & Lee, 1931, includes index. FHL book 974.66 E4p.

■ **1931-1980 Directories**: Ansonia, Derby, Shelton, Seymour Directory: Combining Five Distinct Directories: Governmental Directory, Buyers Directory, Alphabetical Directory, Numerical Directory, Classified Directory, 1931, 1968, 1973-74, 1975-1976, 1980. Originally published New Haven: Price & Lee, 1931 -. FHL book 974.67 E3pa.

Connecticut Censuses & Substitutes Online

■ **1790-1890 Connecticut Censuses.** Originally compiled by Ronald V. Jackson, Accelerated Indexing, Salt Lake City, UT. Electronic files were acquired by Ancestry, Inc. which has these Alabama lists indexed at their website, **www.ancestry.com**. Combined index includes:
- Early Census Index.
- 1790 Federal Census Index
- 1800 Federal Census Index
- 1810 Federal Census Index
- 1820 Federal Census Index
- 1830 Federal Census Index
- 1840 Federal Census Index
- 1840 Pensioners List
- 1850 Federal Census Index
- 1860 Federal Census Index
- 1890 Veterans Schedule

Note: the 1870 and 1880 censuses were added to the collection later.

■ **1790-1930 Connecticut Census Lists Online**. To see what Connecticut federal censuses have been extracted and indexed as databases available on the Internet, go to the Census-Online Web site at **www.census-online.com/links/CT/**. There are county-by-county listings, with links to the Ancestry.com census indexes as well as several other providers.

■ **Connecticut Census Records Online.** (**www.censusfinder.com**). Several Connecticut census lists are available online at various sites. **Statewide listings include**:
- 1636-1776 Colonial Connecticut Records
- 1790-1890 Connecticut Census Search Engine at Ancestry
- 1880 Federal Census images at Ancestry.com
- 1880 Federal Census Search at Family Search

Example of censuses and substitutes:
Fairfield County (formed 1666 - Original County)
- 1790 Federal Census Index of Wilton
- 1810 Federal Census of Wilton.
- 1820 Federal Census of Wilton
- 1840 Census of Revolutionary War Pensioners
- 1850 Federal Census Index of Sherman Twp.
- 1850 Federal Census of Sherman Twp
- 1850 Federal Census of Sherman Twp
- 1850 Federal Census of Stamford
- 1850 Federal Census Index of Wilton
- 1850 Federal Census - Poorhouse Residents
- 1860 Federal Census of Wilton.
- 1880 Federal Census of Stamford
- 1880 Federal Census Index of Wilton
- Early Greenwich Landowners
- Early Settlers of Stamford
- Early Settlers of Stratford
- New Fairfield Congregational Church Records
- 1645-1847 Vital Records for Town of Danbury
- 1820-1850 Barbour Vital Records for Darien
- 1639-1854 Barbour Vital Records for Fairfield
- 1640-1848 Barbour Vital Records for Greenwich
- 1641-1853 Barbour Vital Records Index for Stamford
- 1639-1854 Barbour Vital Records for Stratford
- 1672 Proprietors of Greenwich
- 1688 Inhabitants of Stratford
- 1694-1695 Taxpayers of Greenwich
- 1925 City Directory for Norwalk (actual images)

MAINE

Censuses and Substitutes, 1636-1915

Although part of Massachusetts, federal censuses taken for Maine, 1790-1820, were separate from Massachusetts because the area of Maine was a district of the Federal District Court system. Maine became a state in 1820. No Massachusetts colony-wide or state-wide censuses were taken before 1820, and there are no known district-wide censuses for the area of Maine before statehood. The only state census taken in Maine was authorized by the state legislature in January 1837 to determine disbursement of a federal surplus from the sale of public lands. Some sources incorrectly refer to this state census as the "1837 special federal census." The name lists were compiled by and for each Maine Town jurisdiction. Many of the towns decided to receive federal funds (about $1.75 to each person) based on the number of school age children in a household, and the lists are sometimes referred to as "school censuses." Maine's census substitutes are indicated below, beginning with the oldest known lists, and continuing in chronological order to align with the timeline for New England historical events.

■ **1636 Inhabitants of Saco Bay, York County**, in *York County Genealogical Society Journal*, Vol. 1, No. 4 (Oct 1986).

■ **1676 Blackpoint Garrison, Maine**. Name list in "Inhabitants, 1676, Blackpoint Garrison," in *New England Historical and Genealogical Register*, Vol. 43, No. 1 (Jan 1889).

■ **1687 Town Rate, Jamestown, now Newton, York County**, in *New England Historical and Genealogical Register*, Vol. 32, No. 3 (Jul 1878).

■ **1722 Census, Garrison at Kittery, York County**, in *Old Eliot*, Vol. 1, No. 9 (1897).

■ **1722 Order for Defensible Houses, Kittery, York County**, in *Maine Historical and Genealogical Recorder*, Vol. 3, No. 3 (Jul 1886).

■ **1742 Tax List, Lincoln County**, in *Old Broad Bay Bund und Blatt*, Vol. 3, No. 4 (Oct 1994).

■ **1748 Providence & Town Rate (Falmouth), Cumberland County**, in *Maine Genealogist*, Vol. 8, No. 3.

■ **Tax List, Kittery, York County**, in *Old Eliot*, Vol. 2, No. 11 (Nov 1898).

■ **1755 Tax List, Saco, York County**, in *Maine Historical Magazine*, Vol. 2, NO. 10 (Apr 1887).

■ **1756, 1758, 1770 Tax Lists, Kittery, York County**, in *New England Historical and Genealogical Register*, Vol. 55, No. 3 (Jul 1901).

■ **1759 New Marblehead Tax List**, in *Maine Historical and Genealogical Recorder*, Vol. 4, No. 4 (Oct 1887).

■ **1759 Tax List, North Yarmouth, Cumberland County**, in *Old Times-North Yarmouth, Maine*, Vol. 1, No. 2 (Mar 1877), and Vol. 1, No. 3 (Jul 1877).

■ **1760 Valuation List, Kittery, York County**, in *York County Genealogical Society Journal*, Vol. 15, No. 1 (Jan 2000).

■ **1760 Perfecting or Valuation List, Kittery, York County**, in *York County Genealogical Society Journal*, Vol. 14, No. 4 (Oct 1999).

■ **1770 Tax Assessment, Gorham, Cumberland County**, in *Sprague's Journal of Maine History*, Vol. 14, No. 1 (Jan 1926).

■ **1771 List of Inhabitants, Pownalboro, Cumberland County**, in *Maine Genealogist*, Vol. 9, No. 4 (Nov 1987).

■ **1771 Polls and Estates of Boothbay, Lincoln County**, in *Downeast Ancestry*, Vol. 4, No. 3 (Oct 1980).

■ **1776 Tax List, Families on Penobscot River**, name list in *Maine Historical Magazine*, Vol. 4, No. 7 (Jan 1889).

■ **1776 Valuation List, Kittery, York County**, in *Old Eliot*, Vol. 3, No. 8 (Aug 1899).

■ **1777 Blue Hill, Hancock County, Male Inhabitants**, in *Maine Historical Magazine*, Vol. 4, No. 9-10 (Apr 1889).

■ **1777 Plantation of Gardinerston, (Lincoln County), Male Inhabitants**, in *Maine Genealogist*, Vol. 13, No. 3 (Aug 1991).

■ **1778 Pleasant River Inhabitants, Town of Addison, Washington County, Maine**, in *Maine Historical Magazine*, Vol. 10 (April 1886).

■ **1779-1782 Tax Lists, Shapleigh, York County**, in *York County Genealogical Society Journal*, Vol. 7, No. 2 (Apr 1992).

■ **1780-1781 Taxpayers, Winslow, Clinton, Kennebec County**, in *Maine Historical Magazine*, Vol. 7, No. 1-3 (Jul 1891).

■ **1780-1811 Valuations (Tax Lists).** Microfilm of originals for the Maine District of Massachusetts, located at the State House, Boston. Filmed by the Genealogical Society of Utah, 1974, 8 rolls, as follows:
  • Tax lists for 1780 Cape Elizabeth; 1783 Scarborough; 1784 Arundel, York & Plantation of Wales, FHL film #959904
  • Tax lists for 1784, Plantation of Walpole; 1791 Ballstown, York. FHL film #959905
  • Tax lists for 1792 Ballstown & Woolwich. FHL film #959907.
  • Tax lists for 1800 Augusta – Woolwich, FHL film #959906
  • Tax lists for 1801 Anson – Lewiston, FHL film #959909

  • Tax lists for 1801 Medumcook – Woolwich, FHL film #959908
  • Tax lists for 1811 Bangor – Windham, etc., FHL film #959910
  • Tax lists for Bangor – Wiscasset, and summaries of miscellaneous towns, FHL film #9599911.

■ **1781 Partial Census, Lincoln County, Maine**, in *Downeast Ancestry*, Vol. 7, No. 4 (Dec 1983).

■ **1781 Settlers at Pittston, Kennebec County**, in *Maine Historical and Genealogical Recorder*, Vol. 7, No. 3 (Jul 1893).

■ **1782 Penobscot Journal**. Name list of inhabitants published in *Downeast Ancestry*, Vol. 7, No. 4 (Dec 1983).

■ **1783 Loyalists of Penobscot**, in *Downeast Ancestry*, Vol. 6, No. 1 (Jun 1982), and Vol. 7, No. 4 (Dec 1983).

■ **1784 Penobscot Loyalists at Passamaquoddy**, in *Downeast Ancestry*, Vol. 7, No. 4 (Dec 1983).

■ **1785 Sedgwick, Hancock County, Settlers** in *Maine Historical Magazine*, Vol. 9, No. 7-9 (Jul 1894).

■ **1786 Penobscot Region Tax List**, in *Downeast Ancestry*, Vol. 7, No. 4 (Dec 1983).

■ **1790 Prescots and Whitchers Plantation**, in *New Hampshire/Maine Connection*, Vol. 2, No. 4 (Summer 1999).

■ **1790 Valuation, Blue Hill, Hancock County**, in *Maine Historical Magazine*, Vol. 9, No. 4-6 (Apr 1894).

■ **1794 Bridgton, Cumberland Census**, in *Connections*, (Apr 2000).

■ **1794 Tax List, Rustfield (Norway), Oxford County**, in *Maine Historical and Genealogical Recorder*, Vol. 9, No. 11 (Nov 1898).

■ **1794 Parish Tax List, Wells, York County**, in *Sprague's Journal of Maine History*, Vol. 5, No. 1 (Jul 1917).

■ **1797 Tax List, Eden, Hancock County**, in *Maine Historical Magazine*, Vol. 5, No. 7-9 (Jan 1890).

■ *Massachusetts and Maine Direct Tax of 1798*, microfilm of original records at the New England Historic Genealogical Society, Boston, MA. Filmed with a published index and guide. Indexes are included with first 3 volumes. 18 rolls of film, FHL film #940072-940089. See also *An index and Guide to the Microfilm Edition of the Massachusetts and Maine Direct Tax Census of 1798,* by Michael H. Gorn, published by the New England Historic Genealogical Society, Boston, 1979, 98 pages. FHL book 974.R42i.

■ **1798 Owners of Taxable Land, Poland, Androscoggin County**, in *Forebears in Your Maine Family Tree*, Vol. 3, No. 2 (Summer 1997); and in *Maine Historical and Genealogical Recorder*, Vol. 1, No. 3 (Jul 1884).

■ **1798 Taxpayers, Bristol, Lincoln County**, in *Genealogical Advertiser*, Vol. 3, No. 3 (Sep 1900) and Vol. 3, No. 4 (Dec 1900).

■ **1798 Taxpayers, Medumcook (Friendship), Knox County**, in *Genealogical Advertiser*, Vol. 4, No. 5 (1901).

■ **1798 Taxpayers, Waldoborough, Lincoln County**, in *Genealogical Advertiser*, Vol. 3, No. 4 (Dec 1900), thru Vol. 4, No. 5 (1901).

■ **1798 List of Freeholders, Northerly Eliot, York County**, Maine, in *Old Eliot*, Vol. 6, No. 4 (Dec 1903).

■ **1799 Families, Clinton, Formerly Hancocktown, Kennebec County**, in *New England Historical and Genealogical Register*, Vol. 111, No. 1 (Jan 1957), and Vol. 111, No. 2 (Apr 1957).

■ **1799 Tax List, Gorham, Cumberland County**, in *Maine Historical and Genealogical Recorder*, Vol. 1, No. 4 (Oct 1884).

■ **1801 Tax List, Gouldsborough, Hancock County**, in *Downeast Ancestry*, Vol. 6, No. 3 (Oct 1982).

■ **1803 Taxpayers, Norridgewock, Somerset Co., Maine**, in *New England Historical and Genealogical Register*, Vol. 97, No. 4 (Oct 1943).

■ **1807 Blue Hill Families, Hancock County**, in *Maine Historical Magazine*, Vol. 1, No. 6 (Dec 1885).

■ **1808 Tax List, Kittery, York County**, in *Old Eliot*, Vol. 1, No. 10 (Oct 1897).

■ **1809 Tax Payers, Otisfield, Cumberland County**, in *Maine Historical and Genealogical Recorder*, Vol. 8, No. 4 (Oct 1895).

■ **1810 Highway List, Kittery, York County, Maine**, in *Old Eliot*, Vol. 3, No. 1 (Jan 1899).

■ **1810 Tax List, Kittery, York County**, in *Old Eliot*, Vol. 1, No. 10 (Oct 1897).

■ **1811 Inhabitants & Residents in Town of Lubeck, Washington Co., ME**, in *Downeast Ancestry*, Vol. 10, No. 4 (Dec 1986).

■ **1812 Tax List, Poland, Androscoggin County**, in Rota-Gene, Vol. 4, No. 5 (Dec 1983).

■ **1815 Direct Tax, Hancock County**, in *Maine Historical Magazine*, Vol. 4, No. 1-2 (Jul 1888).

■ **1815 Tax List, North Yarmouth, Cumberland County**, in *Old Time-North Yarmouth, Maine*, Vol. 1, No. 1 (Jan 1877); thru Vol. 1, No. 4 (Oct 1877).

■ **1816 Direct Tax List, Penobscot County, Maine**, in *Hermon Roots News*, Vol. 2, No. 3 (May 1984).

■ **1817 Tax Bills, Dexter, Penobscot County**, in *Dexter Historical Society Newsletter*, (Summer 1997).

■ **1817 Tax List, Dixmont, Penobscot County**, in *Maine Genealogist*, Vol. 12, No. 4 (Nov 1990).

■ **1817 Ratable Polls, Friendship, Knox County**, in *New England Historical and Genealogical Register*, Vol. 83, No. 3 (Jul 1929).

■ **1819 Taxpayers, Sangerville, Piscataquis County**, in *Downeast Ancestry*, Vol. 1, No. 1 (Jun 1977) and in *Sprague's Journal of Maine History*, Vol. 3, No. 3 (Jul 1914).

■ **1821 Tax List, Pownal, Cumberland County**, in *Old Times-North Yarmouth, Maine*, Vol. 4, No. 3 (Jul 1880).

■ **1823 Tax List, North Yarmouth, Cumberland County**, in *Old Times-North Yarmouth, Maine*, Vol. 1, No. 3 (July 1877) thru Vo. 1, No. 4 (Oct 1877).

■ **1824 School Census, Danville, Androscoggin County**, in *Downeast Ancestry*, Vol. 6, No. 5 (Feb 1983).

■ **1829 Poll Tax, Lincoln County, Maine**, in *Mattanawcook Observer*, Vol. 1, No. 1 (Apr 1982).

■ **1829-1831 Tax and Census Records, Orono, Maine**, in *Downeast Ancestry*, Vol. 10, No. 3 (Oct 1986).

■ **1830 Single Poll Tax, Lincoln County**, in *Missing Links-Genealogical Clues*, No. 35 (Jun 1965).

● **1831 Voter List, Berlin, Franklin County**, in *Sprague's Journal of Maine History*, Vol. 7, No. 1 (May 1919).

● **1834 Taxpayers, Vienna, Kennebec County**, in *Sprague's Journal of Maine History*, Vol. 14, No. 1 (Jan 1926).

● **1835 Census, Passadumkeag, Penobscot County**, in *Maine Historical Magazine*, Vol. 2, No. 3 (Sep 1886).

■ **1837 Maine State Census**. The original name lists for Bangor, Portland, and most towns, townships, and plantations are at the Maine State Archives in Augusta. The originals for the town of Eliot, York County, are at the Maine Historical Society in Portland. None have been microfilmed. For information on obtaining copies of the name lists, visit the Maine State Archives site at **www.state.me.us/sos/arc/geneology/** (sic). Only three of the 1837 towns have been extracted/published:
  ● **1837 Census, Gray Surplus & 80 Rod Strip**, in *Maine Genealogist*, Vol.. 12, No. 2 (May 1990).
  ● **1837 State Census, Mount Desert, Hancock County**, in *Maine Genealogist*, Vol. 11, No. 2 (May 1989). See also "1837 State Census, Mount Desert," compiled by Alice MacDonald Long, in *The Maine Seine*, Vol. 11 (1989).
  ● **"1837-1847 South Berwick Persons in Great Works Vicinity, York County,"** in *Downeast Ancestry*, Vol. 13, No. 5 (Feb 1990).

■ **1844 Taxpayers in Townsend (Southport), Lincoln County**, in *Downeast Ancestry*, Vol. 5, No. 4 (Dec 1981).

■ **People from Maine in 1855 and 1865 Massachusetts State Census**, in *Maine Genealogist*, Vol. 11, No. 4 (Aug 1989).

■ **1862-1866 Internal Revenue Assessment Lists for Maine**. Microfilm of original records at the

National Archives, Washington, D.C., series M770, 15 rolls, FHL film #1534403 – 1534417.

■ **1864 Voters List, Harmon, Penobscot County**, in *Harmon Roots News*, Vol. 1, No. 5 (Sep 1983).

■ **1865 Massachusetts State Census, Charlestown (Maine People)**, in "Maine Natives in 1865 census, Charlestown, MA," in *Maine Genealogist*, Vol. 15, No. 1 (Feb 1993).

■ **1865 Census, Fourth school, Penobscot, Maine**, in *Mattanawcook Observer*, Vol. 2, No. 3-4 (Oct 1984).

■ **1871 Non-resident Taxpayers, Dayton, York County**, in *Genealogist's Post*, Vol. 4, No. 8 (Aug 1967).

■ **1879 Tax List, Farmingdale, Kennebec County**, in *Living Tree News*, Vol. 2, No. 3 (Spring 1976) and Vol. 2, No. 4 (Summer 1976).

■ **1892 Voter List, Easton, Aroostook County**, in *Downeast Ancestry*, Vol. 3, No. 1 (Jun 1979).

■ **1905 Census, Town of Lincoln, Penobscot County**, in Mattanawcook Observer, Vol. 2, No. 3-4 (Oct 1984).

■ *1906 Saco Register, with Old Orchard (York County)*, compiled by Mitchell, Daggett, Holt, Lawton, and Sawyer. Published Brunswick, Maine, 1906. This is an attempt to list all residents, street address, occupation, and special genealogical information, such as maiden names of married daughters. FHL book 974.195/S1 H2

■ **1915 Voter List, Medford, Piscataquis County**, in *Tri-City Genealogical Society Bulletin*, Vol. 19, No. 1 (Jan 1979).

Maine Censuses & Substitutes Online

■ **1790-1880 Maine Census Records Online. (www.censusfinder.com/maine.htm**). Several Maine census lists are available online at various sites, accessible via direct links from this Census Finder site.

Statewide listings:
- 1790 Federal Census
- 1800 Federal Census
- 1810 Federal Census
- 1820 Federal Census
- 1830 Federal Census
- 1837 Special Federal Census (sic)
- 1840 Federal Census
- 1840 Revolutionary War Pensioners
- 1850 Federal Census
- 1860 Federal Census
- 1870 Federal Census
- 1880 Federal Census - images
- 1880 Federal Census
- 1880 Federal Census Search at Family Search
- Maine Statewide Databases of Census & Genealogy Records

Example of records from one county
Androscoggin:
- 1790 Federal Census of Leeds (then in Lincoln County)
- 1815 Unpaid Taxes List of Leeds (then in Kennebec County)
- 1860 Federal Census of Leeds
- 1880 Federal Census of Leeds
- 1900 Federal Census Images of Leeds

MASSACHUSETTS

Censuses and Substitutes, 1632-1912

State censuses in Massachusetts were taken every ten years from 1855 to 1945, but the original manuscripts exist only for the years 1855 and 1865. Census substitutes are indicated below, beginning with the oldest known lists, and continuing in chronological order to align with the timeline for New England census jurisdictions.

■ **1632-1634 Tax Lists, Plymouth**, in *New England Historical and Genealogical Register*, Vol. 4, No. 4 (Jul 1850).

■ **1650 Salisbury Tax List, Essex County**, in *New England Historical and Genealogical Register*, Vol. 3, No. 1 (Jan 1849).

■ **Pre-1660 Tax List, Rowley, Essex County**, in *New England Historical and Genealogical Register*, Vol. 15, No. 3 (Jul 1861).

■ **1664, 1681 Topsfield Tax List, Essex County**, in *Topsfield Historical Collections*, Vol. 2 (1896).

■ **1666-1682 List of Freedmen (Plymouth Colony)**. Microfilm of original at Secretary of State, Boston. Filmed by the Genealogical Society of Utah, 1968. FHL film #567791.

■ **1669 Topsfield Tax List, Essex County**, in *Topsfield Historical Collections*, Vol. 1 (1895).

■ **1673 Ipswich Voters, Essex County**, in *Essex Institute Historical Collections*, Vol. 45, No. 4 (Oct 1909).

■ **1679 Billerica Tax List, Middlesex County**, in *New England and Historical Register*, Vol. 5, No. 2 (Apr 1851).

■ **1679 Hatfield Tax List, Hampshire County**, in *Missing Links-Genealogical Clues*, No. 35 (Jun 1965).

■ **1683 Salem Tax List, Essex County**, in *Genealogical Quarterly Magazine*, Vol. 2, No. 3 (1901).

■ **1687 Boston Tax List**, in *New England Historical and Genealogical Register*, Vol. 55, No. 32 (Apr 1901).

■ **1687 Boxford Tax List, Essex County**, in *Essex Institute Historical Collections*, Vol. 56, No. 4 (Oct 1920).

■ **1688 Billerica Town Rate, Middlesex County**, in *New England Historical and Genealogical Register*, Vol. 31, No. 3 (Jul 1877).

■ **1688 Charles Town Rate, Suffolk County**, in *New England Historical and Genealogical Register*, Vol. 34, No. 3 (Jul 1880).

■ **1688 Marlborough Town Rate, Middlesex County**, in *New England Historical and Genealogical Register*, Vol. 36, No. 2 (Apr 1882).

■ **1688 Medford Town Rate, Middlesex County**, in *New England Historical and Genealogical Register*, Vol. 32, No. 3 (Jul 1878).

■ **1688 Newton Town Rate, Middlesex County**, in *New England Historical and Genealogical Register*, Vol. 31, No. 3 (Jul 1877).

■ **1688 Stow Town Rate, Middlesex County**, in *New England Historical and Genealogical Register*, Vol. 32, No. 1 (Jan 1878).

■ **1695 Tax List, Bristol**, in *New England Historical and Genealogical Register*, Vol. 123, No. 3 (Jul 1969).

■ **1700 Salem Tax Lists, Essex County**, in *Genealogical Quarterly Magazine*, Vol. 4, No. 1 (Apr 1903).

■ **1711-1744 Boxford Tax Lists, Essex County**, in *Essex Institute Historical Collection*, Vol. 57, No. 3 (Jul 1921).

■ **1723-1725 Topsfield Tax List, Essex County**, in *Topsfield Historical Collections*, Vol. 3 (1897).

■ **1725-1729 Salem Village Tax Lists**, in *Danvers Historical Collections*, Vol. 24 (1936).

■ **1729-1732 Salem Village Tax Lists**, in *Danvers Historical Collections*, Vol. 25 (1937).

■ **1734 Rate List, Concord, Middlesex County**, in *New England Historical and Genealogical Register*, Vol. 12, No. 1 (Jan 1858).

■ **1735-1748 Boxford Tax Lists, Second Parish, Essex County**, in *Essex Institute Historical Collections*, Vol. 57, No. 4 (Oct 1921).

■ **1738-1752 Omes Ledger of Salem People, Essex County**, in *Essex Institute Historical Collections*, Vol. 47, No. 3 (Jul 1911).

■ **1744-1752 Northborough Taxpayers, Worcester County**, in *Worcester Magazine and Historical Journal*, Vol. 2, No. 3 (Jul 1926?).

■ **1748 Marblehead Tax Lists, Essex County**, in *Essex Institute Historical Collections*, Vol. 43, No. 3 (Jul 1907).

■ **1750 Brookfield Tax List, Worcester County**, in *New England Historical and Genealogical Register*, Vol. 20, No. 2 (Apr 1866).

■ **1752 Danvers Tax List, Essex County**, in *Danvers Historical Collections*, Vol. 3 (1915).

■ **1753 Danvers Voters List, Essex County**, in *Danvers Historical Collections*, Vol. 37 (1949).

■ **1753 Danvers Tax Lists, Essex County**, in *Danvers Historical Collections*, Vol. 39 (1951).

■ **1754 Rockport Tax List, Essex County**, in *New England Historical and Genealogical Register*, Vol. 137, No. 2 (Apr 1983).

■ **1754 Sandy Bay Taxpayers, Essex County**, in *Missing Links-Genealogical Clues*, No. 24 (Jul 1964).

■ **1757 Coach Excise Taxpayers, Worcester County**, in *Genealogical Quarterly Magazine*, Vol. 3, No. 4 (Dec 1902).

■ **1757 Coach Excise Taxpayers, Plymouth County**, in *Genealogical Quarterly Magazine*, Vol. 3, No. 4 (Dec 1902).

■ **1760-1771 Massachusetts Property Valuations and Taxes**, Mass. Dept. of Archives, microfilm of original records. 1760-1770, FHL film #926471; 1770-1771, film #926472; 1768-1771, film #926473; 1771, film #926474.

■ **1761-1778 Norfolk Assessment Roll Family Names**, in *New England Historical and Genealogical Register*, Vol. 36, No. 4 (Oct 1882).

■ **1764 Rehoboth Tax Return, Bristol County**, in *American Genealogist*, Vol. 64, No. 1 (Jan 1989).

■ **1771 Massachusetts Tax Valuations**. Name lists indexed in ***The Massachusetts Tax Valuation List of 1771***, edited by Bettye Hobbs Pruitt, published by Picton Press, Camden, ME, 1998, 945 pages. FHL book 974.4 R4p.

■ **1775 Danvers Tax list, Amos Trask District, Essex County**, in *Essex Institute Historical Collections*, Vol. 29, No. 10 (Oct 1892).

■ **1775 Known Tax Payers, Franklin County**, in *Missing Links-Genealogical Clues*, Vol. 19 (Feb 1964).

■ **1780-1792, 1810-1811 Massachusetts General Court Valuation Committee Tax Lists.** Includes index to taxpayers for all counties and towns of Massachusetts. Filmed by the Genealogical Society of Utah, 1974, 19 rolls, as follows:

- Valuations, (arranged by county) 1780-1841, FHL film #954452.
- Valuations, (arranged by county) 1850-1860, FHL film #954453.
- Amherst to Deerfield 1780, FHL film #953995.
- Dighton to Wilbraham 1780, FHL film #953996.
- Abington to Lynn 1783, FHL film #954454.
- Marshfield to Yarmouth 1783, FHL film #954455.
- Abington to Braintree 1784, FHL film #954458.
- Bridgewater to Foxborough 1784, FHL film #954459.
- Framingham to Lunenburg, 1784, FHL film #954460.
- Lynn to Whately 1784, FHL film #954498.
- Raynham to Warwick 1784, FHL film #954499.
- Watertown to Yarmouth 1784, FHL film #954500.
- Ashburnham to Weymouth 1791, FHL film #953997.
- Ashburnham to Colrain 1792, FHL film #953998.
- Deerfield to Lancaster 1792, FHL film #953999.
- Lee to Sandwich 1792, FHL film #954000.
- Sharon to Williamstown 1792, FHL film #955501.
- Ashfield to Heath 1810-1811, FHL film #959902.
- Leverett to Whately 1811, FHL film #959903.

■ **1781 Northborough Assessment, Worcester County**, in *Hourglass*, Vol. 64 (Jun 1997).

■ **1783 Brookfield Assessors List, Worcester County**, in *Rota-Gene*, Vol. 5, No. 4 (Oct 1984).

■ **1789 Tax Assessors List, Berkshire County**, in *Missing Links-Genealogical Clues*, No. 30 (Jan 1965).

■ **1789 Boston City Directory**, in *New England Historical and Genealogical Register*, Vol. 140, No. 2 (Apr 1986) and No. 3 (Jul 1986).

■ **1789 Pittsfield Assessors List, Berkshire County**, in *Missing Links-Genealogical Clues*, No. 28 (Nov 1964).

■ **1792 Danvers Assessors List, Essex County**, in *Danvers Historical Collections*, Vol. 32, (1944).

■ **1792 Tax Valuation List, Stockbridge, Berkshire County**, in *Berkshire Genealogist*, Vol. 6, No. 2 (Spring 1985).

■ **1796 Raynham Valuations (Tax List), Bristol County**, in *Maine Historical and Genealogical Recorder*, Vol. 7, No. 1 (Jan 1893).

■ **1796-1797 Harwich Tax Books, Barnstable County**, in *Cape Cod Genealogical Society Bulletin*, Vol. 24, No. 3 (Winter 1998).

■ **1798 Boston Taxables**, in *Pennsylvania Traveler-Post*, Vol. 8, No. 2 (Feb 1972).

■ **1798 Massachusetts and Maine Direct Tax of 1798.** Microfilm of original records at the New England Historic and Genealogical Society, Boston, Massachusetts. Filmed with a published index and guide. Indexes are included with first 3 volumes. 18 rolls of film, FHL film #940072-940089. See *An index and Guide to the Microfilm Edition of the Massachusetts and Maine Direct Tax Census of 1798,* by Michael H. Gorn, published by the New England Historic Genealogical Society, Boston, 1979, 98 pages. FHL book 974.R42i.

■ **1799 Savoy Tax List, Berkshire County**, in *Berkshire Genealogist*, Vol. 8, No. 4 (Fall 1987).

■ **1802, 1809-10 Voter Lists, Pittsfield, Berkshire County**, in *Berkshire Genealogist*, Vol. 20, No. 2 (Spring 1999).

■ **1806 Tax Valuation List, Washington, Berkshire County**, in *Berkshire Genealogist*, Vol. 5, No. 3 (Summer 1984).

■ **1808 Tax Document, Worcester County**, in *Rota-Gene*, Vol. 13, No. 1 (Apr 1992).

■ **1814 Windsor Town Tax List, Berkshire County**, name list published in *Berkshire Genealogist*, beginning with Vol. 6, No. 1 (Winter 1985) through Vol. 7, No. 1 (Winter 1986).

■ **1823-1824 Salem Village Tax Lists, Essex County**, in *Danvers Historical Collections*, Vol. 23 (1935).

■ **1830 Voters List, Pittsfield, Berkshire County**, in *Berkshire Genealogist*, Vol. 17, No. 3 (Summer 1996).

■ **1832 Rowe Valuation List, Franklin County**, in *Rowe Historical Society Bulletin*, Vol. 21, No. 4 (Fall 1984).

■ **1837 Census, Town of Danvers, Essex County**. Name list microfilmed. See FHL film #876100, item 9.

■ **1837 Tax Bills, North Ward, Plymouth County**, in *Scituate Historical Society Bulletin*, Vol. 8, No. 3 (Sep 1956).
● **1853 Plymouth Tax List**, in *Scituate Historical Society Bulletin*, Vol. 14, No. 3 (Sep 1962).

■ **1855 & 1865 State Censuses**, Massachusetts Secretary of the Commonwealth, originals at the Massachusetts State Archives, Boston. Filmed and cataloged as one series by the Genealogical Society of Utah, 1974, 68 rolls. Film begins with **1855** Barnstable County, all towns in alphabetical order (film #953973) through 1855 Worcester County (film #953965); followed by **1865** Barnstable County town lists (film #953966) through 1865 Worcester County town lists (film #954384). The contents of the 1855 state census includes names of all members of a household, age, sex, color, occupation, place of birth, and whether a person was deaf, dumb, blind, insane, idiotic, pauper, or convict. The 1865 state census

adds marital status for each person, plus an indication if a male were over the age of 16 and owned enough land to be taxed, and whether the person were of legal age, or a naturalized citizen.

Extracts of the names lists for the 1855 state census for Berkshire County towns were published serially in the *Berkshire Genealogist*. All back issues of this periodical are available from the Berkshire Family History Association of Pittsfield, Massachusetts. For more details, visit their Web site at **www.berkshire.net/~bfha/ membership.htm**.

Ann S. Lainhart published extracts/indexes to the 1855 and 1865 censuses, usually one town per volume. A Web site with general information about accessing the 1855 and 1865 census name lists and the completed town indexes in print is located at **www.mass-doc.com/census_ research_state.htm**.

■ **1872 List of Taxpayers, Franklin County**, in *Rowe Historical Society Bulletin*, Vol. 9, NO. 4 (Fall 1972).

■ **1877-1882 Voter Lists, Washington, Berkshire County**, in *Berkshire Genealogist*, Vol. 9, No. 3 (Summer 1988).

■ **1881 Concord Voter List, Middlesex County**, in *New England Historical and Genealogical Register*, Vol. 38, No. 4 (Oct 1884).

■ **1890 Register of Voters, Pittsfield, Berkshire County**, name list published in *Berkshire Genealogist*, beginning with Vol. 10, No. 1 (Winter 1989) through Vol. 14, No. 3 (Summer 1993).

■ **1892 Webster Poll Tax List, Worcester County**, in *Connecticut Maple Leaf*, Vol. 5, No. 1 (Summer 1991).

■ **1902 Poll Tax List, Southbridge, Worcester County**, in *Connecticut Maple Leaf*, Vol. 4, No. 3 (Summer 1990) through Vol. 4, No. 4 (Winter 1990).

■ **1902 Southbridge Poll Tax List, Worcester County**, in *Connecticut Maple Leaf,* Vol. 5, No., 1 (Summer 1991).

■ **1902 Southbridge Poll Tax List, French-Canadian Surnames**, Worcester County, in *Connecticut Maple Leaf,* Vol. 4, No. 2 (Winter 1989) thru Vol. 4 (Winter 1990).

■ **1905 Hopkinton Tax List, Middlesex County**, in *Massog,* Vol. 17, No. 1 (Jan 1993) thru No. 4 (Oct 1993).

■ **1910 Medway Assessors Report of Valuation and Taxes**, Norfolk County, in *Massog,* Vol. 18, No. 1 (Jan 1994) thru No. 4 (Oct 1994).

■ **1912 Register of the Towns of Manchester, Essex, Hamilton and Wenham (Essex County)**. Published by the Lawton Register, Auburn, ME, 1912. List includes name of every person, wife's maiden name, street address, residence, occupation, and other remarks. See FHL book 974.45 X2r.

Massachusetts Censuses & Substitutes Online

■ **1790-1880 Massachusetts Census Records Online.** Several Massachusetts census lists are available online at various sites, accessible via this site:
www.censusfinder.com/massachusetts.htm.
MA statewide listings include:
 -1790-1890 Federal Census for Massachusetts at Ancestry
 • 1816 Postmasters Statewide
 • 1840 Federal Census Pensioners

• 1880 Federal Census - Search and View the images!
• 1880 Federal Census Search at Family Search
• 1883 Pensioners on the Roll
• Salem Witches Database
• Massachusetts Statewide Databases of Census and Genealogy Records
Records for one Massachusetts county (Barnstable):
• 1790 Federal Census of Truro
• 1790 Federal Census of Orleans
• 1800 Federal Census of Orleans
• 1810 Federal Census of Orleans
• 1820 Federal Census of Orleans

■ **1789-1981 Massachusetts City Directories Online**. A convenient list of city directories which identifies the residents for most towns and cities of Massachusetts, located at **www.mass-doc.com/city_directory_list.htm**. As an example, the list shows Boston City Directories for 1789, 1796, 1798, 1800, 1803, 1805-1807, 1810, 1813, 1815, 1818, 1820-1823, 1825-1865, 1867-1908, 1910-1939, 1940- 1978, and 1981. For a few cities there are direct links to more online name lists.

■ **1800 Boston City Directory Online.** Name list available at **www.distantcousin.com/ Directories/MA/1800/Boston/A.html**.

■ **1904 Boston City Directory Online.** This database is a directory of city residents in that year. In addition to providing the resident's name, it provides their address and occupational information. It includes the names of over 195,000 people, mostly heads of households. There is a page-by-page name list, and full page images from the original book. To access this database and other resources, go to **www.distantcousin.com/Directories/MA/ 1904/Boston/.**

NEW HAMPSHIRE

Censuses and Substitutes, 1648-1921

There were no known official state censuses taken by Connecticut before or after statehood. Censuses of the entire province for 1767, 1775, and 1776 were found and published, but they are, more likely, names from tax lists and other sources. New Hampshire's state census substitutes are indicated below, beginning with the oldest known lists, and continuing in chronological order to align with the timeline for New England census jurisdictions.

■ **1600s New Hampshire Land Grants to Boston Men**, in *Colonial Society of Massachusetts Publications*, Vol. 25 (Mar 1922).

■ **1648 Dover Tax Payers, Strafford County**, in New England Historical and Genealogical Register, Vol. 4, No. 1 (Jan 1850).

■ **1709 Hampton Falls Taxpayers, Rockingham County**, in *New England Historical and Genealogical Register*, Vol. 28, No. 4 (Oct 1874).

■ **1723 Greenland Parish Rate, Rockingham County**, in *New England Historical and Genealogical Register*, Vol. 22, No. 4 (Oct 1868).

■ **1736 Census, Hillsboro County**, in *Ventura County Genealogical Society Quarterly*, (Dec 1996).

■ **1740 Parish Taxpayers, Hillsboro County**, in *New England Historical and Genealogical Register*, Vol. 28, No. 1 (Jan 1874).

■ **1763 New Castle Tax List, Rockingham County**, in *New England Historical and Genealogical Register*, Vol. 105, No. 2 (Apr 1951).

■ **1767 and 1775 Census of New Hampshire**. Microfilm of original records at the Records & Archives Center, Concord, New Hampshire. Filmed by the Genealogical Society of Utah, 1975, 1 roll, #983687.

■ **1775 Hawke Census, Rockingham County**, in *Reminiscences*, Vol. 1 No. 4 (Sep 1995).

■ **1776 New Hampshire Census**. An alphabetized list from the "New Hampshire Association Test of 1776" found in *Miscellaneous Revolutionary Documents of New Hampshire*, published in Manchester, New Hampshire, 1910. Published as *New Hampshire 1776 Census* by Jay Mack Holbrook, (Holbrook Research Institute, Oxford, MA), 1976. See FHL Book 974.2 X2h.

■ **1779 Hudson Tax List, Hillsboro County**, in *Pennsylvania Traveler-Post*, Vol. 8, No. 2 (Feb 1972).

■ **1789 Conway Tax List, Carroll County**, in *Nexus*, Vol. 6, No. 2 (Apr 1989).

■ **1795-1816 Tax Lists, Effingham, Carroll County**, in *New Hampshire Genealogical Record*, Vol. 7, No. 3 (Jul 1990).

■ **1797 Highway Taxpayers List, Rockingham County**, in *Reminiscences*, Vol. 2, No. 10 (Dec 2000).

■ **1802 Cheshire Highway Tax Bill**, in *New Hampshire Genealogical Record*, Vol. 10, No. 4 (Oct 1993.

■ **1803 Delinquent Taxpayers from Dover Sun, Strafford County**, in *Genealogical Record of Strafford County*, Vol. 23, No. 4 (Jul 2000).

■ **1821 Portsmouth Register and Directory**, names published in *Kinship Kronicle*, Vol. 4, No. 3 (Fall 1981) through Vol. 5, No. 1 (Mar 1982).

■ **1826 Highway Tax List, Rockingham County**, in *Detroit Society for Genealogical Research Magazine*, Vol. 35, No. 2 (Winter 1971).

■ **1833 Danville Voter List, Rockingham County**, in *Reminiscences*, Vol. 1, No. 9 (Dec 1996).

■ **1836 Census, Meredith Bridge, Belknap County**, in *New Hampshire Genealogical Record*, Vol. 9, No. 2-3 (Apr 1992).

■ **1836 Middleton Voters, Strafford County**, in *Genealogical Record of Strafford County, NH*, Vol. 23, No. 2 (Mar 2000).

■ **1838 Danville Voter List, Rockingham County**, in *Reminiscences*, Vol. 1, No. 9 (Dec 1996).

■ **1849 New England Mercantile Union Business Directory**, includes all towns of New Hampshire. Filmed by Research Publications, Woodridge, CT. 2 fiche copies at FHL in Salt Lake City, cataloged as film #6044224.

■ **1855 and 1865 Massachusetts State Census (New Hampshire People)**, published serially in *New Hampshire Genealogical Record*, beginning with Vol. 10, No. 4 (Oct 1993).

■ **1860 Milford Taxpayers, Hillsboro County**, in *Genealogist's Post*, Vol. 6, No. 2 (Jun 1969).

■ **1862-1866 Internal Revenue Assessment Lists for New Hampshire**. Microfilm of original records at the National Archives, Washington, D.C. District 1 includes: Belknap, Carroll, Rockingham, and Strafford counties; District 2: Hillsborough and Merrimack counties; and

District 3: Cheshire, Coos, Grafton, and Sullivan counties. Filmed by the National Archives, series M780, 10 rolls. See FHL film #1534780-1534789.

■ **1903 Sandwich Local Returns, Carroll County**, in *Sandwich Historical Society, Annual Excursion Publication*, No. 76 (1995).

■ **1902-1921 New Hampshire State Directories**. Originally published by Union Publishing Co. and others, microfilmed by Research Publications, Woodridge, CT, 1980-1984. Copies at FHL in Salt Lake City, cataloged as follows: **1902**, film #1841735; **1903**, film #1841735; **1904**, film #1841735; **1905**, film #1841735; **1906**, film #1841736; **1907**, film #1841736; **1909**, film #1841736; **1910**, film #1841736; **1911**, film #1841737; **1912**, film #1841737; **1913**, film #1841737; **1914**, #1841738; **1915**, film #1841738; **1916**, film #1841738; **1917**, film #1841739; **1919**, film #1841739; and **1921**, film #1841739.

New Hampshire Censuses & Substitutes Online

■ **1790-1880 New Hampshire Census Records Online**. (CensusFinder.com). Several New Hampshire census lists are available online at various sites, accessible thru this site: **www.censusfinder.com/new_hampshires.htm**.

CT statewide listings include:
• 1790-1930 New Hampshire Census at Ancestry
• 1840 Federal Census Pensioners
• 1880 Federal Census - images
• 1880 Federal Census Search at Family Search
• 1880 Federal Census of Norwegians
• New Hampshire State Databases of Census & Genealogy Records
Records for one NH County (Belknap):
• 1800 Federal Census Index of Sanbornton
• 1810 Federal Census of Sanbornton
• 1830 Federal Census Index of Sanbornton
• 1882 Annual Report for Gilford (actual images)

RHODE ISLAND

Censuses and Substitutes, 1636-1935

Colonial censuses were taken in Rhode Island for several years, but except for the statistics of the population figures, the name lists for only a few exist today – those that survive are identified below. More than any other New England state, the several state censuses taken for Rhode Island provide many census options between federal census years. Rhode Island began taking state censuses beginning in 1865 and every ten years thereafter, the last in 1935. All of the name lists are extant, except that no record of the 1895 census can be found. Rhode Island's state censuses and substitutes are indicated below, beginning with the oldest known lists, and continuing in chronological order to align with the timeline for New England census jurisdictions.

■ **1636-1792 Records of the Colony of Rhode Island and Providence Plantations in New England**, printed extracts of the *Rhode Island Colonial Record*, printed by order of the legislature, transcribed and edited by John Russell Bartlett, 10 vols., publ. Providence: A.C. Green, 1856-1865. Title also known as *Rhode Island Records*. This is an excellent source for finding a reference to a resident of Rhode Island during the Colonial period. Includes a name index, and includes statistics from censuses taken in 1698, 1708 (+ name list), 1730, 1747, 1748-9, 1754, 1776, 1777, and 1782. FHL book 974.5 N29. Also on microfilm, filmed by the Genealogical Society of Utah, 1966, 1971. 7 rolls. Volumes 1,3: film 496842; Vol. 2: 421547; Vol. 4: 418117; Vol. 5: 421548; Vol. 6-7: 496843; Vol. 8-9: 496844 ; Vol. 10: 496845.

■ **1649 Providence Tax List**, in *Rhode Island Historical Society Proceedings* (1893).

■ **1600s. Rhode Island Deed Abstracts**. Names of land buyers and sellers in *Rhode Island Historical Magazine*, Vol. 2, No. 3 (Jan 1882).

■ **1659 Rhode Island Deeds**. Names of land buyers and sellers in *Narragansett Historical Register*, Vol. 3, No. 1 (Jul 1884).

■ **1668-1759 Rhode Island Freemen**, in *Genealogical Reference Builders Newsletter*, Vol. 5, No. 2 (May 1971) and No. 3 (Aug 1971).

■ **1676-1695 Newport Will List and Witnesses**, in *Newport Historical Magazine*, Vol. 3, No. 1 (Jul 1882).

■ **1687 Rochester Town Rate, Kingston**, in *New England Historical and Genealogical Register*, Vol. 35, No. 2 (Apr 1881).

■ **1687 Providence Militia List**, in *Rhode Island Historical Publications*, Vol. 7, No. 4 (Jan 1900).

■ **1688-1689 Bristol Census**, name list in *The American Genealogist*, Vol. 68, No. 3 (Jul 1993); and in *New England Historical and Genealogical Register*, Vol. 34 (1880), p. 404-5.

■ **1692, 1698 Tiverton Inhabitants**, name lists in *Newport Historical Magazine*, Vol. 1, No. 4 (Apr 1881).

■ **1695 Bristol Tax List**, in *New England Historical and Genealogical Register*, Vol. 123, No. 3 (Jul 1969).

■ **1711-1717 Rhode Island Freemen**, in *Genealogical Reference Builders Newsletter*, Vol. 5, No. 4 (Nov 1971).

■ **1719-1738 Rhode Island Freemen**, in *Genealogical Reference Builders Newsletter*, Vol. 6, No. 1 (Feb 1972).

■ **1730-1738 Rhode Island Freemen**, in *Genealogical Reference Builders Newsletter*, Vol. 6, No. 2 (May 1972).

■ **1730 Rhode Island Colonial Census, Portsmouth**, transcribed by Mildred Mosher Chamberlain in *Rhode Island Roots*, Vol. 7, No. 2 (Jun 1981).

■ **1730 Rhode Island Colonial Census, South Kingstown, Washington County**, in *Rhode Island Roots*, Vol. 10, No. 1 (Mar 1984).

■ **1731-1773 Accounts of the Agents of the Colony of Rhode Island**. Original manuscripts in the Rhode Island Archives, Providence. This is the written accounts of agents Richard Partridge, 1731-1759; and Joseph Sherwood, 1760-1773, who were London-based agents of the Rhode Island Colony. Includes many names of people coming to Rhode Island from England during the 18th century. Filmed by the Genealogical Society of Utah, 1974, film #954960.

■ **1738-1760 Rhode Island Freemen**, in *Genealogical Reference Builders Newsletter*, Vol. 6, No. 3 (Nov 1972).

■ *1742 Rhode Island Census*, edited by Ronald Vern Jackson, Accelerated Indexing, North Salt Lake, 1988. See FHL book 974.5 X22r.

■ **1747 Rhode Island Census**, see *A Census of the Freeman of 1747 as Found in the Supplement to the Rhode Island Colonial Records*, by Frank T. Calef. Filmed by the Genealogical Society of Utah, 1950, 1 roll. See FHL film #22390 Item 2. Indexed as **Rhode Island, 1747**, Ronald Vern Jackson, editor, Accelerated Indexing, North Salt Lake, UT, 1988, FHL book 974.5 X22r. See also *Supplement to the Rhode Island Colonial Records Comprising a List of the Freemen Admitted from May 1747 to May 1754*, originals filmed by the Genealogical Society of Utah, 1950, 1 roll, film #22393.

■ **1747 Warren, Male Inhabitants**, in *Rhode Island Historical Magazine*, Vol. 6, No. 2 (Oct 1885).

■ *1747-1755 Rhode Island Freemen: A Census of Registered Voters*, compiled by Bruce C. MacGunnigle, published by Genealogical Publishing Co., Inc., 1977, 49 pages. FHL book 974.5 A1 No. 7. Taken from the index cards at the Rhode Island State Archives, the Freedmen lists comprise a record of the men eligible to vote in Rhode Island for this period, and thus, a fairly complete listing of the head of households of Rhode Island.

■ **1748 Proprietors of Warwick, Kent County**, in *Narragansett Historical Register*, Vol. 2, No. 2 (Oct 1883).

■ **1760-1762 Freemen, North Kingstown**, in *Rhode Island Roots*, Vol. 12, No. 1 (Mar 1986).

■ **1760-1762 Men Made Freemen, Portsmouth**, in *Rhode Island Roots*, Vol. 12, No. 2 (Jun 1986).

■ **1760-1762 Freemen, Richmond**, in *Rhode Island Roots*, Vol. 12, No. 2 (Jun 1986).

■ **1760-1762 Men Made Freemen, Scituate**, in *Rhode Island Roots*, Vol. 12, No. 3 (Sep 1986).

■ **1760-1762 Freemen, Smithfield**, in *Rhode Island Roots*, Vol. 12, No. 3 (Sep 1986).

■ **1760-1762 Freemen, South Kingstown & Westerly**, in *Rhode Island Roots*, Vol. 12, No. 4 (Dec 1986).

■ **1760-1762 Freemen, Tiverton,** in *Rhode Island Roots*, Vol. 12, No. 4 (Dec 1986).

■ **1760-1762 Freemen, Warwick & W. Greenwich, Kent County**, in *Rhode Island Roots*, Vol. 12, No. 4 (Dec 1986).

■ **1763 Warwick Voters, Kent County**, in *American Monthly Magazine*, Vol. 82, No. 2 (Feb 1948).

■ **1774 Rhode Island Census**, see *Census of the Colony of Rhode Island, 1774,* microfilm of manuscripts in the Rhode Island State Archives. Filmed by the Genealogical Society of Utah, 1973. See FHL film #947359 item 1. See also, *Census of the Inhabitants of the Colony of Rhode Island and Providence Plantations 1774*, Rhode Island Secretary of State, reprint of the 1858 edition, arranged by John R. Bartlett, published Hunterdon House, Lambertville, NJ, 1984, 243 pages. FHL book 974.5 X2pb.

■ **1774-1805, Card Index to Rhode Island Military and Naval Records**. Originals in Rhode Island State Archives, Providence. Filmed by the Genealogical Society of Utah, 1974, 1980, 19 rolls, beginning with film #934758.

■ *1776 Rhode Island Military Census,* edited by Ronald Vern Jackson, Accelerated Indexing, North Salt Lake, UT, 1988, 66 pages. FHL book 974.5 X22j.

■ *The Rhode Island 1777 Military Census*, compiled by Mildred M. Chamberlain. Published under the direction of the Rhode Island Genealogical Society, Originally published in installments in *Rhode Island Roots* between December 1981 and September 1984. Reprinted with an added index by Genealogical Publishing Co., Inc., Baltimore, 1985, 181 pages. Originals cataloged as *List of all male persons 16 years of age and upwards, 1777*, Rhode Island. General Assembly, microfilm of manuscripts in the National Archives in Washington. Includes a list of men on the alarm list of Westerly, and signers of the Test Act. A letter by the State Record Commissioner of 1916 reads "I have examined with great care the original manuscripts of the census for 1777 and I find that the following towns are omitted: Exeter, Little Compton, Middletown, Newport, New Shoreham and Portsmouth. Undoubtedly this was due to the occupation of the British." Filmed by the Genealogical Society of Utah, 1973, 1 roll. FHL film #947359 Item 2. See also *Rhode Island 1777 State Census Index* (sic), (Running title: *Rhode Island Military Census 1777*), edited by Ronald Vern Jackson, Accelerated Indexing, North Salt Lake, UT, 1988. FHL book 974.5 X22.

■ **1778 Gloucester Tax List**, in *Rhode Island Roots*, Vol. 19, No. 4 (Dec 1993) through Vol. 20, No. 4 (Dec 1994).

■ **1778 Smithfield Tax List**, in *Rhode Island Roots*, Vol. 21, No. 1 (Mar 1995) through Vol. 23, No. 1 (Mar 1997).

■ **1779 Scituate Census**, in *National Genealogical Society Quarterly*, Vol. 14, No. 2 (Jun 1925).

■ **1780 Newport Strangers Tax**, in *Newport Historical Magazine*, Vol. 2, No. 1 (Jul 1881).

■ **1782 Rhode Island Census**. Microfilm of manuscripts at Rhode Island Historical Society in Providence. Filmed by the Genealogical Society of Utah, 1950, 1 roll, FHL film #22390 Item 1. See also *Rhode Island 1782 Census*, by Jay Mack Holbrook, published by Holbrook Research Institute, Oxford, MA, 1979, 240 pages. From preface: "This book. is a reconstructed census using the original manuscript [Rhode Island General Assembly, Census for the State of Rhode Island for 1782] and tax lists of the same time period to replace lost records." FHL book 974.5 X2h. Also, name lists from the 1782 Rhode Island census were published serially in the *New England Historical and Genealogical Register*, beginning with Vol. 127, No. 1 (Jan 1973).

■ *1798-1872 Rhode Island Passenger Lists, Port of Providence, 1798-1808, 1820-1872; Ports of Bristol and Warren, 1820-1871*, compiled by Maureen A. Taylor, published by Genealogical Publishing Co., Inc., Baltimore, 245 pages. FHL book 974.5 W3t. Compiled from the Custom House Papers in the Manuscript Department of the Rhode Island Historical Society, and supplemented by a National Archives microfilm publication containing copies of passenger arrival lists.

■ **1830 West Greenwich Town Tax Bill**, Kent County, in *Rhode Island Roots*, Vol. 6, No. 2 (Summer 1980).

■ **1855 New York State Census (Rhode Island People)**. Name lists for people born in Rhode Island, in *Rhode Island Roots*, Vol. 21, No. 1 (Mar 1995) and No. 2 (Jun 1995).

■ **1855 & 1865 Massachusetts State Census (Rhode Island People).** Name lists for people born in Rhode Island, in *Rhode Island Roots*, Vol. 19, No. 1 (Mar 1993) through Vol. 20, No. 4 (Dec 1994).

■ **1862-1866 Internal Revenue Tax Assessment Lists for Rhode Island**. Microfilm of original records in the National Archives, Washington, D.C., 7 rolls. FHL film #1299309-1299315.

■ **1865 Rhode Island State Census and Index**. Original manuscript records at the Rhode Island State Archives, Providence. The census schedules and a card index compiled by the archives was filmed together in one series by the Genealogical Society of Utah, 1998, 29 rolls, beginning with film #2135474 (Index, Baillayon to Boardman) through #2115175 (Index, Wood to Zuel); followed by the census schedules, Vol. 1 (#2130153) through Vol. 23 (#2130267). **Contents:** name of all members of a household, age, sex, color, place of birth, nativity of parents, whether a person over 15 could read or write, occupation, naturalization info, if attended school, deaf and dumb, blind, insane or idiotic; employment in military or navy since 1860. It should be noted that for those persons born in Rhode Island, this census listing gives their exact Rhode Island Town of birth.

■ **1875 Rhode Island State Census**. Original manuscripts at the Rhode Island State Archives, Providence. Filmed by the Genealogical Society of Utah, 1973, 9 rolls. FHL film #947361-947369. A card index was prepared by the Rhode Island State Archives, which was also filmed as *Rhode Island 1875 State Census Index Cards* by the Genealogical Society of Utah, 2000, 48 rolls, film #2223509 through #2242805. Contents: name of each member of a household, age, sex, color, relationship to head of household, marital status, nativity of parents, read/write, occupation, voter info, number of months in school (whether Public, Select or Catholic school).

■ **1885 Rhode Island State Census**. Original manuscripts at the Rhode Island State Archives, Providence. Filmed by the Genealogical Society of Utah, 1975, 13 rolls, film #953910 through #953912. The 1885 census was published as *Rhode Island State Census, 1885,* by E.L. Freeman, Printers to the State, Providence, 1887, 660 pages. Includes a name index for each town, one for males, another for females. See FHL book 974.5 X2. **Contents:** name of each member of a household, sex, relationship to head of household, color/race, age, marital status, place of birth, nativity of parents, occupation, read/write, number of months in school, whether blind, deaf and dumb, idiotic, or insane; voting info for males over 21, and naturalization info.

■ **1888 Bristol, Rhode Island Tax List – Index**. This name list is a free online database available at **http://distantcousin.com/Directories/ RI/Bristol/1888/**

■ **1905 Rhode Island State Census**. Original records at the Rhode Island State Archives, Providence. Filmed by the Genealogical Society of Utah, 1997-1999, 445 rolls, beginning with film #2070397. The name lists are organized by town, with separate alphabetized listing of males and females. **Contents:** name of all members of a household, relationship to head of household, color/race, age, marital status, date of birth, number of children, place of birth, read/write, year of immigration to the U.S., number of years in the U.S., number of years a resident of Rhode Island, number of months (of the census year) a resident of the Town, birthplace of father and mother, occupation, number of months unemployed, whether a Union soldier, sailor or marine during Civil War/Spanish American War, pension, and religion.

■ **1915 Rhode Island State Census**. Original manuscripts at the Rhode Island State Archives, Providence. Filmed by the Genealogical Society of Utah, 1991, 25 rolls, beginning with film #1763723. The census schedules are organized by enumeration districts. An index to the districts, Barrington to Westerly, is on the last roll (#1769155). **Contents:** names of all members of a household, relationship to head of household, sex, color, age, place of birth, place of birth of father and mother, whether alien or naturalized, occupation, nature of business; employer, employee, or working on own account; and whether out of work.

■ **1925 Rhode Island State Census**. Original manuscripts at the Rhode Island State Archives, Providence. Filmed by the Genealogical Society of Utah, 1991, 1997, 20 rolls, beginning with film #1769232. The census schedules are organized by enumeration districts. **Contents:** names of all members of a household, relationship to the head of household, sex, color, age, place of birth, and citizenship.

■ **1935 Rhode Island State Census**. (Although referred to officially as the "1935 census," the schedules are dated January 1936). Original manuscripts at the Rhode Island State Archives, Providence. Filmed as "Census, 1936" by the Genealogical Society of Utah, 1991, 132 rolls, beginning with film #1753773. Names from the census schedules are in alphabetical order for each town. **Contents:** names of all members of a household, sex, race, place of birth, date of birth, marital status, read/write, citizenship, if at school, name of school, grade, any physical handicaps, occupation, whether unemployed and how long.

Rhode Island Censuses & Substitutes Online

■ **1740-1930 Rhode Island Censuses**. Most of the databases (thru 1860) were compiled by Ronald Vern Jackson, Accelerated Indexing, North Salt Lake, UT. Electronic files were acquired by Ancestry, Inc. which has these Rhode Island lists indexed at their Web site, **www.ancestry.com**. Combined index includes:
- 1740-43 Colonial Census Index
- 1747 Colonial Census Index
- 1777 Military Census Index
- 1782 Census Index
- 1790 Federal Census Index
- 1800 Federal Census Index
- 1810 Federal Census Index
- 1820 Federal Census Index
- 1830 Federal Census Index
- 1840 Federal Census Index
- 1840 Pensioners List
- 1850 Federal Census Index
- 1860 Federal Census Index
- 1870 Federal Census Index
- 1890 Veterans Schedules
- 1900 Federal Census Index
- 1910 Federal Census Index
- 1920 Federal Census Index
- 1930 Federal Census Index

VERMONT

Censuses and Substitutes, 1761-1924

There were no official state censuses taken in Vermont. Tax lists for virtually every town in Vermont have been taken annually. Called a "Grand List," they are hard to find, since they may appear in town or proprietor meeting records, town clerk's offices, or at the Vermont Public Records Division. A few of these town name lists have been published, which are shown below. Other census substitutes are indicated below, beginning with the oldest known lists, and continuing in chronological order to align with the timeline for New England census jurisdictions.

■ **1700s – 1800s. Manuscript Vermont State Papers**: 18th and 19th Century government records (mostly pre-1840), including legislative records, grand lists, petitions, some court records, and federal documents. The **Nye Index** is a name and subject index referencing the manuscripts and provides a useful tool for genealogists. For more information, visit the Vermont State Archives Web site at **http://vermont-archives.org/guide/aguide.htm**.

■ **1761 Cornwall Grantees**, in *Missing Links-Genealogical Clues*, No. 12 (Jul 1963).

■ **1761 Leicester Land Grantees**, in *Missing Links-Genealogical Clues*, No. 12 (Jul 1963).

■ **1761 Peru Original Grantees**, in *Missing Links-Genealogical Clues*, No. 61 (Aug 1967).

■ **1761 Addison's Original Grantees**, in *Missing Links-Genealogical Clues*, No 56 (Mar 1967).

■ **1763 Jericho Original Grantees**, in *Missing Links-Genealogical Clues*, No. 47 (Jun 1966).

■ *1770s – 1860s. Index to State of Vermont Military Records: Revolutionary War, Civil War, War of 1812: Salvaged From the State Arsenal Fire, September 1, 1945,* author/publisher not stated, 65 pages. FHL Book 974.3 M22i. Also on microfilm. Filmed by the Genealogical Society of Utah, 1971. 1 roll, film #824107, Item 2.

■ **1770-1832. Orange County Tax Records, 1789-1832; Miscellaneous Records, 1770-1781**, Microfilm of original records at Chelsea, Vermont. Includes record of taxes paid and land sold, peddlers licenses, licenses to preach, clergyman's appointments, deputations and recognizances, and docket and records referred to in the Judicial history of Vermont. Filmed by the Genealogical Society of Utah, 1952, FHL film #28622.

■ **General Index to Vital Records of Vermont, Early to 1870**, Microfilm of original records in the Office of the Secretary of State, Montpelier, Vermont.. Coverage for every town of Vermont. Index includes births, deaths and marriages. With the lack of census records for Vermont, this index provides an outstanding substitute. Filmed by the Genealogical Society of Utah, 1951, 287 rolls, beginning with film #27455.

■ **1771 Census, Windham, Vermont**, name list from unknown sources in *Branches and Twigs*, Vol. 8, No. 3 (Summer 1979).

■ **1782 Wells Poll List, Rutland County**, in *Detroit Society for Genealogical Research Magazine*, Vol. 13, No. 5 (Jun 1950).

■ **1788 Starsborough Road Tax**, name list in *Missing Links-Genealogical Clues*, No. 22 (May 1964).

■ **1788 Addison Tax for Roads and Bridges**, in *Missing Links-Genealogical Clues*, No. 12 (Jul 1963).

■ **1793 Chittenden Delinquent Tax Records, Rutland County**, in *Rooted in the Green Mountains*, Vol. 2, No. 2 (Jul 1998).

■ **1793 Rutland Delinquent Tax Records**, in *Rooted in the Green Mountains*, Vol. 2, No. 3 (Jul 1998).

■ **1793 Brattleboro Tax List, Windham County**, in *Vermont Genealogy*, Vol. 5, No. 4 (Oct 2000).

■ **1796-1959 General Alphabetical Card Index to Estate Files, Chittenden District Probate Court**, Microfilm of original records. FHL film #1913864-1913866.

■ **1807 Cavendish Legal Voters, Windsor County**, in *Branches and Twigs*, Vol. 21, No. 3 (Summer 1992).

■ **1807 Poultney Grand List, Rutland County**, in *Rooted in the Green Mountains*, Vol. 2, No. 1 (Jan 1998).

■ **1813, 1815, 1816 Williston Federal District Tax, Chittenden** County, in *Vermont Genealogy*, Vol. 6, No. 2 (Apr 2001).

■ **1815 Grand List for New Haven, Addison County**, in *Vermont Genealogy*, Vol. 6, No. 1 (Jan 2001).

■ **1827-1833 Rutland Freemen**, in *Missing Links-Genealogical Clues*, No. 41 (Dec 1965).

■ **1828 Windsor Tax Rates**, in *Vermont Historical Society Proceedings*, Vol. 23, No. 2 (Apr 1955).

■ **1832 Brattleboro Voters List**, in *Missing Links-Genealogical Clues*, No. 42 (Jan 1966).

■ **1843 Derby Census, Orleans County**, in *Vermont Genealogy*, Vol. 4, No. 4 (Oct 1999).

■ **1852-1959 General Alphabetical Card Index to Case Files, Addison District, Vermont.** Microfilm of original records in the Probate Court, Middlebury, Vermont. FHL film #1913861-191382.

■ **1855-1860 Statewide Directories for Vermont**, microfilmed by Research Publications, Woodbridge, Conn., 1980-1984. These directories are essentially heads of household censuses for the entire state of Vermont. There are microfilm copies for this series of directories at the FHL, for the following years:
  ● **1855 Vermont Directory,** by W. W. Atwater, FHL film # 6044609, 6044610.
  ● **1856 Vermont Directory,** by W. W. Atwater, FHL film # 6044611.
  ● **1857 Vermont Directory**, by W. W. Atwater, FHL film #6044612.
  ● **1858 The Vermont Directory**, by W. W. Atwater, FHL film #6044613.
  ● **1859 Vermont Directory**, by W. W. Atwater; published by G. A. Tuttle & Co., FHL film #6044614.
  ● **1860 Vermont Directory**, by W. W. Atwater; published by G. A. Tuttle & Co., FHL film # 6044615.

■ **1861-1866 Internal Revenue Tax Assessment Lists for Vermont**. Microfilm of original records in the National Archives, Washington, D.C., series M792, 7 rolls. FHL film #1578444-1578450.

■ **1865 Vermont Directory**, prepared by Alice I. Noble. Reproduction of original book published 1865, 144 pages, FHL book 974.3 E4. Also on microfilm, roll #1440652.

■ **1869 Rutland, Incomes in the County**, in *Rooted in the Green Mountains*, Vol. 3, No. 4 (Oct 1999).

■ **1871-1908. General Index to Vital Records of Vermont**. Microfilm of original records in the State Capitol Building, Montpelier, VT. Coverage for every town of Vermont. This incredible index offsets the lack of census records for Vermont. Index includes births, deaths and marriages. Filmed by the Genealogical Society of Utah, 1967, 1994-1995, 122 rolls, beginning with film #540051.

■ **1874 Newfane Grand List, by School Districts, Windham County**, in *Branches and Twigs*, Vol. 23, No. 2 (Spring 1994).

■ *1880-1881 Gazetteer and Business Directory of Bennington County, Vermont*, compiled and published by Hamilton Child, 1880, Syracuse, NY, 500 pages. FHL film #1486499. See also *Index of Gazetteer of Bennington County, Vt., 1880-81 by Hamilton Child*, compiled by Charles D. Townsend, Sarasota, FL, Aceto Booment, 1989, 41 pages. FHL book 974.38 E42c.

■ *1881-1882 Gazetteer and Business Directory of Rutland County, Vermont*, compiled and published by Hamilton Child, 1882, 642 pages. Includes historical notes of the county and the towns. FHL book 974.37 E4c.

■ *1881-1882 Gazetteer and Business Directory of Addison County, Vermont*, compiled and published by Hamilton Child, Syracuse, N.Y., 1882, 541 pages. FHL film #1415262. See also, *Index of Gazetteer of Addison County, Vermont, 1882.* FHL book 974.35 E4c.

■ *1882-1883 Gazetteer and Business Directory of Chittenden County, Vermont.* Compiled and published by Hamilton Child, Syracuse, N.Y., 1882, 584 pages. FHL book 974.317 E4c.

■ *1882-1883 Gazetteer and Business Directory of Franklin and Grand Isle Counties, Vermont*, compiled and published by Hamilton Child, Syracuse, NY, 1883, 612 pages. Includes a history

of the counties with biographical sketches. FHL film #1000626.

■ *1883-1884 Gazetteer and Business Directory of Windsor County, Vermont*, compiled and published by Hamilton Child, Syracuse, NY, 1884, 664 pages. FHL book 974.365. See also *Index, gazetteer of Windsor County, VT, for 1883-84, compiled and published by Hamilton Child*, compiled by Charles D. Townsend, publ. 1999, Sarasota, FL, Aceto Bookmen, 63 pages. FHL book 974.365 E5.

■ *1883-1884 Gazetteer and Business Directory of Lamoille and Orleans Counties, Vermont*, compiled and published by Hamilton Child, Syracuse, NY, 1884, 658 pages. FHL film #1000626.

■ *1884 Gazetteer and Business Directory of Windham County, Vermont*, compiled and published by Hamilton Child, Syracuse, NY, 1884, 600+ pages. Includes a history of the county, with biographical sketches. FHL book 974.39 E4c. See also, *Index of Gazetteer of Windham County, Vermont, Hamilton Child, 1884*, compiled by Charles D. Townsend, Sarasota, FL, Aceto Bookmen, 1987, 203 pages. FHL book 974.39 E4c index.

■ *1887-1888 Gazetteer of Caledonia and Essex Counties*, Vermont, Part 2, compiled and published by Hamilton Child, Syracuse, NY, 1888. Part 1 includes a history of the counties with biographical sketches. FHL book 974.3 E4c.

■ *1888 Gazetteer of Orange County, Vermont*, compiled and published by Hamilton Child, Syracuse, NY, 1888. Includes a history of the county with biographical sketches. Filmed by the Genealogical Society of Utah, 1974, FHL film #962543.

■ *1889 Gazetteer of Washington County, Vermont,* compiled and published by Hamilton Child, Syracuse Journal Company, 1889. Includes a history of the county with biographical sketches. FHL book 974.34 E4c.

■ **1895-1924. St. Albans District Manifest Records of Aliens Arriving From Foreign Contiguous Territory: Records of Arrivals Through Small Ports in Vermont**. United States Immigration and Naturalization Service. Microfilmed by National Archives, series M1462, 6 rolls. Records of all U.S./Canadian border crossings from the Pacific to the Atlantic were collected at St. Albans, VT. This six-roll series is for Vermont only. Records include Primary Inspection Memorandum cards, Card Manifests, Record of Registry cards, and Resident Aliens Border Crossing Cards (from Canada to the U.S.). The records are arranged alphabetically for each port of entry in Vermont. FHL film #1430987-1430992.

Vermont Censuses & Substitutes Online

■ **1790-1880 Vermont Census Records Online.** (CensusFinder.com). Several Vermont census lists are available online at various sites, accessible thru this site:
www.censusfinder.com/vermont.htm
VT statewide records:
- 1790-1930 Vermont Census Records at Ancestry
- 1840 Census of Revolutionary War Pensioners
- 1880 Federal Census - Images
- 1880 Federal Census Search at Family Search
- Vermont State Databases of Census & Genealogy Records

Records for one county (Addison):
- 1785 State Census (sic)
- 1790 Federal Census index
- 1800 Federal Census – Shoreham District
- 1835 Pensioners

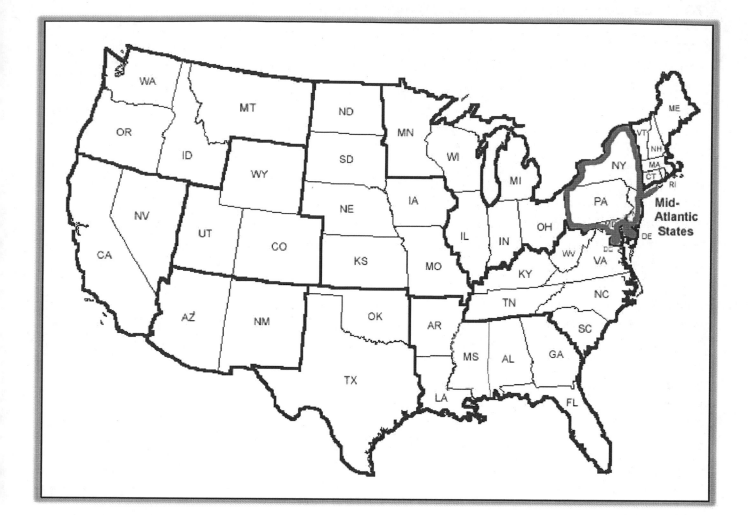

Chapter 3E – Mid-Atlantic States

Delaware, District of Columbia, Maryland, New Jersey, New York, and Pennsylvania

Timeline of Historical Events, Mid-Atlantic Jurisdictions

1497 English Discovery. John Cabot of England explores the Atlantic coast, claiming the area for the English King, Henry VII. Cabot is the first of many European explorers to seek a Northwest Passage from the Atlantic to the Pacific, which was not navigated until 461 years later (by the submarine Nautilus).

1524 French Exploration. Giovanni da Verrazano explores the Middle Atlantic region. An Italian hired by the King of France, he sailed past the New Jersey coast, entered New York bay and reached the Hudson River, then headed north to New England. The bridge named after him was not there yet.

1608 Virginia, Maryland & Delaware. English Capt. John Smith (of the Jamestown Colony) explores Chesapeake Bay. He was looking for crab cakes.

1609 New York. Samuel de Champlain explored the upstate New York area, after dropping down from the St. Lawrence River. He claimed the region as part of New France.

1609 Delaware Bay and River. Henry Hudson, an Englishman sailing for the Dutch East India Company, discovers Delaware Bay and River. A year later, Captain Samuel Argall, an English sea captain, names the bay and river after Lord De La Warr, the governor of Virginia.

1613 Manhattan Island. A Dutch trading post is set up on lower Manhattan Island. The Dutch discover that a string of beads will buy just about anything from the Indians.

1624. Fort Orange established by the Dutch. It was the first permanent white settlement in the New York region, located on the Hudson River, just south of present-day Albany.

1626 Manhattan Island. Dutchman Peter Minuit purchased Manhattan from the Indians for $24.00 worth of beads and baubles. The value of the purchase has increased a little due to inflation and Donald Trump.

1631 Delaware. Dutch colonists settle Zwaanendael, site of present-day Lewes, Delaware. After a year of Indian attacks, the colonists were all wiped out.

1632 Maryland Charter. Maryland Charter granted to Cecilius Calvert, 2nd Lord Baltimore, by King Charles I.

1634 Maryland Settlement (Maryland Day, March 25). After setting sail from Cowes, England four months earlier, the first Calvert party aboard the *Ark* and *Dove* lands at St. Clement's (now Blakistone) Island. Calvert party soon purchases Indian land and builds a fort, which they call St. Mary's City.

1638 New Sweden Colony. Peter Minuet leads a group of Swedes to the Delaware and establishes Fort Christiana (now Wilmington), the first permanent settlement on the Delaware and the founding of the New Sweden Colony.

1651 Delaware. Peter Stuyvesant, Dutch governor of New Netherland, builds Fort Casimir (now New Castle) just a few miles south of Fort Christina on the Delaware, but the Swedes are not pleased with the Dutch intrusion.

1654 Delaware. The Swedes capture Fort Casimir and rename it Fort Trinity. A year later the Dutch defeat the Swedes, ending the New Sweden colony, and Delaware becomes part of New Netherland. But, several Swedish communities continued to thrive.

1660 New Jersey. Bergen is established by the Dutch, the first permanent town in present New Jersey.

1664 New York and New Jersey. The Dutch colony of New Netherland becomes controlled by the English after Gov. Peter Stuyvesant surrenders to the British following a naval blockade. The British also take control of New Jersey from the Dutch.

1664 Delaware. Sir Robert Carr drives the Dutch off the Delaware and claims the land for James, Duke of York. Delaware then becomes an English colony.

1664 New York. England takes control of New Amsterdam. The English renamed the territory after the Duke of York, the same who is later granted a royal charter from his brother, King Charles II.

1669. Frenchmen Rene-Robert Cavelier and Sieur de La Salle, explored the Niagara region. These two eventually floated down the entire length of the Ohio and Mississippi Rivers, claiming everything they saw for France.

1673 New York and Delaware. Dutch military forces take back New York and Delaware from the British.

1674 Delaware. The English take back control of the Delaware colony.

1674. The Treaty of Westminster ends hostilities between the English and Dutch and officially returns all Dutch colonies in America to the English. This ends the Dutch presence in North America – but many of the Dutch settlements continue under British rule, particularly along the Hudson River of New York, and East Jersey.

1676 New York Royal Grant. Charles II grants to his brother, James, the Duke of York, the following: *"…main land between the two rivers there, called or known by the several names of Conecticut or Hudsons river… and all the lands from the west side of Conecticut, to the east side of Delaware Bay."* When Charles II died without issue, his brother became James II.

1676 New Jersey. The colony is divided into **East Jersey** and **West Jersey.** The diagonal dividing line runs from the Northwest corner to the Southeast corner. East Jersey is settled by mostly English Puritans and Anglicans, while West Jersey is settled mostly by English Quakers.

1676 New Jersey. Still in England, William Penn is heavily involved in the transportation of Quakers to the West Jersey Colony. He was a trustee in the colony's establishment, and was responsible for drawing up the first set of laws. They would become the basis for the Great Experiment he envisioned for Pennsylvania a few years later.

1681 Pennsylvania. William Penn is granted land in North America by Charles II and establishes the colony of Pennsylvania. He arrived in October 1682 on the ship *Welcome.* He visited Philadelphia, just laid out as the capital city, and soon after his arrival, summoned a General Assembly, called for uniting Delaware with Pennsylvania, and created the first three Pennsylvania counties of Bucks, Chester, and Philadelphia.

1682 Delaware. James, The Duke of York, transfers control of the Delaware Colony to English Quaker William Penn.

1694 Maryland. Capital moved from St. Mary's City to Anne Arundel Town. Soon after, Anne Arundel Town renamed Annapolis.

1702 New Jersey. East and West Jersey combined into one colony. However, the East and West Jersey proprietorships retained ownership of the land as originally granted to them. They remained intact as Land Commissions, solely for the purpose of granting land to individuals. Both commissions still exist today.

1715 Maryland. William and Mary declare Maryland a royal colony and appoint Sir Lionel Copley governor. Maryland governed as a royal colony rather than as a proprietary province.

1721 New Jersey. William Trent started a village called "Trent's Town," which eventually became Trenton in 1790 and the state's capital city.

1755 French and Indian War. Gen. Edward Braddock led an expedition through Maryland and Pennsylvania to the west, building Braddock's Road, the first overland route from Maryland to the Ohio River, but French-led Indians defeated Braddock's forces near Fort Duquesne (now Pittsburgh).

1758. Gen. John Forbes, the British commander, builds "Forbes Road," through Pennsylvania, takes possession of Ft. Duquesne, renames it Ft. Pitt, as the British force the French out of the western wilderness.

1763 Treaty of Paris. The French and Indian War ends. Great Britain gains control of all lands previously held by France. The Mississippi River becomes the dividing line between British North America and Spanish lands.

1764 Pennsylvania and Maryland. After years of arguments between the Penn Family and the Calvert Family, Charles Mason and Jeremiah Dixon survey the Maryland-Pennsylvania boundary, which becomes known as the "Mason-Dixon Line." It becomes the dividing line between the northern and southern British colonies, later, free versus slave states. Along the length of the Mason-Dixon Line, stone monuments were erected every five miles, each with the engraved coat of arms of the Penn Family on the side of the stone facing north, the arms of the Calvert family facing south.

1775 Delaware. The three Lower Counties break away from Pennsylvania. They adopt a constitution and become the "Delaware State," the first of all the colonies to call themselves a state.

1776-1783 Revolutionary War. 1783 Treaty of Paris ends the War, and the United States of America is officially recognized as an independent nation by Britain, France, and Spain.

1787 – Dec. 7. **Delaware** ratifies the U.S. Constitution and becomes the 1st state in the Union.

1787 – Dec. 12. **Pennsylvania** is the 2nd state to ratify the Constitution.

1787 – Dec. 12. **New Jersey** becomes the 3rd state to join the union by ratifying the U.S. Constitution just a few hours after Pennsylvania.

1788 – April 28. **Maryland** ratifies the U.S. Constitution, making it the 7th state in the Union.

1788 – Jul. 26, 1788. **New York** ratifies the U.S. Constitution and becomes the 11th state.

Important Name Lists For the Middle Colonies

■ *Immigrants to the Middle Colonies: A Consolidation of Ship Passenger Lists and Associated Data From the New York Genealogical and Biographical Record,* edited by Michael Tepper, published by Genealogical Publishing Co., Inc., 1978, 190 pages. See FHL book 973 W3te.

■ *Genealogical Miscellanea of Pennsylvania Families: With Related Records from New Jersey, Maryland, Delaware, New York,* researched and compiled into this book by Mildred Corson Williams, published at Danboro, PA, 1983, 569 pages. One of the better lists of the earliest families of the Middle Colonies. See FHL book 974.8 D2w.

■ *The Colonial Clergy of the Middle Colonies: New York, New Jersey, and Pennsylvania 1628-1776,* by Frederick Lewis Weis, originally published by American Antiquarian Society, 1957; reprint by Genealogical Publishing Co., Inc., Baltimore, 1978, 184 pages. From intro: "The history of the towns of the British Colonies in North America during the colonial period was in large measure that of their churches, and the history of these churches was largely that of their clergy. The ministers of that period were the leaders in theology, law, medicine, education, and to a considerable degree, in politics and Indian warfare. Often they were the only educated persons in a community." FHL book 973 D3wf.

■ *The Ministry and Churches of all Denominations in the Middle Colonies From the First Settlements Until the Year 1800,* by Edward

T. Corwin. This unpublished manuscript was prepared by ecclesiastical historian Edward T. Corwin and sent after his death in 1914 to A.J.F. Van Laer, Archivist and Dutch translator with the New York State Library. The manuscript consists of two parts. Part I. "Minutes of all Denominations in the Middle Colonies, before the year 1800," is an alphabetical list of clergy giving their denominations, location, dates of birth and death (when known) and of residence in each community, and frequently a citation to a biographical sketch. Part II. "Churches of All Denominations in the Middle Colonies, before the Year 1800," lists churches alphabetically by community, giving their denomination, year established (if known), and the names and dates of pastors. The states or colonies included in this manuscript are New York, Pennsylvania, Delaware, New Jersey, Maryland, and Virginia. Access the NYSL Excelsior catalog at **http://nysl.nysed.gov/**, then "all libraries," to reach the "search the library catalog" box. Enter the keywords "Middle Colonies Corwin" to find this exact reference. Information about obtaining a copy of the Corwin manuscript is available at the same site.

■ *Scots in the Mid-Atlantic Colonies, 1635-1783*, by David Dobson, published by Genealogical Publishing Co., Inc., Baltimore, 2002, 150 pages; and *Scots in the Mid-Atlantic States, 1783-1883*, 150 pages. Both books name about 3,000 Scots immigrants to the mid-Atlantic region, before and after the Revolutionary War. Both books provide a series of sketches conveying such information as the immigrant's place and date of birth and death, occupation, date of arrival and place of settlement in the U.S., and names of spouse and children. The most informative source of vital data on Scots who settled abroad is the birth, marriage, and death columns of local newspapers. These compilations depend heavily on such sources, together with certain documentary sources in the National Archives of Scotland, as well as a few other sources both printed and manuscript. These are two volumes in Dobson's regional immigration series, which includes *Directory of Scots in the Carolinas, Scots on the Chesapeake, Scots in Georgia and the Deep South,* and *Scots in New England*.

DELAWARE

Censuses and Substitutes, 1609-1934

During its colonial period, a few censuses for Delaware were taken, but after statehood, Delaware took no state censuses. The bibliography below indicates the colonial censuses and census substitutes.

■ **1609-1888 Index to Delaware History**. The definitive work is *History of Delaware* by J. Thomas Scharf, publ. 1888. The index to the names mentioned in this 1,100 page history comprises an excellent census substitute of Delaware residents. See FHL book 975.1 H22s v.1-3. Also on microfiche: film #6088424-6088426.

■ **Anglo-Americans in Spanish Archives: Lists of Anglo-American Settlers in the Spanish Colonies of America; A Finding Aid,** by Lawrence H. Feldman, published by Genealogical Publishing Co., Inc., Baltimore, 1991. Includes a few names of people living in Delaware in the 17th Century. See FHL book 973.X2.

■ **1644 New Sweden Census**, in *Swedish Colonial News*, Vol. 1, No. 9 (Spring 1994).

■ **1646-1679 Land Titles in Delaware**. Commonly known as *Duke of York Records*. Subtitle: *Being an Authorized Transcript From the Official Archives of the State of Delaware, and Comprising the Letters, Patents, Permits, Commissions, Surveys, Plats, and Confirmations by* *the Duke of York and Other High Officials, From 1646 to 1649, With Revised Index.* Original published Wilmington, DE., by Sunday Star Printing Co., n.d., FHL has reprinted copy by Family Line Publications, Westminster, MD, 1988, 199 pages, includes index. See FHL book 975.1R2o.

■ **1647 Census of New Sweden**, in *Swedish Colonial News*, Vol. 1, No. 15 (Spring 1997).

■ *Early Delaware Census Records, 1665-1697*, Ronald V. Jackson, ed., published by Accelerated Indexing, Bountiful, UT, 1977. See FHL book 975.1 X2. As was typical for many of the Jackson indexes, the source for these "census records" was not given.

■ **1676 Taxables, New Castle County**, in *Pennsylvania Magazine of History and Biography*, Vol. 1 (No. 1, Jan 1895).

■ **1677 Taxables, New Castle County, Delaware**, in *Pennsylvania Magazine of History and Biography*, Vol. 3, No. 3 (Jul 1879).

■ **1680-1934 Delaware Vital Records**. Filmed by the Genealogical Society of Utah, 1949, under the title, *Index Cards of Delaware Marriages, Baptisms, Births and Deaths, ca. 1680-1934*, microfilm of original index (typescript) at the Delaware State Archives in Dover. Contains an alphabetical listing of names from primary and secondary sources, including: bibles, church records, marriage bonds and licenses, newspapers, probate records, magazines, and *Sketch of Ecclesiastical Affairs in New Castle, Delaware and History of Immanuel Church* by Thomas Holcomb. Delaware required official recording of vital statistics in 1913; record collections prior to 1913 are considered incomplete. 18 rolls, FHL film #6416-1643.

■ **1681-1714 Colonial Delaware Records**, compiled by Bruce A. Bendler, published by

Family Line Publications, Westminster, MD, 1990, 84 pages, includes index. Book title: *Colonial Delaware records 1681-1713*. Contains Kent County rent roll 1681-1688; Sussex County rent roll 1681-1688; 1693 tax assessment list of New Castle County; 1693 tax assessment list of Kent County; 1693 tax assessment list of Sussex County; Kent County, quitrents, c1701-1713; and Sussex County quitrents, 1702-1713. See FHL book 975.1 R2b.

■ *1682-1759 Warrants and Surveys of the Province of Pennsylvania: Transcribed From the Records of the Surveyor General's and Proprietaries Secretary's offices by John Hughes, Recorder of Warrants and Surveys Under the Act of Assembly July 7, 1759; With a Guide to the Books and Index, an Historical Background and a Copy of the Act*, compiled by Charles E. Hughes, Jr., city archivist; Thomas E. Slattery, archival examiner. Microfilm of original published: Philadelphia: Dept. of Records, 1957, original manuscripts (9 volumes) in the Dept. of Records, City Archives, Philadelphia. Vol. 3, 4, 5, 7 & 8 include records for New Castle, Kent, and Sussex counties, Delaware, including an identification of the first land grants of Delaware. See FHL film #981096-981097. (See an official recap of these records made public in "1759 Warrants and Surveys" below).

■ **1684 Colonial Delaware Census, Kent County**, see "Census, 1684," in *Maryland and Delaware Genealogist*, Vol. 27, No. 1 (Jan 1986).

■ **1685 Landholders, Sussex County, Delaware**, in *Genealogical Society of Pennsylvania Publications*, Vol. 40, No. 3 (Spring 1998).

■ **1686 Colonial Delaware Census, Kent County**, see "Census, 1686," in *Delaware Genealogical Society Journal*, Vol. 3, No. 3 (Apr 1986).

■ **1688 Colonial Delaware Census, Kent County**. A census listing for Kent County was published in *The Pennsylvania Genealogical Magazine*, Vol. 37 (1991), which appears more complete than the earlier list, "1688 Kent County Census," in *Delaware Genealogical Journal*, Vol. 3 (1986).

■ **1693 Tax List, New Castle, Delaware**, in *Genealogical Researcher's Record Round-Up*, Vol. 6, No. 2 (1973) through Vol. 6, No. 4 (1973).

■ **1693 Census, Swedes on the Delaware**. Name list in *Swedish American Genealogist*, Vol. 9, No. 3 (Sep 1989) through Vol. 12, No. 1 (Mar 1992).

■ **1693 Provincial Delaware Tax Lists**. Name lists in *The Pennsylvania Genealogical Magazine* Vol. 37, No. 1 (1991).

■ **1693 Tax List, Province of Pennsylvania and the Three Lower Counties**, abstracted and indexed by Adams Apple Press, Bedminster, PA, 64 pages, includes index. Contains Philadelphia County, Bucks County, and Chester County in Pennsylvania; New Castle, Kent, and Sussex counties in Delaware. See FHL book 974. A1 No. 643.

■ **1726 Tax List, Kent County, Delaware**, in *Maryland and Delaware Genealogist*, Vol. 27, No. 4 (Oct 1986); Vol. 28, No. 1 (Jan 1987); and Vol. 28, No. 2 (Spring 1987).

■ **1755 Tax List, Kent County, Delaware**. Name list published serially in *Maryland and Delaware Genealogist*, Vol. 29, No. 1 (Winter 1988), through Vol. 29, No. 4 (Fall 1988).

■ **1759 Warrants and Surveys of the Province of Pennsylvania Including the Three Lower Counties**, compiled by Allen Winberg and Thomas E. Slattery under the directory of Charles E. Hughes, Jr., 1965 edition published by Department of Records, Philadelphia. The Provincial Assembly representing the people of Pennsylvania was in conflict with the sons of

William Penn who were the Proprietaries of the Province of Pennsylvania. Records of Warrants under the control of the Proprietaries and which ordered surveys to be made were not public records. This created confusion over property rights and boundaries. In 1759 the Assembly passed a law for recording warrants and surveys. The Proprietaries in 1760 brought the law before the King who vetoed it. In the meantime, the warrants were transcribed and made public. This is an index of names recorded in the warrants in the present-day Pennsylvania counties of Berks, Bucks, Chester, Cumberland, Lancaster, Northampton, Philadelphia, and York; and the three counties Kent, Newcastle, and Sussex making up Delaware. FHL has a reprint by The Bookmark, Knightstown, IN, 1975, 91 pages. See FHL book 974.8 R2w.

■ **1779 Delaware, Kent County Tax List**, see "Duck Creek Hundred Levy and Taxes for 1779," in *Maryland and Delaware Genealogist*, Vol. 16, No. 4 (Fall 1985).

■ **1782 Colonial Delaware Census**. Manuscripts survive for a colonial census taken for Brandywine, Christiana, and St. Georgia's hundreds in New Castle County; Duck Creek and Little Creek hundreds in Kent County; and Lewes Town Hundred in Sussex County. Two versions of the name lists have been published: *1782 Delaware Tax Assessment and Census*, compiled by Ralph D. Nelson, et al, published by the Delaware Genealogical Society, Wilmington, DE, 1994, 404 pages. See FHL book 975.1 X2; and *The Reconstructed Delaware State Census of 1782*, Harold B. Hancock, ed., (Delaware Genealogical Society, Wilmington, DE, 1983), 233 pages. See FHL book 975.1 X2.

■ **1785 Tax List for Kenton Hundred, Kent County, Delaware**, in *Maryland and Delaware Genealogist*, Vol. 5, No. 3 (Jul 1964) and No. 4 (Oct 1964).

■ **1790 Delaware Census (Reconstructed).** The 1790 federal census for Delaware was lost. A reconstructed name list was compiled by Leon DeValinger, Jr. from tax lists, land records, and other local sources, and published serially in the *National Genealogical Society Quarterly,* later as NGS Special Publication No. 10: *Reconstructed 1790 Census of Delaware,* 1954, 83 pages. See FHL book 975.1 X2.

■ **1800 Tax List, Dover, Kent County, Delaware,** in *Delaware Genealogical Society Journal,* Vol. 8, No. 4 (Oct 1996).

■ **1800 Road Tax, New Castle, Delaware.** Names of taxpayers listed in *Maryland and Delaware Genealogist,* Vol. 26, No. 1 (Jan 1985).

■ **1800 Tax List, Pencader, New Castle County, Delaware,** in *Delaware Genealogical Society Journal,* Vol. 8, No. 4 (Oct 1996).

■ **1807 Road Tax, New Castle, Delaware.** Names of taxpayers in *Maryland and Delaware Genealogist, Vol. 26, No. 2 (Apr 1985).*

■ **1850-1880 Delaware Mortality Schedules.** Microfilmed by the Delaware Division of Historical and Cultural Affairs, 1971, under the title, *United States Census of Delaware; Persons Who Died During the [Census] Year, 1850-1880,* original records at the Hall of Records, Dover, DE. Lists names of individuals who died during the year ending 1 Jun of the census years 1850-1870 and during the year ending 31 May 1880. FHL film #1421306. Another copy filmed as #1549980.

■ **1859-1860 Delaware (State) Directory.** Microfilm of original published as *Boyd's Delaware State Directory,* by Research Publications, Woodbridge, CT, 1980, "...containing the names of all persons in business on their own account, also the censers, manufacturing statistics, and names of the inhabitants of Wilmington city," by William H.

Wilmington and Andrew Boyd. See FHL film #6043859.

■ **1862-1866 Internal Revenue Assessment Lists for Delaware.** Microfilm of original records in the National Archives, Washington, DC, 1988, series M759, 8 rolls. FHL film #1578436 through #1578443.

■ **1862-1872 Delaware Income & Manufacturers Tax.** Name list in *Delaware History,* Vol. 14, No. 4 (Oct 1971).

Delaware Censuses & Substitutes Online

■ **1680-1925 Probates: An Online Index.** This large database is an index to Delaware estate files, including names of deceased, heirs, executors, administrators, and other names associated with county probate cases during this period. The database is freely accessible, and searchable online at **www.state.de.us/sos/dpa/collections/probate.htm**.

■ **1790-1930 Federal Census Records for Delaware** (**www.ancestry.com**). Indexes originally compiled by Ronald V. Jackson, Accelerated Indexing Systems, Salt Lake City, UT. 1790-1860 electronic files were acquired by Ancestry, Inc. which has these Delaware lists plus several updates, 1870-1930, all indexed online.

■ **1790-1930 Delaware Statewide Census Records Online.** (CensusFinder.com). Direct links to Internet Web sites where census name lists have been published online can be found at **www.censusfinder.com/delaware.htm**. Censuses links arranged by state, thereafter by county, as shown below:
Delaware Statewide Censuses:
• 1790-1890 Delaware Census Search Engine at Ancestry
• 1880 Federal Census - Images
• 1880 Federal Census Search at Family Search

- Delaware Statewide Databases of Census & Genealogy Records

Kent County
- 1860 Federal Census Images
- 1693 Tax List
- 1782 Tax List Images of Little Creek Hundred
- 1840 Census of Revolutionary War Pensioners
- 1851 Thomson's Mercantile and Professional Directory
- WWI Draft Registrations

New Castle County
- 1850 Federal Census Index - Surnames
- 1850 Federal Census of Newcastle
- Early Pioneer Residents of Wilmington
- 1693 Tax Assessment
- 1696 / 1697 Tax list
- 1777 Tax List of Brandywine Hundred
- 1840 Census of Revolutionary War Pensioners
- 1851 Thomson's Mercantile and Professional Directory
- 1859 City Directory of Wilmington
- WWI Draft Registrations

Sussex County
- 1850 Federal Census Index of Georgetown Broadkiln Hundred
- 1870 Federal Census Images
- Orphan's Court Records
- 1693 Tax Records
- 1800s-1900s Baptism Records of Sound Methodist Church
- 1851 Thomson's Mercantile and Professional Directory
- WWI Draft Registrations

■ **1790-1930 Links to Online Census Records**. (CensusOnline.com). This is another Web site featuring links to census records online. Go to **www.census-online.com/links/DE/** to review any Delaware census records online. Examples for Delaware's three counties are shown below:

New Castle County
- 1859 City Directory - Wilmington

Kent County
- 1860 Federal Census Images

Sussex County
- 1870 Federal Census Images

District of Columbia

The District of Columbia holds a unique status in this country's political system, functioning as a state, county, and city. The Governments of the District and the City are the same. Some functions are done under the name District of Columbia, others under the name of the city of Washington, DC.

Specific functions usually performed by state–level governments include state courts, driver licensing, liquor control, unemployment compensation, food and drug inspection, and professional licensing, just to name a few. It is the mayor of the city of Washington who administers these state-level functions; plus the mayor manages city-level functions such as police and fire departments.

Also a unique governmental system, the "state court" of the District of Columbia is a circuit division of the Supreme Court of the United States, and the "state judge" is usually the Chief Justice of the Supreme Court.

This current system was preceded by several different governmental structures, jurisdictions and names; and local political control changed several times. For genealogists looking for records in which their ancestors may be mentioned, an understanding of the territory, county, city, and district jurisdictions is necessary.

Origins of the District

The U.S. Constitution, ratified in 1789, gave the first President of the United States the job of finding a site for a new federal capital district, "not to exceed 100 square miles in size." George Washington chose a site not far from his Mount Vernon plantation on the Potomac River.

What is known today as the District of Columbia began as a ten-mile square tract of land straddling the Potomac River, incorporating the established towns of Georgetown, Maryland and Alexandria, Virginia. In 1791, the northern part was ceded by Maryland to the federal government, and the southern part ceded by Virginia. Before the cessions, the area was within Montgomery and Prince Georges County, Maryland; and Fairfax County, Virginia. Another connection to George Washington: the Virginia portion was land originally owned by Martha Dandridge Custis Washington's first husband, Daniel Parke Custis, a prominent Virginia planter. Custis died in 1757, and Martha, the widow, held title to the land for two years, until she married George Washington, and he became the owner. But Washington had divested himself of that specific piece of land well before it was purchased by the federal government in 1791.

Within the area which became the new federal district north of the Potomac, Georgetown was a well established town, part of Montgomery County, Maryland; while the town of Alexandria was the county seat of Fairfax County, Virginia.

Since 1746, when the first wagon road across the Blue Ridge Mountains was opened, Alexandria had become a busy immigration port, the site of the start of the Pioneer's Road – the route to Winchester, Virginia on the Shenandoah River was followed by many of the Scots-Irish coming to America before the Revolutionary War. Georgetown, founded in 1751, had a similar history, located just upriver from Alexandria, and became a starting point to reach Braddock's Road (since the French and Indian War of the mid-1750s), into western Maryland and Pennsylvania.

After the 1790 Act to authorize the **Territory of Columbia**, Congress was not inclined to include the Alexandria area, but Alexandria-based supporters were successful in getting their area included in the new federal capital district. However, in the 1791 enabling Act, Congress prohibited the construction of federal facilities on the Alexandria side, which hampered any government-related economic development there. The prohibition eventually led to the retrocession of the area back to Virginia.

The present **District of Columbia** is the area ceded by Maryland only, as Virginia retroceded its area in 1846. The area of Alexandria City/County, DC, 1791-1846, included what is now Arlington County and the older section of the City of Alexandria, Virginia.

Timeline of D.C. Jurisdictions

1790. The 1790 federal census included the areas of the District as part of Montgomery and Prince Georges counties, Maryland; and part of Fairfax County, Virginia.

1791. The City of Washington was first laid out in 1791, but Georgetown remained the main community in the northern part of the District for several more years.

1800. The capital of the United States was officially moved from Philadelphia to Washington in December. The 1800 federal census taken for the inhabitants of the Territory of Columbia was included with the Maryland and Virginia enumerations. The population of the Georgetown side was 8,144, while the Alexandria side had 5,959 residents.

1801. The Organic Act of 1801 established **"the territory called Columbia"** as a jurisdiction exclusively under the control of Congress. This Act established the territorial judicial system, provided for a committee in Congress to manage the affairs of the district; and created two counties, Washington County on the northern side of the Potomac, and Alexandria County on the southern side. From 1790-1801, both Virginia and Maryland considered the residents in their ceded areas as citizens, qualified to vote in state and federal elections; and included them in the federal censuses taken there in 1790 and

1800 as part of Virginia and Maryland. The 1801 Act essentially disenfranchised the District residents, who now had no representation in Congress, and virtually no home rule. As late as 1990, challenges were filed in Congress questioning the constitutionality of the Organic Act of 1801, as well as asking for the restoration of Maryland citizenship for the District residents.

1802. Congress granted the City of Washington its first municipal charter. Voters, defined as white males who paid taxes and had lived in the city for at least a year, received the right to elect a 12-member council. The mayor was appointed by the president.

1810. In the 1810 federal census, the Territory of Columbia was enumerated as a separate district for the first time. The population of the area was 15,471 residents in the two counties of Washington and Alexandria.

1812. Congress amended the charter of the City of Washington to provide for an eight-member board of aldermen and a 12-member common council. The aldermen and the common council elected the mayor.

1814. British troops burned the capitol and other federal buildings during the War of 1812. Contrary to popular belief, no original federal censuses were lost in the fires, with the possible exception of the 1810 District of Columbia schedules. None of the federal census name lists had been moved to Washington yet. That did not happened until after an 1830 law asked for the clerks of the district courts in all states to send the original copies to the U.S. Secretary of State's Office in Washington, DC.

1820. Congress amended the Charter of the City of Washington for the direct election of the mayor by resident voters.

1846. Congress passed a law returning the city of Alexandria and Alexandria County to the state of Virginia.

1848. Congress adopted a new charter for the City of Washington and expanded the number of elected offices to include a board of assessors, a surveyor, a collector and a registrar.

1871. The elected mayor and council of Washington City and Georgetown, and the County Levy Court were abolished by Congress and replaced by a governor and council appointed by the president. An elected House of Delegates and a non-voting delegate to Congress were created. In this Act, the jurisdiction and territorial government came to be called the **District of Columbia**, combining the governments of Georgetown, the City of Washington and the County of Washington.

1874. The territorial government of the District of Columbia was abolished, including the non-voting delegate to Congress. Three temporary commissioners and a subordinate military engineer were thereafter appointed by the president.

1878. In the Organic Act of 1878, Congress established the District of Columbia government as a municipal corporation governed by three commissioners appointed by the President. This form of government continued until 1973.

1895. Although no longer a city, the area of Georgetown was officially added to the city of Washington. The boundaries of the City of Washington and the District of Columbia were now the same.

1961. The 23rd Amendment to the Constitution gave District residents the right to vote for president.

1973. Congress approved the District of Columbia Self-Government and Governmental Reorganization Act, which established an elected mayor and a 13-member council.

1978. Congress approved the District of Columbia Voting Rights Amendment, which would have given District residents voting representation in the House and the Senate. However, the proposed constitutional amendment was not ratified by the necessary number of states (38) within the allotted seven years.

1980. District electors approve the District of Columbia Statehood Constitutional Convention of 1979, which called for convening a state constitutional convention.

1982. After a constitutional convention, a Constitution for the **State of New Columbia** was ratified by District voters. But, no action by Congress was taken over the next ten years.

1992. The U.S. House of Representatives approved an enabling act for statehood for Washington, DC, but the U.S. Senate did not approve the measure. Drives for statehood continue.

D.C. Census Substitutes

The District of Columbia/City of Washington has never taken a census apart from the federal censuses. But, there are numerous name lists that can serve as substitutes. The following bibliography is arranged in chronological order, including name lists from Alexandria and Georgetown prior to the formation of the District of Columbia.

■ *Abstracts of Wills in the District of Columbia, 1776-1815: Compiled From Records in the Office of the Register of Wills,* compiled by Mrs. Alexander H. Bell, 2 vols., published 1945-1946, Washington, DC, Includes index. FHL book 975.3

S2b v.1-2. Also on microfilm, FHL film #207695 (Vol. 1 only); and microfiche, FHL fiche #6051443 (vol. 1) and fiche #6051444 (vol. 2).

■ **1783-1870 Deeds, Alexandria City/County, Virginia.** See *Deed Books, 1783-1865; Index, 1793-1870,* microfilm of original records in the Alexandria City Courthouse in Alexandria, Virginia. Includes a general index. Most volumes are also individually indexed. Alexandria County was formed in 1789 from Fairfax County and included Alexandria City. It was formally established in 1801 as a county in the District of Columbia. In 1846 the county was given back to Virginia and organized in 1847 as a Virginia county. Alexandria County underwent a name change in 1920, becoming Arlington County. The city of Alexandria became an independent city in 1852. The 1783-1801 records were registered with the Hustings Court in the city of Alexandria. From 1801 to 1847 the deeds were recorded in the Circuit Court of the District of Columbia which was held for the county of Alexandria. After 1847 they were recorded with the County Court (later the Circuit Court, then Corporation Court) for the city and county of Alexandria. Filmed by the Genealogical Society of Utah, 1951, 37 rolls, beginning with FHL film #30168.

■ **1783-1801 Deed Index.** See *Alexandria, Virginia, Alexandria Hustings Court Deeds,* compiled by James D. Munson, published by Heritage Books, Bowie, MD 1991, 2 vols. Includes indexes to grantors and grantees. Contents: vol. 1: 1783-1797; vol. 2: 1797-1801. The deed books cover the time period when Alexandria's first court of record, the Alexandria Hustings Court, began recording deeds in 1782 through 1801. The deeds indexed are those issued prior to Alexandria County becoming part of the District of Columbia in 1801. FHL book 975.5296 R2m v 1-2.

■ **1791-1800 Land Owners.** See *District of Columbia Original Land Owners, 1791-1800,* compiled by Wesley E. Pippenger, published by W.E. Pippenger, Westminster, MD, 1999, 156 pages. FHL book 975.3 R2p.

■ **1792-1886 Land Records; General Index to Deeds, 1792-1919,** microfilm of original records in the District of Columbia Courthouse, Washington, DC. Filmed by the Genealogical Society of Utah, 1972, 694 rolls, beginning with FHL film #89525 (General index to deeds v. 1-4 1792-1828).

■ **1795-1863 Records of Coffin Sales,** see *William King's Mortality Books,* transcribed from the originals by Jan Donovan and Carlton Fletcher, published by Heritage Books, Bowie, MD, 2001, 2004, 2 vols. William King was a cabinet maker in Georgetown, and kept careful records of every coffin constructed for Georgetown and Washington families, including the name of the deceased and the person paying for the coffin. FHL book 975.3/G1 V3k vol. 1 (1795-1832) and FHL book 975.3/G1 V3k vol. 2 (1833-1863).

■ **1798 Direct Tax, District of Columbia,** see *Federal Assessment, 1790-1805, Maryland, District of Columbia,* microfilm of manuscripts (hand and typewritten) held by the Maryland Hall of Records, Annapolis, MD. Filmed by the Hall of Records, 1965, 9 rolls, for all Maryland counties, including "District of Columbia, Maryland," which was mainly a name list of tax payers from Georgetown and environs. The name list for the District of Columbia is on FHL film #499897.

■ **1800-1878 Will books; Index to Wills, 1800-1951, Alexandria County, District of Columbia (1801-1846); Arlington County, Virginia (1846-1920); and Alexandria, Virginia, an Independent City (1920 to date),** microfilm of original records at the Alexandria City Courthouse in Alexandria, Virginia and the Arlington County Courthouse in Arlington, Virginia. Includes general index. Most volumes

are also individually indexed. Includes accounts, inventories and other related probate matters. Contains probate records 1800-1801 for the Hustings Court and the Corporation Court for Alexandria City. From 1801 to 1846 the court was the Orphans Court for Alexandria County while the county was part of the District of Columbia. In 1846, when Alexandria County was returned to Virginia, the court became the County Court. Alexandria was renamed Arlington County in 1920. Filmed by the Genealogical Society of Utah, 1951, 6 rolls, beginning with FHL film #30499 (Index to wills, 1800-1951).

■ **1800-1879 Tax Lists.** See *Georgetown Property Tax Records, 1800-1820, and 1862-1879,* microfilm of originals at the National Archives, Washington, DC. From intro: "This microfilm publication reproduces records of the local government of the city of Georgetown, 1800-1879. Georgetown, which was founded in Maryland in 1751, was governed by its own mayor and council until 1871, when Congress revoked its charter. Georgetown retained its name as a topographical designation, however, until 1895, when Congress abolished its existence as a separate city, consolidating it with Washington, D.C." Some volumes are indexed. Filmed by the Archives, series M605, 9 rolls, as follows:
- Tax records, 1800-1813, FHL film #1024464.
- Tax records, 1815, 1818-1820, FHL film #1024465.
- Tax records, 1862-1868, FHL film #1024475.
- Tax records, 1865-1873, FHL film #1024466.
- Tax records, 1871-1872, FHL film #1024471.
- Tax records, 1874-1875, FHL film #1024467.
- Tax records, 1875-1876, FHL film #1024468.
- Tax records, 1875-1877, FHL film #1024469.
- Tax records, 1878-1879, FHL film #1024470.

■ *1800-1850 Marriage and Death Notices from the National Intelligencer (Washington, D.C.),* by George Martin and Frank J. Metcalf, indexed by Margaret Elliott Higgins, published as Special Publication No. 41, National Genealogical Society, Washington, DC, 1976, microfilmed on 3 rolls, FHL film #929472 (Index, Notices 1800-1834); FHL film #929473 (Notices, 1835-1846); and FHL film #929474 (Notices, 1847-1850).

■ **1801-1838 Georgetown Marriage and Death Notices,** see *Georgetown, District of Columbia, Marriage and Death Notices, 1801-1838,* by Wesley E. Pippenger, published by Heritage Books, Bowie, MD, 2004, 330 pages. Includes index. This compilation of marriage and death notices was taken from nine newspapers that were published in Georgetown during the period 1801-1838. There are some gaps due to missing newspapers. FHL book 975.3/G1 V28p.

■ **1801-1930 Probate Records, District of Columbia, Register of Wills,** microfilm of originals at the Office of Public Records, Washington, DC. Folders are arranged alphabetically by year. These are loose papers. General index is to files by number but by using the date the will was filed or other date it is possible to locate the will. Filmed by the Genealogical Society of Utah, 1996-1997, 133 rolls, beginning with FHL film #2050077 (Index: A – Buchoff, 1801-1929). An index to wills, 1801-1950 can be found in *Index to District of Columbia Wills,* prepared by Dorothy S. Provine, published by Willow Bend Books, Westminster, MD, 1996, 2 vols. This index provides the name, year, and box number. Contents: Vol. 1: 1801-1920; Vol. 2:1921-1950. FHL book 975.3 P22P v.1-2.

■ **1801-1808 Orphan's Court.** See, *Proceedings of the Orphan's Court: Washington County, District of Columbia, 1801-1808,* compiled by Wesley E. Pippenger, published by Willow Bend Books, Westminster, MD, 1998, 94 pages. FHL book 975.3 P2p.

■ **1802-1928 Guardianships.** See *District of Columbia Guardianship Index, 1802-1928,* compiled by Wesley E. Pippenger, published by

Willow Bend Books, 1998, 401 pages. FHL book 975.3 P22pw.

■ **1802-1909 Naturalizations.** See *Index to Naturalization Records of the U.S. Supreme Court for the District of Columbia, 1802-1909,* microfilm of original records located at the National Archives, Washington, DC. From intro: "On the single roll of this microfilm publication is the index to naturalization records for the U.S. Supreme Court for the District of Columbia, 1802-1909. These records are part of the Records of the District Court of the United States, Record Group 21." Filmed by the Archives, 1999, series M1827, 1 roll. FHL has film #2311054 (Index, 1802-1909).

■ **1811-1830 Marriage Licenses.** See *Marriage Licenses of Washington, D.C., 1811-1830,* compiled by F. Edward Wright, published by Family Line Publications, Silver Spring, MD, 1988, 159 pages. Arranged in alphabetical order for both males and females. FHL book 975.3 V28w.

■ **1822 Directory.** See *Washington Directory: Showing the Name, Occupation, and Residence of Each Head of a Family and Person in Business, the Names of the Members of Congress, and Where They Board; Together With Other Useful Information,* by Judah Delano, microfilm of original book published by W. Duncan, Washington, DC, 1822, 148 pages. Filmed by the Genealogical Society of Utah, 1966, 4 microfiche, FHL fiche #6125565. See also *Washington Directory of 1822,* reprint of original by Family Line Publications, Silver Spring, MD, ca1985, 43 pages. FHL book 975.3 E4w.

■ **1822-1935 City Directories.** See *Washington D.C. City Directories,* microfilm of originals published by various publishers. Filmed by Research Publications, Woodbridge, CT, 1980-1984, 44 microfiches, beginning with FHL fiche #6044618 (1822: The Washington Directory by

William Duncan (3 fiches). 1822 followed by directories for the years 1827, 1843 1846, 1850, 1853, 1855, 1858, 1860, and a complete run of years from 1862 through 1935.

■ **1847-1938 Burial Records.** See *Register of Burials of the Joseph F. Birch Funeral Home: January 1, 1847 - December 31, 1938*, transcribed by Paul E. Sluby, Sr.; Stanton L. Wormley, published by the Columbian Harmony Society, Washington, DC, 1989, 4 vols. Includes copies of the original records of this Georgetown funeral home. Includes surname index for each volume. The funeral home was apparently known by slight variations of the name over a period of time. FHL book 975.3 V39r v. 1-4.

■ **1853 Directory.** See *The Washington and Georgetown Directory*, compiled and published by Alfred Hunter; revised by Wesley E. Pippenger, originally published by Kirkwood & McGill, 1853. Reprinted by Colonial Roots, Lewes, DE, 2004, 160 pages. FHL book 975.3 E4h.

■ **1855-1964 Death Records, District of Columbia.** See *Interments, 1855-1874; Death certificates, 1874-1931; Index to (1) Interments, (2) Death Certificates, (3) "Foreign" Death Certificates, 1855-1949; Stillbirth Certificates, 1874-1964*, microfilm of original records at the Health Department in Washington, D.C. Certificates are loose papers. This material has some missing or non-readable pages. "Foreign" deaths refers to death certificates for a person who died outside of DC but the body was brought to DC for burial. Filmed by the Genealogical Society of Utah, 1995, 1998-1999, 130 rolls, beginning with FHL film #1994618 (Index to old register of deaths, 1855-1874; Index, vol. 1-2, 1874-1882).

■ **1855-1870 Deaths.** See *Daily National Intelligencer, Index to Deaths, 1855-1870*, compiled by Wesley E. Pippenger, published by Heritage Books, Westminster, MD, 2004, 137 pages. Arranged in alphabetical order by surname. From preface: "The present work is an index of death notices that appeared primarily under the column heading 'Deaths' as found most often in the earlier years on the front page of each four-page issue. By 1865, notices typically appeared on page three of each issue. Each entry in the present index contains as much information from the death notice that can be inserted on a single line. The compiler did not analyze each issue for death information that might be contained in other articles or editorials. Researchers should consult the newspaper for the complete notice. During the war years, one will find an occasional list of dead as submitted by the Navy Department; not all of these lists were indexed." FHL book 975.3 B32p.

■ **1860-1869 Georgetown Land Transfers.** See *Real Estate Belonging to the District of Columbia, 1860-1869*, microfilm of original manuscript at the National Archives, Washington, DC. The book contains some transfers of property up to 1873. Filmed by the Archives, series M605, 1965, 1 roll, FHL film #1024477.

■ **1861-1865 Civil War Soldiers.** See *Index to Compiled Service Records of Volunteer Union Soldiers Who Served in Organizations From the District of Columbia*, microfilm of original records at the National Archives, Washington, DC. Filmed by the Archives, 1964, series M538, 3 rolls. FHL has series, beginning with FHL film #881964 (Index, A-G, 1861-1865)

■ **1862-1866 Internal Revenue Assessment Lists for the District of Columbia**, microfilm of originals at the National Archives in Washington, DC Records indicate a name and place of residence for each person subject to the tax. (generally, land owners, but occasionally those with personal property only). Filmed by the Archives, 1969, series M760, 8 rolls, beginning with FHL film #1578491 (Annual tax lists, divisions 1-8, 1863-1864).

■ **1865-1876 Vital Records.** See *The Georgetown Courier Marriage and Death Notices: Georgetown, District of Columbia, November 18, 1865 to May 6, 1876,* compiled by Wesley E. Pippenger, published by Willow Bend Book, Westminster, MD, 1998, 206 pages. FHL book 975.3 V4p.

■ **1874-1897 Birth Records, District of Columbia,** see *District of Columbia Birth Records, 1874-1897; Indexes, 1874-1897,* microfilm of originals at the Health Department, Washington, DC. Includes indexes to certificate numbers. The certificates are loose papers. Filmed by the Genealogical Society of Utah, 1995, 1998, 31 rolls, beginning with FHL film #2020343 (Index, 1874-1889).

■ **1889-1941 Directories.** See *Boyd's District of Columbia Directory,* certain years available in book form at the FHL, with FHL book 975.3 E4b (year); and microfilm of other years, beginning with FHL film #1000737. FHL Library has: 1889 (film only), 1891 (film only), 1893 (film only), 1894 (film only), 1897 (film only), 1898 (film only), 1904, 1907-1909, 1910 (film only), 1912 (film only), 1913, 1915-1919, 1921 (film only), 1929, 1930, 1939, and 1941

■ **1908-1909 Biographies.** See *American Biographical Directories, District of Columbia: Concise Biographies of its Prominent and Representative Contemporary Citizens, and Valuable Statistical Data, 1908-1909,* with an historical sketch by Henry B. F. MacFarland, published by Potomac Press, Washington, DC,

1908, 589 pages. Filmed by W. C. Cox Co., Tucson, AZ, 1974. FHL has 1 roll, FHL #1000157.

■ **1912-1931 Suburban Directories.** See *Washington, D.C. Suburban Directories,* microfilm of original records located in various libraries and societies. Filmed by Primary Source Microfilm, Woodbridge, CT, ca1995, 4 rolls, beginning with FHL #2310369 (1912-1913) and continuing with directories for 1914, 1915, 1916, 1917, 1918, 1923, 1927-1928, and 1930-1931.

■ **Online Resources at the Washington, DC RootsWeb Website.** Web address: **www.rootsweb.com/~dcgenweb/.** The following categories can be accessed:
- Washington DC GenWeb Research Links
- Obtaining Church Records
- Educational Institutions
- D.C. History
- African American Links
- Genealogical Societies
- Cemetery Records
- Maps and Gazetteers
- Library of Congress Books on D.C.
- Extracts from *The Daily National Intelligencer*
- Early Churches and Synagogues
- Obituaries
- Bible Records
- Early Georgetown Information
- Irish, German, Jewish, Italians in D.C.
- Memories
- About the DC GenWeb
- Mailing Lists
- Records of the Congress Street Methodist Protestant Church
- Queries
- Museums

MARYLAND

Censuses and Substitutes, 1633-1969

During its colonial period, Maryland took a census of its entire population in 1776 and 1778, as well as several colony-wide tax lists. But after statehood, no state censuses were ever taken in Maryland. Census substitutes are shown below. If you have a Maryland ancestor, start with the time period when the person lived there to see if any census substitutes exist for a Maryland town, county, or region.

■ **1633-1680.** The definitive list of the founders of Maryland was compiled from original land records in the MD state archives. See *The early settlers of Maryland: An Index to Names of Immigrants Compiled From Records of Land Patents, 1633-1680, in the Hall of Records, Annapolis, Maryland*, compiled by Gust Skordas, published by Genealogical Publishing Co., Inc., Baltimore, 1968, 536 pages. FHL book 975.2 W2s.xi

■ **1636-1969 Archives of Maryland**. In 1883, the state of Maryland began publishing the *Archives of Maryland*, a serial that (re)publishes historical documents that "form the constitutional, legal, legislative, judicial, and administrative basis of Maryland's government" from the 17th century through the present day. It is published by the Maryland State Archives. The first volume of the *Archives* came out in 1883, covering proceedings and acts of the General Assembly starting in 1637. These legislative session minutes often mention the names of persons petitioning the Assembly, and the index of names is like a census of Maryland during the colonial period. As of the start of 2000, there were 140 printed volumes in the series, covering proceedings of various sorts from 1636-1969. More volumes are still being issued, at irregular intervals. To see the titles and contents of the online volumes, go to the main Maryland State Archives Web site at **www.mdarchives.state.md.us/**. From that page, find the "Archives of Maryland Online," then "All Volumes," where any of the tiles can be accessed as digitized textual pages. Included are tax lists, voter lists, lists of officers in county, colonial and state government, and dozens of other name lists. The *Archives of Maryland* is also available online at the **www.ancestry.com** site, but the MD Archives site has better indexes and better page-locating tools (and it is free).

■ **1654-1685 Immigrants.** See *Bristol and America, a Record of the First Settlers in the Colonies of North America 1654-1685: Including the Names With Places of Origin of More than 10,000 Servants to Foreign Plantations Who Sailed From the Port of Bristol to Virginia, Maryland, and Other Parts of the Atlantic coast, and Also to the West Indies From 1654 to 1685*, compiled by W. Dodgson Bowman, N. Dermott Harding, and R. Hargreaves-Mawdsley, this list was compiled and published from records of the Corporation of the City of Bristol, England, originally published in London: [R.S. Glover], 1929, 1931, reprinted by Genealogical Publishing Co., Inc., Baltimore, 1970, 210 pages. Includes an index that was originally issued in a separate volume. See FHL book 973 W3b.

■ **1659-1750 Census Substitutes**. See *Citizens of the Eastern Shore of Maryland, 1659-1750*, compiled by F. Edward Wright, Published by Family Line Publications, Silver Spring, MD, 1986. Includes index. Contents: Listings of taxables, petitioners, bounty recipients, overseers of roads, militiamen, cattle mark registrants, charity cases, persons reimbursed by the court and persons fined. See FHL book 975.21 D2w.

■ **1689 Public Levy in Colonial Maryland**, in *Maryland Historical Magazine*, Vol. 53, No. 3 (Sep 1958).

■ **1689 Somerset County (Maryland) Inhabitants**, in *Southeast Alabama Genealogical Society Quarterly*, Vol. 16, No. 4 (Apr 2000).

■ **1692 Tax List, Baltimore County, Maryland**, in *Notebook of the Baltimore County Genealogical Society*, Vol. 13, No. 3 (Sep 1997).

■ **1693 List of Taxables, Northside Patapsco Hundred, Baltimore County, Maryland**, in *Notebook of the Baltimore County Genealogical Society*, Vol. 13, No. 4 (Dec 1997).

■ **1699 List of Taxables, Baltimore County, Maryland**, in *Maryland Historical Magazine*, Vol. 12, No. 1 (Mar 1917); and in *Maryland and Delaware Genealogist*, Vol. 1, No. 2 (Dec 1959).

■ **1700 List of Taxables, Baltimore County, Maryland**, in *Maryland and Delaware Genealogist*, Vol. 1, No. 3 (Mar 1960) and Vol. 1, No. 4 (Jun 1960).

■ **1701 List of Taxables, Baltimore County, Maryland**, in *Maryland and Delaware Genealogist*, Vol. 2, No. 1 (Fall 1960, through Vol. 3, No. 3 (Mar 1962).

■ **1702 List of Taxables, Baltimore County, Maryland**, in *Maryland and Delaware Genealogist*, Vol. 4, No. 1 (Jan 1963) through Vol. 4, No. 4 (Oct 1963).

■ **1718 Tax Assessment List, Baltimore County, Maryland**, in *History Trails*, Vol. 30, No. 1-2 (1995).

■ **1719 Anglican Inhabitants, Prince George's County, Maryland**, in *Prince George's County Genealogical Society Bulletin*, Vol. 10, No. 6 (Feb 1979).

■ **1724 Tax Lists, Somerset County, Maryland**, in *National Genealogical Society Quarterly*, Vol. 61, No. 3 (Sep 1973) through Vol. 61, No. 4 (Dec 1973).

■ **1725 Taxables, Annamessex Hundred, Somerset County, Maryland**, in *Maryland Genealogical Society Bulletin*, Vol. 31, No. 2 (Spring 1990).

■ **1725 Tax List, Somerset County, Maryland**, in *Maryland Connections Queries*, Vol. 10, No. 2 (Jan 2000) through Vol. 11, No. 5 (Jul 2001).

■ **1727-1882 Western Maryland**. See *Western Maryland Pioneers: Marriages, Early Settlers, Births and Deaths With Location*, arranged and alphabetized by Hilda Chance, original published: [Liberty, PA, H. Chance, 196?] 2 vols., filmed by the Genealogical Society of Utah, 1968. **Contents, Vol. 1:** *Frederick County Marriages Before 1830; Wills of Frederick County Before 1800; Frederick County Early Settlers, Land Grants, Land Purchasers, Some of These Were Local Officials. Frederick County Births and Deaths; Births and deaths of Early Washington County From Cemetery and Newspaper Obits. Early Marriages of Hagerstown, Washington County.* **Contents, Vol. 2:** *Early marriages of Allegany County; Early marriages of Garrett County; Early Marriages of Montgomery County; Early Settlers, Montgomery County; Land Grants and Purchases, Births and Deaths of Montgomery County; Births and Deaths of Carroll County; Early marriages of Carroll County; First Settlers of Carroll County from 1727; First Wills of Carroll County.* From preface: "This is not a history of Maryland but lists, alphabetically arranged, of 8,000 early settlers, marriages, births and deaths, with dates, from cemeteries and newspapers, land grants and early wills index. These are taken from two large volumes of Thomas Scharf, 1882." See FHL film #560192.

■ **1732-1733 Taxables, St. Mary's County, Maryland**, in *Calvert County Maryland Genealogy Newsletter*, Vol. 3, No. 12 (Mar 1989).

■ **1732-1733 Tax Lists, Calvert County, Maryland**, in *Maryland and Delaware Genealogist*, Vol. 30, No. 3 (Summer 1989); Vol. 30, No. 4 (Fall 1989) and Vol. 31, No. 2 (Spring 1990).

■ **1732-1733 Tax Lists, St. Leonard's Creek Hundred, Calvert County, Maryland**, in *Maryland and Delaware Genealogist*, Vol. 31, No. 1 (Winter 1990).

■ **1733 Eltonhead Hundred Taxables, Calvert County, Maryland**, in *Calvert County Maryland Genealogy Newsletter*, Vol. 8, No. 4 (Jul 1993).

■ **1733 Taxables, Prince George's County, Maryland**, in *Western Maryland Genealogy*, Vol. 3, No. 3 (Jul 1987).

■ **1733 List of Taxables, Monocacy Hundred, Frederick County, Maryland**, in *Maryland's Colonial Families Newsletter*, Vol. 3, No. 1 (Spring 1994).

■ **1740 Tax List, Anne Arundel County, Maryland**, in *Maryland Genealogical Society Bulletin*, Vol. 18, No. 1 (Winter 1977).

■ **1752-1930 Baltimore City Directories**, Microfilm of originals published by various publishers, filmed by Research Publications, Woodbridge, CT, 1980-1984. Most of these directories include suburban areas surrounding Baltimore city. They are available at the FHL for the following years: 1752, 1796, 1799, 1800-1801, 1802, 1803, 1804, 1807, 1808, 1810, 1812, 1814/15, 1816, 1817/18, 1819, 1822/23, 1824, 1827, 1829, 1831, 1833, 1835/36, 1837/38, 1840/41, 1842 (2), 1843, 1845, 1847/48, 1849/50, 1851, 1853/54, 1855/56, 1856/57, 1858, 1858/59, 1859/60, 1860, 1863/64, 1865/66, 1867/68, and one for each year from 1870 through 1917, then 1918/19, followed by one for each year from 1920 through 1930.

■ **1756 & 1757 Tax on Bachelors, Harford County, Maryland**, in *Harford County Historical Society Newsletter*, (Jan 2001).

■ **1756-1762 Tax on Bachelors, Baltimore County, Maryland**, in *Maryland Connections Queries*, Vol. 2, No. 2 (Dec 1991).

■ **1760-1761 Rent Rolls, Frederick County, Maryland**, in *Western Maryland Genealogy*, Vol. 2, No. 3 (Jul 1986).

■ **1761 Taxables in Old Town and Sugarland Hundred, Frederick County, Maryland**, in *Western Maryland Genealogy*, Vol. 6, No. 3 (Jul 1990).

■ **1763 Taxables, Soldiers Delight Hundred, Baltimore County, Maryland**, in *Maryland Connections Queries*, Vol. 10, No. 2 (Jan 2000) through Vol. 10, No. 6 (Aug 2000).

■ **1763 Census of Acadians in Maryland**, in *Louisiana Genealogical Register*, Vol. 21, No. 4 (Dec 1974).

■ **1768 St. Inigoes Census, St. Mary's County, Maryland**, name list in *Maryland Connections Queries*, Vol. 5, No. 3 (Feb 1995) through Vol. 9, No. 2 (Jan 1999).

■ **1769 St. Inigoes Census, St. Mary's County, Maryland**, in *Maryland Connections Queries*, Vol. 8, No. 5 (Jul 1998).

■ **1775-1778 Census, Charles County, Maryland**, name list in *Southern States Courier*, Vol. 3, No. 1 (Jan 1986).

■ **1776 & 1778 Provincial Maryland Censuses**. Originals at Maryland State Archives in Annapolis. The 1776 name lists are extant for Anne Arundel, Baltimore, Caroline, Dorchester,

Frederick, Harford, Prince George's, Queen Anne, and Talbot Counties. The 1778 name lists are extant for Caroline, Charles, and Queen Anne's Counties only. The 1776 & 1778 colonial name lists are included in a database (with names from the 1870 and 1880 federal censuses). This searchable database is freely accessible online at **www.mdarchives.state.md.us/ msa/refserv/html/censussearch.html** where one can search for any surname. In addition, a published name list with the title, *1776 Census of Maryland*, was produced by Bettie Stirling Carothers, published Lutherville, MD, 197?, 212 pages. Indexed. See FHL book 975.2 X2p. (Name lists from the 1776 Census of Maryland were also published in several Maryland county genealogical society periodicals, as well as in the Brumbaugh book described below).

■ **1776-1864 Censuses & Substitutes.** See *Maryland Records: Colonial, Revolutionary, County and Church, From Original Sources*, compiled by Gaius Marcus Brumbaugh, FHL has microfilm of original 2-vol. book published Baltimore: Williams & Wilkins, 1915, and Lancaster, PA, Lancaster Press, 1928. (A reprint was published by Genealogical Publishing Co., Inc., Baltimore, 1993, but is currently out of print). Includes index. Contents: I. Provincial census of August 31, 1776, Prince George's county: Marriage licenses issued at Upper Marlborough, Prince George's county, 1777-1800: Two muster rolls, militia, Prince George's county: French war, 1799: Provincial census of 1776, Frederick County; Earliest records of marriages and births of All Saints' parish, Frederick, MD (1727-1781); Tombstone inscriptions from the old cemetery of All Saints' parish. Frederick, MD; Poll list of presidential election, November 9-12, 1796, Frederick County, MD; Constable's census of Charles County, 1775-1778; Marriage licenses of St. Mary's County, 1794-1864; and the Provincial census of 1776, Anne Arundel County. Vol. 2: State of his Lordship's manor, 1776, 1767, 1768; Census of 1776; Oaths of fidelity and

support; Early Maryland Naturalizations; Kilty's Laws; Revolutionary war pensions; some original commissions, etc.; and marriage records. It should be noted that Brumbaugh's 1915 extraction of the 1776 Maryland Census differs from the Carothers 1977 extraction, in that Brumbaugh chose to group some family names together, even though they may not have appeared together in the census lists. Carothers' lists are as they appeared on the originals, and an index to the names can be used to find the original arrangement. The Brumbaugh book is available on FHL film #1033832, and is included as a Maryland online census source at www.ancestry.com.

■ **Baltimore Residents Before 1776,** in *Maryland Historical Magazine*, Vol. 42, No. 1 (Mar 1947).

■ **1776 Provincial Maryland Census**. See "Census, 1776, Deptford Hundred, Fells Point," in *Maryland Historical Magazine*, Vol. 25, No. 3 (Sep 1930).

■ **1776 Straight Hundred, Dorchester County, Maryland**, name list in *Dorchester County Genealogical Magazine*, Vol. 3, No. 4 (Nov 1983).

■ **1776 Naticoke Hundred, Dorchester County, Maryland**, name list in *Dorchester County Genealogical Magazine*, Vol. 3, No. 1 (May 1983).

■ **1776 Census, Harford County, Maryland**, in *Genealogy*, Vol. 6, No. 12 (Dec 1916).

■ **1776 Census, Formerly Frederick Co. Hundred, Montgomery County, Maryland**, in *Mason County Genealogical Society Newsletter*, Vol. 8, No. 3 (1990).

■ **1776 Tax List, Transquakin Hundred, Dorchester County, Maryland**, name list published serially in *Dorchester County Genealogical Magazine*, Vol. 3, No. 5 (Jan 1984) through No. 6 (Mar 1984).

■ **1776 Taxables, Carroll County, Maryland**, in *Carrolltonian*, Vol. 9, No. 4 (Jun 1990).

■ **1777 Tax List, Montgomery County, Maryland**, in *Maryland Connections Queries*, Vol. 6, No. 5 (Jun 1966), through Vol. 10, No. 1 (Nov 1999).

■ **1778 Tax List, Harford County, Maryland**, in *Maryland Genealogical Society Bulletin*, Vol. 18, No. 1 (Winter 1977).

■ **1781 Assessment Records, Choptank Hundred, Caroline County, Maryland**, in *Maryland Genealogical Society Bulletin*, Vol. 35, No. 4 (Fall 1994).

■ **1781-1782 Residents Who Paid Taxes, Somerset County, Maryland**, in *More From the Shore*, Vol. 3, No. 1 (Spring 1984).

■ **1782 Tax List, Frederick County, Maryland**, in *Western Maryland Genealogy*, Vol. 15, No. 1 (Jan 1999).

■ **1783 Provincial Maryland Tax List**. See the book with names extracted from the originals at the Maryland State Archives with the title, *1783 Tax List of Maryland*, compiled by Bettie Stirling Carothers, published Lutherville, MD, 1977, indexed. FHL has Vol. 1: Cecil, Talbot, Harford, and Calvert Counties only. FHL book 975.2 R4c.

■ **1783 Tax Assessment, Washington County, Maryland**, in *Western Maryland Genealogy*, Vol. 7, No. 2 (Apr 1991) through Vol. 9, No. 3 (Jul 1993).

■ **1783 Tax List, Harford County, Maryland**, in *Harford Historical Bulletin*, No. 24 (Spring 1985).

■ **1783 Patapsco Hundred Tax List, Anne Arundel County, Maryland**, in *Anne Arundel Readings*, Vol. 2, No. 1 (Jan 1999).

■ **1783 Tax List, Dorchester County, Maryland**, in *Dorchester County Genealogical Magazine*, Vol. 9, No. 3 (Sep 1989).

■ **1783 Tax list, Herring Point-Hog Range, Dorchester County, Maryland**, in *Dorchester County Genealogical Magazine*, Vol. 9, No. 1 (May 1989).

■ **1783 Tax List, Dorchester County, Maryland**, in *Dorchester County Genealogical Magazine*, Vol. 3, No. 2 (Jul 1983) through Vol. 12, No. 5 (Jan 1993).

■ **1783 Tax Records, Dorchester County, Maryland**, in *Dorchester County Genealogical Magazine*, Vol. 4, No. 2 (Jul 1984).

■ **1785 Tax Lists, Carroll County, Maryland**, in *Carrolltonian*, Vol. 13, No. 2 (Dec 1993).

■ **1788 Name List, Patapsco Lower, Carroll County**, in *Maryland Genealogical Society Bulletin*, Vol. 7, No. 1 (Feb 1966).

■ **1790-1930 Maryland Census Records Online (www.ancestry.com).** 1790-1860 indexes originally compiled by Ronald V. Jackson, Accelerated Indexing Systems, Salt Lake City, UT. Electronic files were acquired by Ancestry, Inc., which has these Maryland lists plus several updates, 1870-1930, all indexed online. A membership is required to access the records.
Maryland Statewide Census Records
- 1790-1930 United States Federal Census
- Maryland Census, 1772-1890
- Maryland Colonial Census, 1776
- Maryland Records Colonial, Revolutionary, County, and Church from Original Sources, Vol. I (Brumbaugh)

■ **1793 Tax Assessment, Allegany County, Maryland**, in *Western Maryland Genealogy*, Vol. 6, No. 2 (Apr 1990) through Vol. 6, No. 4 (Oct 1990).

■ **1793 Tax List, Taylorsville Area, Carroll County, Maryland**, in *Western Maryland Genealogy*, Vol. 5, No. 4 (Oct 1989).

■ **1793 Tax Assessment, Unity and Burnt Woods, Frederick County, Maryland**, in *Western Maryland Genealogy*, Vol. 13, No. 2 (Apr 1997).

■ **1793 Tax Assessment, District 1, Frederick County, Maryland**, in *Western Maryland Genealogy*, Vol. 13, No. 1 (Jan 1997).

■ **1793 Tax Assessment, Montgomery County, Maryland**, in *Western Maryland Genealogy*, Vol. 12, No. 1 (Jan 1996) through Vol. 12, No. 4 (Oct 1996).

■ **1795 Inhabitants of Georgetown, Montgomery County, Maryland**, in *Maryland Genealogical Bulletin*, Vol. 12, No. 2 (Apr 1941).

■ **1797 Tax List, Baltimore County, Maryland**, in *National Genealogical Society Quarterly*, Vol. 66, No. 3 (Sep 1978).

■ **1797 Taxables, Queen Anne's County, Maryland,** in *Chesapeake Cousins*, Vol. 20, No. 1 (Fall 1993).

■ **1798 Federal Assessment Rolls, Maryland & District of Columbia**, with some 1790, 1799, and 1800 name lists added. This is basically the contents of the 1798 Federal Direct Tax List for Maryland, but with some added name lists for certain counties for subsequent years. Originals microfilmed by Maryland Hall of Records Commission, 1965. Includes 1798 taxpayer name lists for Ann Arundel Co.; Caroline Co.; Baltimore County & City, District of Columbia (Washington County, DC, the portion formerly in Maryland); Prince Georges Co.; Queen Anne's Co.; and added lists for 1798-1800 Baltimore City; Baltimore County, 1798 (mostly) with some 1799 & 1800; 1798-1800 Charles Co.; 1798-1800 Harford Co.; 1798-1800 St. Mary's Co.; 1798-1800

Somerset Co.; and a 1790 Talbot County list. 13 rolls of microfilm available at the FHL as film #499893 through #499905. **See also**, "1798 Federal Direct Tax (Maryland)," a name list published in *Maryland Genealogical Society Bulletin*, beginning with Vol. 5, No. 4 (Oct 1934).

■ **1798 Federal Assessment Rolls, Maryland**. In addition to the above, several Maryland county-wide name lists have been published:
  • **Allegany County**, see "1798 Property Owners in Assessment Book," published in *The Old Pike Post*, Vol. 15, No. 1 (Mar 1998) through Vol. 15, No. 3 (Sep 1998).
  • **Baltimore County**, see "1798 Tax Assessment List," in *Maryland and Delaware Genealogist*, published serially, beginning with Vol. 18, No. 3 (Apr 1977).
  • **Carroll County**, see "1798 Tax Assessment," in *Historical Society of Carroll County, Maryland Newsletter*, Vol. 26, No. 1 (Jan 1976).
  • **Frederick County,** see "1798 Tax Assessment List", in *Western Maryland Genealogy*, Vol. 10, No. 2 (Apr 1994) through Vol. 14, No. 4 (Oct 1998); and in *Antietam Ancestors*, Vol. 1, No. 3 (Summer 1984) through Vol. 2. No. 1 (Winter 1985).
  • **Prince George's County**, see "1798 Tax List, Prince George's County, Maryland," in *Prince George's County Genealogical Society Bulletin*, Vol. 5, No. 8 (Oct 1974).

■ **1804 Baltimore County Tax Assessment Lists**. Name lists (by hundreds) serialized in *Maryland Genealogical Society Bulletin*:
  • **Unnamed Hundred**, in Vol. 41, No. 3 (Summer 2000).
  • **Patapsco Hundred**, in Vol. 42, No. 2 (Spring 2001).
  • **Mine Run Hundred**, in Vol. 41, No. 4 (Fall 2000).
  • **Soldiers Delight Hundred**, in Vol. 42, No. 2 (Spring 2001).
  • **Middle River Hundred**, in Vol. 42, No. 2 (Spring 2001).
  • **North Hundred**, in Vol. 41, No. 2 (Spring 2000).

■ **1804-1812 Tax List, Allegany County, Maryland**, in *Western Maryland Genealogy*, Vol. 16, No. 1 (Jan 2000) through Vol. 16, No. 4 (Oct 2000).

■ **1804-1820 Tax Lists, Allegany County, Maryland**, in *Western Maryland Genealogy*, Vol. 17, No. 1 (Jan 2001) through Vol. 17, No. 4 (Oct 2001).

■ **1825 Tax List, Somerset County, Maryland**, in *Maryland Genealogical Society Bulletin*, Vol. 31, No. 1 (Winter 1990).

■ **1831 Tax List, Martins District #4, Dorchester County, Maryland**, in *Dorchester County Genealogical Magazine*, Vol. 5, No. 4 (Nov 1985) and Vol. 5, No. 5 (Jan 1986).

■ **1831 Tax List, Hooper Island District No. 6, Dorchester County, Maryland**, in *Dorchester County Genealogical Magazine*, Vol. 5, No. 3 (Sep 1994) through Vol. 5, No. 6 (Mar 1986).

■ **1831-1838 Tax Assessment, Dorchester County**, (Relationships Shown) in *Dorchester County Genealogical Society Magazine*, Vol. 16, No. 6 (Mar 1997).

■ **1832 Tax List, Dorchester County, Maryland**, in *Dorchester County Genealogical Magazine*, Vol. 6 (Mar 1985).

■ **1832 Tax List, Neck District #8, Dorchester County, Maryland**, in *Dorchester County Genealogical Magazine*, Vol. 5, No. 2 (Jul 1985).

■ **1835 Tax List, Somerset County, Maryland**, in *Maryland Connections Queries*, Vol. 10, No. 5 (Jul 2000).

■ **1836 Tax List, Dorchester County, Maryland**, in *Dorchester County Genealogical Magazine*, Vol. 4, No. 5 (Jan 1985).

■ **1836 Tax Records, Lakes District #5, Dorchester County, Maryland**, in *Dorchester County Genealogical Magazine*, Vol. 5, No. 1 (May 1985).

■ **1837 Tax List, Dorchester County, Maryland**, in *Dorchester County Genealogical Magazine*, Vol. 6, No. 6 (Mar 1987).

■ **1844 Tax List, Dorchester County, Maryland**, in *Dorchester County Genealogical Magazine*, Vol. 6, No. 3 (Sep 1987) through Vol. 7, No. 6 (Mar 1988).

■ **1845 Dorchester County Tax Lists,** name lists published serially in *Dorchester County Genealogical Magazine,*
  • **Fork District**, in Vol. 5, No. 3 (Sep 1985).
  • **Neck District**, in Vol. 14, No. 1 (May 1994).
  • **Parson Creek**, in Vol. 6, No. 2 (Jul 1986).
  • **School #10, Parents and Children**, in Vol. 26, No. 2 (Spring 2000).

■ **1862-1866 Internal Revenue Assessment Lists for Maryland**. Originals at the National Archives, Washington, DC., Records of the Internal Revenue Service, Record Group (RG) 58. These are name lists of taxpayers taken during the Civil War in all Union States. A tax was levied for all annual incomes exceeding $600. Legacies and distributive shares of personal property were also taxed. All persons, partnerships, firms, associations, and corporations were to submit a list to the assistant assessor of their division showing the amount of their annual income, articles owned subject to special tax or duty, and the quantity of taxable goods made or sold. The name lists for Maryland are organized as follows: District 1: Caroline, Cecil, Dorchester, Kent, Queen Anne's, Somerset, Talbot and Worcester counties; District 2: Baltimore city (wards 1-7) and Baltimore (districts 5-7, 9-12) and Harford counties; District 3 includes Baltimore city (wards 8-20); District 4: Allegany, Carroll, Frederick and Washington counties; and District 5: Anne Arundel, Baltimore (districts 1-4, 8, 13), Calvert, Charles, Howard, Montgomery, Prince George's and St. Mary's counties. Some records are damaged, some are missing and some are filed out of order. Most are arranged by year or month, then division of district and then alphabetically. FHL has microfilm copies, 21 rolls, #1534367 through #1534387.

■ **1862 Tax Assessment, Maryland**, name lists extracted in *Chesapeake Cousins*, beginning with Vol. 4, No. 1 (1976).

■ **1873 Tax List, Dorchester County, Maryland**, in *Dorchester County Genealogical Magazine*, Vol. 10, No. 6 (Mar 1991).

■ **1901-1902 Public School #1 Register, Dorchester County, Maryland**, in *Dorchester County Genealogical Magazine*, Vol. 15, No. 1 (May 1995).

Maryland Censuses & Substitutes Online

■ **1790-1930 Maryland Statewide Census Records Online. (Censusfinder.com).** Direct links to Internet Web sites where census name lists have been published. Go to **www.censusfinder.com/maryland.htm.** Censuses links are arranged by state, thereafter by county, as the examples shown below:

Maryland Statewide Censuses:
- Maryland Statewide Census Records Online:
- 1678-1682 Statewide Tax Lists
- 1772 - 1890 Maryland Census Records at Ancestry
- 1783 Tax List Index for the State of Maryland

- 1835 Pension Roll for the State of Maryland
- Early Settlers of Maryland Search Engine
- 1880 Federal Census - Images
- 1880 Federal Census at Family Search
- Maryland Statewide Databases of Census & Genealogy Records

Baltimore County Censuses
- 1810 Federal Census Index of Dorsey Surname Only
- 1820 Federal Census Index of 3rd Election District
- 1820 Federal Census of 3rd Election District
- 1830 Federal Census of 3rd Election District
- 1830 Federal Census of 3rd Election District
- 1840 Pensioners Census
- 1850 Federal Census Includes Index
- 1850 Federal Census 1st & 6th Districts
- 1850 Federal Census 2nd & 6th Districts
- 1910 Federal Census of District 12
- 1910 Federal Census & Index of ED 41

Other Records
- 1842-1853 Runaway Slave Ads
- 1783 Tax List Index

■ **1790-1930 Links to Online Census Records. (www.census-online.com).** The **www.census-online.com/links/MD/** site is another Web site featuring links to Maryland census records online (separate from the Ancestry.com site). An example of what is available for one Maryland county is shown below:

Baltimore County
Censuses
- 1790 Federal Census
- 1790 Federal Census - Baltimore City
- 1820 Federal Census
- 1840 Federal Census - Baltimore City Pensioners
- 1840 Federal Census - Pensioners
- 1850 Federal Census - Academy of the Visitation, Located at Baltimore City,

- 1850 Federal Census - Baltimore Wards 1 and 2
- 1850 Federal Census - Fort McHenry
- 1860 Federal Census - Baltimore
- 1860 Federal Census - Baltimore
- 1900 Federal Census - German Orphanage
- Index to 1790 Federal Census
- Index to 1790 Federal Census – Baltimore City

Miscellaneous

- 1915 Farmer's Directory - Baltimore

NEW JERSEY

Censuses and Substitutes, 1600-1915

State Censuses: New Jersey began taking a state census for the purpose of apportionment of its state legislature in 1855, continuing every ten years thereafter until the last one in 1915.

Ratable Lists: For the period of the 1700s through the 1800s, numerous tax lists were prepared at the county level in New Jersey. A person named in one of these assessment lists of county residents was called a "ratable." Many of the original Ratable Lists were collected from the counties by the State Archives for preservation. Although not complete for all years, at least one ratable list exists for each county.

Substitutes: In addition to these state-wide tax lists and censuses, several other census substitutes were published, which are shown in the bibliography below.

■ **1600-1825 Ship Passenger Lists, New York and New Jersey**, compiled and indexed by Carl Boyer, III, Newhall, CA: publ. by C. Boyer, 1978, 333 pages. Contains reprints of passenger lists named in Lancour's *Bibliography of Ship Passenger Lists*. See FHL book 973 W3.

■ **1650-1856 Deeds, Surveys and Commissions.** Originals and indexes from all West Jersey and East Jersey counties. Original records from the Department of State, located at the New Jersey State Archives. Includes Grantee-Grantor indexes for all New Jersey counties, which can serve as a better list of residents in an area than a heads of household census. Visit the New Jersey Archives Web site for the list of 69 microfilm reels, with contents for each. Go to **www.njarchives.org/ links/guides/sstse023r.html.** In addition, the FHL has 7 rolls of film for the series, *Index to Deeds, Grantee and Grantor.* (Starting with FHL film #539948, remaining rolls not in sequence). Title gives no dates, but it is believed that these indexes are from the same *Deeds, Surveys and Commissions* at the New Jersey Archives.

■ **1660-1775 Colonial Documents Index.** See *General index to the documents relating to the colonial history of the state of New Jersey: first in series, in ten volumes; published under and by virtue of an act entitled "An act for the better preservation of the early records of the state of New Jersey," passed March twenty-ninth, one thousand and eight hundred and seventy-two*, prepared by Frederick W. Ricord, originally published Newark, NJ, 1888, reprint by Genealogical Research Society of New Orleans, 1994, 198 pages. See FHL book 974.9 H22r.

■ **1677 Assessment Lists, Settlers of Delaware Shores, Salem County**, in *Genealogical Magazine of New Jersey*, Vol. 13, No. 1 (Jan 1938).

■ **1684 Assessment List, Burlington County**, in *Pennsylvania Magazine of History and Biography*, Vol. 15, No. 3 (Jul 1891).

■ **1687 Tax List of the Lower Division, Gloucester County**, in *Genealogical Magazine of New Jersey*, Vol. 13, No. 1 (Jan 1938).

■ **1693 Census, New Sweden, Wiacaco Congregation**, in *Swedish American Genealogist*, Vol. 9, No. 3 (Sep 1989).

■ **1704 Census, Cape May County**, in *Cape May County Magazine of History and Genealogy*, Vol. 2, No. 4 (Jun 1942).

■ **1709 Census, Northampton**, in *American Genealogist*, Vol. 1, No. 5 (Jul 1899) and in *New Jersey Historical Society Proceedings*, Vol. 4, No. 1 (1849).

■ **1722 Heads of Families, Maidenhead**, in *Hunterdon Historical Newsletter*, Vol. 13, No. 2 (Spring 1977).

■ **1722 Tax Lists, Hunterdon County**, in *Hunterdon Historical Newsletter*, Vol. 13, No. 2 (Spring 1977).

■ **1735, 1745 Rate List, Franklin Township, Hunterdon County**, in *Genealogical Magazine of New Jersey*, Vol. 42, No. 3 (Sep 1967).

■ **1735 Tax List, Franklin, Somerset County**, in *Our Home: A Monthly Magazine*, Vol. 1, No. 8 (Oct 1873).

■ **1739 Tax List, Gloucester County**, in *Gloucester County Historical Society Bulletin*, Vol. 5, No. 5 (Sep 1956).

■ **1745 Census, Lower Penns Neck**, in *Genealogical Magazine of New Jersey*, Vol. 52, No. 1 (Jan 1977).

■ **1745 Tax Payers, Franklin, Somerset County**, in *Our Home: A Monthly Magazine*, Vol. 1, No. 9 (Sep 1873).

■ **1750 Freeholders List, Middlesex County**, in *New Jersey Historical Society Proceedings*, Vol. 13, No. 2 (1894).

■ **1751 Ratables, Lower Precinct, Cape May County**, in *Genealogical Magazine of New Jersey*, Vol. 14, No. 2 (Apr 1939).

■ **1751 Ratables, Maurice River Precinct, Cumberland County**, in *Genealogical Magazine of New Jersey*, Vol. 14, No. 2 (Apr 1939).

■ **1755 Freeholders List, Essex County**, in *New Jersey Historical Society Proceedings*, Vol. 13, No. 1 (1894).

■ **1761 Middletown Assessment**, in *Monmouth Connection* .Vol. 13, No. 2 and Vol. 13, No. 5 (May 2002).

■ **1765-72 Cobblers Census, Three-Mile Run, Somerset County**, in *Somerset County Historical Quarterly*, Vol. 6, No. 2 (Apr 1917).

■ **1768-1846. County Tax Lists (Ratables)**. Microreproduction of originals in the Division of the State library, Archives and History, Trenton, New Jersey. These are tax lists for all New Jersey counties, on 27 rolls of film. To see the reel list and contents, go to the NJ archives website at **www.state.nj.us/state/ darm/links/guides/ sas00001.html#contain**.
Refer to *Index to Tax Lists, 1700's-1800's: Listing of Counties and Townships and Years of Taxes*, by the NJ Bureau of Archives and History, typescript, microfilmed by the Genealogical Society of Utah, 1972, see FHL film #913174. From these original lists, several township/county name lists were published, shown below in the order of the dates of each tax list (or ratables).

■ **1768 Ratables, Lower Precinct, Cape May County,** in *Genealogical Magazine of New Jersey*, Vol. 14, No. 3 (Jul 1939).

■ **New Jersey Tax Lists, 1772-1822**, edited by Ronald V. Jackson, Accelerated Index, Bountiful, UT. See FHL book 974.9 R42.

■ **1773-1774 Ratables.** Name lists published serially in *Genealogical Magazine of New Jersey* for several county areas, in the following issues:

Burlington County:
- **Unnamed Precinct,** in Vol. 36, No. 2 (May 1961).
- **Newton Township,** in Vol. 60, No. 2 (May 1985).
- **Dover Township,** in Vol. 59, No. 3 (Sep 1984).
- **Chester-Evesham Townships,** in Vol. 36, No. 3 (Sep 1961).
- **L. Egg Harbor-Hanover,** Vol. 37, No. 1 (Jan 1962).
- **Northampton-Nottingham Twps,** in Vol. 37, No. 2 (May 1962).
- **Springfield-Will Townships,** in Vol. 37, No. 3 (Sep 1962).

Cape May County:
- **Ratables,** in Vol. 37, No. 3 (Sep 1962) and Vol. 38, No. 1 (Jan 1963)

Cumberland County:
- **Deerfield-Fairfield Townships,** in Vol. 38, No. 2 (May 1963).
- **1773-1774 Greenwich-Stow Creek Townships,** in Vol. 38, No. 3 (Sep 1963).

Gloucester County:
- **Gloucester-Great Egg Harbor Townships,** in Vol. 39, No. 1 (Jan 1964).
- **Greenwich Township,** in Vol. 39, No. 2 (May 1964).

Hunterdon County:
- **Ratables,** Hunterdon County, in Vol. 39, No. 2 (May 1964).

Monmouth County:
- **Dover Township,** in Vol. 59, No. 3 (Sep 1984).

Salem County:
- **Mannington-Salem Townships,** in Vol. 40, No. 1 (Jan 1965).
- **Upper Alloways-Upper Penns Townships** in Vol. 40, No. 2 (May 1965).
- **Elsnboro & Lower Alloways Townships,** in Vol. 39, No. 3 (Sep 1964).

Sussex County:
- **Newton Township,** in Vol. 60, No. 2 (May 1985).
- **Greenwich Township** in Vol. 40, No. 2 (May 1965).
- **Hardistown-Walpack Townships, in** Vol. 40, No. 3 (Sep 1965).

■ **1777 Tax List, Gloucester County,** in *Gloucester County Historical Society Bulletin,* Vol. 4, No. 8 (Jun 1955).

■ **1778-1780 Ratables.** Name lists by county/township published serially in *Genealogical Magazine of New* Jersey in the following issues:

Bergen County:
- **Franklin Township,** in Vol. 41, No. 1 (Jan 1996).
- **Barbadoes Township,** in Vol. 41, No. 2 (May 1966).
- **Saddle River Township,** in Vol. 41, No. 3 (Sep 1966).

Burlington County:
- **Chesterfield Township,** in Vol. 42, No. 1 (Jan 1967).

Essex County
- **Acquackanonk Township,** in Vol. 42, No. 2 (May 1967).
- **Elizabeth Township,** Essex County, in Vol. 42 No. 3 (Sep 1967) through Vol. 44, No. 3 (Sep 1969).

Gloucester County:
- **Newton and Waterford** Townships, in Vol. 46, No. 3 (Sep 1971).
- **Woolwich** Township, in Vol. 47, No. 1 (Jan 1972).

Hunterdon County:
- **Amwell Township,** in Vol. 47, No. 2 (May 1972).
- **Bethlehem Township,** in Vol. 47, No. 3 (Sep 1972).
- **Hopewell Township,** in Vol. 48, No. 1 (Jan 1973).
- **Kingwood Township,** in Vol. 48, No. 2 (May 1973).
- **Lebanon and Maidenhead Townships,** in Vol. 48, No. 3 (Sep 1973).
- **Reading and Trenton Townships,** in Vol. 49, No. 1 (Jan 1974).

Middlesex County:
- **New Brunswick Township,** in Vol. 51, No. 1 (Jan 1976).
- **Perth Amboy & South Amboy Townships,** in Vol. 50, No. 3 (Sep 1975).
- **Piscataway Township,** in Vol. 51, No. 2 (May 1976).
- **Windsor Township,** in Vol. 51, No. 3 (Sep 1976).
- **Woodbridge Township,** in Vol. 52, No. 1 (Jan 1977).

Monmouth County:
- **Dover and Freehold Townships**, in Vol. 49, No. 2 (May 1974).
- **Middletown** Township, in Vol. 49, No. 3 (Sep 1974).
- **Shrewsbury** Township, in Vol. 50, No. 1 (Jan 1975).
- **Upper Freehold** Township, in Vol. 50, No. 2 (May 1975).

Morris County:
- **Hanover** Township, in Vol. 45, No. 1 (Jan 1970) and Vol. 45, No. 2 (May 1970).
- **Mendham** Township, in Vol. 45, No. 3 (Sep 1970).
- **Morris** Township, in Vol. 46, No. 1 (Jan 1971).
- **Pequannock** Township, in Vol. 45, No. 2 (May 1970).
- **Roxbury** Township, in Vol. 46, No. 2 (May 1971).

Somerset County
- **Bedminster** Township, in Vol. 52, No. 2 (May 1977).
- **Bernards** Township, in Vol. 52, No. 3 (Sep 1977).
- **Bridgewater** Township, in Vol. 53, No. 1 (Jan 1978).
- **Eastern and Western Precincts**, in Vol. 53, No. 3 (Sep 1978).
- **Hillsborough** Township, in Vol. 53, No. 2 (May 1978).

■ **1779 Ratables List, Roxbury, Morris County**, in *Detroit Society for Genealogical Research Magazine*, Vol. 25, No. 1 (Fall 1961).

■ **1779 Wheat Levy, Somerset County**, in *Somerset County Genealogical Quarterly*, Vol. 2, No. 1 (Mar 1984).

■ **1779 Cumberland County Ratables,** Name lists by township published serially in *Vineland Historical Magazine* in the following issues:
- **Maurice River Township**, in Vol.44, No. 1 (Jun 1965).
- **Downe Township**, in Vol. 43, No. 3- 4 (Jul 1964).
- **Fairfield Township**, Vol. 40, No. 1-2 (Jan 1955).
- **Greenwich Township** in Vol. 41, No. 1-2 (Jan 1956).
- **Hopewell Township** in Vol. 41, No. 3-4 (Jul 1956).
- **Stow Creek Township**, in Vol. 40, No. 3-4 (Jul 1955).

■ **1780 Ratables, Galloway Township**, in *Atlantic County Historical Society Yearbook*, Vol. 6. No. 3 (Oct 1970).

■ **1781 Ratables, Egg Harbor Township**, in *Atlantic County Historical Society Yearbook*, Vol. 7, No. 2 (Oct 1973).

■ **1781 Tax List, Squankum, Gloucester County**, in *Gloucester County Historical Society Bulletin*, Vol. 7, No. 4 (Jun 1960).

■ **1783 Ratables, Gloucester County**, in *Gloucester County Historical Society Bulletin*, Vol. 18, No. 2 (Dec 1981).

■ **1784 Census, Gloucester County, New Jersey.** Name lists by towns or townships, published serially in *Gloucester County Historical Society Bulletin*, in the following issues:
- **Unnamed Area**, in Vol. 20, No. 6 (Dec 1986) and Vol. 20, No. 7 (Mar 1987), and Vol. 8, No. 3 (Mar 1962).
- **Newton**, in Vol. 20, No. 2 (Dec 1985) and Vol. 20, 3 (Mar 1986).
- **Lower Township**, in Vol. 19, No. 8 (Jun 1985) through Vol. 20, No. 1 (Sep 1985).
- **Upper Township**, in, Vol. 19, No. 3 (Mar 1984).
- **Deptford**, in Vol. 19, No. 5 (Sep 1984) and Vol. 19, No. 6 (Dec 1984).
- **Middle Township**, in Vol. 19, No. 3 (Mar 1984) & Vol. 19, No. 4 (Jun 1984).

■ **1784 Hillsborough Census**, in *Somerset County Genealogical Quarterly*, Vol. 2, No. 3 (Sep 1984).

■ **1784-1786 Ratables, Alexandria Township, Hunterdon County**, in *Genealogical Magazine of New Jersey*, Vol. 54, No. 2-3 (May 1979).

■ **1784-1786 Ratables, Stafford Township, Monmouth County**, in *Genealogical Magazine of New Jersey*, Vol. 54, No. 2-3 (May 1979).

■ **1784-1786 Ratables, Bergen Township, Bergen County,** in *Genealogical Magazine of New Jersey*, Vol. 54, No. 2-3 (May 1979).

■ **1784-1786 Ratables, Eastern Precinct, Somerset County,** in *Genealogical Magazine of New Jersey*, Vol. 54, No. 1 (Jan 1979).

■ **1785 Ratables, Bedminster Township, Somerset County,** in *Somerset County Genealogical Quarterly*, Vol. 3, No. 2 (Jun 1985) and Vol. 3, No. 3 (Sep 1985).

■ **1785 Ratables, Bedminster Township, Somerset County,** in *Somerset County Genealogical Quarterly*, Vol. 3, No. 2 (Jun 1985); Vol. 3, No. 3 (Sep 1985); Vol. 4, No. 2 (Jun 1986); Vol. 4, No. 1 (Mar 1986); and Vol. 4, No. 2 (Jun 1986).

■ **1785 Ratables, Bedminster Township, Somerset County,** in *Somerset County Genealogical Quarterly*, Vol. 3, No. 2 (Jun 1985); Vol. 3, No. 3 (Sep 1985); Vol. 4, No. 2 (Jun 1986); Vol. 4, No. 1 (Mar 1986); and Vol. 4, No. 2 (Jun 1986).

■ **1788 Ratables, Salem City, Salem County**, in *Fenwick Colony Gazette*, Vol. 2, No. 3 (Mar 1995).

■ **1790 Tax List, Mannington, Salem County**, in *Salem County Historical Society Newsletter*, Vol. 43, No. 4 (Dec 1998).

■ **1801 Taxable Married Men, Fairfield Township, Cumberland County**, in *Vineland Historical Magazine*, Vol. 14, No. 2 (Apr 1929).

■ **1809 Tax List, Martha Company, Burlington County,** in *South Jersey Magazine*, Vol. 7, No. 1 (Jan 1978).

■ **1825 Assessor List, Franklin Township, Somerset County**, in *Somerset County Historical Quarterly*, Vol. 7, No. 1 (Jan 1918) and Vol. 7, No. 2 (Apr 1918).

■ **1834 Tax Ratables, Upper Penns Neck, Salem County**, in *Genealogical Magazine of New Jersey*, Vol. 76, No. 1 (Jan 2001).

■ **1855 New Jersey State Census**. Original state census manuscripts from the New Jersey State Board of Assessors, originals located at the New Jersey State Library of Archives and History, and microfilmed by the NJ Archives in 1962. **Contents:** Name, usually only the head of household; number of adults in each household, native-born or foreign-born, colored or white, sex; and number of children aged 5-16, by race and gender. A few township lists include all names of family members. The FHL cataloged 1855 and 1865 censuses together as one series, 8 rolls of film, but contents of film held by FHL differs from reel contents list from NJ archives. Microfilm available at the NJ Archives & FHL: NJ reel #1 (FHL film #802944): Atlantic, Bergen, Camden, Cumberland, and Gloucester Counties. NJ Reel #2 (no FHL film): Essex County (7th Ward of Newark only); NJ reel #3 (FHL film #802945): Hunterdon, Hudson, Monmouth, and Morris Counties. NJ reel #3 (FHL film #802946): Somerset, Passaic, Sussex, and Warren Counties. Visit the New Jersey Archives site for a reel list for the 1855 State Census on microfilm at **www.njarchives.org/links/guides/sstce001.html**.

■ **1855 New Jersey State Census, Atlantic City**, name list published in *Atlantic County Historical Society Yearbook*, Vol. 2, No. 1 (Oct 1952).

■ **1864 Tax Assessment, Washington Township, Mercer County**, in *Mercer County Genealogical Quarterly*, Vol. 6, No. 1 (Mar 1997).

■ **1865 New Jersey State Census**. Original state census manuscripts from the New Jersey State Board of Assessors, originals located at the New Jersey State Library of Archives and History, and microfilmed by the NJ Archives in 1962.

Contents: Name of each member of a household, sex, whether native or foreign-born, colored or white, or at school. **Microfilm:** The FHL cataloged 1855 and 1865 censuses together as one series, 8 rolls of film, but contents of 1865 film held by FHL differs from reel contents list from NJ archives. NJ reel #1 (FHL film #802947): Atlantic, Bergen, Burlington, and Camden Counties. NJ reel #2 (FHL film #802948): Cumberland, Gloucester, Hudson, and Hunterdon Counties. NJ reel #3 (no FHL film): Essex County (partial) includes Newark (ward unknown, 4th, 5th and 11th wards), Caldwell, Clinton, Milburn, Orange (1st Ward) and West Orange. NJ reel #4 (FHL film #802949): Middlesex, Monmouth, and Passaic counties (FHL film notes say "Leader indicates Passaic, which is not on the roll". FHL copy of Passaic County is on FHL film #802950). NJ reel #5 (FHL #802951): Salem and Union Counties. NJ reel #6 (no FHL film): Sussex County. Visit the New Jersey Archives site for a reel list for the 1865 State Census on microfilm at **www.njarchives. org/links/guides/sstce002.html**.

■ **1875 New Jersey State Census.** Fragments of the originals exist for Essex, Hunterdon, Monmouth, and Sussex Counties only, located at the New Jersey State Archives. **Contents:** Names of each member of a household, age, sex, native/foreign born, color, birthplace of each person, birthplace of each person's parents, and occupation. **Microfilm** by NJ State Archives on 11 rolls of film (FHL does not have copies) as follows: Reel #1: Essex County (Belleville and Caldwell). Reel #2: Essex County (Clinton, Newark, 1st - 2nd Wards. Reel 3: Essex County: Newark (3rd - 6th Wards). Reel #4: Essex County: Newark (7th - 10th Wards. Reel #5: Essex County: Newark (10th - 14th Wards) Reel #6: Essex County: Newark (15th Ward) & Agriculture Schedules. Reel #7: Essex County: Manufacturing & Mining. Reel. #8: Hunterdon County: Alexandria - Raritan (p. 4). Reel #9: Hunterdon County: Raritan (p. 5) - West Amwell.

Reel #10: Monmouth County. Reel #11: Sussex County. Visit the New Jersey Archives site for a reel list for the 1875 State Census on microfilm at **www.njarchives.org/links/guides/sstce003.html**.

■ **1885 New Jersey State Census.** Original state manuscripts at the New Jersey State Archives, Trenton. Microfilm by the archives, complete for all New Jersey counties. **Contents:** Name of each member of a household, sex, race, age (in categories, under 5, 5-20, 20-60, and over 60), native or foreign born (indicating Irish, German, and Other). Microfilm: FHL has complete set (45 rolls) of NJ Archives film. See FHL film, beginning with #865499 & 865500, then #888601 - #888643. Roll #45 of the NJ film (FHL #888643) is a summary of census statistics for the entire state, arranged by county then by township within each county. Visit the New Jersey Archives site for a reel list for the 1885 State Census on microfilm at **www.njarchives.org/links/guides/sstce004.html**.

■ **1895 New Jersey State Census.** Original state manuscripts at the New Jersey State Archives, Trenton. Microfilm by the archives, complete for all New Jersey counties. **Contents:** Name of each member of a household, sex, age, race, age in categories of under 5, 5-20, 20-60, and over 60, native or foreign born, (indicating Irish, German, and Other). **Microfilm**: See FHL film #888644-888675, #1026332, #888678, #1404109, #1026333, #929465, and #888680-#888696. (FHL film notes: film #888677 (Hunterdon County) and 888697 (part of Warren County) are missing from the vault and not available). Visit the New Jersey Archives site for a reel list for the 1895 State Census on microfilm at **www.njarchives.org/links/guides/sstce005.html**.

● **1905 New Jersey State Census.** Original state manuscripts at the New Jersey State Archives, Trenton. Microfilm by the archives, complete for all New Jersey counties. **Contents:** Name of each member of a household, color, sex, month and year of birth, marital status, birthplace, parents' birthplaces, number of years in the U.S., citizenship status, occupation, read/write English, house owned or rented. Within towns, street addresses are shown for the dwellings. **Microfilm**, by NJ Archives on 49 rolls. Film held by FHL (film #1688587-1688628) seems to cover the same content, but on 42 rolls. Visit the New Jersey Archives site for a reel list for the 1905 State Census on microfilm at **www.njarchives. org/links/guides/sstce006.html.**

■ **1915 New Jersey State Census.** Original state manuscripts at the New Jersey State Archives, Trenton. Microfilm by the archives, complete for all New Jersey counties. **Contents:** Name of each member of a household, color, sex, month and year of birth, marital status, birthplace, parents' birthplaces, number of years in the U.S., citizenship status, occupation, read/write English, house owned or rented. Within towns, street addresses are shown for the dwellings. **Microfilm**, by NJ Archives on 70 rolls. Film held by FHL (film #1465501-1465563) seems to cover the same content, but on 63 rolls. Visit the New Jersey Archives site for a reel list for the 1915 State Census on microfilm at **www.njarchives. org/links/guides/sstce007.html.**

New Jersey Censuses & Substitutes Online

■ **1790-1930 New Jersey Census Records Online (www.ancestry.com).** 1790-1860 indexes originally compiled by Ronald V. Jackson, Accelerated Indexing Systems, Salt Lake City, UT. Electronic files were acquired by Ancestry, Inc., which has these New Jersey lists plus several updates, 1870-1930, all indexed online. A membership is required to access the records.

New Jersey Census Records
- 1830-1930 United States Federal
- 1890 United States Federal Census Fragment (Jersey City)
- New Jersey Census, 1772-1890

■ **1790-1930 New Jersey Statewide Census Records Online. (Censusfinder.com).** Direct links to Internet Web sites where census name lists have been published. Go to **www.censusfinder.com/newjersey.htm.** Censuses links are arranged by state, thereafter by county, as the examples shown below:

New Jersey Statewide Census Records:
- 1772-1890 New Jersey Census at Ancestry
- 1840 Federal Census of Revolutionary War Pensioners
- 1880 Federal Census - images
- 1880 Federal Census at Family Search
- 1880 Federal Census of Norwegians
- New Jersey State Databases of Census & Genealogy Records

Burlington County Censuses:
- 1850 Federal Census of North Hanover - partial
- 1850 Evesham Township - partial
- 1850 Medford Township - partial
- 1850 Federal Census of New Hanover Twp.
- 1850 Pemberton Township - partial
- 1850 Southampton Township – partial
- 1850 Washington Township - partial
- 1860 Federal Census
- 1860 Egg Harbor Township - partial
- 1860 Lumberton Township - partial
- 1860 Medford Township-partial
- 1860 Northampton Township-partial
- 1860 Shamong Township - partial
- 1870 Evesham Township - partial
- 1870 Medford Township - partial
- 1880 Evesham Township-partial
- 1880 Medford Township - partial
- 1885 State Census Index of New Hanover Township
- 1885 State Census of New Hanover Township
- 1885 State Census of Washington Township
- 1895 State Census Index of New Hanover Township
- 1895 State Census of Hanover Township
- 1900 Evesham Township - partial
- 1900 Medford Township - partial
- 1900 Riverside Township - partial
- 1900 Shamong Township - partial
- 1910 Evesham Township - partial
- 1910 Medford Township - partial
- 1910 Riverside Township - partial

- 1910 Shamong Township - partial
- 1910 Southampton Township- partial
- 1910 Tabernacle Township - partial
- 1920 Mount Laurel Township - partial

■ **1790-1930 Links to Online Census Records.**
(www.census-online.com). The **www.census-online.com/links/NJ/** site is another Web site featuring links to New Jersey census records online (separate from the Ancestry.com site).

New Jersey Statewide:
- 1840 Federal Census - Pensioners

Censuses and Substitutes by County (number of online databases): Atlantic (2); Bergen (1); Burlington (0); Camden (0); Cape May (2); Cumberland (0); Essex (4); Gloucester (0); Hudson (0); Hunterdon (2); Mercer (21); Middlesex (1); Monmouth (10); Morris (2); Ocean (0); Passaic (2); Salem (0); Somerset (0); Sussex (4); Union (3); and Warren (2).

NEW YORK

Censuses & Substitutes, 1630-1930

New York has a wealth of state census records, more so than any other state in the Union. For the purpose of apportionment of the State Assembly, the legislature authorized censuses for 1795, 1801, 1807, 1814, and 1821, but few of these early "electoral censuses" included the names of inhabitants.

More formalized state censuses for New York began with an act in 1825, "An act to provide for taking future enumerations of the inhabitants of this state, and for procuring useful statistical tables." State censuses were taken in 1825, 1835, 1845, 1855, 1865 and 1875; then one in 1892, followed by one in 1905, again in 1915, and the last one in 1925. The primary purpose of these state censuses was for apportionment of the State Assembly. The state began using the federal decennial census counts for apportioning the New York state legislature in 1930.

When adding the decennial federal censuses taken for New York state, this review of state censuses incorporates a comprehensive coverage of the population schedules in five-year intervals, beginning with the 1825 state census through the federal census of 1930.

No other state has a 105-year array of population schedules in five-year increments available to genealogists. As a result, New York has more options for locating families living there, and for a longer period of time than any other state.

■ **1630-1930 Census Substitutes**. See *An Index of Albany County Records Covering Materials Within the Dates 1630-1930,* compiled by Lydia Hammond Gale, publ. Albany, 1933, 137 pages. Microfilm of original published Albany, 1933. Contains a bibliography of sources to Albany County history from 1630 to 1930. Includes index. Before the Revolutionary War, Albany County comprised most of the upstate population, including New York's claim to the area that became Vermont in 1792. Filmed by UMI, 1987. FHL film # 6062167.

■ *New York State Censuses & Substitutes: An Annotated Bibliography of State Censuses, Census Substitutes, and Selected Name Lists in Print, on Microform, or Online; with County Boundary Maps, 1683-1915; and State Census Examples and Extraction Forms, 1825-1925,* by William Dollarhide, published by Genealogical Publishing Co., Inc., Baltimore, 2006, 250 pages, FHL book 974.7 X23d. This book expands the bibliography of census substitutes and state census records to each of New York's sixty-two counties. An example from the book for Albany County is shown on page 114.

■ **1760-1768**. See *Upstate New York in the 1760's, Tax Lists and Selected Militia Rolls of old Albany County, 1760-1768*, compiled by Florence Christoph, Camden, ME, includes index, 320 pages. Albany County comprised a large area of upstate New York before the Revolutionary War, including New York's claim to the area that became Vermont. See FHL book 974.7 R4u.

■ **1675-1920 New York,** CD-ROM publication, entitled: "New York 1675-1920," originally published by Broderbund, 1998. Part of the Family Tree Maker Archives, Genealogical Records, No. 301. (FHL CD-ROM no. 9 pt. 238). This is an index of more than 600,000 individuals who lived in New York between 1675 and 1920. It indexes passenger lists, land records, city directories, and census records.

■ **1784-1829 American Deaths and Marriages**, compiled by Joseph Gavit. Marriages and obituaries from 65 New York state newspapers. FHL book 974.7 B32s. Also on 2 rolls of microfilm, FHL film #1022833-1022834. Indexed as *Joseph Gavit's American Deaths and Marriages: Index to Non-principals in Microfilm Copies of Abstracts in the New York State Library, Albany, New York*, compiled by Kenneth Scott, Published by Polyanthos, New Orleans, 1976, in cooperation with the New York Historical Society, the New York State Library, and the New York Genealogical and Biographical Society. This index accompanies two roles of microfilm reproducing a card file prepared by Joseph Gavit for the New York State Library, Albany, New York. See FHL book 974.7 B32s index.

■ **1792-1906 Index (Soundex) to New York Naturalization Records**. Microfilm of originals at the National Archives, Northeast Region, New York, New York. Indexes the following courts: City Court of Brooklyn, 1836-1894; Kings County Court, 1806-1906; New York City Marine Court, 1806-1849; New York County Common Pleas

Court, 1792-1895; New York County Superior Court, 1828-1895; New York City and County Supreme Court, 1868-1906 Queens County Court, 1799-1906; Queens County Surrogate Court, 1888-1898; Richmond County Court, 1869-1906; U.S. Circuit Court Southern District, 1846-1876; U.S. District Court Eastern District, (Kings, Queens, Nassau and Suffolk counties), 1865-1906; and U.S. District Court Southern Court Southern District, (New York, Bronx and also Dutchess, Orange, Putnam, Richmond, Rockland, Sullivan and Westchester counties), 1824-1906. Federal, state and local courts located in New York City include New York, Kings, Queens and Richmond counties. Some cards are filmed out of order. Some of the more obvious are noted with the roll numbers. Filmed by the Genealogical Society of Utah, 1985-1987, 294 microfilm rolls, beginning with FHL film #1419807 (Aha, Ambrose – Abramowitz, Harry).

■ **1861-1865 - Index to Compiled Service Records of Volunteer Union Soldiers Who Served in Organizations From the State of New York**, microfilm of original records in the National Archives, Washington, D.C., series M0551. 157 microfilm rolls. FHL film begins with #882057.

■ **1862-1866 Assessment Lists of the Federal Bureau of Internal Revenue**. FHL film title, "Internal Revenue Assessment Lists for New York and New Jersey." Microfilm of original records in The National Archives, Washington, D.C., series M0603, 218 rolls. New York name lists begin with FHL film #1534827.

■ **1917-1918 Civilian Draft Registration Cards, New York**. FHL Title: "New York, World War I Selective Service System draft registration cards, 1917-1918." Microfilm of original records in the National Archives in East Point, Georgia. Cards are in rough alphabetical order. Occasionally while filming, lost cards would be found. If these cards were found, they would be filmed after the

Z's of the locality they belonged to. The draft cards are arranged alphabetically by state, then alphabetically by county or city, and then alphabetically by surname of registrants. New York begins with FHL film #1711815.

■ **1825-1925 New York State Censuses**. Most of the originals (or duplicates) of state censuses taken from 1825-1905 are still in the hands of the county wherein the census was taken. For each of the 62 New York counties, the original censuses may be at a county courthouse, county historian's office, or a local library. In some cases, the state archives received an original copy, while the county retained a duplicate original copy.

Microfilming of the county census records was done by the Genealogical Society of Utah, which began in the early 1950s, and was completed in the early 1970s.

For the 1915 and 1925 State Censuses, the originals (or duplicates) for all counties are located at the New York State Archives. All of the state copies of the 1915-1925 state censuses for each county were microfilmed by the Genealogical Society of Utah.

Complete sets of the state census microfilm, 1825-1925, can be found at the Family History Library in Salt Lake City where they are all available on interlibrary loan to their Family History Centers. The New York State Library in Albany has a complete set, but the microfilm must be used in person at the library. In addition, much of the microfilm can be used at the New York Genealogical and Biographical Society Library, or the New York Public Library, both located in New York City.

There are virtually no complete New York State Censuses in digitized format, mainly because the ownership of the censuses remains with each of the counties, while the microfilm copies are held by the Family History Library (FHL) in Salt Lake City.

The contents of the New York State Censuses were as follows:

1825. Name of head of family; number of males in family, including its head, if male; females in family, including its head, if female; males subject to militia duty between the ages of 18 and 45; males eligible to vote; male aliens, not naturalized; paupers; colored not taxed; colored taxed; colored taxed and qualified to vote for state and county officers; married females under 45; unmarried females between the ages of 16 and 45; unmarried females under 16; marriages occurring in the same family, where such female married person resided, during the preceding year; male and female births in the same family during the preceding year; male and female deaths in the same family during the preceding year; family's acres of improved land, animals, cloth manufactures, mills, carding machines, factories, iron works, trip hammers, distilleries, asheries; deaf and dumb, idiots and lunatics.

1835. Name of head of family; number of males in family, including its head, if male; females in family, including its head, if female; males subject to militia duty; males eligible to vote; male aliens, not naturalized; paupers; colored not taxed; colored taxed; colored taxed and eligible to vote; married females under 45; unmarried females between the ages of 16 and 45; unmarried females under 16; marriages occurring in the same family, where such female married person resided during the preceding year; male and female births in the same family during the preceding year; male and female deaths in the same family during the preceding year; family's acres of improved land, animals, and cloth manufactures; deaf and dumb, blind, idiots and lunatics.

1845. Name of head of family; number of males in family, including its head, if male; females in family, including its head, if female; males in family subject to militia duty; persons entitled to vote; aliens, not naturalized; paupers; colored not taxed; colored taxed; colored voters; married females under 45; unmarried females between the ages of 16 and 45; unmarried females under 16; marriages in the family during the preceding year; male and female births in family during year; male and female deaths in family during year; family members born in New York State; born in New England; born in any other state of the Union; born in Mexico, or South America; born in Great Britain, or its possessions; born in France; born in Germany; born in other parts of Europe; children between the ages of 5 and 16; children attending common schools; children attending private or select incorporated schools; children attending academies or unincorporated seminaries of learning other than colleges; children attending colleges and universities; family's cloth manufactures, acres of improved land, crops and animals.

1855. Dwelling numbered in order of visitation; material of which dwelling is built; value; family numbered in order of visitation; every name; age, sex and color (black or mulatto); relation to head of family; place of birth (county of New York State, other state or foreign country); married; widowed; years resident in this city or town; profession, trade or occupation; native and naturalized voters; aliens; colored not taxed; over 21 who cannot read and write; owners of land; deaf, dumb, blind, insane or idiotic.

1865. Dwelling numbered in order of visitation; material of which dwelling is built; value; family numbered in order of visitation; every name (including that of anyone absent in army or navy); age, sex and color (white, black or mulatto); relation to head of family; place of birth (county of New York State, other state or foreign country); parent of how many children; number of times married; whether now married, widowed or single; profession, trade or

occupation; usual place of employment; native and naturalized voters; aliens; colored not taxed; owners of land; over 21 who cannot read and write; deaf and dumb, blind, insane or idiotic; servicemen (lists those now or formerly in the army or navy of the United States).

1875. Dwelling numbered in order of visitation; material of which dwelling is built; value; family numbered in order of visitation; every name; age, sex and color (white, black, mulatto or Indian); relation to head of family; place of birth (county of New York State, other state or foreign country); whether now married, widowed or single; profession, trade or occupation; usual place of employment (those in military service list former home); native and naturalized voters; aliens; owners of land; over 21 who cannot read and write; deaf and dumb, blind, insane or idiotic.

1892. Every name; sex, age and color; country of birth; citizen or alien; occupation.

1905. Address; every name; relation to head of family; color, sex and age; place of birth (U.S. or foreign country); number of years in United States; citizen or alien; occupation; inmates of institutions (residence at time of admission).

1915. Address; every name; relation to head of family; color, sex and age; place of birth (U.S. or foreign country); number of years in United States; citizen or alien; occupation, inmates of institutions (residence at time of admission); infants under one year.

1925. Address; every name; relation to head of family; color, sex and age; place of birth (U.S. or foreign country); number of years in United States; citizen or alien; if naturalized, when and where; occupation, inmates of institutions (residence at time of admission); infants under one year.

New York Censuses & Substitutes Online

• **New York Statewide Census Records Online.** Two Internet Web sites have links to hundreds of New York databases online. These are **www.censusfinder.com/** and **www.census-online.com**. To locate statewide information on the former type the following: **www.censusfinder.com/new_york.htm**.

The following statewide lists are available:
- 1790-1890 New York Census Records at Ancestry
- 1840 Census of New York Pensioners
- 1880 Federal Census (images)
- 1880 Federal Census Search at Family Search
- RootsWeb Search
- New York State Databases of Census & Genealogy

To access databases organized by county enter **www.censusfinder.com/**. Click on "New York Census Records," and scroll to the menu of "New York Census Finder – Counties" at the bottom of the page. Ten groups of counties organized alphabetically will be presented. Click on the appropriate category and scroll as needed to the desired county and named database. The second Web site should be accessed at **www.census-online.com/links/NY/"county name."**

• **New York Wills Online.** W. David Samuelsen has been transcribing and indexing New York county records for many years. Much of his work is now online with name indexes for the testators from wills from virtually every New York county. Each entry gives the name of the testator, place of residence, county, and volume and page number from the original will books. There are also links to Web sites for each NY county with more transcribed data. Access Samuelsen's free Web site for New York wills at: **www.sampubco.com/wills/ny/newyork.htm**.

Census Substitutes & State Censuses for one New York County
Extracted from
New York State Censuses & Substitutes

As an example of the types of census substitutes available for each New York county, a bibliography for Albany County is shown below. Note that the State Census originals on microfilm at the FHL are indicated, along with published census abstracts and/or indexes. In addition, any census substitutes, such as tax lists, history indexes, and deed indexes are shown in this example. (Deed indexes may provide a better list of residents in a county than those found in heads of household censuses). A similar list shown below for Albany County may be repeated for any of New York's sixty-two counties.

Albany County

Albany was one of twelve original counties formed by the New York Provincial Assembly on 1 Nov 1683. It was named after James Stuart (1633-1701), the Duke of York and the Duke of Albany, who became James II, King of England, Scotland, and Ireland following the death of his brother Charles II in 1685. The county seat is located at Albany, New York. From 1683 to 1770, Albany County encompassed all of New York north of Ulster and Dutchess counties, an area from which 53 of New York's 62 modern counties were established. New York's expansion began in Albany County, and many historical records relating to that expansion exist in the form of censuses and lists of inhabitants. Many of the early county records are now located at the Albany County Hall of Records, the largest county archives in the state, operated by the Albany County Clerk's Office and the City of Albany. Address: Albany County Hall of Records, 95 Tivoli Street, Albany, NY 12207. Phone: (518) 436-3663. Resources can be reviewed at their Web site: **www.albanycounty. com/achor/**.

State Census Originals, Extracts, Indexes, Etc.

• *State Census of Albany County Towns in 1790,* compiled by Kenneth Scott, published by Genealogical Publishing Co., Inc., Baltimore, 1975. This county census was unique to Albany County. The author has compared the 1790 county name lists with those from the 1790 federal census. See FHL book 974.742 X2s.

• **1855-1905 New York State Censuses, Albany County, New York,** microfilm of original records from the county clerk's office, now located at the Albany County Hall of Records, Albany, New York, filmed by the Genealogical Society of Utah, 1967, 16 rolls, as follows:
  • **1855** State Census, 3 rolls, FHL film #521922-521924.
  • **1865** State Census, 4 rolls, FHL film #521927-521930.
  • **1875** State Census, 4 rolls, FHL film #521936-521939.
  • **1892** State Census, 2 rolls, FHL film #521944-521945.
  • **1905** State Census, 3 rolls, FHL film #521946-521948.

• **1855 New York State Census, Albany County, New York,** published on CD-ROM, 2003. For more details on contents and availability of the CD, contact the Capital District Genealogical Society, PO Box 2175, Albany, NY 12220-0175.

• **1855 New York State Census, 6th Ward, City of Albany,** listing of wives by maiden names, *The CAPITAL,* Vol. 3, No. 2 (1988) through Vol. 5, No. 1 (Spring 1990), published by KiNSHip, Rhinebeck, NY.

■ **Card Index to 1892 New York State Census, Albany County, New York,** located at the Albany County Hall of Records, 95 Tivoli St., Albany, NY 12207. Phone: (518) 436-3663. Not on microfilm.

■ **1915 and 1925 New York State Censuses, Albany County, New York,** microfilm of the state's duplicate original copies at the New York State Archives. Filmed by the Genealogical Society of Utah, 1970, 9 rolls, as follows:
  • **1915,** 5 rolls, FHL film #521949-521953.
  • **1925,** 4 rolls, FHL film #462889-462890 and #523472-523473.

■ **Card Index to 1925 State Population Census Schedules, City of Albany and Albany County, New York,** original card file at the New York State Archives, Albany, NY. This series consists of approximately 21,000 index cards created for the purpose of indexing the 1925 state census schedules for the City of Albany and Albany County. Information on each card includes a head of household, members of household, and census book and page number. The cards were created ca1959 by members of the Daughters of the American Revolution acting as volunteers for the New York State Library. Card file transferred to the state archives, call no. 1) B1724.

Original Federal Censuses

■ **1860 Federal Census, Albany County, New York,** microfilm of county originals at the Albany County Hall of Records, Albany, New York. Filmed by the Genealogical Society of Utah, 1967, 3 rolls, as follows:
  • **1860** Federal Census, county's original copy, Vol. 1, City of Albany, wards 1-6, FHL film #521925.
  • **1860** Federal Census, county's original copy, Vol. 2, City of Albany, wards 7-10, FHL film #521926.
  • **1860** Federal Census, county's original copy, Vol. 3-4, Bethlehem, Berne, Coeymans, Knox, New Scotland, Rensselaerville, West Troy, Watervliet, Westerlo, FHL film #521935.

■ *The Matched Mortality and Population Schedules of 1860 Census of Albany City and County, New York,* compiled by David Paul Davenport; copyrighted by Arthur C.M. Kelly, published by Palatine Transcripts (now KiNSHiP), Rhinebeck, NY, 1987, 133 pages. Includes index. FHL book 974.742 X2d.

• **1870 Federal Census, Albany County, New York,** microfilm of county originals at the Albany County Hall of Records, Albany, New York. Filmed by the Genealogical Society of Utah, 1967, 4 rolls, as follows:
  • **1870** Federal Census, county's original copy, Vol. 1, Albany, wards 1-7, FHL film #521931.
  • **1870** Federal Census, county's original copy, Vol. 2, Albany, wards 8, 10, FHL film #521932.
  • **1870** Federal Census, county's original copy, Vol. 3, Bethlehem, Berne, Cohoes, Coeymans, Green Island, Guilderland, FHL film #521933.
  • **1870** Federal Census, county's original copy, Vol. 4, Knox, New Scotland, Rensselaerville, Westerlo, Watervliet, West Troy, FHL film #521934.

■ **1880 Federal Census (Short Form), Albany County, New York,** microfilm of county originals at the Albany County Hall of Records, Albany, New York. Filmed by the Genealogical Society of Utah, 1968, 4 rolls, as follows:
  • **1880 Short Form,** vol. 1, Albany, wards 1-5, FHL film #521940.
  • **1880 Short Form,** vol. 2, Albany, wards 6-9, FHL film #521941.
  • **1880 Short Form,** vol. 3, Guilderland, Knox, New Scotland, Rensselaerville, Westerlo, Bethlehem, Berne, Coeymans, FHL film #521942.
  • **1880 Short Form,** Vol. 4, Cohoes, West Troy, Watervliet, Green Island, Watervliet, FHL film #521943.

Census Substitutes & Selected Name Lists

■ *An Index of Albany County Records Covering Materials Within the Dates 1630-1930,* compiled by Lydia Hammond Gale, publ. Albany, 1933, 137 pages. Microfilm of original published Albany, 1933. Contains a bibliography of sources to Albany County history from 1630 to 1930. Includes index. Before the Revolutionary War, Albany County comprised much of the upper population, including New York's claim to the area that became Vermont. Filmed by University Microfilms International, 1987. FHL film #6062167.

■ **1630-1966 Grantee-Grantor Index to Deeds, Albany County, New York.** Microfilm of original records in the Albany County courthouse, Albany, New York. Filmed by the Genealogical Society of Utah, 1968, 268 rolls, beginning with FHL film #464896 (Grantors, A-B, 1630-1894).

■ **1653, 1697, 1699, and 1742 Name Lists.** See *The Annals of Albany,* by Joel Munsell, photocopy of original published Albany, NY, 1850-1859, 4 vols., includes index. Includes Albany name lists for 1653 (oaths), 1697 (census), 1699 (oaths), and 1742 (freeholders). FHL book 974.743 H2m vol. 1-4.

■ *1683-1700 Residents, Albany, New York,* as extracted from the Albany Reformed Church member list by Arthur C. M. Kelly, published by KiNSHip, Rhinebeck, NY, 2003, 23 pages.

■ **1684 Freeholders, Albany County, New York.** Transcription published in *New York Genealogical & Biographical Society Record*, Vol. 3, page 71. Includes town of Schenectady.

■ **1697 Inhabitants, City of Albany, Albany County,** heads of household giving numbers of men, women, and children, *The Capital*, Vol. 9, No. 2 (1994) through Vol. 10, No. 1 (1995), published by KiNSHip, Rhinebeck, NY.

■ **1702 and 1720 Freeholders List.** See *The Documentary History of the State of New York,* arranged under direction of the Christopher Morgan, Secretary of State, by E. B. O'Callaghan, published by Wee, Parson, Public Printers, Albany, NY, 1849, 4 vols. Includes 1702 and 1720 Freeholders List for Albany County. FHL book 974.7 H2o vol. 1-4. Indexed in *Lists of Inhabitants of Colonial New York: Excerpted From The Documentary History of the State of New York by Edmund Bailey O'Callaghan,* indexed by Rosanne Conway, published by Genealogical Publishing Co., Inc., 1979, 351 pages, FHL book 974.7 D4L and FHL fiche #6046723.

■ **1701 Albany County.** See *Documents Relative to the Colonial History of the State of New York: Procured in Holland, England, and France,* by John Romeyn Brodhead, agent; edited E. B. O'Callaghan, 15 vols., published by Weed, Parsons and Company, Albany, NY, 1853-1887. 1701 Name List in Vol. 4, page 939. FHL book 974.7 H2d v. 1-15.

■ **1730-1769 Patentees, Albany County,** giving date, acreage and description of the Patent and to whom granted, *The Capital,* Vol. 8, No. 3 through Vol. 8, No. 4, published by KiNSHip, Rhinebeck, NY.

■ **1756 Stockade Inhabitants, City of Albany, Albany County,** lists households and their ability to quarter troops, *The Capital,* Vol. 1, No. 3 (Fall 1986), published by KiNSHip, Rhinebeck, NY.

■ **Census Records Online, Albany County, New York.** The following census/name lists are available on the Internet, each accessed with a direct link via **www.censusfinder.com**
Census Records
  • 1720 Census of Freeholders in the city and county of Albany
  • 1790 Federal Census of Catskill
  • 1790 Federal Census of Coxsackie
  • 1790 Federal Census Index of Rensselaerville
  • 1790 Federal Census of Rensselaerville
  • 1790 Federal Census Index of Watervliet
  • 1790 Federal Census of Watervliet
  • 1790 Federal Census of towns that became part of Saratoga County in 1791
Census Substitutes
  • 8th Regiment - Albany Militia
  • 1683-1689 Records of the Reformed Dutch Church of Albany
  • 1690-1835 Probate Index - Old Volume 1
  • 1690-1835 Probate Index - Old Volume 2
  • 1779 Tax List
  • 1787-1791 Probate Index Volume 1
  • 1791-1802 Probate Index Volume 2
  • 1802-1809 Probate Index Volume 3
  • 1809-1817 Probate Index Volume 3

PENNSYLVANIA

Censuses & Substitutes, 1680-1950

Many historians report that the Commonwealth of Pennsylvania has never taken a state census. But in fact, "septennial censuses" for virtually every Pennsylvania county were taken every seven years, from 1779 through 1863. The counts from these statewide septennial lists were intended to provide a basis for apportioning the state legislature, based on population. They are now more often called "tax lists' because the names are for taxpayers. An argument of the semantics of "census" versus "tax list" is probably moot, because, unfortunately, very few of the name lists of the septennial censuses survive. Most of those that do exist have been published as part of the *Pennsylvania Archives* series.

Making up for the lack of state censuses, particularly during the era of the Penn family's proprietorship of Pennsylvania, 1681-1776, there were some important census-type manuscripts produced, listing the names of inhabitants for the earliest settlements along the Delaware River. And since the Society of Friends (Quakers) were such good record keepers, published abstracts of Quaker Monthly Meetings provide excellent census substitutes for the first few decades (1680s-1720s) when the Quakers were the predominate group of people living in Pennsylvania.

Pennsylvania's early federal period is also represented with several census substitutes, such as federal tax lists, county tax lists, and other statewide compilations. Pennsylvania has a long history of preservation of historical documents, probably more so than any other state, and most of the surviving original censuses or tax lists have been transferred to the State Archives for safe keeping.

Since the 1880s, the Pennsylvania State Archives has published its holdings in the 136 volume series, *Pennsylvania Archives*, which is now a "Who's Who" for finding Pennsylvania ancestors. Samplings of census substitutes are shown below.

■ **1682-1950 Index to Names of Land Purchasers**. Microfilm of original records located at the Bureau of Land Records, Harrisburg, PA, filmed by the Genealogical Society of Utah, 1976. The FHL cataloged these records as *Warrant Register, 1682-1950*. A warrant register is an index to the land surveys, warrants, and patents issued by the Proprietorship and Commonwealth of Pennsylvania to individuals. The resulting name list of land buyers is a valuable census substitute, naming a large percentage of the adult, white, male population of Pennsylvania. Locating a name of an ancestor in the warrant registers will connect the person to an exact land description for a certain parcel of land. Any subsequent sale of the same land would be recorded (as a deed) in the courthouse of the county wherein the land was located. Subsequent genealogical research can begin at that point for further evidence of a family in a particular county. The real value of the warrant registers is that they can lead a family historian to the later county deed records, where the hidden genealogical treasures may lie. The Pennsylvania warrant registers are organized by survey districts (usually one county) as follows:

- **Warrant registers, Vol. 1-3**: Adams, York, Allegheny, Armstrong, Cambria, Fayette, Greene, Indiana, and Somerset counties, FHL film #1003194.
- **Warrant registers, Vol. 4-7**: Beaver, Butler, Crawford, Erie, Lawrence, Mercer, Venango, Warren, Bedford, Berks, Schuykill, Blair, and Clarion counties, FHL film #1003195.
- **Warrant registers Vol. 8-12**: Bradford, Columbia, Montour, Sullivan, Susquehanna, Tioga, Wyoming, Cameron, Clearfield, Elk, Forest, Jefferson, Lycoming, McKean, Potter, Carbon, Lackawanna, Luzerne, Monroe, Centre, Clinton, and Huntingdon counties, FHL film #1003196.
- **Warrant registers, Vol. 13-16**: Dauphin, Lebanon, Franklin, Fulton, Juniata, Mifflin, Perry, Snyder, and Union counties, Northumberland lottery, Baynton and Wharton survey, Cumberland and Lancaster counties, FHL film #1003197.
- **Warrant registers, Vol. 17-20**: Northampton, Northumberland, Philadelphia, Chester, Bucks, Montgomery, Delaware, Wayne, Pike, and Lehigh counties, FHL film #1003198.
- **Warrant registers, Vol. 21**: Westmoreland and Washington counties, FHL film #1003199.

■ **1759 Warrants and Surveys of the Province of Pennsylvania Including the Three Lower Counties**, compiled by Allen Winberg and Thomas E. Slattery under the directory of Charles E. Hughes, Jr., 1965 edition published by Department of Records, Philadelphia. The Provincial Assembly representing the people of Pennsylvania was in conflict with the sons of

William Penn who were the Proprietaries of the Province of Pennsylvania. Records of Warrants under the control of the Proprietaries and which ordered surveys to be made were not public records. This created confusion over property rights and boundaries. In 1759 the Assembly passed a law for recording warrants and surveys. The Proprietaries in 1760 brought the law before the King who vetoed it. In the meantime, the warrants were transcribed and made public. This is an index of names recorded in the warrants in the present-day Pennsylvania counties of Berks, Bucks, Chester, Cumberland, Lancaster, Northampton, Philadelphia, and York; and the three counties Kent, Newcastle, and Sussex making up Delaware. FHL has a reprint by The Bookmark, Knightstown, IN, 1975, 91 pages. See FHL book 974.8 R2w.

■ **1680s-1900s Grantee-Grantor Indexes to Deeds, Pennsylvania Counties.** Indexes to land sellers (grantors) and buyers (grantees) exist for every Pennsylvania county. All of Pennsylvania's county deed indexes were microfilmed by the Genealogical Society of Utah in the 1970s. These name lists are a better overview of the heads of households for a county than a pre-1850 census. To find a particular Pennsylvania county's deed index, go to the **www.familysearch.org** site and do a "Place Search" for "(county name)", part of "Pennsylvania," then look for "Land and Property," as one of a long list of categories. During the colonial period, Pennsylvania deeds are wordy and full of pedantic legalese (the clerks were paid by the word, which explains why there are so many repeated and unnecessary words in the deed transcripts). Nevertheless, the deed transcripts often contain sources of genealogical links that may be found no where else. For example, clerks often made reference to the original patent for the land being sold, naming the first land holder, subsequent land owners, and in the process, giving father-to-son relationships for several generations.

■ **1680-1938 Quaker Monthly Meeting Records, New Jersey and Pennsylvania.** See *Encyclopedia of American Quaker Genealogy. Vol. II: (New Jersey and Pennsylvania Monthly Meetings)*, compiled by William Wade Hinshaw, originally published 1938, republished by Genealogical Published Co., Inc., Baltimore, 1994, 1,126 pages. The second volume of the Great Encyclopedia is complete for the New Jersey and Pennsylvania monthly meetings which were part of the Philadelphia Yearly Meeting. It includes all records of genealogical value, both Orthodox and Hicksite, known to be in existence for the meetings from the last quarter of the seventeenth century down to the time the work was originally published in 1938. The records are of two principal classes: (1) births and deaths and (2) minutes and marriages, and they are arranged in alphabetical order, by family name, under their corresponding monthly meeting. The marriages are arranged by the names of both brides and grooms. Also provided are abstracts of Quaker certificates of removal, which enable genealogists to trace Quaker ancestors from one monthly meeting to another. Also available on microfilm, see FHL film # 432600-432601.

■ **1760s-1790s Pennsylvania Tax Lists.** The published *Pennsylvania Archives* consists of 136 volumes of early Pennsylvania government records, grouped into ten series. Volumes 11-22 of the Third Series contain tax lists from the 1760s to the early 1790s. These lists were transcribed and compiled from original tax lists for their permanent preservation in the late 1880s, and several have been published separate from the PA Archives series. The years and type of tax vary from county to county, but in all cases, the names of tax payers are listed by township and most include the number of acres, horses and cattle owned by each taxpayer. Of special note is the Land Return Tax of 1783 for Westmoreland and of 1784 for Bucks and Bedford counties, along with the List of Inhabitants for York County in 1783. These lists contain names of all inhabitants and can serve as a complete census substitute for those counties. The importance of these tax lists from the *Pennsylvania Archives* series has seen several publications released. Most recently, for example, Retrospect Publishing of Alexandria, Virginia released a CD-ROM containing Volumes 11-22 of the Third Series, a digitized textual reproduction in which every word is indexed for finding surnames or places. An earlier publication was *Returns of Taxables for the Counties of Bedford (1773 to 1784), Huntingdon (1788), Westmoreland (1783, 1786), Fayette (1785, 1786), Allegheny (1791), Washington (1786), A Census of Bedford (1784) and Westmoreland (1783),* edited by William Henry Egle, State Archivist, microfilm of original published in Harrisburg, PA, by W.S. Ray, 1897, 782 pages, in *Pennsylvania archives,* third series, vol. 22. Filmed by the Genealogical Society of Utah, 1966, 1 roll, FHL film #432614.

■ **Pennsylvania in the 1700's: An Index to Who Was There and Where**, by Donna Beers, Published Warrensburg, MO, 1998, 119 pages. Sources from which information was found: v. 1. *Lancaster Co., PA 1771 Census* from Series 3, Vol. 17 of the Published PA Archives; *PA Soldiers in the Provincial Service 1746-1759; The PA militia in 1777,* by Hannah Benner Roach; *Berks Co. PA births 1705-1800,* by Jeffrey J. Howell; Berks Co. *PA land warrants 1730-1868,* by Howell & Paul; Bucks Co. PA land warrants 1730-1868; Chester Co. PA land warrants 1730-1868; East District PA land warrants 1730-1868; Lancaster Co. PA land warrants 1730-1868; Philadelphia Co. PA land warrants 1730-1868; Northampton Co. PA Land Warrants 1730-1868; Berks Co. PA Land Warrants 1730-1868; Bucks Co. PA deed book 5, 1713-1731; Bucks Co. PA Wills & Admin. Index 1684-1850; Cumberland Co. PA Marriages 1761-1812; History of Big Spring Presbyterian Church, Cumberland Co. PA; *Encyclopedia American Quaker Genealogy Vol. II PA* (Phil. MM Bucks Co.; Falls MM Bucks Co.); *Quaker Arrivals at*

Philadelphia 1682-1750 by Albert Cook Myers 1971; *An Index to the Will Books and Intestate Records of Lancaster Co. PA 1729-1850,* by Eleanore Jane Fulton & Barbara Kendig Mylin 1981; Lancaster Co. *PA Tax Lists 1751-1756-1757-1758* by Dr. Albert H Gerberich 1933; *Index to the 1718-1727 Tax Records of Chester Co. Relating to Areas Later Part of Lancaster Co. PA* by Gary T. Hawbaker. Information extracted: name, age when given, event, date, source and page number. See FHL book 974.8 H22b.

■ *Pennsylvania in 1780: A Statewide Index of circa 1780 Pennsylvania Tax Lists*, compiled by John D. and E. Diane Stemmons, published by Southwest Pennsylvania Genealogical Services, Laughlintown, PA, 1978, 217 pages. Includes the counties of Bedford, Berks, Bucks, Chester, Cumberland, Lancaster, Northampton, Northumberland, Philadelphia, Westmoreland, and York. FHL book 974.8 R42.

■ **United States Direct Tax of 1798, Tax Lists for the State of Pennsylvania**, microfilm of original records at the National Archives, Washington, DC. Filmed by the National Archives, series M0372, 24 rolls. Name lists organized as follows:
- **Philadelphia** City, FHL film #351594- 351595.
- **Philadelphia** County, FHL film #351596-351598.
- **Lancaster** County, FHL film #351599.
- **Chester** (part) and **Delaware** counties, FHL film #351600.
- **Bucks** County, FHL film #351601.
- **Montgomery** County, FHL film #351602.
- **Berks** County, FHL film #351603.
- **Dauphin** County, FHL film #351604.
- **Northampton** and **Wayne** counties, FHL film #351605.
- **Luzerne** County, FHL film #351606.
- **York** County, 351607-351609.
- **Cumberland** County, FHL film #351610.
- **Franklin** County, FHL film #351611.
- **Northumberland, Lycoming,** and **Mifflin** counties, FHL film #351612.
- **Bedford** County, FHL film #351613.
- **Huntingdon** and **Somerset** counties, FHL film

#351614.

- **Westmoreland** County, FHL film #351615.
- **Fayette** County, FHL film #351616.
- **Green, Washington,** and **Allegheny** counties, FHL film #351617.

■ *Encyclopedia of Pennsylvania Biography*, by John W. Jordan, publication New York, Lewis Historical Pub., 1914, 32 volumes. The biographies cover all eras but the main focus is 19th and early 20th century. FHL book 974.8 D3. Also on microfilm. Filmed by the Genealogical Society of Utah, 1989. 4 rolls, FHL film #1697289, 1320892, 1320852, 1698080, and 1320892. All 32 volumes of the *Encyclopedia of Pennsylvania Biography* was indexed in **Index to the Encyclopedia of Pennsylvania Biography, volumes I-XXXII**, compiled by Frederic A. Godcharles; index to Volumes XXI-XXXII compiled by Walter D. Stock Publication. Published by Clearfield, Baltimore, MD, 1996, 277 pages. From preface: "A cumulative index to volumes 1-20 containing about 16,000 names was published in 1932. A cumulative index to volumes 21-32 containing about 26,000 names was compiled in 1994 at the Free Library of Philadelphia." See FHL book 974.D3e.

■ *Pennsylvania Biographical Dictionary: People of all Times and all Places Who Have Been Important to the History and Life of the State*, published by American Historical Publications, Wilmington, DE, 1989, 446 pages, includes index. See FHL book 974.8 D3p.

■ *Pennsylvania, 1740-1900*, CD-ROM publication, originally published Broderbund, 1998, part of Family Tree Maker's Archives. (FHL CD: County and Family Histories, No. 193). Contains images of pages of the following books: *History of Beaver County, Pennsylvania: And its Centennial Celebration*, by Joseph H. Bausman (vols. 1-2); *History of Butler County, Pennsylvania* (vols. 1-2); *Commemorative Biographical Record of Central Pennsylvania: Including the Counties of Centre, Clearfield, Jefferson and Clarion; History of*

Erie County, Pennsylvania; History of Luzerne County, Pennsylvania: With Biographical Selections, H.C. Bradsby, editor; *Byram-Crawford and Allied Families Genealogy*, by Eunice Bryam Roberts; *Bibliography of Pennsylvania History: Second Edition of Writings on Pennsylvania history, a Bibliography*, compiled by Norman B. Wilkinson; *The descendants of John Cadwallader of Wales, Horsham and Warminster*, by Anna H. Baker; *Family Record and Biography*, compiled by Leander James McCormick; *Chester (and its vicinity), Delaware County in Pennsylvania: With Genealogical Sketches of Some Old Families*, by John Hill Martin; *Monnet family genealogy: An Emphasis of a Noble Huguenot Heritage*, by Orra Eugene Monnette; *Pennsylvania Archives (vols. 2, 9); A Pennsylvania Pioneer: Biographical Sketch With a Report of the Executive Committee; The Strassburger Family and Allied Families of Pennsylvania: Being the Ancestry of Jacob Andrew Strassburger, Esquire, of Montgomery County, Pennsylvania*, by his son Ralph Beaver Strassburger.

■ **1887-1893 Pennsylvania City Directories.** CD-ROM publication published by Ancestry, Inc., Provo, UT, 2001, titled **City Directories: Pennsylvania 1887-1893**. With 967,776 records, this is a good census substitute for the lost 1890 federal census records for Pennsylvania. The CD-ROM database allows you to search for a surname, given name, age, address, home address, occupation, and other information. City directories for these localities included: Allentown, Erie, Pittsburgh, Bethlehem, Harrisburg, Reading, Bradford, Norristown, Scranton, Chester, Philadelphia, and Wilkes-Barre.

■ **1870 Federal Census.** A special extraction database was sorted from every state in the 1870 census, entitled **Heads-of-Household Listing Pennsylvania as Birthplace in the 1870 U.S. Federal Census**, a CD-ROM publication by Heritage Quest, North Salt Lake, UT, 2001. This CD provides a good search tool for locating lost ancestors in the 1870 U.S. Census, regardless of which state. It is a nationwide extraction, recording 993,869 heads-of-household in 1870 America who listed Pennsylvania as their birthplace.

Pennsylvania Censuses & Substitutes Online

■ **1700s - 1900s Pennsylvania Censuses and Substitutes. Genealogical Databases Online (www.ancestry.com)** Membership required. Pennsylvania censuses, military lists, immigration lists, and city directories are some of the substitutes included. This is perhaps the largest list of online genealogical databases for any state:

Pennsylvania Census Records
- 1790 United States Federal Census
- 1800 United States Federal Census
- 1810 United States Federal Census
- 1820 United States Federal Census
- 1830 United States Federal Census
- 1840 United States Federal Census
- 1850 United States Federal Census
- 1860 United States Federal Census
- 1870 United States Federal Census
- 1880 United States Federal Census
- 1890 United States Federal Census
- 1920 United States Federal Census
- 1930 United States Federal Census
- Pennsylvania 1910 Miracode Index
- Pennsylvania Census, 1772-1890
- Vitelli Soundex of the U.S. Census

Pennsylvania Military Records
- Pennsylvania Pensioners, 1835
- Pennsylvania Volunteers in the War of 1812
- Revolutionary War Courts-Martial
- Revolutionary War Officers
- Revolutionary War Pension Index
- Revolutionary War Pensioner Census,1840
- Revolutionary War Service Records, 1775-83
- U.S. Army Historical Register, 1789-1903
- U.S. Military Records, 1925: Official National Guard Register
- U.S. Military: Great White Fleet (Atlantic Fleet bound for the Pacific, 16 December 1907)
- U.S. Naval Deaths, World War I

- U.S. World War I Mothers' Pilgrimage, 1930
- Vietnam Casualty Index
- War of 1812 Service Records
- War of the Rebellion
- World War I Draft Registration Cards, 1917-191
- World War II and Korean Conflict
- Veterans Interred Overseas

Pennsylvania Immigration & Naturalization Records
- American Emigrant Ministers, 1690-1811
- Boston, New York, Philadelphia and Baltimore Steamship Arrivals, 1890-1930
- Early American Immigrations
- Immigrants in Pennsylvania, 1727-76
- Immigration of Irish Quakers to Pennsylvania, 1682-1750
- Irish Quaker Immigration into PA
- Naturalizations in America and the West Indies
- New York, 1820-1850 Passenger and Immigration Lists
- Passenger and Immigration Lists Index, 1500s-1900s
- Passenger Arrivals in the U.S., 1819-1820
- Pennsylvania Foreign Oaths of Allegiance
- Pennsylvania German Pioneers
- Pennsylvania Irish Quaker Immigrants, 1682-1750
- Pennsylvania Naturalizations, 1740-73
- Persons of Quality Original Lists
- Philadelphia German Immigration, 1700-75
- Philadelphia Quaker Arrivals, 1682-1750
- Philadelphia, 1789-1880 Naturalization Records
- Philadelphia, 1800-1850 Passenger and Immigration Lists
- Philadelphia, Pennsylvania Indentures, 1771-73
- Rensselaerswyck, New York Settlers, 1630-58
- Ship Passenger Lists from Ireland to America: Miscellaneous Ships
- Ship Passenger Lists to Pennsylvania: Miscellaneous Ships
- Swiss Emigrants in the 18th Century

Pennsylvania Court, Land, Probate Records
- Berks County, Pennsylvania Estate Records, 1752-1914
- Chester County, Pennsylvania Wills, 1713-1825
- Early Pennsylvania Land Records
- English Origins of American Colonists
- Lancaster, Pennsylvania Probate Index, 1729-1850
- Philadelphia County, Pennsylvania Wills, 1682-1819
- U.S. House of Representatives Private Claims
- York County, Pennsylvania Wills, 1749-1819

Pennsylvania Directories & Membership Lists

- 1994 Phone and Address Directory
- 2000 Phone and Address Directory
- Allentown, Pennsylvania Directories, 1887, 1890
- Bethlehem, Pennsylvania Directory, 1890
- Bradford, Pennsylvania Directories, 1887-93
- Chester City, Pennsylvania Directory, 1888-89
- Erie, Pennsylvania City Directories, 1889-93
- Harrisburg, Pennsylvania Directories, 1887-90
- Indiana County, Pennsylvania Normal School Directory, 1909-10
- LDS Member Name Index, 1830-45
- Norristown, Pennsylvania Directories, 1888-1893
- Philadelphia City Directory, 1890
- Pittsburgh, Pennsylvania Directories, 1888-92
- Presbyterian Ministerial Directory 1898
- Protestant Episcopal Church Clerical Directory, 1898
- Reading, Pennsylvania Directories, 1887-90
- Scranton, Pennsylvania Directories, 1890-92
- Susquehanna County, Silver Lake Township, PA,1878-79 Tax Rolls
- U.K. and U.S. Directories, 1680-1830
- Wilkes-Barre, Pennsylvania Directories, 1889-1892
- Williamsport, Pennsylvania Directories, 1889-92

■ **1680s–1900s Pennsylvania Census Links Online. (census-online).** Links to databases available online are arranged by county at **www.census-online.com/links/PA/.** For each county, the number of databases online are indicated below.

Statewide (1); Adams (3); Allegheny (27); Armstrong (11); Beaver (36); Bedford (93); Berks (36); Blair (46); Bradford (243); Bucks (52); Butler (30); Cambria (70); Cameron (12); Carbon (6); Centre (2); Chester (93); Clarion (3); Clearfield (16); Clinton (61); Columbia (39); Crawford (17); Cumberland (5); Dauphin (21); Delaware (46); Elk (12); Erie (62); Fayette (24); Forest (0); Franklin (17); Fulton (3); Greene (24); Huntingdon (8); Indiana (30); Jefferson (8); Juniata (3); Lackawanna (2); Lancaster (18); Lawrence (24); Lebanon (33); Lehigh (101); Luzerne (9); Lycoming (32); McKean (26); Mercer (58); Mifflin (8); Monroe (57); Montgomery (2); Montour (1); Northampton (145); Northumberland (32); Perry (15); Philadelphia (6); Pike (1); Potter (71); Schuylkill (108); Snyder (19); Somerset (142); Sullivan (61); Susquehanna (5); Tioga (183); Union (2); Venango (20); Warren (6); Washington (14); Wayne (11); Westmoreland (34); Wyoming (1); and York (5).

Chapter 4E – The Old South

Kentucky, North Carolina, South Carolina, Tennessee, Virginia, and West Virginia

Historical Timeline for the Old South

1558 England. The reign of Queen Elizabeth I begins. During her 45-year rule, all of the great explorations of North America take place, and the first attempts at English colonization begin.

1584 Virginia. Sir Walter Raleigh claims and names Virginia for the "Virgin Queen," Elizabeth I, an area from Maine to Florida, "sea to sea" and everything else on a northwestern line to Alaska. Soon after, he sends several shiploads of people to establish the New World's first English colony on North Carolina's Roanoke Island. By 1586 the colonists are forced to return to England due to hardships.

1587 Virginia (North Carolina). Jul 2: John White establishes a second English colony at Roanoke. Aug 18: Virginia Dare is born, becoming the first English child christened on American soil. Aug 22: White returns to England for more supplies.

1590 Virginia (North Carolina). White returns to Roanoke to find that the settlers have all disappeared. The word "CROATOAN" is found carved into a tree, but the fate of The Lost Colony still remains a mystery.

1603 England. James VI of Scotland becomes James I of England.

1607 Virginia. Apr 26, three ships under the command of Capt. Christopher Newport sought shelter in Chesapeake Bay. The forced landing led to the founding of Jamestown on the James River, the first permanent English settlement, consisting of 104 men and boys. A year later, about 100 new settlers arrive, finding only 38 survivors from the first group. In 1610, recently appointed governor of Virginia, Thomas West (Lord De La Warr) arrives at Jamestown to find only 60 settlers.

1623 Carolina. First charter for Carolina Colony granted to Sir Robert Heath by King Charles I. Charter would never be used.

1633 Virginia. Founding of Middle Plantation in Virginia, later to become Colonial Williamsburg.

1641 Virginia. William Berkeley appointed governor. Over the next 35 years, he transforms the colony, emulating the culture of southwest England's plantation system.

1649 England. King Charles I is tried by a court of Puritans, convicted of treason, and beheaded. Oliver Cromwell comes to power.

1650 Carolina. First settlements near Albemarle Sound, by frontiersmen from Virginia.

1660 England. Cromwell dies and his son, Richard, is too weak politically to take power. Parliament offers the throne to the deposed Scottish King, son of Charles I, who accepts, becoming Charles II.

1663 England. Charles II, as repayment for their political support against the forces of Cromwell, grants eight ex-generals, the Lords Proprietors, title to Carolina. The charter is later amended to include the Albemarle Sound settlements. The name Carolina comes from "Carolus" the Latin form of Charles.

1669, en route to Carolina. In November, colonists sail from London on three ships: the *Albemarle*, the *Port Royal*, and the *Carolina*. At Barbados, the ships are struck by a hurricane. The *Albemarle* is destroyed and the *Port Royal* and *Carolina* are damaged.

1670 Carolina. In March, the *Carolina* arrives in Seewee Bay, and proceeds to anchor at the north end of Bull's Island. In April, Charles Town is founded as the capital city of Carolina.

1682 Carolina. First four counties created by the Lords Proprietors: Berkeley, Colleton, Craven, and Granville.

1699 Virginia. The capital moved from Jamestown to the newly established town of Williamsburg.

1705 Carolina. Bath, the first town in North Carolina, is built.

1712 North and South Carolina. The territory of Carolina is divided into North and South, each having its own governor.

1721. South Carolina becomes a royal colony. General Sir Francis Nicholson made Governor.

1729. North Carolina becomes a royal English colony after 7 of the 8 Lords Proprietors sell their interest back to the Crown. Lord Granville retains control of the northern half of present-day North Carolina.

1745-1750 Western Virginia/North Carolina. The Great Wagon Road of the Shenandoah Valley provides the route for thousands of Scots-Irish immigrants coming into Western Virginia as well as the Granville District of North Carolina, and eventually, as far as the Clinch, Holston, and Powell River valleys leading into Eastern Tennessee.

1750 Kentucky. Thomas Walker explores Kentucky through the Cumberland Gap.

1768 Tennessee. William Johnson, the northern Indian Commissioner, signs a treaty with the Iroquois Indians to acquire much of the land between the Tennessee and Ohio rivers for future settlement.

1768 Virginia (West Virginia). Iroquois cession includes lands north of the Little Kanawha River (Treaty of Fort Stanwix).

1769 Kentucky. Daniel Boone and John Finley first saw the far distant Bluegrass atop Pilot Knob, now in Powell County.

1770 North Carolina. Tryon Palace is completed at New Bern, becoming North Carolina's colonial capitol building.

1774 Kentucky. James Harrod and 32 others establish the first permanent settlement in Kentucky at Fort Harrod, now Harrodsburg.

1774 Virginia (West Virginia). William Morris, Sr. is the first permanent English settler in Kanawha county, Cedar Grove at the mouth of Kelly's Creek.

1775 Kentucky. Indians give Richard Henderson land between the Ohio and Cumberland rivers for the Transylvania Land Company. Under Henderson's employ, Daniel Boone blazes the Wilderness Trail and establishes Fort Boonesborough. Between 1775 and 1783, it is estimated that 60,000 settlers used the Wilderness Trail to move into Kentucky. They did it in single file using pack teams.

1784. Eastern Tennessee settlers declared their area an independent state and named it Franklin; a year later the Continental Congress rejected it.

1786. South Carolina capital is moved from Charleston to Columbia.

1788. South Carolina (Mar 23) becomes the 8th state.

1788. Virginia (June 25) Virginia becomes the 10th state.

1789. North Carolina. (Nov 21) North Carolina becomes the 12th state.

1789 Virginia (West Virginia). Road from Winchester reaches Clarksburg, opening the gates to large numbers of settlers in the Monongalia region.

1792. Kentucky (Jun 1) Kentucky becomes the 15th state, with capital at Frankfort.

1794 North Carolina. The capital of North Carolina is moved from New Bern to Raleigh.

1796 Kentucky. Wilderness Road opened to wagons. Although a pack team trail and primary route into Kentucky since 1775, only in this year did it become possible for a fully loaded horse-drawn wagon to make the trip.

1796 Tennessee (Jun 1) – Tennessee becomes the 16th state of the union.

1800 West Virginia. 78,000 people in 13 counties of Virginia that later became West Virginia, with 35,000 west of the Alleghenies.

1863. West Virginia (Jun 20) officially separates from Virginia, becomes the 35th state.

1875 Kentucky. First Kentucky Derby run at Churchill Downs.

KENTUCKY

Census Substitutes, 1773-1886

There have been no state-sponsored censuses taken in Kentucky. However, from its first year of statehood in 1792, annual state-wide tax lists were authorized, and cover virtually all Kentucky counties. The annual lists compiled by county tax assessors were published in the reports of the State Board of Equalization. Extracts of many of the name lists have been published and are shown in chronological order below.

Kentucky County (Virginia) was established in 1777, matching the modern boundaries of the State of Kentucky (except the extreme western region still under control of the Chickasaws). In 1780, the name Kentucky was dropped and the same area was carved into the three counties of Fayette, Jefferson and Lincoln. Any census substitutes prior to statehood from these three counties are identified since they represent the entire area of present-day Kentucky. Tax lists, deeds, etc., from other early counties and later statewide census substitutes are also identified.

■ *Early Kentucky Land Records, 1773-1780*, by Neal O. Hammon, published by the Filson Club, Louisville, 1992, 292 pages. Includes general index with names arranged in alphabetical order. FHL book 976.9 R28h.

■ *1774-1796 Virginia Land Grant Surveys in Kentucky*, microfilm of originals and typescript at the Kentucky State Land Office, Frankfort. Filmed by the Genealogical Society of Utah, 1962, 7 rolls, beginning with FHL film #272939 (Index to Virginia Land Grant Surveys). See also *Virginia Land Grants, 1782-1792*, microfilm of originals at the Kentucky State Land Office, Frankfort. These are part of the land grants of Virginia transferred to Kentucky when it became a state in 1792. FHL film #1464015. Above records indexed in *Master Index, Virginia Surveys and Grants 1774-1791*, compiled by Joan E. Brookes-Smith, published by the Kentucky Historical Society, 1976, FHL book 976.9 R22b and FHL film #1320833.

■ **1780-1909 Deed Books**, microfilm of original records at the Kentucky Historical Society, Frankfort. Filmed by the society, 1966, 13 rolls, beginning with FHL film #551280 (Index, Deed Books, A-Z, 1796-1798).

■ **1781-1839 Abstracts**. See *Kentucky Genealogical Records & Abstracts*, vol. 1, 1781-1839; vol. 2, 1796-1839. compiled by Sherida K. Eddlemon, published by Heritage Books, Bowie, MD, 1997. Includes early Kentucky tax lists. Surname index, each volume. FHL book 976.9 D28e v. 1 & 2.

■ **1782-1787**. For early tax lists of Fayette and Lincoln counties, Kentucky, see *Virginia Tax Payers, 1782-1787, Other Than Those Published by the United States Census Bureau*, by Augusta B. Fothergill and John Mark Naugle, published Richmond, 1940, 142 pages. Reprinted Genealogical Publishing Co., Inc., Baltimore, 1978. FHL book 975.5 R4f.

■ **1792-1894 Tax Books, Nelson County, Kentucky**, microfilm of original records at Frankfort and Lexington. Lists are arranged by district and then alphabetically by the first letter of the surname. Filmed by the Genealogical Society of Utah, 1952-1953, 1957-1958, 1991, beginning with FHL film #8178 (1811-1826).

■ **1787 Tax List**. Kentucky areas included in *The 1787 Census of Virginia: An Accounting of the Name of Every White Male Tithable Over 21 Years, the Number of White Males Between 16 & 21 Years, the Number of Slaves Over 16 & Those Under 16 Years, Together With a Listing of Their Horses, Cattle & Carriages, and Also the Names of all Persons to Whom Ordinary Licenses and Physician's Licenses Were Issued*, compiled by Netti Schreiner-Yantis and Florene Speakman Love. Includes records of counties presently in the states of Kentucky and West Virginia. FHL book 975.5 R4sn, 3 vols.

■ **1787-1811 Lincoln County, Kentucky.** See *Early Kentucky Landholders, 1787-1811*, compiled by James F. Sutherland, published by Genealogical Publishing Co., Inc., Baltimore, 1986, 376 pages. Compiled from land data contained in Lincoln County, Kentucky tax records. Forty-six of Kentucky's fifty-four counties came out of Lincoln County in this time period and so names disappear from the list over the years. Names of land owners arranged in alphabetical order. FHL book 976.9 R2su.

■ **1787-1875 Tax Books, Lincoln County, Kentucky**, microfilm of original records at the Kentucky Historical Society, Frankfort. Filmed by the society, 1952-3, 5 rolls, beginning with FHL film #8114 (Tax books, 1787-1788, 1790-1797).

■ **1787-1811 Annual Tax Lists**. See *Early Kentucky Householders, 1787-1811*, compiled by James F. Sutherland, published by Genealogical Publishing Co., Inc., Baltimore, 1986, 209 pages. Names are arranged in alphabetical order. This book was compiled from annual tax lists used by county tax commissioners. FHL book 976.9625 R4s.

■ **1788-1875 Tax Books, Fayette County, Kentucky**, microfilm of original records at the Kentucky Historical Society, Frankfort. Filmed by the society, 1952-3, 24 rolls, beginning with

FHL film #7957 (Tax Books, 1787-1797, 1799-1804).

■ **1789-1892 Tax Books, Jefferson County, Kentucky**, microfilm of original records at the Kentucky Historical Society and the Dept. of Libraries and Archives, Frankfort. Filmed by the society, 1952, 1953, 1957, 1958, 1990, 160 rolls, beginning with FHL film #8050 (1789-1797; 1799-1801).

■ **Some Pre-1800 Kentucky Tax lists For the Counties of: Fayette, 1788; Mason (later Floyd), 1790; Mercer, 1789; Washington, 1792**, compiled by Levi Todd, et al, published by Borderland Books, Anchorage, KY, 1965, 28 pages. FHL book 976.9 R4t and FHL film #1320548.

■ **1790s-1800s Census Substitutes.** See *Early Kentucky Tax Records, From the Register of the Kentucky Historical Society,* with an index by Carol Lee Ford. Published by Genealogical Publishing Co., Inc., Baltimore, 1984, 318 pages. Excerpted and reprinted from the Register of the Kentucky Historical Society, with added publisher's note, contents, index. FHL book 976.9 R4e. See also *Kentucky Historical Society Index to Tax List*, prepared by Microfilm Department, Kentucky Historical Society, Lexington, published by the society, 1973, 339 pages. FHL book 976.9 R4k and FHL film #1036831. And for same period, see *Kentucky Pioneer and Court Records, Abstracts of Early Wills, Deeds and Marriages From Court Houses and Records of Old Bibles, Churches, Graveyards, and Cemeteries Copied by American War Mothers, Genealogical Material Collected From Authentic Sources: Records From Anderson, Bourbon, Boyle, Clark, Estill, Fayette, Garrard, Harrison, Jessamine, Lincoln, Madison, Mercer, Montgomery, Nicholas and Woodford counties*, compiled by Mrs. Harry Kennett McAdams, published by Keystone, Lexington, KY, 1929, 382 pages. Filmed by the Genealogical Society of Utah, 1968, 1 roll, FHL film #459632.

■ *1792-1830 Index, Old Kentucky Survey and Grants; Index for Tellico Surveys and Grants*, compiled from the original records at the Kentucky Historical Society, Frankfort. Published by the society, 1975, 186 pages. This coordinated index is organized in alphabetical and chronological order, giving the survey number and name surveyed for, acreage, county, watercourse, survey date, original survey book and page, grant date, and original grant book and page for all the Old Kentucky land grants from 1776 to 1838. Tellico claims covered Cherokee lands extending into Southeast Kentucky. FHL book 976.9 R2k and FHL film #1492856.

■ **1792-1913 Record of Resident and Non-resident Lands Forfeited to the State and Sold for Taxes**, microfilm of the original records at the Kentucky State Land Office, Lexington. Filmed by the Genealogical Society of Utah, 1958, 30 rolls, beginning with FHL film #174962 (Index of forfeited resident lands to 1846).

■ *1792-1796 Residents of Nelson County, Virginia (now Kentucky)* [sic] *Recorded in Tithable and Tax Lists*. compiled by Margaret Johnson Schroeder and Carl A. Schroeder, published Bardstown, KY, 1988, 4 vols. Old Nelson was definitely in Virginia in 1790, but in 1792, Nelson was one of the original counties of the state, and at that time included more than 15 modern counties of central Kentucky. FHL book 976.9 R48s. Vol. 1-4.

■ **1793-1836 Tax Lists.** See *Early Hardin County, Kentucky Census and Tax Lists, 1793-1836*, compiled by Carolyn Wimp, Mary Sabetti; indexed by Judy Nacke, published by Ancestral Trails, Vine Grove, KY, 1998, 195 pages. Includes every-name index to 1793-1797, 1799-1800, 1805, 1815, 1825, 1836 tax lists; and 1810, 1820, 1830 census lists. From preface: "Includes portions of Kentucky later know as Breckinridge, Daviess, Grayson, Hancock, LaRue, Meade, Ohio, as well as portions of Butler, Edmonson, and Hart Counties, Kentucky." FHL book 976.9845 R4w.

■ **1794-1805 Nonresident Tax List of Kentucky**, microfilm of originals in Lexington, Kentucky. Filmed by the Genealogical Society of Utah, 1958, 1 roll, FHL film #175004.

■ **1794-1817 Fee Books of the Land Office of Kentucky**, microfilm of originals at Lexington, Kentucky. Name lists of early land buyers, based on records recording fees paid by each. Filmed by the Genealogical Society of Utah, 1958, 1 roll, FHL film #74993.

■ **1795 Tax Lists**. See *The 1795 Census of Kentucky*, by T.L.C. Genealogy, Miami, FL, 1991, 195 pages. This is an alphabetical list of names from the 1795 tax lists. FHL book 976.9 R48t.

■ **1796-1808 Tax Ledgers**, microfilm of originals at Lexington, KY. (Historical Society?). Filmed by the Genealogical Society of Utah, 1958, 2 rolls, FHL film #174989 (Ledgers, 1796-1798), and #174990 (Ledgers, 1804-1808).

■ **1797-1866 Land Grants South of the Green River**, microfilm of originals in the Kentucky Land Office, Frankfort. Filmed by the Genealogical Society of Utah, 1962, 15 rolls, beginning with FHL film #272827 (Index to Grants, 1797-1866).

■ *Kentucky Marriages, Early to 1800: A Research Tool*, compiled, extracted & transcribed by Liahona Research; edited by Jordan R. Dodd, published by Precision Indexing, div. of AGLL, Bountiful, UT, 1990, 242 pages. Names are arranged in alphabetical order. FHL book 976.9 V28k.

■ **1800 Tax Lists**. See *Second Census of Kentucky: A Privately Compiled and Published Enumeration of Tax Payers Appearing in the 79 Manuscript Volumes Extant of Tax Lists of the 42 Counties of Kentucky in Existence in 1800*, compiled by Garrett Glenn Clift, published by the Kentucky Historical Society, Frankford, KY, 1954, 333 pages. A good substitute for the lost 1800 federal census for Kentucky. FHL book 976.9 X2p and FHL film #390838.

■ **1820-1900 Land Grants West of the Tennessee River**, microfilm of original records at the Kentucky Land Office, Frankfurt. Filmed by the Genealogical Society of Utah, 1962, 4 rolls, beginning with FHL film #272865 (Index to grants 1820-1858).

■ **1851-1900 Kentucky Marriages**, see *Kentucky, 1851-1900*, CD-ROM publication by Broderbund, 1998 (Family Tree Archives No. 233), originally prepared by Liahona Research, Orem, Utah.

Contains information of approximately 318,000 individuals who were married in sixty-two Kentucky counties between 1851-1900. FHL CD-ROM no. 9, pt. 233.

■ **1859-1860 George W. Hawes's Kentucky State Gazetteer and Business Directory**, filmed by Research Publications, Woodbridge, CT, 1980, FHL film #6044020.

■ **1860-1936 General Index to Court of Appeals**, microfilm of originals at the Margaret I. King Library, University of Kentucky in Lexington, Kentucky. Filmed by the Margaret I. King Library, 1955, 5 rolls, as follows:
- General index, Vols. 1-2 1860-1877, FHL film #8661.
- General index, Vols. 3-4 1878-1898, FHL film #8662.
- General index, Vols. 4-5 [5-6] 1898-1909, FHL film #8663.
- General index, Vols. 7-8 1909-1924, FHL film #8664.
- General index, Vols. 9-10 1925-1936, FHL film #8665.

■ **1861-1865 Confederate Soldiers**. See *Index to Compiled Service Records of Confederate Soldiers Who Served in Organizations From the State of Kentucky*, microfilm of original records in the National Archives, Washington, DC, series M319, 14 rolls, beginning with FHL film #881380 (Index, A-Bi 1861-1865).

■ **1861-1865 Union Soldiers**. See *Index to Compiled Service Records of Volunteer Union Soldiers Who Served in Organizations From the State of Kentucky*, microfilm of original records in the National Archives, Washington, DC, series M386, 30 rolls, beginning with FHL film #881492 (Index, A, 1861-1865).

■ **1862-1866 Internal Revenue Assessment Lists for Kentucky**, microfilm of originals at the National Archives, Washington, D.C. Divisions are often not in order but names are generally in alphabetical order. Some are arranged by division and then year. What rolls have a county on them are noted at the front of each roll. National Archives microfilm, series M0768, 24 rolls, beginning with FHL film #1491176.

■ **1895-1896 Directory**. See *Kentucky Places and People: R. L. Polk & Co.'s Kentucky State Gazetteer and Business Directory for 1895-96*, originally published, R.L. Polk & Co., 1895. Reprinted by McDowell Publications, Utica, KY, 1984, 323 pages. FHL book 976.9 E4k.

Kentucky Censuses & Substitutes Online

The following databases are available online at these sites:

www.ancestry.com
- 1810 United States Federal Census
- 1820 United States Federal Census
- 1830 United States Federal Census
- 1840 United States Federal Census
- 1850 United States Federal Census
- 1860 United States Federal Census
- 1870 United States Federal Census
- 1880 United States Federal Census
- 1890 United States Federal Census Fragment
- 1910 United States Federal Census
- 1920 United States Federal Census
- 1930 United States Federal Census
- Daviess County, Kentucky Census, 1900
- Daviess County, Kentucky Census, 1920
- Kentucky 1910 Miracode Index
- Kentucky Census, 1810-90
- Kentucky Census, Reconstructed, 1790
- Vitelli Soundex of the U.S. Census
- Abstract of Graves of Revolutionary Patriots
- Bourbon County, Kentucky Marriage Records, 1786-1800
- Caldwell County, Kentucky Marriage Records, 1809-28
- Carroll County, Kentucky Marriages, 1838-1920
- Fayette County, Kentucky Marriage Records, 1803-14
- Fleming County, Kentucky
- Marriage Records, 1798-1851
- Franklin County, Kentucky Marriage Records, 1790-1815, Volume I
- Jessamine County, Kentucky
- Marriage Records 1799-1820
- Kentucky Death Index, 1911-2000
- Kentucky Marriages to 1850

www.censusfinder.com
- 1786 Militia Lists for Central Kentucky
- 1810-1890 Federal Census of Kentucky at Ancestry
- 1835 Federal Pension List – Statewide
- Kentucky Lawyers in 1859 – Statewide Index

- 1880 Federal Census - images.
- 1880 Federal Census Search at Family Search
- 1883 Pensioners on the Roll –Statewide
- KY Revolutionary War Soldiers – Statewide
- Kentucky Civil War Rosters Search Engine - Statewide
- Korean War Missing Personnel from the State of Kentucky
- Viet Nam POW / MIA - Kentucky Statewide
- Kentucky Statewide Databases of Census & Genealogy Records

www.census-online.com
- 1790 Federal Census –Reconstructed Searchable
- 1840 Federal Census - Pensioners
- Revolutionary War Pensioners

North Carolina

Census Substitutes, 1663-1913

In 1784, the North Carolina General Assembly asked for a list of inhabitants, which was completed for all counties by 1787 (and may have actually been two name lists combined into one). But North Carolina has not taken a state-wide census since. Land, tax and other lists provide substitutes for the entire state, which are identified below:

• **1600-1957 Land Records; Indexes, 1693-1959**, microfilm of original records at the North Carolina State Archives, Raleigh. Filmed by the NC archives, 1980-2003, 591 rolls, beginning with FHL film #1942649 (Western country land documents (now Tennessee, in alphabetical order); FHL film #1942644 (Index cards to land records of Bath, Bute, Dobbs, Glasgow & Tryon counties, in alphabetical order within each county); and FHL film #1942545 (Index cards, in alphabetical order, to Lord Proprietor grants in old Albemarle County, ca. 1704-1736); followed by land grant index cards in alphabetical order by county.

• *North Carolina Headrights: A List of Names, 1663-1744*, compiled by Carolina B. Whitley; prepared for publication by Susan M. Trimble, published by the Division of Archives and History, NC Dept. of Cultural Resources, 2001, Raleigh, NC. 312 pages. Includes index. See FHL book 975.6 R2wc.

• *1663-1900 Index to North Carolina Wills*, compiled by William Perry Johnson, published by the author, 196?. Contents: v. 1. Alamance, Alexander, Alleghany, Anson, Ashe, Beaufort counties -- v. 2. Bertie, Bladen, Brunswick, Buncombe, Burke counties -- v. 3. Cabarrus, Caldwell, Camden, Carteret, Caswell, Catawba, Chatham, Cherokee counties -- v. 4. Chowan, Clay, Cleveland, Columbus counties. FHL has bound volumes 1-4 into one volume, FHL book 975.6 P2j and FHL film #1036601.

• **1679-1790 Tax Lists**. See *North Carolina Taxpayers*, compiled by Clarence E. Ratcliff, published Genealogical Publishing Co., Inc., Baltimore, 1987-1989, vol. 1: 1701-1786; vol. 2: 1679-1790. FHL book 975.6 R4rc v.1-2.

• **1690-1760 North Carolina Wills**, see *Abstract of North Carolina Wills [1690-1760] Compiled From Original and Recorded Wills in the Office of the Secretary of State*, compiled by J. Bryan Grimes, Reprint. Originally published: Raleigh, N. C., 1910. Reprinted Genealogical Publishing Co., Inc., Baltimore, 1967, 670 pages. Includes index. FHL book 975.6 P2gr, also on microfiche, FHL film #6046876. See a supplement to Grimes' lists in *Abstract of North Carolina Wills From About 1760 to About 1800*, prepared from the originals and other data by Fred A. Olds, microfilm of typescript edition on file in the Library of Congress, Washington, DC, published by the Family History Library, FHL film #496782, indexed in *Index to abstract of North Carolina wills from about 1760 to about 1800 prepared...by Fred A. Olds*, compiled and typed by the FHL, see FHL film #1033627.

• *The Granville District*, by W.N. Watt, 1992, includes index. Includes information about land

ownership, tax records and public officials. FHL book #975.6 R2w.

• **1700s-1900s**. See *Early North Carolina settlers, 1700s-1900s*, CD-ROM publication by Broderbund, 2000, as Family Tree Maker's Family Archives: Genealogical Records, No. 524. Produced in collaboration with the Genealogical Publishing Co., Inc., Baltimore. Contents: *Historical Sketches of North Carolina from 1584 to 1851: Compiled From Original Records, Official Documents and Traditional Statements With Biographical Sketches of her Distinguished Statesmen, Jurists, Lawyers, Soldiers, Divines, etc.*, by John Hill Wheeler (vols. I-II); *Sketches of Western North Carolina, Historical and Biographical*, by C.L. Hunter; *Marriage and Death Notices From Raleigh Register and North Carolina State Gazette, 1799-1825*, compiled by Carrie L. Broughton; *Marriage and Death Notices From Raleigh Register and North Carolina State Gazette, 1826-1845*, compiled by Carrie L. Broughton; *Marriage and Death Notices from Raleigh Register and North Carolina State Gazette, 1846-1867*, compiled by Carrie L. Broughton; *The North Carolina Historical and Genealogical Register*, J.R.B. Hathaway, editor (vols. I-III); *Reminiscences and Memoirs of North Carolina and Eminent North Carolinians*, by John H. Wheeler; *North Carolina Land grants in South Carolina*, by Brent H. Holcomb. FHL CD-ROM No. 9, pt. 524.

• **1720-1764 Tax Lists, North Carolina Counties**, FHL title: "Tax lists of various counties of North Carolina," microfilm of originals at the Secretary of State's Office, Raleigh, NC. Includes Anson County, 1763; Beaufort County, 1764; Bladen County, 1763; Brunswick County, 1769; Caswell County, 1777; Craven County, 1720 and 1769; Granville County, 1769; Onslow County, 1769 and 1770; Pasquotank County, 1754 and 1769; and Pitt County, 1762. Names are arranged alphabetically within the county. Filmed by the Genealogical Society of Utah, 1941, 1 roll, FHL film #18071.

• **1735-1775 North Carolina Land Patents**, see *Colony of North Carolina, Abstracts of Land Patents*, by Margaret M. Hofmann, published by the author, Roanoke Rapids, NC, 1982-1984, vol. 1: 1735-1764; vol. 2, 1765-1775. FHL book 975.6 R2hm.

• **1741-1868 North Carolina Marriages**. See *An Index to Marriage Bonds Filed in the North Carolina State Archives*, microfiche of original records at the NC Div. of Archives and History, Raleigh. Marriage bonds were statements of intent documenting bonds taken out by the groom, usually from the county in which the bride resided. Index lists bride's and groom's names, date of bond, bondsmen's and witness' names, a code for the county where the bond was taken out and the volume and page of the abstracted marriage bond. Filmed by the archives, 88 microfiches, beginning with FHL film #6330241 (Bride list, Anonymous to Andrews, Julia C.).

• **1748-1763 Land Grants**. See *The Granville District of North Carolina, 1748-1763: Abstracts of Land Grants*, by Margaret M. Hofmann, published by Roanoke News, Weldon, NC, 1986, 5 vols., FHL book 975.6 R28h, v.1-5.

■ **1776-1783**. See *Index to Compiled Service Records of Volunteer Soldiers Who Served During the Revolutionary War in Organizations From the State of North Carolina*, microfilm of original records in the National Archives. This is an alphabetical card index to the compiled service records of volunteer soldiers of North Carolina containing names of soldiers to which references were found in the records used in compiling the service records. The cards give the name of the soldier, his rank, and the unit in which he served. There are cross-reference cards for soldiers' names that appeared in the records under more than one spelling. National Archives microfilm series M0257, 2 rolls, FHL film #821595 (Index, A-Q); #821596 (Index, R-Z).

■ **1778-1795 Index to North Carolina Land Entries**, by A. B. Pruitt. Published by the author, Whitakers, NC, vol. 1: surnames A-F; vol. 2, surnames G-N; vol. 3, surnames O-Z. FHL book 975.6 R22pa v.1-3.

■ **1784-1787 Census**. See *State Census of North Carolina, 1784-1787: From Records in the North Carolina Department of Archives and History*, transcribed and indexed by Alvaretta Kenan Register, microfilm of original published Norfolk, VA, 1971, 240 pages. Includes index. Filmed by the Genealogical Society of Utah, 1972, FHL film #897274. See reprint, *State Census of North Carolina, 1784-1787*, by Alvaretta Kenan Register, reprinted by Genealogical Publishing Co., Baltimore, 1993, 233 pages. FHL book 975.6 X2r.

■ **1786 State Census, Granville County, North Carolina**, microfilm of originals by the North Carolina Division of Archives and History, Raleigh, Filmed by the Archives, 197-, 1 roll, FHL film 1014833.

■ **1799-1825 Marriages and Death Notices**, see *Index to Marriage and Death Notices in Raleigh Register and North Carolina State Gazette*, published by Oakland Genealogy Library, FHL book 975.6 V2b and FHL film #824074, another filming: FHL film #844969.

■ **1835 Poll Books, North Carolina: 12th Congressional District for the Counties of Burke, Haywood, Yancey, Macon, Rutherford and Buncombe**, edited by Charles David Biddix, published by Old Buncombe County Genealogical Society, Asheville, NC, 1988, 103 pages. FHL book 975.6 N4p.

■ **1864-1866 Internal Revenue Assessment List for North Carolina**, microfilm of originals in the National Archives in Washington, D.C. Contains information for the following districts: DISTRICT 1: Beaufort, Bertie, Camden, Chowan, Currituck,

Gates, Halifax, Hertford, Hyde, Martin, Northampton, Pasquotank, Perquimans, Tyrrell, and Washington.- DISTRICT 2: Carteret, Craven, Duplin, Edgecombe, Greene, Jones, Lenoir, New Hanover, Onslow, Pitt, Wayne, and Wilson. DISTRICT 3: Anson, Bladen, Brunswick, Columbus, Cumberland, Harnett, Montgomery, Moore, Richmond, Robeson, Sampson, and Stanly. DISTRICT 4: Chatham, Franklin, Granville, Johnston, Nash, Orange, Wake, and Warren. DISTRICT 5: Alamance, Caswell, Davidson, Forsyth, Guilford, Person, Randolph, Rockingham, Stokes, and Surry. DISTRICT 6: Alexander, Cabarrus, Catawba, Davie, Gaston, Iredell, Lincoln, Mecklenburg, Rowan, Union, Wilkes, and Yadkin. DISTRICT 7: Alleghany, Ashe, Buncombe, Burke, Caldwell, Cherokee, Clay, Cleveland, Haywood, Henderson, Jackson, Macon, Madison, McDowell, Mitchell, Polk, Rutherford, Transylvania, Watauga, and Yancey. For further information see note at the beginning of first film. Filmed by the Genealogical Society of Utah, 1988, 2 rolls, FHL 1578467 (District 1-2, 1864-1866); film #1578468 (District 3-7).

■ **1934-1954 North Carolina Population Relocation Files**, Tennessee Valley Authority (records of relocation of people due to the development of dams and reservoirs). Microfilm of originals housed in the National Archives Record Office, East Point, Georgia. Lists name, address, marital status, birthplace of parents, number of and ages of children, occupation, real estate, religion, for families in Cherokee and Swain counties. Filmed by the Genealogical Society of Utah, 1996, 3 rolls, beginning with FHL film #2033919 (Hiwassee project, Cherokee County, 1936-1944, 970 files).

■ **1934-1954 Master File Relocation Card Index for Grave and Cemetery Removal and Relocation**, Tennessee Valley Authority (records of relocation of burials due to the development of dams and reservoirs). Microfilm of originals housed in the National Archives, East Point,

Georgia. Lists cemetery name and number, deceased, date of birth, date of death, age, type and condition of marker and inscription, nearest living relative or source of information, source's address and relationship to deceased. Filmed by the Genealogical Society of Utah, 1996, North Carolina begin with FHL film #2050608 (North Carolina Grave removal master card index).

■ **Pre-1914 Cemetery Inscription Card Index**, prepared by the Historical Records Survey Service Division, Work Projects Administration, microfilm of originals in the North Carolina Department of Archives and History in Raleigh, North Carolina. Surname index cards list county, name of cemetery, town, person, date of birth, death date, age, spouse or parents, location of grave, military information. Cemetery cards are organized alphabetically by county, alphabetically by town and then alphabetically by cemetery name. Filmed by the archives, 23 rolls, beginning with FHL film #882944 (Surnames Aa-At).

■ **Post-1914 Cemetery Inscription Card Index**, prepared by the Historical Records Survey Service Division, Work Projects Administration, microfilm of originals in the North Carolina Department of Archives and History in Raleigh, North Carolina. The cards give county, name of cemetery, town, name of person, birth date, death date, age, spouse or parents, location of grave, and military information, if known. Filmed by the archives, 5 rolls, beginning with FHL film #882965 (Surnames A-C).

North Carolina Censuses & Substitutes Online

The following databases are available online at these sites:
www.ancestry.com
- 1790 United States Federal Census
- 1800 United States Federal Census

- 1820 United States Federal Census
- 1830 United States Federal Census
- 1840 United States Federal Census
- 1850 United States Federal Census
- 1860 United States Federal Census
- 1870 United States Federal Census
- 1880 United States Federal Census
- 1890 United States Federal Census Fragment
- 1910 United States Federal Census
- 1920 United States Federal Census
- 1930 United States Federal Census
- North Carolina Census, 1790-1890
- Vitelli Soundex of the U.S. Census
- Abstract of Graves of Revolutionary Patriots
- American Marriages Before 1699
- Bertie County, North Carolina Vital Statistics, 1700s-1920
- Edgecombe County, North Carolina Vital Records, 1720-1880
- Encyclopedia of American Quaker Genealogy, Vol. 1
- Hopkins Family Marriage Records in the United States, 1628-1865
- Nash County, North Carolina Vital Records Abstracts
- North Carolina Deaths, 1968-69
- North Carolina Deaths, 1970-74
- North Carolina Deaths, 1975

www.censusfinder.com

- North Carolina Statewide Census Records Online:
- 1790-1890 North Carolina Census at Ancestry
- 1793-1840 Black Craftsmen of North Carolina
- 1835 Federal Pension List – Statewide
- 1838 Indian Removal - North Carolina Regiment
- 1840 Pensioners - Military Service
- 1852 Federal Pension List – Statewide
- 1880 Federal Census - mages
- 1880 Federal Census Search at Family Search
- North Carolina Civil War Soldier Database
- The Proprietors of Carolina
- North Carolina State Databases of Census & Genealogy Records

www.census-online.com

- 1840 Federal Census - Pensioners
- 1838 Indian Removal Regiment

SOUTH CAROLINA

Censuses & Substitutes, 1600s - 1944

South Carolina has a long history of state censuses, but very few of the census manuscripts have survived. All of the surviving state census schedules are located today at the South Carolina Department of Archives and History in Columbia, South Carolina. The earliest known state-wide census for South Carolina was taken in 1829, but only Fairfield and Laurens districts are extant. In addition, an 1839 state census of Kershaw and Chesterfield districts is extant.

South Carolina's state constitution of 1868 provided for state censuses for 1869, 1875, and every ten years thereafter. An enumeration was taken showing the number of inhabitants of twenty counties, dated 1868, under the Bureau of Agriculture, and a year later, a listing of the population was published. A few of the 1869 district lists survive and name lists were published in various genealogical periodicals. In 1875, the jurisdiction of the census was transferred to the Secretary of State, and the name lists for just three complete counties exist: Clarendon, Newberry, and Marlboro, with partial listings for Abbeville, Beaufort, Fairfield, Lancaster, and Sumter counties. Although authorized, there is no record of a state census taken after 1875. In the state constitution of 1895, state censuses were authorized for 1901 and every ten years thereafter; but allowed the state to use the decennial federal censuses to determine apportionment of the General Assembly, and again, no state censuses have been found. Census substitutes of land, tax, and other name lists are shown below. References to "mesne" land transfers refer to those lands granted by agents of the Lords Proprietors of early Carolina.

■ **1600s-1800s**. See *Early South Carolina Settlers, 1600's-1800's*, CD-ROM publication, originally published by Broderbund in collaboration with the Genealogical Publishing Co., Inc., Baltimore, Family Tree Maker's Family Archives – Genealogical Records No. 517. **Contents:** *A Compilation of the Original Lists of Protestant Immigrants to South Carolina, 1763-1773*, compiled by Janie Revill; *Scotch-Irish Migration to South Carolina, 1772; Rev. William Martin and His Five Shiploads of Settlers*, by Jean Stephenson; *Passenger Arrivals at the Port of Charleston, 1820-1829*, transcribed by Brent H. Holcomb; *South Carolina Naturalizations, 1783-1850*, compiled by Brent H. Holcomb; *The Jury Lists of South Carolina, 1778-1779*, compiled by Ge Lee Corley Hendrix and Morn McKoy Lindsay; *Heads of Families at the First Census of the United States Taken in the Year 1790: South Carolina, Index to the 1800 Census of South Carolina*, compiled by Brent H. Holcomb; *North Carolina Land Grants in South Carolina*, by Brent H. Holcomb; *Warrants for Lands in South Carolina, 1672-1711*, edited by A.S. Salley (vols. I-III); *Indexes to the County Wills of South Carolina*, compiled by Martha Lou Houston; *Index to Wills of Charleston County, South Carolina, 1671-1868*, compiled under the direction of the Charleston Free Library. FHL CD-ROM No. 9 pt. 517.

■ **1600s-1800s**, see *South Carolina Name Index to Genealogical Records Collected by South Carolina Daughters of the American Revolution (DAR)*, 25,666 pages filmed by the Genealogical Society of Utah, 1988. An alphabetical list of surnames, vol./page number of records collection, on 102 microfiche, FHL film #6052835 (fiche #1: A. Pearl – Abbott, Moses S.).

■ **1695-1775 Index to Royal Land Grants; Royal Land Grants, 1731-1775**, microfilm of original records at the Secretary of State's Office, Columbia, South Carolina. Filmed by the Genealogical Society of Utah, 1951, 17 rolls, beginning with FHL film #22581 (Index to Land Grants, A-Z, 1695-1775).

■ **1695-1925 Combined Alphabetical Index**, microfilm of original manuscript at the South Carolina Department of Archives and History, Columbia, South Carolina. This is a computer-generated microfilm finding aid to thirty early record series held either in the original or on microfilm. Reference numbers are given for each entry in the consolidated index so that patrons may order photocopies of the original documents. The index is on 19 rolls of microfilm, beginning with FHL #1690457 (A.C. Tuxberry Land – Berkeley County).

■ *1719-1785 Index to Deeds of the Province and State of South Carolina; and Charleston District, 1785-1800, from Register of Mesne Conveyance, Charleston County, South Carolina*, published by Southern Historical Press, Easley, SC, 1977, 841 pages. FHL book 975.7 R2c.

■ **1732 Tax Return, Edisto Island**, in *South Carolina Magazine of Ancestral Research*, Vol. 18, No. 4 (Fall 1990).

■ **1733-1742 South Carolina Tax List**, compiled by Tony Draine and John Skinner, typescript published by Congaree Publications, Columbia, SC, 1986, 100 pages. Arranged in alphabetical order by surname. FHL book 975.7 R48.

■ **1734-1777 Land Owner References**. See *Petitions for Land from the South Carolina Council Journals*, by Brent H. Holcomb, published by SCMAR, Columbia, SC, 1996, 7 vols., name and place indexes, Vo. 4 &7. FHL book 975.7 R2h v.1-7.

■ **1734-1860 Mortgage Records; Index, 1709-1840**, microfilm of original records at the Historical Commission in Columbia, South Carolina. Records predominantly "mortgages of negroes." Includes sale of land, bonds, furniture, livestock, and miscellaneous property. Also includes cattle marks. Includes index. Filmed by the Genealogical Society of Utah, 1951, 27 rolls, beginning with FHL film #22627 (Index to Mortgages, Aaron – Zylstra, 1766-1840).

■ **1771-1868 Miscellaneous Court Records**, microfilm of original records at the Secretary of State's Office, Columbia, South Carolina. Includes bonds, mortgages, bills of sale (including slaves), manumissions, powers of attorney and other miscellaneous records. Includes general index. Filmed by the Genealogical Society of Utah, 1950-1951, 56 rolls, beginning with FHL film #22662 (Index to v. A-Z, 1777-1857).

■ *1772-1773-1774 South Carolina Quitrents*, compiled by Theresa M. Hicks and Frances S. Osburn, published Peppercorn Publications, Columbia, SC, 1998, 200 pages. FHL book 975.7 R2hi.

■ **1776-1785 Land Records**. See *Register of Mesne Conveyances: Conveyance Books, 1776-1785*, microfilm of original records at the South Carolina Department of Archives and History, Columbia, South Carolina. This series is commonly called the "Charleston Deeds." Its alphabetical volume designations continue on from the earlier Conveyance Books kept by the Public Register, 1719-1776. It is itself followed by the volumes in the Conveyance Books series, 1785-1915, of the Charleston County Register of Mesne. Property descriptions for real estate usually include acreage; physical location including natural features, boundaries, and surrounding landholders; buildings and other improvements on the property, if any; and previous owners of the property. The descriptions of previous owners (chains of title) usually provide a history of property ownership back to the original land grant. South Carolina Archives Series Description: *Conveyance Books, 1776-1785*, Call No. S 36300.

■ **1784-1883 South Carolina Land Grants**, microfilm of original records at the Secretary of State's Office in Columbia, South Carolina.

Includes partial general index. Also, some volumes individually indexed. Filmed by the Genealogical Society of Utah, 1950-1951, 50 rolls, beginning with FHL film #22531 (Index to grants, A-Z, 1790-1821).

■ **1783 Tax List, St. Bartholomew Parish, Charleston District, South Carolina**, in *South Carolina Magazine of Ancestral Research*, Vol. 2, No. 4 (Fall 1974); and Vol. 3, No. 3 (Summer 1975).

■ **1786 Tax Returns, St. Bartholomew's Parish, Charleston District, South Carolina**. Name lists were published in the *South Carolina Magazine of Ancestral Research*, Vol. 9, No. 2 (Spring 1981); through Vol. 10, No. 3 (Summer 1982). Note: St. Bartholomew's Parish in 1786 had the same boundaries as Colleton County has today.

■ **1786 Tax Returns, St. Paul's Parish, Charleston District, South Carolina**, in *South Carolina Magazine of Ancestral Research*, Vol. 9, No. 2 (Spring 1981). Note: the area of St. Paul's Parish was added to Colleton County by 1800, but has been in Charleston County since 1910.

■ **1787 Tax List, Barnwell District, South Carolina** in *Georgia Genealogical Magazine*, Vol. 49 (Summer 1973); and "1787 Winton County, Barnwell District," in *Carolina Genealogist*, Vol. 11 (Summer 1972).

■ **1802-1813 Voter Lists**, microfilm of original typescript at the South Carolina Historical Commission, Columbia. Includes registered voters 18 Nov. 1811, Parish of St. Matthews; election held at William Fanner, Sr. in Nov. 1813 for Senator for Orange Parish; list of persons who voted at Richard Tredaway, 1802, Winton Co. Filmed by the Genealogical Society of Utah, 1974, 1 roll, FHL film 954252.

■ **1829 Census of Laurens District**, in *South Carolina Magazine of Ancestral Research*, Vol. 4, No. 2 (Spring 1976); and Vol. 4, No. 3 (Summer 1976).

■ **1839 South Carolina State Census, Lexington District**, in *South Carolina Magazine of Ancestral Research*, Vol. 25, No. 3 (Summer 1997).

■ **1839 South Carolina State Census, Chesterfield District**, in *Darlington Flag*, "A-E," in Vol. 7, No. 2 (Spring 1995); "G-M" in Vol. 7, No. 3 (Summer 1995); and "M-S" in Vol. 7, No. 4 (Fall 1995).

■ **1864-1866 Internal Revenue Assessment Lists for South Carolina**, microfilm of originals at the National Archives, Washington, DC. Includes index that references counties to districts and indicates whether the county is represented on reel 1, reel 2, or, both reels. This index is found at the beginning of each reel of film. Film by the National Archives, series M789, 2 rolls, FHL film 1578451 (Districts 1-2, 1865-1866); and FHL film #1578452 (District 2-3, 1864-1866).

■ **1865 Darlington Tax Returns**, in *Darlington Flag*, Vol. 7, No. 2 (Spring 1995); and Vol. 7, No. 3 (Summer 1995).

■ **1869 South Carolina State Census, Lexington & Newberry,** in *Dutch Fork Digest*, Vol. 14, No. 2 (Apr 1999); through Vol. 16, No. 1 (Jan 2001).

■ **1869 South Carolina State Census, Blacks in York County**, in *Family Records Today*, Vol. 6, No. 1 (Jan 1985).

■ **1875 South Carolina State Census, Agricultural, York County**, in *Broad River Notebook*, (Sep 1997).

■ **1915-1944 Death Certificate Indexes,** microfilm of original records of the State Board of Health, now at the South Carolina Department of Archives and History, Columbia, South Carolina. Index cards include name, vol. no., certificate no., county, date of death, and age. 53 microfiches, in alphabetical order, are divided chronologically: 1915-1924, 1925-1934, and 1935-1944, beginning

with FHL film #6334927 (fiches 1-12), Aanes, Bennett to Murray, Potter, 1915-1924).

South Carolina Censuses & Substitutes Online

The following databases are available online at these sites:
www.ancestry.com
- 1790 United States Federal Census
- 1800 United States Federal Census
- 1810 United States Federal Census
- 1820 United States Federal Census
- 1830 United States Federal Census
- 1840 United States Federal Census
- 1850 United States Federal Census
- 1860 United States Federal Census
- 1870 United States Federal Census
- 1880 United States Federal Census
- 1890 United States Federal Census Fragment
- 1910 United States Federal Census
- 1920 United States Federal Census
- 1930 United States Federal Census
- Laurens County, South Carolina Census, 1800
- South Carolina Census, 1790-1890
- Vitelli Soundex of the U.S. Census
- Abstract of Graves of Revolutionary Patriots
- Aiken County, South Carolina Cemetery Inscriptions
- Aiken County, South Carolina Cemetery Inscriptions: Graniteville
- Aiken County, South Carolina: Cemetery Records
- American Marriages Before 1699
- Charleston Observer (South Carolina), Marriages and Deaths
- Charleston, Charleston County, South Carolina Black Deaths 1871-89
- Columbia, South Carolina Newspaper Marriage and Death Notices
- Columbia, South Carolina Obituaries, 1859-77
- Greenville, South Carolina Marriage and Death Notices, 1826-63

www.censusfinder.com
- 1716-1783 Early South Carolina Colonists
- 1770 Tryon County, NC (contains many residents in present day SC boundaries)
- 1779 Census of the 96th District
- 1781 Residents of Unknown Counties of SC
- 1790 Federal Census Statewide

- 1790 Federal Census Images Statewide
- 1790 Census Transcriptions Statewide
- 1835 Federal Pension List – Statewide
- 1840 Federal Census Pensioners Statewide Surnames A-L
- 1840 Federal Census Pensioners Statewide Surnames M-Z
- 1865 Federal Pensioners Statewide
- 1870 Federal Census Mortality Schedule Statewide
- 1880 Federal Census - images
- 1880 Federal Census Search at Family Search
- South Carolina Statewide Databases of Census & Genealogy Records

www.census-online.com

- 1790 Federal Census Images
- 1840 Federal Census - Pensioners
- 1870 Federal Census - Mortality Schedule

TENNESSEE

Censuses & Substitutes, 1778-1891

There are several references to enumerations authorized in the state constitutions of 1796 and 1834, but there are no known state-sponsored censuses for Tennessee until 1891. In that year, the state authorized an enumeration of all males over the age of 21 years, citizens of the state. A number of tax lists have been published that substitute for the federal census for 1790 (Southwest Territory), which was a tally list without names; the lost Tennessee federal censuses of 1800 and 1810; and the 1820 federal census for which only about half of the county name lists survive. Earlier names lists from the counties of Greene, Hawkins, Knox, and Washington cover the first areas of settlement in East Tennessee; while lists from the Middle Tennessee counties of Davidson, Montgomery, Robertson, and Sumner cover the rest of the population up to about 1800. Name lists from other early counties, and any statewide land, tax, and other name lists can serve as state-wide census substitutes, as shown below:

■ **1778-1885 Tax Books, Washington County, Tennessee**, microfilm of original records at the Trustee's Office, Washington County Courthouse, Jonesboro, Tennessee. Filmed by the Tennessee State Library and Archives, 1969, 4 rolls, beginning with FHL film #825545 (Tax Books, 1778-1846).

■ **1784-1946 Deed Records & Grantee-Grantor Index, Davidson County, Tennessee,** microfilm of original records at the office of the Register of Deeds, Davidson County Courthouse, Nashville, Tennessee. Filmed by the State Library & Archives, 1965, 547 rolls, beginning with FHL film #392082 (Grantee Index A-K 1784-1871).

■ **1786-1962 Deeds Records, Montgomery County, Tennessee**, microfilm of original records at the Tennessee State Library and Archives in Nashville, Tennessee. Includes general index with some volumes individually indexed. Filmed by the Tennessee State Library and Archives, 1963, 95 rolls, beginning with FHL film #320851 (Index, 1786-1869).

■ **1787-1794 Tax Lists, Sumner County, Tennessee**, prepared by the Historical Records Project (WPA), microfilm of typescript at the Tennessee State Library and Archives in Nashville. Includes index. Filmed by the Genealogical Society of Utah, 1940, 1 roll, FHL film #24839.

■ **1787-1967 Deed Records & Indexes, Sumner County, Tennessee**, microfilm of transcript (hand and typewritten) at the Tennessee State Library and Archives, Nashville. Filmed by the state library, 1966-1967, 161 rolls, beginning with FHL film #467510 (Direct Index to Deeds, A-D, 1787-1947).

■ **1787-1791 Land Grants**, see *Partial Census of 1787 to 1791 of Tennessee as Taken From the North Carolina Land Grants*, compiled by Lucy Kate McGhee, typescript filmed by the

Genealogical Society of Utah, 1990, 2 rolls, FHL film #1728882 (parts 1 &2); and FHL film #1683130 (part 3).

■ **1791-1966 Deed Records & Index, Knox County, Tennessee**, microfilm of original records at the Knox County Courthouse, Knoxville, Tennessee. Filmed by the Tennessee State Library and Archives, 1966, 1,564 rolls, beginning with FHL film #464119 (Deed Index, A-C).

■ **1796-1963 Deed Books; Index to Deeds, 1796-1965, Robertson County, Tennessee,** microfilm of original records at the Tennessee State Library and Archives, filmed by the Genealogical Society of Utah, 1965, 90 rolls, beginning with FHL film #422467 (Index to Deeds, 1796-1907); and FHL film #422468 (Reverse Index to Deeds, A-Z, 1900-1965). See also *1796-1838 General Index to Deeds, Robertson County, Tennessee*, microfilm of typescript prepared by the Historical Records Survey (WPA) at the Tennessee State Library and Archives, Nashville. Filmed by the Genealogical Society of Utah, 1941, 1 roll, FHL film #24802 (Index to deeds, 1796-1838).

■ *1798 Property Tax List and 1820 Census of Montgomery County, Tennessee*, transcribed, indexed and published by Ursula S. Beach and Ann E. Alley, Clarksville, TN, 1969, 43 pages. FHL book 976.845 X2p and FHL film #1033729. See also, *Montgomery County, Tennessee 1798 Tax List*, James L. Douthat, published by Mountain Press, Signal Mountain, TN, 2000, 32 pages, FHL book 976.845 R4d and FHL film #6003699.

■ *Tennessee Marriages, Early to 1800: A Research Tool*, compiled, extracted and transcribed by Liahona Research; edited by Jordan R. Dodd; published by Precision Indexing, div. of AGLL, Bountiful, UT, 1990, 69 pages. FHL book 976.8 V22t.

■ *1801-1825 Tennessee Marriages*, compiled, extracted & transcribed by Liahona Research, Inc.; edited by Jordan R. Dodd, published by Heritage Quest, North Salt Lake, 2001, 270 pages, FHL book 976.8.

■ **1806 Tax List, Knox County, Tennessee**, author and publisher unknown, name list published in FHL book 976.885 R4ka and FHL film #1320525.

■ **1809-1817 Tax Books, Greene County, Tennessee**, prepared by the Historical Records Project (WPA), microfilm of typescript at the State Library and Archives, Nashville, Tennessee. Includes index. Filmed by the Genealogical Society of Utah, 1939, 1 roll, FHL film #film 24667 (Tax books, 1809-1817).

■ **1809-1812 Tax List, Hawkins County, Tennessee**, author and publisher unknown, 13 page typescript at the FHL as FHL book 976.8 A1 No. 95.

■ *The Reconstructed 1810 Census of Tennessee: 33,000 Long-lost Records From Tax Lists, Court Minutes, Church Records, Wills, Deeds and Other Sources*, by Charles A. Sherrill, published by the author, Mt. Juliet, TN, 2001, 576 pages. Names listed in alphabetical order. FHL book 976.8 X2s.

■ *1812 Davidson County, Tennessee, Tax List: Taken From the Microfilm Copy Found in the Tennessee State Archives*, by James L. Douthat, published by Mountain Press, Signal Mountain, TN, 2000, 28 pages. FHL book 976.855 R4d and FHL film #6003700.

■ **1814-1819 Tax Lists, Washington County, Tennessee**, microfilm of typescript prepared by the Historical Records Project (WPA) at the Tennessee State Library & Archive, Nashville. Includes index. Filmed by the Genealogical Society of Utah, 1940, 1 roll, FHL film #24853.

■ *Early Tennessee Settlers, 1700's-1900's*, CD-ROM publication, originally published by Broderbund in collaboration with Genealogical Publishing Co., Inc., Baltimore, 2002, Family Tree Maker's Family Archives, Genealogical Records No. 511. **Contents:** *Pioneers of Davidson County, Tennessee*, compiled by Edythe Rucker Whitley; *Red River Settlers: Records of the Settlers of Northern Montgomery, Robertson, and Sumner counties, Tennessee*, by Edythe Rucker Whitley; *Tennessee Genealogical records: Henry County "old time stuff,"* researched, compiled and published by Edythe Rucker Whitley:; *Tennessee Genealogical Records: Records of Early Settlers From State and County Archives*, by Edythe Rucker Whitley; *Overton County, Tennessee, Genealogical Records.* compiled by Edythe Rucker Whitley; *1770-1790 Census of the Cumberland Settlements: Davidson, Sumner and Tennessee counties (in what is now Tennessee)*, compiled by Richard Carlton Fulcher; *Index to the 1820 census of Tennessee*, compiled by Elizabeth Petty Bentley; *Tennessee Records: Bible Records and Marriage Bonds*, compiled by Jeannette Tillotson Acklen; *Sumner County, Tennessee: Abstract of Will Books 1 and 2, 1788-1842*, compiled by Edythe Rucker Whitley; *Tennessee Records: Tombstone Inscriptions and Manuscripts: Historical and Biographical*, compiled by Jeannette Tillotson Acklen; *Tennessee Soldiers in the Revolution*, by Penelope Johnson Allen; *Some Tennessee Heros of the Revolution: Compiled from Pension Statements*, by Zella Armstrong; *Twenty-four Hundred Tennessee Pensioners; Revolution - War of 1812*, by Zella Armstrong; and *Record of Commissions of Officers in the Tennessee Militia, 1796-1815*, compiled by Mrs. John Trotwood Moore. See FHL CD-ROM No. 9, Part 511.

■ **Early Tennessee Court and Miscellaneous Records**, see *Tennessee*, a series of records compiled by Carol Wells and others. CD-ROM publication by Heritage Books, Bowie, MD, 2001, 3 CDs. edited by Carol Wells. **Contents: Vol. 1:** *Davidson County, Tennessee, County Court minutes,*

v. 1-3, by Carol Wells; **Vol. 2:** *Robertson County, Tennessee, Court Minutes, 1796-1807; Williamson County, Tennessee, County Court minutes, 1806-1812; Williamson County, Tennessee, County Court minutes, 1812-1815*, compiled by Carol Wells; *Abstracts of Giles County, Tennessee, County Court minutes, 1813-1816*, and *Circuit Court minutes, 1810-1816*, by Carol Wells; *Rhea County, Tennessee, Circuit Court minutes, September 1815-March 1836*, by Carol Wells; *Rhea County, Tennessee, tax lists, 1832-1834 & County Court minutes, volume D, 1829-1834*, by Carol Wells; *Dickson County, Tennessee County and Circuit Court minutes, 1816-1828 and witness docke*, by Carol Wells; *Notable men of Tennessee, from 1833 to 1875*, by Oliver P. Temple; compiled and arranged by his daughter, Mary B. Temple; **Vol. 3:** *Davidson County, Tennessee, Deed Books*, by Mary Sue Smith; *Historic Sumner County, Tennessee with genealogies of the Bledsoe, Cage and Douglas families*, by Jay Guy Cisco, indexed by Vera Meek Wimberly; *History of Sweetwater Valley, Tennessee*, by William Ballard Lenoir; *Historical sketches of the Holston valleys*, by Thomas Wilson Preston. These books are published in Adobe Acrobat PDF format. FHL CD-ROM No. 678.

■ **Early 1800s Tax Lists**, see *Early East Tennessee Tax Lists*, compiled by Mary Barnett Curtis, published by Arrow Point, Ft. Worth, TX, 1964, 93 pages. A compiled list of residents of the area covered in 22 East Tennessee counties for which there is no census record prior to 1830. These lists are composed of names of those people who appear on tax lists or petitions for the early 1800's. Names are listed in alphabetical order within each tax list. FHL book 976.8 R4c. See also, *Early East Tennessee Taxpayers*, compiled by Pollyanna Creekmore, published by Southern Historical Press, Easley, SC, 1980, 277 pages. FHL book 976.8 R4 and FHL film #1486601. Indexed in *Revised Index to Early East Tennessee Taxpayers*, by S. Emmett Lucas, published by Southern Historical Press, Easley,

SC, 1982, 36 pages. Index was revised because of error made in pagination of original book. Includes names from footnotes, not originally indexed. FHL book 976.8 R4cp index.

■ *Index to Early Tennessee Tax Lists*, transcribed and indexed by Byron and Barbara Sistler, published by the authors, Evanston, IL, 1977, 217 pages. FHL book 976.8 R4s and FHL film #1697905.

■ *1831-1870 Tennessee Convicts: Early Records of the State Penitentiary*, by Charles A. Sherrilland Tomye M. Sherrill, published by the authors, Mt. Juliet, TN, 1997-2002, 2 vols., includes index of places (vol. 1) and full-name indexes (vols. 1 & 2). FHL book 976.8 J6s v.1-2.

■ *1836 Hawkins County, Tennessee Civil District and Tax List*, compiled by James L. Douthat, published by Mountain Press, Signal Mountain, TN, 1994, 32 pages. FHL book 976.895 R4 and FHL film #2055166.

■ *1836 Robertson County, Tennessee Civil District and Tax List*, compiled by James L. Douthat, published by Mountain Press, Signal Mountain, TN, 1999, 49 pages. FHL book 976.8464 R4 .

■ **1851-1900 Tennessee Marriages**, see *Tennessee, 1851-1900*, CD-ROM publication by Genealogy.com, 2000. (Family Tree Maker's Family Archive, Marriage Index, CD No. 235). Lists approximately 439,000 individuals from Tennessee who were married between 1851 and 1900. FHL CD-ROM No. 9 pt. 235.

■ **1853 History**. See *The annals of Tennessee to the End of the Eighteenth Century: Comprising its Settlement, as the Watauga Association, From 1769 to 1777; a Part of North-Carolina, from 1777 to 1784; the state of Franklin, From 1788 to 1790; the territory of the US South of the Ohio, From 1790 to 1796; and the State of Tennessee, From 1796 to 1800*, by James Gettys McGready Ramsey, reprint of original published: Charleston: Walker and James, 1853. Filmed with *Fain's Critical and Analytical Index and Genealogical Guide to Ramsey's Annals of Tennessee: Embracing All Proper Names as Well as Important Topical Subjects*, compiled by John Tyree Fain, original published: Nashville: Paul Hunter, 1920, 86 pages. History and Index on FHL film #24525.

■ **1853 Directory**. See *The Nashville, State of Tennessee, and General Commercial Directory*, microfilm of original published by American Book and Job Printing Office, Nashville, 5 vols., includes index. Filmed by the Tennessee State Library and Archives, 1 roll, FHL film #570814.

■ *1860-1861 John L. Mitchell's Tennessee State Gazetteer, and Business Directory*, microfilm of originals, filmed by Research Publications, Woodbridge, CT, 1980-1984. 8 microfiches, FHL film #6044535.

■ **1861-1865 Assessment Lists of the United States Direct Tax Commission for the District of Tennessee**, microfilm of original records at the National Archives, Washington, DC. Filmed by the National Archives, series T0227, 6 rolls, as follows:
- Anderson County, districts 1-11 thru Coffee County, districts 1-13. FHL film #157841
- Coffee County, districts 1-13 (cont.) thru Gibson County, districts 1-21, FHL film #1578416.
- Gibson County, districts 1-21 (cont.) thru Hancock County, districts 1-14, FHL film #1578417.
- Hancock County, districts 1-14 (cont.) thru Madison County, districts 1-8, FHL film #1578418.
- Marion County, districts 1-13 thru Roane County, districts 1-16, FHL film #1578419.
- Robertson County, districts 1-17 thru Wilson County, districts 1-25 FHL film #1578420.

■ **1861-1865**. *Index to Questionnaires of Civil War Veterans*, compiled by the Tennessee State Library and Archives, 1962, Nashville, 33 pages. FHL book 976.8 M2ti and FHL film #982038.

■ **Confederate Patriot Index**, compiled by the Tennessee Division, United Daughters of the Confederacy, 1976-1978. Includes a name index to soldiers from Tennessee. Vol. 1: 1894-1924; Vol. 2: 1924-1978. FHL book 976.8 M2u and FHL film #6046695.

■ **1891 Tennessee State Census**. See *Enumeration of Male Inhabitants of Twenty-one Years of Age and Upward, Citizens of Tennessee, January 1, 1891, as Provided for by an Act of General Assembly of Tennessee, Passed January 15, 1891, and Approved January 22, 1891*, abstracted and indexed by Sue S. Reed, published by the author, Houston, TX, 1989, 7 vols., each volume indexed. Contents: v. 1: Anderson, Blount, Knox, and Sevier counties; v. 2. Benton, Carroll, Henry, Houston, and Stewart counties; v. 3. Dyer, Gibson, Lake, Obion, and Weakley counties; v. 4. Shelby county; v. 5. Cumberland, Fentress, Jackson, Loudon, Morgan, Overton, Putnam, Roane, and Scott counties; v. 6. Campbell, Clay, Hancock, Macon, Pickett, Smith and Trousdale counties; v. 7. Carter, Greene, Hawkins, Johnson, Sullivan, Unicoi, and Washington counties; v. 8. Cheatham, Dickson, Hickman, Humphreys, Lawrence, Lewis, Perry, Wayne and Williamson counties. FHL book 976.8 X2r v. 1-8.

Tennessee Censuses & Substitutes Online

The following databases are available online at these sites:

www.ancestry.com
- 1810 United States Federal Census
- 1820 United States Federal Census
- 1830 United States Federal Census
- 1840 United States Federal Census
- 1850 United States Federal Census
- 1860 United States Federal Census
- 1870 United States Federal Census
- 1880 United States Federal Census
- 1890 United States Federal Census Fragment
- 1910 United States Federal Census
- Abstract of Graves of Revolutionary Patriots
- Dickson County, Tennessee Marriages, 1850-70
- Greene County, Tennessee Cemetery Records
- Loudon County, Tennessee Cemetery Inscriptions
- Obituary Collection
- Social Security Death Index
- Tennessee Marriage and Bible Records
- Tennessee Marriages to 1825
- Tennessee Marriages, 1851-1900

www.censusfinder.com
- 1810-1891 Tennessee Census Records at Ancestry
- 1835 Tennessee Pension Roll – Statewide
- 1880 Federal Census - images
- 1880 Federal Census Search at Family Search
- 1908-1912 Tennessee Death Records Index
- 1914-1925 Tennessee Death Records Index
- RootsWeb Search
- Tennessee State Databases of Census & Genealogy Records

www.census-online.com
- 1840 Federal Census - Pensioners
- 1851 Chapman Rolls Eastern Cherokees

VIRGINIA

Censuses & Substitutes, 1600s - 1852

Virginia's earliest federal censuses do not provide much help to genealogist looking for ancestors there. The entire 1790 federal census was lost; and only two counties are extant for the 1800 federal census. For the 1810 census, about one fourth of its counties were lost. The first full statewide census which exists for Virginia is the 1820 federal census.

The state of Virginia has never taken a state census, so to find substitute lists of the names of inhabitants, one must turn to tax lists, land grants, deed indexes, and other name lists to find them. For example, back in 1908, the Census Bureau published the *Heads of Families* list of names for 1790 Virginia using extant county tax lists from 1782-1785. There are a few other published name lists for Virginia that have been compiled for the entire state, but to find the names of people living in Virginia before 1820, it is usually a matter of searching at the county level. The bibliography below identifies statewide census substitutes as well as a few county-wide lists for the early period.

■ *Virginia Colonial Records, 1600s-1700s*, CD-ROM publication, originally published by Broderbund, 1999, (Family Tree Maker Archives No. 503), **Contents**: *1623-1666, Early Virginia Immigrants*, by George Cabell Greer; *Some Emigrants to Virginia*, by W. G. Stanard (2nd edition, enlarged); *Virginia Colonial Abstracts, vols. I-III*, by Beverley Fleet; *Virginia Gleanings in England: Abstracts of 17th and 18th Century Wills and Administrations Relating to Virginia and Virginians*, by Lothrop Withington; *Colonial records of Virginia; The Colonial Virginia Register: A List of Governors, Councilors, and Other High Officials, and Also of Members of the House of Burgesses, and the Revolutionary Conventions of the Colony of Virginia*, compiled by William G. and Mary Newton Stanard; *English duplicates of Lost Virginia Records*, compiled by Louis de Cognets, Jr.; *Personal Names in Henings Statutes at Large of Virginia and Shepherd's Continuation*, by Joseph J. Casey; *Cavaliers and Pioneers: Abstracts of Virginia land Patents and Grants, 1623-1666*, Abstracted and Indexed by Nell Marion Nugent; *The Quit Rents of Virginia, 1704*, compiled by Annie Laurie Wright Smith; *List of Colonial Soldiers of Virginia; Virginia County Records, Vol. II: Virginia Colonial Militia, 1671-1776*, edited by William Armstrong Crozier; and *Virginia's Colonial Soldiers*, by Lloyd

DeWitt Bockstruck. See FHL CD-ROM No. 9, pt. 503.

■ *Virginia in the 1600's, an index to who was there!---and where!*, a serial publication compiled and edited by Harold Oliver, published by D&H Pub. Co., Riverside, CA, 1992. (FHL has only book 1, June 1992). From intro: "Each issue is arranged in alphabetical order and gives name, age if known, event, date, and source. Each contains a list of sources used by that issue to create the index. Periodical is a series of indexes to individuals named in various Virginia sources for the time period of the 1600's. Sources consist of immigration records, periodicals, court records, deeds, wills, historical accounts, tax records, and many other records." (It is not known whether any further books were produced under this title). Book 1: FHL book 975.5 H22v.

■ **1619-1930 References**. See **Virginia Historical Index: In Two Volumes**, Earl Gregg Swem, originally published Roanoke, Virginia: Stone Printing, 1934-1936, 2 vols. This is often referred to as "Swem's Index," an analysis of the information that relates to Virginians in the following periodicals and books: *The Virginia Magazine of History and Biography*, volumes 1-38, 1893-1930; the *William and Mary College Quarterly Historical Magazine*, first series, ... volumes 1-27, 1892-1919; the *William and Mary College Quarterly Historical Magazine*, second series, volumes 1-10, 1921-1930; *Tyler's Quarterly Historical and Genealogical Magazine*, volumes 1-10, 1919-1929; *Virginia Historical Register and Literary Advertiser*, volumes 1-6, 1848-1853; the *Lower Norfolk County Virginia Antiquary*, volumes 1-5, 1895-1906; *Hening's Statutes at Large*, ... 1619-1792, volumes 1-13; *Calendar of Virginia State Papers and other manuscripts preserved in the Capitol at Richmond, 1652-1869*, volumes 1-11."--V. 1, pref. Contents: v. 1. A-K -- v. 2. L-Z. FHL book 975.5 H22s v. 1-2 and FHL film #604696. See also *Virginia*

Historical Index, by E. G. Swem, digitized images of reprint published: Gloucester, Mass.: P. Smith, 1965. 2 v., published by Broderbund, 1998, Family Tree Maker's Family Archives, Genealogical Records, CD #202.

■ **1623-1990 Index to Land Patents and Grants,** microfilm of original records at the Virginia State Library, Richmond,. Filmed under the title: *Land Office Card Catalog 1623-1990: Patents and Grants.* Arranged by name of patentee (grantee), each card shows the date of patent (grant), the county in which the land was located when granted, the number of acres in each tract, a brief description of the property and the volume and beginning page where the record appears. Filmed by the Genealogical Society of Utah, 1991-1992, 55 rolls, beginning with FHL film #1854108 (ABC Enterprises – Antwerp).

■ *Cavaliers and Pioneers: A Calendar of Virginia Land Grants, 1623-1800,* compiled by Nell M. Nugent, published Dietz Print Co., Richmond, 1929-1931, 272 pages. Often referred to as "Nugent's List," which was his first list of the names of the founders of Virginia, based on the earliest land grants. This first edition was filmed by the Genealogical Society of Utah, 1991, 1 roll, FHL film #1320992. Over the years, additional volumes were added to form a seven-volume set. For the full series, see *Cavaliers and Pioneers: Abstracts of Virginia Land Patents and Grants.* The 1963, 1979, and 1983 editions of vol. 1 were published by Genealogical Publishing Company, Inc., Baltimore. Vols. 1-3 were abstracted and indexed by Nell Marion Nugent. Vol. 4 was abstracted by members of the Virginia Genealogical Society and edited by Denis Hudgins, while vols. 5-7 were edited by Dennis Ray Hudgins. Vols. 2-3 published by the Virginia State Library, Richmond. Vols. 4-7 published by the Virginia Genealogical Society, Richmond. Volumes are individually indexed. **Contents:** vol. 1: 1623-1666; vol. 2: 1666-1695; vol. 3: 1695-1732;

vol. 4: 1732-1741; vol. 5: 1741-1749; vol. 6: 1749-1762; and vol. 7: 1762-1776. FHL book 975.5 R2n v. 1-7. Also on microfilm: FHL film #1320779.

■ *1632-1800 Virginia Wills and Administrations: An Index of Wills Recorded in Local Courts of Virginia, 1632-1800, and of Administrations on Estates Shown by Inventories of the Estates of Intestates Recorded in Will (and other) Books of Local Courts, 1632-1800.* compiled by Clayton Torrence, originally published by William Byrd Press, Richmond, 1932, 483 pages. Filmed by the Genealogical Society of Utah, 1955, 1 roll, FHL film #29274; another filming FHL film #485954.

■ *Virginia in 1720: A Reconstructed Census,* by T.L.C. Genealogy, Miami Beach, FL, 1998, 221 pages. From intro: "This book, which is based on primary records (deeds, wills, tax lists, order books, etc.), is an alphabetical list of Virginia inhabitants, their county of residence, and the source of the information about them." FHL book 975.5 X22t 1720.

■ **1736-1820 Marriage and Obituary Notices.** See *Abstracts of Marriage and Obituary Notices in Virginia Newspapers Before 1820,* compiled by Viginius Cornick, microfilm of original records at the Virginia Historical Society in Richmond, Virginia. Abstracts are on cards which are in alphabetical order by name. Information on the cards varies but gives at least a name, the date of the event or newspaper, and the newspaper's name. Filmed by the Genealogical Society of Utah, 1987, 4 rolls, beginning with FHL film #1508537 (Abbot, Mrs. Josiah to Dean, Samuel).

■ *Virginia in 1740: A Reconstructed Census,* by T.L.C. Genealogy, Miami Beach, FL, 1992, 308 pages. From intro: "This book, which is based on deeds, wills, tax lists, order books, etc., is an alphabetical list of Virginia inhabitants, their county of residence, and the source of the information about them." FHL book 975.5 X22t

1740 and FHL film #697799.

■ *Virginia in 1760: A Reconstructed Census*, by T.L.C. Genealogy, Miami Beach, FL, 1996, 375 pages. From intro: "This book, which is based on primary records (deeds, wills, tax lists, order books, etc.), is an alphabetical list of Virginia inhabitants, their county of residence, and the source of the information about them." ISBN: 1574450204.

■ *Annals of Southwest Virginia, 1769-1800,* by Lewis Preston Summers, originally published by the author, Abingdon, VA, 1929, 2 vols. Reprinted by Southern Historical Press, Greenville, SC, 1992, 2 vols., 1,732 pages. Contains minutes of county courts, land surveys, wills, deeds, marriage licenses, list of forts and soldiers stationed therein, list of Revolutionary soldiers, etc. Covers the counties of Botetourt, Fincastle, Montgomery, Washington, and Wythe. FHL book 975.5 H2sL v. 1-2).

■ "A Short Census of Virginia, 1779," by William H. Dumont, photocopy of an article in the *National Genealogical Society*, Vol. 46, No. 4 (Dec 1958), p.163-211. From page 163: "A short census of Virginia for 1779 can be found in one of the old loan records of the United States Treasury. Over 4,200 Virginians turned in their paper money to the Virginia Loan office in 1779 and 1780." Tables 3-4 gives name, county and/or state, entry no., and amount deposited. Tables 1-2 and 5 are statistical. Table 2 also gives the county with its abbreviation. FHL book 975.5 X2p 1779 and FHL film 908198.

■ **1779-1978 Land Surveys; Index to Land Surveys, 1779-1924**, microfilm of original records of the Virginia Land Office now at the Virginia State Library, Richmond. Contains recorded plats and descriptions of lands on which grants have been issued since the establishment of the Commonwealth Land Office. The name of the individual for whom the survey was made, the

county in which the land was located, the number of acres in the tract, its metes and bounds, the date of the survey, and the names of the chain carriers and the surveyor are given. Accompanying papers, such as assignments, are recorded along with the survey, but accompanying warrants are not recorded. Filmed by the Virginia State Library, 1949, 92 rolls, beginning with FHL film #29542 (Index to surveys, 1779-1819).

■ **1779-1860 Bounty Warrants**, microfilm of original records at the Virginia State Library in Richmond. Filmed under the titles: Revolutionary War bounty warrants index, Revolutionary War bounty warrants. Includes typed card index. Contains documentation accepted for proof of military service. Filmed by the Genealogical Society of Utah, 1954, 31 rolls, beginning with FHL film #29850 (Index, Aaron, William to Payner, Wm.)

■ **1782-1785 List of Inhabitants (Virginia)**, microfilm of typescript and original records at the Virginia State Library in Richmond, Virginia. This series of original Virginia tax lists was used by the U.S. Census Bureau for its 1908 *Heads of Families* as a substitute for the lost 1790 Virginia federal census. There are lists for thirty-nine counties and the town of Williamsburg, Information found in the lists for 1782 and 1783 include the name of the head of the household, the number of white inhabitants, and the number of slaves, while the lists for 1784 and 1785 include the heads of households, the number of whites, and the numbers of dwelling houses and "outhouses." The lists were created by Virginia by four acts passed by the General Assembly. The county courts were to appoint justices to make lists of people in their precincts. The county court clerks were to collect the lists and send them to the Governor. The premise for the creation of these lists was taxation but they have been used as a census. **Contents:** Albermarle 1785; Amelia 1782, 1785; Amherst 1783, 1785;

Bedford 1783 (summary only); Charlotte 1782 (summary only), 1783; Chesterfield 1783; Cumberland 1782, 1784; Essex 1783; Fairfax 1782, 1785; Fluvanna 1782; Frederick 1782; Gloucester 1783, 1784; Greenbrier 1783; Greensville 1783, 1785; Halifax 1782, 1784; Hampshire 1782, 1784; Hanover 1782; Harrison 1785; Isle of Wight 1782; Lancaster 1783, 1785; Mecklenburg 1782; Middlesex 1783; Monongalia 1782; Nansemond 1783, 1784, 1785; New Kent 1782, 1784; Norfolk 1782, 1784, 1785; Northumberland 1782, 1784; Orange 1782, 1785; Pittsylvania 1782, 1785; Powhatan 1783; Prince Edward 1783, 1785; Princess Anne 1783, 1785; Richmond 1783; Rockingham 1784; Shenandoah 1783, 1785; Southampton 1783, 1785; Stafford 1785; Surry 1782, 1784; Sussex 1782; Warwick 1782, 1784; Williamsburg City 1782. Filmed by the Genealogical Society of Utah, 1992, 1 roll, FHL film #1854091. The extracted name lists in the *Heads of Families* printed volume can be found on FHL film #29681 (Heads of families at the first census of the United States taken in the year 1790: records of the state enumerations, 1782-1785, Virginia).

■ *1785 Botetourt County, Virginia, Enumeration*, copied and indexed by Charles T. Burton, published by mimeograph, Troutville, Virginia, 197?, 11 pages. Includes index. "The area enumerated included all or parts of the present-day counties of Botetourt, Alleghany, Bath, Craig, and Roanoke." Gives name of family, number of white people in family, number of dwellings, and number of other buildings. FHL book 975.583 X2b and FHL film #928249.

■ **1787 Virginia Tax Lists**. See *The 1787 Census of Virginia: An Accounting of the Name of Every White Male Tithable Over 21 Years, the Number of White Males Between 16 & 21 Years, the Number of Slaves Over 16 & Those Under 16 Years, Together With a Listing of Their Horses, Cattle & Carriages, and Also the Names of all Persons to Whom Ordinary Licenses and*

Physician's Licenses Were Issued, compiled by Netti Schreiner-Yantis and Florene Speakman Love. Published by Genealogical Books in Print, Springfield, VA, 1987, 3 vols. Includes records presently in the states of Kentucky and West Virginia. FHL book 975.5 R4sn, 3 vols.

■ *1809-1848 Burned County Data, as Found in the Virginia Contested Election Files*, compiled by Benjamin B. Weisiger, III, published by the author, Richmond, VA, 1986, 103 pages. The depositions regarding qualifications of the voters are from the counties of Hanover, Buckingham, Charles City, Gloucester, New Kent, James City and Caroline. Contains information about land ownership, age, length of residence in the county, and other information. This other information were proofs of status from attached wills, deeds, marriage data, Bible records, etc. Voter or poll lists were not included in book because they were too lengthy. Includes index. FHL book 975.5 P2w and FHL film #1697900.

■ *A Supplement to the 1810 Census of Virginia: Tax Lists of the Counties for Which the Census is Missing*, transcribed and edited by Netti Schreiner-Yantis, published by Genealogical Books in Print, Springfield, VA, 1971, 324 pages. FHL book 975.5 R4s.

■ *1815 Directory of Virginia Landowners (and Gazetteer)*, abstracted by Roger G. Ward, published by Iberian Publishing Co., Athens, GA, 1997-2000, 6 vols. Arranged in alphabetical order within each county. **Contents:** vol. 1: Central region (comprising the counties of Albemarle, Amelia, Amherst, Buckingham, Charles City, Chesterfield, Cumberland, Dinwiddie, Fluvanna, Goochland, Hanover, Henrico, Louisa, Nelson, New Kent, Nottoway, Powhatan, Prince George, & the independent cities of Petersburg and Richmond); vol. 2: South central region (comprising the counties of Bedford, Brunswick, Campbell, Charlotte, Franklin, Greensville, Halifax, Henry, Lunenburg, Mecklenburg,

Patrick, Pittsylvania, Prince Edward, Southampton, and Susses; vol. 3: Eastern region (comprising the counties of Accomack, Caroline, Elizabeth City, Essex, Gloucester, Isle of Wight, James City, King and Queen, King George, King William, Lancaster, Mathews, Middlesex, Nansemond, Norfolk, Northampton, Northumberland, Princess Ann, Richmond, Surry, Warwick, Westmoreland, and York, and the independent city of Norfolk) -- vol. 4: Northern region (comprising the counties of Alexandria, Culpeper, Fairfax, Fauquier, Frederick, Independent City of Alexandria, Independent City of Fredericksburg, Independent City of Winchester, Loudoun, Madison, Orange, Prince William, Rockingham, Shenandoah, Spotsylvania and Stafford); vol. 5: Southwest region (comprising the following counties of Augusta, Bath, Botetourt, Giles, Grayson, Greenbrier, Lee, Monroe, Montgomery, Pendleton, Rockbridge, Russell, Scott, Tazewell, Washington, and Wythe, and the independent city of Staunton); and vol. 6: Northwest region (comprising the counties of Berkeley, Brooke, Cabell, Hampshire, Hardy, Harrison, Jefferson, Kanawha, Mason, Monongalia, Ohio, Pendleton, Randolph, Tyler, and Wood). Includes Given name, personal identifiers (if any); location/place-name of land; and miles/direction from the 1815 courthouse. FHL book 975 E4w, vol. 1-6.

■ *Virginia Tax Records: From the Virginia Magazine of History and Biography, the William and Mary College Quarterly, and Tyler's Quarterly*, with an index by Gary Parks, published by Genealogical Publishing Co., Inc., Baltimore, 1983, 663 pages. Excerpted and reprinted with added publisher's note, contents, and index. FHL book 975.5 R4v.

■ *1828-1938 Index to Marriage Notices in the Religious Herald*, prepared by the Historical Records Survey of Virginia, Division of Community Service Programs, Works Projects Administration, 1941. Reprinted by Genealogical Pub. Co., 1996, 316 pages. The *Religious Herald* was published in Richmond, Virginia, as a weekly newspaper since January 1828. FHL book 975.5 V22in.

■ *Index to Marriage Notices in the Southern Churchman, 1835-1941*, prepared by the Historical Records Survey of Virginia, Service Division, Work Projects Administration, sponsored by the Virginia Conservation Commission. 1942, 2 vols., Vol. 1: A-K; Vol. 2: L-Z. FHL book 975.5 V22i, v.1&2 and FHL film #908352.

■ *Index to the Virginia Genealogist: Volumes 1-20, 1957-1976*, compiled by John Frederick Dorman, published by Genealogical Books in Print, Springfield, VA, 1981, 941 pages. FHL book 975.5 B2vg v. 1-20 index.

■ *Index to the Virginia Genealogist: Volumes 21-35, 1977-1992*, compiled by John Frederick Dorman, published by the author, Falmouth, VA, 1994, 1,011 pages. FHL book 975.5 B2vg v. 21-35 index.

■ **1861-1865 Military Records**. See *Index to Compiled Service Records of Confederate Soldiers Who Served in Organizations From the State of Virginia*, microfilm of original records in The National Archives, Washington, D.C., filmed by the National Archives, series M0382, 62 rolls, beginning with FHL film #881395 (Index, A-Am).

■ **1861-1865 Military Records**. See *Index to Compiled Service Records of Volunteer Union Soldiers Who Served in Organizations From the State of Virginia*, microfilm of original records in the National Archives. Filmed by the National Archives, series M0394, 1 roll, FHL film #881594.

■ *1852 Elliott & Nye's Virginia Directory and Business Register*, by Elliott & Nye, printers, microfilm of originals published by Research

Publications, Woodbridge, CT, 1980-1984, 7 microfiches, FHL film #6044617.

Virginia Censuses & Substitutes Online

The following databases are available online at these sites:

www.ancestry.com

- 1810 United States Federal Census
- 1820 United States Federal Census
- 1830 United States Federal Census
- 1840 United States Federal Census
- 1850 United States Federal Census
- 1860 United States Federal Census
- 1870 United States Federal Census
- 1880 United States Federal Census
- 1910 United States Federal Census
- 1920 United States Federal Census
- 1930 United States Federal Census
- Rockingham County, Virginia Census, 1900
- Virginia 1910 Census Miracode Index
- Virginia Census, 1800-90
- Vitelli Soundex of the U.S. Census
- Abstract of Graves of Revolutionary Patriots
- Accomack County, Virginia Births, 1853-65
- Accomack County, Virginia Births, 1866-73
- Accomack County, Virginia Births, 1874-77
- Accomack County, Virginia Births, 1878-81
- Accomack County, Virginia Births, 1882-92
- Accomack County, Virginia Births, 1893-96
- Albemarle County, Virginia Births, 1886-89
- Albemarle County, Virginia Births, 1890-96
- Albemarle, Virginia Record of Families, 1744-1890
- Virginia Court, Land, Probate Records
- English Origins of American Colonists
- New Kent County, Virginia Land Tax Records, 1782
- Norfolk County, Virginia Will Abstracts, 1710-53
- Prince William County, Virginia Wills, Part 1, 1734-1925
- Prince William County, Virginia Wills, Part 2, 1734-1920
- Shenandoah County, Virginia Wills, 1771-91
- Spotsylvania, Virginia County Records, 1721-1800
- U.S. House of Representatives Private Claims, Vol. 1
- U.S. House of Representatives Private Claims, Vol. 2
- U.S. House of Representatives Private Claims, Vol. 3
- Virginia County Records, Volume IX
- Virginia County Records, Volume VI
- Virginia County Records, Volume VII
- Westmoreland County, Virginia Wills, 1654-1800
- 1994 Phone and Address Directory
- 2000 Phone and Address Directory
- Danville, Virginia Directories, 1888-93
- Norfolk, Virginia Directories, 1888-1891
- Presbyterian Ministerial Directory 1898
- Protestant Episcopal Church Clerical Directory, 1898
- Richmond, Virginia City Directories, 1889-90
- U.K. and U.S. Directories, 1680-1830
- Virginia Periodicals & Newspapers
- Daily Index (Petersburg, Virginia) Daily Index, The (Petersburg, Virginia)
- PERiodical Source Index
- Petersburg Daily Index (Petersburg, Virginia)
- Petersburg Index, The (Petersburg, Virginia)
- Richmond, Virginia Newspaper Obituaries, 1804-38
- Virginia Genealogical Society Quarterly
- Virginia Military Records
- American Civil War Battle Summaries
- American Civil War General Officers
- American Civil War Regiments
- American Civil War Soldiers American Revolutionary War Rejected Pensions
- American Soldiers of World War I
- Civil War Pension Index
- Civil War Service Records
- Confederate States Field Officers
- Korean Conflict Death Index

www.censusfinder.com

- 1600s Irish Immigrants to America
- 1704-1705 Rent Roll of Virginia
- Revolutionary War Pensioners Surnames A-K Statewide Index
- Revolutionary War Pensioners Surnames L-Z Statewide Index
- 1800-1890 Virginia Census Records at Ancestry
- 1810 Federal Census Statewide Extraction of "Other Free" Heads of Households
- 1835 Pension Roll - Statewide
- 1840 Pensioners Census
- 1861 Members of the Virginia Convention

- 1880 Federal Census - images
- 1880 Federal Census Search at Family Search
- 1890 Union Veterans Census of Southwest Virginia Counties
- Virginia State Databases of Genealogy and Census Records

www.census-online.com

- 1790 Tax List
- 1800 Tax List
- 1840 Federal Census - Veterans
- 1704 Virginia Rent Rolls

WEST VIRGINIA

Censuses & Substitutes, 1600s - 1900

At the time of West Virginia's first settlements in the mid 1770s, county government for the area was in Augusta, Botetourt, Hampshire, and Frederick counties, Virginia. Early tax lists, deed lists, and other name list for the early counties provide census substitutes prior to the Revolutionary War. Since West Virginia separated from Virginia in 1863, there have been no state censuses taken. Statewide census substitutes are shown below along with county-wide tax lists for the pre-1802 Virginia counties making up the area of modern West Virginia.

■ **1600s-1900s Census Substitutes**. See *Early West Virginia settlers, 1600s-1900s,* CD-ROM publication, originally published by Broderbund in collaboration with the Genealogical Publishing Co., Inc., Baltimore, 2000, part of Family Tree Makers's Family Archives, CD No. 520. **Contents**: *Genealogies of West Virginia Families: From the West Virginia Historical Magazine Quarterly, 1901-1905; Cabell County Annals and Families,* by George Selden Wallace; *Capon Valley: Its Pioneers and Their Descendants, 1648 to 1940,* by Maud Pugh (vols. I-II); *Genealogy of Some Early Families in Grant and Pleasant Districts, Preston County, West Virginia; Greenbrier Pioneers and Their Homes,* by Ruth Woods Dayton; *Roane*

County, West Virginia Families, by William H. Bishop; *Pioneers and Their Homes in the Upper Kanawha,* by Ruth Woods Dayton ; *Marriage Records of Berkeley County, Virginia For the Period 1781-1854, Located at Berkeley County Court House, Martinsburg, WV,* compiled and edited by Guy L. Keesecker; *Mason County, West Virginia, Marriages, 1806-1915,* compiled and edited by Julie Chapin Hesson, Sherman Gene Hesson, & Jane J. Russell; *Early Records, Hampshire County, Virginia, now West Virginia,* compiled by Clara McCormack Sage and Laura Sage Jones; *West Virginia Estate Settlements: An Index to Wills, Inventories, Appraisements, Land Grants, and Surveys to 1850,* compiled by Ross B. Johnson; *West Virginia Revolutionary Ancestors: Whose Services Were Non-military, and Whose Names, Therefore, Do Not Appear in Revolutionary Indexes of Soldiers and Sailors,* compiled by Anne Waller Ready; *West Virginians in the American Revolution,* compiled by Ross B. Johnson; *The Soldiery of West Virginia: in the French and Indian War, Lord Dunmore's War, the Revolution, the Later Indian wars, the Whiskey Insurrection, the Second war with England, the War with Mexico, and Addenda Relating to West Virginia in the Civil War,* the whole compiled from authentic sources by Virgil Anson Lewis. FHL CD-ROM No. 9 pt. 520.

■ **1777-1850 Census Substitutes**, see *Early West Virginia Wills,* compiled by K. T. H. McFarland, published by Closson Press, Apollo, PA, 1993. Includes surname indexes. Contains abstracts of wills for the northwestern-most section of what is now West Virginia. Shows name of deceased or estate; names of heirs, executors, witnesses; date of will and date probated. Contents: v. 1. Ohio Co., 1777-1850 -- Marshall Co., 1835-1850 -- Tyler Co., 1815-1850 -- Wetzel Co., 1847-1850 -- Doddridge co., 1849-1850. FHL book 975.4 P28m.

■ **1787 Virginia Tax Lists**. For West Virginia counties, see *The 1787 Census of Virginia: An Accounting of the Name of Every White Male Tithable Over 21 Years, the Number of White*

Males Between 16 & 21 Years, the Number of Slaves Over 16 & Those Under 16 Years, Together With a Listing of Their Horses, Cattle & Carriages, and Also the Names of all Persons to Whom Ordinary Licenses and Physician's Licenses Were Issued, compiled by Netti Schreiner-Yantis and Florene Speakman Love. Published by Genealogical Books in Print, Springfield, VA, 1987, 3 vols. Includes records presently in the states of Kentucky and West Virginia. FHL book 975.5 R4sn, 3 vols.

■ **1782-1907 Land Book, Berkeley County, Virginia/West Virginia**, microfilm of original records at the State Auditor's Office, Charleston, West Virginia. Lists of landowners subject to taxation. Each book organized by surname in loose alphabetical order. Filmed by the Genealogical Society of Utah, 1968, 15 rolls, beginning with FHL film #531232 (Land book, 1782-1803). See also, *Land owners, Berkeley County: 1784-1799*, microfilm of index prepared by the Historical Records Survey, WPA, 1940. Includes Berkeley County index to wills, inventories, sale bills, etc., a typewritten list of names only, arranged by year. Filmed by the Genealogical Society of Utah, 1958, 1 roll, FHL film #163713.

■ **1782-1850 Personal Property Tax Lists, Greenbrier County, Virginia**, microfilm of original records at the Virginia State Library in Richmond, Virginia. Tax lists give name of person taxed or tithed, type and amount of taxable property, amount of tax, and the county statistics. Greenbrier County kept taxpayers lists by years, 1782 one list, 1783 five lists, 1784 two lists, 1785-1786 one list, 1787-1798 two lists, 1799-1800 one list. From 1801-1850 they kept two lists. Filmed by the Virginia State Library, 1986, 3 rolls, beginning with FHL film #2024557 (Tax lists, 1782-1816).

■ **1782-1860 Hampshire County, Virginia.** See *Early Records, Hampshire County, Virginia, now*

West Virginia: Including at the Start Most of Known Va. Aside From Augusta District, by Clara McCormack Sage and Laura Elisabeth Sage Jones, printed by the Delavan Republican, Delavan, WI, 1939, 138 pages. Contains a synopsis of wills from originals up to 1860; grantee with acreage-location, wife's name and witnesses; grantor deeds up to 1800; marriage records 1824-1828 and alphabetical arrangement of state census 1782 and 1784; Revolutionary soldiers pensions residing in the county 1835. FHL book 975.495 R2s and FHL film #833355.

■ **1782 Census, Hampshire County, Virginia (now West Virginia).** See *The First Census of Hampshire County*, a booklet prepared by the West Virginia Workers of the Federal Writers' Project, Works Progress Administration, microfilm of original published: Romney, WV: School for the Deaf and the Blind, 1937, 68 pages. In 1782, when the first census was taken, Hampshire County included within its boundaries the counties of Hardy, Grant, Mineral and portions of Morgan and Pendleton. Filmed by the Genealogical Society of Utah, 1990, 1 rolls, FHL film #1697283.

■ **1783-1900 Land Tax (with Hardy County Births), Hardy County, Virginia/West Virginia**, microfilm of name index in the W. Guy Tetrick Collection, Clarksburg, West Virginia, prepared by the Historical Records Survey, WPA, 1940. A typewritten list of names. Filmed by the Genealogical Society of Utah, 1958, 1 roll, FHL film #163718.

■ **1783-1850 Personal Property Tax Lists, Monongalia County, Virginia**, microfilm of original records at the Virginia State Library and Archives in Richmond, Virginia. Arranged in alphabetical order by the first letter of the surname within each year Lists give name of person taxed or tithed, type and amount of taxable property, amount of tax, and the county statistics. Filmed by the Genealogical Society of

Utah, 1992, 3 rolls, beginning with FHL film #1854104 (Tax lists, 1783-1821).

■ **1785-1850 Personal Property Tax lists, Harrison County, Virginia**, microfilm of original records at the Virginia State Library in Richmond, Virginia. Tax lists give name of person taxed or tithed, type and amount of taxable property, amount of tax, and the county statistics. Harrison County kept one list of taxpayers per year from 1785 to 1799, they kept two lists from 1800-1850. Filmed by the Virginia State Library, 1986, 4 rolls, beginning with FHL film #2024579 (Tax lists, 1785-1808).

■ **1787-1850 Personal Property Tax Lists, Randolph County, Virginia**, microfilm of original records at the Virginia State Library and Archives in Richmond, Virginia. Lists 1787-1802 are arranged in alphabetical order by the first letter of the first or given name within each year. Lists 1803-1850 are arranged in alphabetical order by the first letter of the surname within each year. Lists give name of person taxed or tithed, type and amount of taxable property, amount of tax, and the county statistics. Filmed by the Genealogical Society of Utah, 1992, 2 rolls, beginning with FHL film #1905702 (Tax lists 1787-1829).

■ **1789-1850 Personal Property Tax Lists, Pendleton County, Virginia**, microfilm of original records at the Virginia State Library and Archives in Richmond, Virginia. Arranged in alphabetical order by the first letter of the surname for each year. Lists give name of person taxed or tithed, type and amount of taxable property, amount of tax, and the county statistics. Filmed by the Genealogical Society of Utah, 1992, 3 rolls, beginning with FHL film #1870195 (Tax lists, 1789-1816).

■ **1792-1850 Personal Property Tax Lists, Kanawha County**, Virginia, microfilm of original records at the Virginia State Library in Richmond, Virginia. Tax lists give name of person taxed or tithed, type and amount of taxable property, amount of tax, and the county statistics. Kanawha County kept one list from 1792 to 1850, with some of the years missing, 1794-1795, 1797-1800. Filmed by the Virginia State Library, 1986, 3 rolls, beginning with FHL film #2024596 (Tax lists, 1792-1832).

■ **1797-1899 Records, Pendleton County, Virginia/West Virginia**, microfilm of original typescripts at the County Clerk's Office, Pendleton County, West Virginia, for Births, 1853-1862; deaths, 1853-1892; land owners; 1789-1804; voters, 1790-1797; surveys, 1789-1797; marriages, 1843-1899; and wills, etc., 1791-1818, 1825-1899. FHL film #464975.

■ **1797-1851 Personal Property Tax Lists, Brooke County, Virginia**, microfilm of original records at the Virginia State Library in Richmond, Virginia. Tax lists give name of person taxed or tithed, type and amount of taxable property, amount of tax, and the county statistics. Brooke County kept two taxpayers lists per year. Filmed by the Virginia State Library, 1986, 3 rolls, beginning with FHL film #2024492 (Tax lists, 1797-1804).

■ **1799-1850 Personal Property Tax Lists, Monroe County, Virginia**, microfilm of original records at the Virginia State Library and Archives in Richmond, Virginia. Arranged in alphabetical order by the first letter of the surname within each year. Lists give name of person taxed or tithed, type and amount of taxable property, amount of tax, and the county statistics. Filmed by the Genealogical Society of Utah, 1992, 2 rolls, beginning with FHL film #1854107 (Tax lists, 1799-1834).

■ **1800 Census Substitute**. See *Virginians in 1800, Counties of West Virginia*, by Steven A. Bridges, published by the author, Trumbull, CT, 1987, 167 pages. Includes name lists taken from tax assessment lists of Virginia counties that became West Virginia. FHL book 975.4 R4b.

■ **1801-1850 Personal Property Tax Lists, Wood County**, Virginia, microfilm of original records at the Virginia State Library in Richmond, Virginia. Tax lists give name of person taxed or tithed, type and amount of taxable property, amount of tax, and the county statistics. Wood County kept two taxpayers lists per year. Filmed by the Virginia State Library, 1986, 3 rolls, beginning with FHL film #2026409 (Tax lists, 1801-1830).

■ *A Supplement to the 1810 Census of Virginia: Tax Lists of the Counties for Which the Census is Missing*, transcribed and edited by Netti Schreiner-Yantis, published by Genealogical Books in Print, Springfield, VA, 1971, 324 pages. Includes tax lists for the lost (West Virginia) counties of Cabell, Greenbrier, Hardy, and Tazewell. FHL book 975.5 R4s.

■ **1811-1850 Personal Property Tax Lists, Ohio County, Virginia**, microfilm of original records at the Virginia State Library and Archives in Richmond, Virginia. Arranged in alphabetical order by the first letter of the surname for each year. Lists give name of person taxed or tithed, type and amount of taxable property, amount of tax, and the county statistics. Some of the census years have two lists, one for the upper district and one for the lower district. Filmed by the Genealogical Society of Utah, 1992, 3 rolls, beginning with FHL film #1870185 (Tax lists, 1811-1814).

■ **1862-1866 Internal Revenue Assessment Lists for West Virginia**, microfilm of originals at the National Archives. Includes an index of what counties are on which rolls and which kinds of reports are involved. Records include place of residence. Front of each roll includes an

explanation of the set. Morgan, Berkley, Jefferson, Hampshire and Hardy counties are with district 3 of Virginia for 1862. District 1 - Established 10 Oct. 1862 with Brooke, Hancock, Marion, Marshall, Ohio, Pleasants, Preston, Taylor Tyler & Wetzel counties. Reorganized 3 May 1865 with Brooke, Calhoun, Dodderidge, Gilmer, Hancock, Harrison, Marion, Marshall, Ohio, Pleasants, Ritchie, Roane, Tyler, Wetzel & Wirt counties. Louis County transferred to District 1 on 1 Aug. 1865 and Wood County on Mar. 14, 1866. District 2 - Established 10 Oct 1862 with Barbour, Braxton, Cabell, Calhoun, Clay, Kanawha, Lewis, Mason, Putnam, Randolph, Ritchie, Roane, Tucker, Upshur, Webster, Wirt & Wood counties. Reorganized 3 May 1865 with Barbour, Berkeley, Hampshire, Hardy, Jefferson, Lewis, Monongalia, Morgan, Pendleton, Pocahontas, Preston, Randolph, Taylor, Tucker, Upshur & Webster counties. Marion County transferred here 1 Aug. 1865. District 3 - Established 3 May 1865 with Boone, Braxton, Cabell, Clay, Fayette, Greenbrier, Jackson, Kanawha, Logan, McDowell, Mason, Mercer, Monroe, Nicholas, Putnam, Raleigh, Wayne, Wood and Wyoming counties. Districts are divided into divisions. The number of these may vary. Some may be missing or not be filmed in order. Filmed by the National Archives, 1972, series M0795, 4 rolls, beginning with FHL #1578241 (District 1).

■ **1899-1900 Directory**. See *Pruden's Combined Business Directory and Gazetteer: Embracing the Following Cities: Wheeling, Sistersville, Parkersburg, Huntington, Charleston, &c., &c., W. Va., East Liverpool, Steubenville, Bellaire, Marietta, Ironton, Portsmouth, Ohio, and Ashland and Catlettsburg, Ky., for the Years 1899-1900*, by M.M. Pruden, compiler, published, Pruden Pub. Co, Charleston, WV, 1900, 353 pages. Filmed by the Genealogical Society of Utah, 1973, 1 roll, FHL film #940405.

West Virginia Censuses & Substitutes Online

The following databases are available online at these sites:

www.ancestry.com
- 1810 United States Federal Census
- 1820 United States Federal Census
- 1830 United States Federal Census
- 1840 United States Federal Census
- 1850 United States Federal Census
- 1860 United States Federal Census
- 1870 United States Federal Census
- 1880 United States Federal Census
- 1910 United States Federal Census
- 1920 United States Federal Census
- 1930 United States Federal Census
- The Charleston Daily Mail (Charleston, West Virginia)
- West Virginia Marriage Records, 1863-1900
- American Revolutionary War Rejected Pensions
- Bluefield Daily Telegraph (Bluefield, West Virginia)

www.censusfinder.com
- 1860-90 West Virginia Census Search Engine at Ancestry
- 1880 Federal Census - Search and View the images
- 1880 Federal Census Search at Family Search
- West Virginia Statewide Databases of Census & Genealogy Records

www.census-online.com
- 1810 Federal Census Index (VA)
- Links to county databases (no. of links):

Barbour (8); Berkeley (3); Boone (7); Braxton (8); Brooke (6); Cabell (8); Calhoun (9); Clay (6); Doddridge (3); Fayette (3); Gilmer (3); Grant (3); Greenbrier (12); Hampshire (17); Hancock (1); Hardy (5); Harrison (2); Jackson (3); Jefferson (2); Kanawha (16); Lewis (7); Lincoln (5); Logan (21); Marion (12); Marshall (11); Mason (6); McDowell (4); Mercer (0); Mineral (3); Mingo (5); Monongalia (3); Monroe (22); Morgan (5); Nicholas (16); Ohio (19); Pendleton (29); Pleasants (7); Pocahontas (5); Preston (3); Putnam (1); Raleigh (10); Randolph (15); Ritchie (15); Roane (2); Summers (0); Taylor (2); Tucker (5); Tyler (10); Upshur (3); Wayne (11); Webster (15); Wetzel (10); Wirt (4); Wood (8); and Wyoming (13).

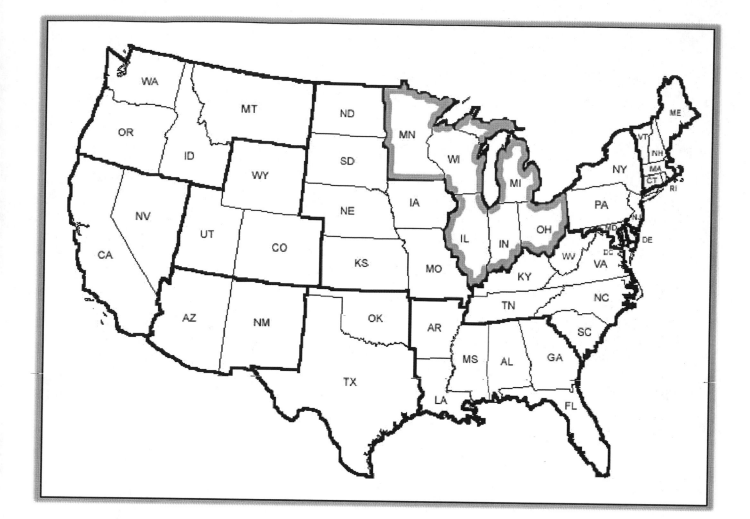

Chapter 5E – The Old Northwest

Illinois, Indiana, Michigan, Minnesota
Ohio, and Wisconsin

Historical Timeline for the Old Northwest

1614-1615 Ohio Country. Samuel de Champlain, governor of New France and the founder of Québec, was believed to be the first of the French explorers to visit the Ohio country. He is believed to have seen the Maumee River in 1614 or 1615.

1668 Great Lakes region. Jacques Marquette and Claude Dablon establish the first mission at Sault Sainte Marie.

1670 Great Lakes region. René-Robert Cavelier explores and claims the Ohio country for France.

1673 Mississippi River. French explorers Marquette and Jolliet discover the upper portion of the Mississippi River. They then descend the Mississippi to the Arkansas River and return to present-day Wisconsin via the Illinois River.

1675 Illinois Country. Marquette founds a mission at the Great Village of the Illinois River, near present Utica, Illinois.

1680 Illinois Country. French traders Cavelier, LaSalle, and deTonti build Fort Crèvecoeur on the Illinois River, near present-day Peoria.

1696 Illinois Country. Jesuit priest Pierre François Pinet establishes a mission at present-day Chicago.

1699 Illinois Country. Québec priests found a mission at Cahokia, the first permanent settlement in the Illinois country.

1717. Illinois becomes part of the French colony of Louisiana.

1721 Indiana. Fort Philippe, later called Fort Miami, was built on the St. Mary's River, near present Fort Wayne, where the St. Mary's, St. Joseph's and Maumee Rivers meet.

1732 Indiana. Vincennes established, becoming Indiana's first permanent settlement.

1750 Ohio Country. The Ohio Company of Virginia asserts the British claim to the Ohio region for England, and begins sending fur trading parties to the area. The British encroachment into "New France" leads to a war between England and France.

1756-1763 French and Indian War in North America. In Europe, it was called the "Seven Years War." Britain was declared the winner at the Treaty of Paris of 1763. As a result, the French surrendered all land in North America to Britain. Britain's ally, Spain, received Louisiana from France in compensation for its loss of Florida during the Seven Years War. Great Britain wins and retains its claim to all of Canada and all of the rest of North America east of the Mississippi River. The Brits rename the entire area "British North America."

1764 Wisconsin Country. Charles Langlade settled at Green Bay, the first permanent settlement in present-day Wisconsin.

1774 Québec Act. After deciding not to repeat the evacuation of all French Acadians from Nova Scotia in the mid 1750s, the British Parliament passed the Québec Act, permitting the French Canadians to retain French laws and customs, and allowing the Catholic Church to maintain all its rights. The early French settlements in present-day Michigan, Indiana, Illinois and Wisconsin, were by the act included in the Province of Québec, under British rule.

1783. Post-Revolutionary War. The 1783 Treaty of Paris recognizing the United States of America as an independent nation defined its borders from the Atlantic Ocean to the Mississippi River. Although the settlements in the Great Lakes region (formerly part of the Province of Québec) were to be included within the United States, British military forces continued to maintain control of much of the Great Lakes area for several years after the Revolution.

1781 Wisconsin Country. First American settlement at Prairie du Chien, on the Mississippi River.

1784 Ohio Country. Connecticut, Virginia and Massachusetts relinquish their claim to lands in the Ohio Country. Title transferred to the "public domain" of the United States Government. Connecticut retains ownership of the "Western Reserve" on Lake Erie, then sells the tract to the Connecticut Land Company in 1795.

1787 Northwest Territory. The Ordinance of 1787 establishes the "Territory Northwest of the River Ohio," and defines the procedure for any territory to obtain statehood. Present states carved out of the original area of the Northwest Territory include Ohio, Indiana, Illinois, Michigan, Wisconsin, and that part of Minnesota east of the Mississippi River.

1787-1812 Flatboat Travelers. The main transportation on the Ohio River beginning at Pittsburgh or Wheeling was flatboats and rafts constructed of lumber and nails that could be disassembled by a migrating family when they arrived at their new homesite along the Ohio River and tributaries. The flatboat era continued until steamboats were first introduced on the Ohio River in 1812.

1788 Ohio Country. Marietta was Ohio's first permanent settlement. It was founded in 1788 by General Rufus Putnam and named in honor of Marie Antoinette. Putman's New Ohio Company purchased a large tract of land above the Ohio River and sold parcels to the first settlers of Ohio, most of whom arrived at Marietta by flatboat via Pittsburgh.

1795. Treaty of Greenville ends the Indian Wars in Ohio. The "Greenville Line" defined the extent of areas opened to settlement by whites (about three-fourths of present-day Ohio).

1796 Great Lakes Region. The British evacuate Detroit and abandon their posts on the Great Lakes, the last of the British hold-outs in the Old Northwest.

1800. Indiana Territory was established from the Northwest Territory with William Henry Harrison as the first Governor and Vincennes the capital. Area included all of present-day Indiana, Illinois, Wisconsin, and the western half of Michigan. The Northwest Territory was reduced to the present-day area of Ohio and the eastern half of Michigan.

1803. Ohio admitted to the Union as the 17th state, with Chillicothe as the state capital. The portion of Michigan included in the Northwest Territory 1800-1803 became part of Indiana Territory. Upon Ohio's statehood, the name Northwest Territory was dropped.

1804 Louisiana District (Minnesota Portion). The United States purchases Louisiana from France in 1803, land described as "the drainage of the Mississippi and Missouri Rivers." Louisiana District, created in 1804, included that portion of present-day Minnesota west of the Mississippi River.

1805. Michigan Territory separated from the Indiana Territory. The original area was between Lake Michigan and Lake Huron, as today, but did not include the Upper Peninsula, which was still under control of Indiana Territory.

1809. Illinois Territory separated from Indiana Territory, with Kaskaskia the capital. The original area included present-day Illinois, Wisconsin, a portion of the Upper Peninsula of Michigan, and that portion of Minnesota east of the Mississippi River.

1810 Ohio. Zanesville named state capital of Ohio.

1811 Battle of Tippecanoe (Indiana). Tecumseh defeated at the Battle of Tippecanoe. American forces were led by William Henry Harrison, who later gained the presidential nickname "Tippecanoe." The victory over a large force of Indians opened up much of Indiana for settlement.

1812 Ohio. Fort Meigs constructed to protect Ohio from invasion during the War of 1812.

1812-1815 Steamboats. First introduced in 1812, by 1815 steamboats had quickly become the main mode of transportation on the Ohio and Mississippi Rivers.

1816 Ohio. Columbus named state capital of Ohio.

1816 Wisconsin Country. The establishment of Fort Howard at Green Bay and Fort Shelby rebuilt at Prairie du Chien (renamed Fort Crawford), opens the region to settlement.

1813 Indiana Territory. Capital moved to Corydon.

1814 Treaty of Ghent. The War of 1812 ended, freeing up American settlement of the Old Northwest.

1816. Indiana becomes the 19th state with the same boundaries as today. The state capital was at Corydon.

1818. Illinois becomes the 21st state, with the same boundaries as today. Kaskaskia was the first state capital.

1818 Minnesota Country. By treaty with Britain, the northern boundary of Minnesota was set at the 49th parallel.

1825 Indiana. Indianapolis becomes the state capital of Indiana.

1825 Erie Canal opened. This New York route from the Hudson River to Lake Erie provided direct access to the Ohio Country. Western New

York and the State of Ohio were impacted the most, with many settlements attributed to the early Erie Canal travelers.

1830s Wisconsin Country. Heavy settlement began along the Lake Michigan shoreline at the sites of present-day Milwaukee, Racine, and Kenosha.

1835 Toledo War. Boundary disputes cause the "Toledo War" over the Michigan-Ohio boundary. Michigan was not admitted to the Union because she would not surrender her claim to the Toledo strip. As an adjoining state, Ohio asserted its veto power over the first attempt for statehood for Michigan Territory. The disputed area was finally surrendered in exchange for the western section of the Upper Peninsula. Ohio gained the Toledo strip from Michigan, and Michigan gained the Upper Peninsula (from Indiana). Ohio gave up nothing and was the clear winner of the "Toledo War."

1836. Wisconsin Territory created, which included unpopulated lands west of the Mississippi River to the Missouri River until 1838 (when Iowa Territory was created). The first Wisconsin Territory capital was at Belmont.

1837. Michigan is admitted to the Union as the 26th state.

1839 Illinois. Springfield becomes the state capital of Illinois. Also in this year, the National Road was completed from Cumberland, Maryland, to Vandalia, Illinois. It became the most heavily traveled highway in America. (The National Road followed the same general line that Interstate 70 follows today).

1846. Mormons leave Nauvoo, Illinois for the Great Salt Lake Basin in Utah.

1846. Donner party leaves Springfield, Illinois by wagon train for California; forty-two perish in Sierra Mountains snowstorms.

1848. Wisconsin admitted into the union as the 30th state, leaving residents of the area between the Mississippi and St. Croix rivers (present-day eastern Minnesota) without a territorial government or legal system.

1849. Minnesota Territory formed with present day eastern and southern boundaries set. The original area included present Minnesota, extending from the Mississippi River to include that portion of present North and South Dakota east of the Missouri River.

1858. Minnesota becomes the 32nd state admitted to the Union.

1908 Detroit, Michigan. The first Ford Model T is manufactured.

1911 Indianapolis, Indiana. The first Indy 500 car race takes place.

1945. Chicago Cubs win the National League pennant, but lose the World Series to the Detroit Tigers.

ILLINOIS

Censuses & Substitutes, 1600s - 1869

Censuses and substitutes were created by the French in settlements along the Mississippi River before the British took over the region after the French and Indian War of 1754-1763. Land records from both the French and English eras exist today. As American soil, Illinois Territory was created in 1809 from Indiana Territory, and the first actual census taken there was the 1810 territorial census, which was separate from the federal census of 1810. A territorial census was also taken in 1818, a few weeks before statehood in the same year. After statehood, the Illinois legislature authorized state censuses for 1820, 1825, 1830, 1835, 1840, 1845, 1855, and 1865, all separate from the federal censuses. Unfortunately only the 1820, 1855, and 1865 state censuses have survived reasonably intact. Most of the county returns for 1825, 1830, 1835, and 1845 are missing and nearly half of the 1840 state census has been lost. Since Illinois chose to conduct several of its state censuses in the same years as the federal censuses, it may not be obvious to genealogists that there are potentially two statewide name lists available for 1810, 1820,

1830, and 1840 (although the state versions are mostly incomplete for those years). The bibliography below shows state censuses and substitutes, and adds federal censuses when they can be used as comparisons with state versions. County-wide lists are shown for the earliest counties only.

■ **1600s-1800s Illinois, Indiana, Kansas, Michigan, and Missouri People**, see *Midwest pioneers, 1600s-1800s*, a CD-ROM publication, part of Broderbund's Family Tree Maker Archives in collaboration with Genealogical Publishing Co., Inc., Baltimore, 1999. (FHL CD-ROM no. 9, pt. 508). Contents: *Pioneer families of the Midwest*, by Blanche L. Walden (vols. I-III); *Illinois Census Returns, 1810 and 1818*, edited with introduction and notes by Margaret Cross Norton; *Illinois Census Returns, 1820*, edited by Margaret Cross Norton; *Revolutionary Soldiers Buried in Illinois*, by Harriet J. Walker; *Revolutionary Soldiers Buried in Indiana*, with supplement, compiled by Margaret R. Waters; *Revolutionary Soldiers Buried in Indiana, a Supplement: 485 names not listed in the roster of soldiers and patriots in the American Revolution buried in Indiana*, by Margaret R. Waters; *Roster of Soldiers and Patriots of the American Revolution buried in Indiana*, compiled and edited by Mrs. Roscoe C. O'Byrne; *Detroit River Connections: Historical and Biographical Sketches of the Eastern Great Lakes Border Region*, by Judy Jacobson; *Michigan Military records: the DAR. of Michigan historical collections: records of the Revolutionary soldiers buried in Michigan, the pensioners of territorial Michigan, and the soldiers of Michigan awarded the "Medal of Honor,"* by Sue Imogene Silliman; *An index of pioneers from Massachusetts to the West, especially the state of Michigan*, compiled by Charles A. Flagg; *Missouri marriages before 1840*, compiled by Susan Ormesher; *A history of the pioneer families of Missouri, with numerous sketches, anecdotes, adventures, etc., relating to early days in Missouri;* by Wm. S. Bryan and Robert Rose; and *Kansas Territorial Settlers of 1860 who were born in Tennessee, Virginia, North Carolina and South Carolina*, by Clara Hamlett Robertson.

■ **1678-1814 Land Records, Consolidated Index for the Raymond H. Hammes Collection at the Illinois State Archives**, microfilm of original manuscripts at the Illinois State Archives, Springfield, IL. Filmed by the Genealogical Society of Utah, 1988, 1 roll, FHL film #1543598. See also *1722-1784 Land Records*, microfilm of original records at the Illinois State Archives, Springfield, IL, part of the Raymond H. Hammes Collection. This volume contains abstracts of Illinois land transactions, 1722-1784, translated from the original French. Includes general index that indexes by transaction number. Some personal names are found under "Occupations" in the index. Lists of military & religious personnel are also found in the index. Filmed by the Genealogical Society of Utah, 1988, 1 roll, FHL film 1543598, Item 1 (Land Records).

■ **1763-1916 Illinois Marriage Records Index**, compiled by the Illinois State Genealogical Society, records located at the Illinois State Archives, Springfield, IL. This index is an ongoing project of the Illinois State Archives and the Illinois State Genealogical Society to produce an index of Illinois marriages prior to 1901. Filmed by the Archives and the Society, 1994, 94 microfiches, beginning with FHL film #6334564 Unknown/incomplete names - Adams, David). See also a CD-ROM publication by the Illinois State Genealogical Society, 1997, *Index of Illinois Marriages, Earliest to 1900* (FHL CD-ROM No. 76).

■ **1799-1813 Land and Property Records, St. Clair County, Illinois**, microfilm of original manuscripts at the Illinois State Archives, Springfield, IL. St. Clair (with Randolph) was one the two original counties of Illinois, and covered the northern 3/4ths of the present state of Illinois. These records are mostly for the first settled areas along the Mississippi River north of Fort Kaskaskia. Some marriage information may be found among the deeds. Filmed by the state archives, 1985, 1 roll. FHL film #1689031.

■ **1800-1850 Randolph County, Illinois Information**, compiled by the Randolph County Genealogical Society, Chester, IL, 369 pages. Title page title: *Randolph County, Where Illinois Began*. Includes surname index. Includes: 1807, 1825 & 1840 censuses; marriages; deeds; court cases (participants only); deaths from administrators' lists, 1844-1848; cemetery records (those born before 1851); and probate index. FHL book 977.392 V3r.

■ **1804-1814 Kaskaskia French and English Deed Records**, microfilm of original records at the Randolph County Courthouse, Chester, IL (1977). Kaskaskia was the first capital of Illinois Territory, and these records provide names of land owners during the transition from the early French to the English; and later American settlements in Illinois. Filmed by the Genealogical Society of Utah, 1977, 3 rolls, as follows:

- Deeds vol. A45-B46 1804-1806, FHL film #1012401.
- Deeds vol. C47-D48 1804-1814, FHL film #1012402.
- Translation of French deeds in vol. A-D, vol. 49 1804-1814, FHL film #1012403.

■ **1807 Census of Indiana Territory**, facsimile of the original manuscript, published by the Indiana Historical Society, 1980, 57 pages. In 1807, Indiana Territory included St. Clair and Randolph counties, now in Illinois. (Illinois Territory was formed in 1809). Includes name index. FHL book 977.2 X2c and FHL film #1033927.

■ **1810 Federal Census of Illinois Territory**, an alphabetized name list, compiled by Accelerated Indexing Systems, North Salt Lake, UT, 1987, 27 pages. Includes only Randolph County, Illinois Territory, which then included the area of several modern counties of southern Illinois. (The only other Illinois county in 1810 was St. Clair, whose 1810 census schedules were lost). See FHL book 977.3 X28i.

■ **1810 & 1818 Illinois State Censuses**. See *Illinois Census Returns, 1810-1818*, edited by Margaret Cross Norton, originally published by the Trustees of the Illinois State Historical Library, Springfield, IL, 1935, as *Collections of the Illinois State Historical Society*, vol. 24, (reprint, Genealogical Publishing Co., Inc., Baltimore, 1969), 329 pages. The volume is devoted to the schedules available from the 1810 state census, to returns from the 1818 state census, and to an index of names. FHL book 977.3 B4i v. 24. Also on FHL film #897331.

■ **1810-1855 Combined Index to Illinois Territory, State, and Federal Censuses, and Other Records**. See *Name Index to Early Illinois Records*, microfilm of indexes located at the Illinois State Archives, Springfield, IL. With the filmed equivalent of 500,000 typescript pages, this includes indexes to the state and federal censuses of 1810, 1818, 1820, 1825, 1830, 1835, 1840, 1845, 1850, and 1855; executive record to 1861; election returns of 1818-1847; House and Senate journals through 1830's; early laws to 1849; as part of the Perrin Collection at the State Archives. Filmed by the archives, 1975, 248 16mm rolls. FHL film begins with film #1001592 (Aacer – Adams).

■ *1814-1872 Original Land Patents, Randolph County, Illinois*, abstracted by Lola Frazer Crowder, 1991, 174 pages. As one of two original counties of Illinois, the federal land sales during the early period represent a large part of the early population. These name lists are county records relating to the original public land buyers in Randolph County. FHL book 977.392 R28c. See also *Kaskaskia Land Warrants, Military Certificates, Randolph County, Illinois*, by Peggy Lathrop Sapp of Springfield, Illinois, from film at the Illinois State Archives. Includes four alphabetical indexes. See FHL book 977.392 R2s.

■ *1818 Illinois State Census Index*, edited by Ronald Vern Jackson, et al, Accelerated Indexing, North Salt Lake, UT, 1997, 93 pages. The name list was generated from the Illinois State Historical Society's originals. FHL book 977.3 X28i.

■ **1818-1848 Illinois Election Returns**, edited by Theodore Calvin Pease, published by the Trustees of Illinois State Historical Library, vol. 18, *Collections of the Illinois State Historical Library: Statistical Series*, 1923. Filmed by the Genealogical Society of Utah, 1984, 1 roll, FHL book 977.3 B4i v.18 and FHL film #1035628.

■ **1820-1825 Randolph County, Illinois**, see *Residents of early Randolph County, Illinois*, compiled by Lucille Wittnenborn Wiechens, published 1989, 26 pages. Names are in alphabetical order. Includes names from the 1825 state census and names from 1820 land records. Includes short history of Illinois and Randolph County. FHL book 977.392 X2w.

■ *1820 Illinois Census Returns*, (State census, separate from the 1820 federal census), edited by Margaret Cross Norton, published Springfield,

IL: Trustees of the Illinois State Historical Library, 1934, 466 pages, as part of *Collections of the Illinois State Historical Library, Statistical Series,* Vol. 3. From preface: "This book contains not only the 1820 state census schedules but also notes comparing all discrepancies between the names as written in the 1818 territorial, the 1820 state, and the 1820 federal censuses." Includes an index of names FHL book 977.3 B4i v. 26 and FHL film #6051147.

■ *1820 Federal Census of Illinois,* compiled by Lowell M. Volkel and James V. Gill, published by Heritage House, Danville, IL, 1966, 79 pages. FHL book 977.3 X2v.

■ *1825 Illinois State Census Index,* compiled by W. David Samuelsen, published by Accelerated Indexing Systems, North Salt Lake, 1985, 26 pages. FHL book 977.3 X2j.

■ *1825 Census of Randolph County, Illinois,* transcribed by Mrs. Harlin B. Taylor, published by Vio-Lin Enterprises, Decatur, IL, 1972, 29 pages. Includes index.

■ **1826-1873 Index to Public Domain Sales Land Tract Record Listing for Illinois,** microfilm of original computer print-out (29,931 pages) made in 1984 at the Illinois State Archives, Springfield, IL. Includes name of purchaser, type of sale, description of the land purchased (including section, township, range, and principal meridian), number of acres purchased, total purchase price, date of purchase, and volume and page of the original land record on which the transaction was entered. This project was originally called the Public Domain Computer Conversion Project. It indexes over 550,000 individual entries obtained from sales records of the U.S. General Land Office, Illinois officials, and the Illinois Central Railroad. Alphabetically arranged. Filmed by the IL State Archives, 1984, 144 microfiche, beginning with FHL fiche #6016848.

■ *1830 Illinois State Census Index,* by W. David Samuelsen, et al, published by Accelerated Indexing Systems, Bountiful, UT, 1984, 34 pages. FHL book 977.3 X2j. Genealogist have two

published indexes to the 1830 Illinois federal census that can be used to compare with names listed on the 1830 state census. See *Index to the 1830 Federal Census,* compiled by James V. Gill and Maryan R. Gill, published by Illiana Genealogical Pub. Co., Danville, IL, 1968, 4 vols., FHL book 977.3 X22g 1830. See also *Illinois 1830 Census Index,* edited by Ronald Vern Jackson, et al, published by Accelerated Indexing Systems, Bountiful, UT, 1976, 63 pages. FHL book 977.3 X2ja 1830. The 1830 IL federal census names are also online at several sites (see the online census sites shown below).

■ *1835 Illinois State Census Index,* edited by W. David Samuelsen, et al, published by Accelerated Indexing Systems, Bountiful, UT, 1984, 58 pages. FHL book 977.3 X2j 1835.

■ **1835 Illinois State Census, Cass, Morgan, Scott Counties,** in *Jacksonville, Illinois Genealogical Society Journal,* Vol. 26, No. 1 (Mar 1998).

■ **1835 Illinois State Census, Edwards County,** in *Edwards County Historical Society Newsletter,* Vol. 4, No. 2-3 (Summer 1983).

■ **1835 Illinois State Census, Iroquois County,** in *Iroquois Stalker,* Vol. 31, No. 2 (2001).

■ **1835 Illinois State Census, Union County,** in *Saga of Southern Illinois,* Vol. 5, No. 1 (Spring 1978), and Vol. 23, No. 3 (Fall 1996).

■ **1840 Illinois State Census,** microfilm of original records at the Illinois State Archives, Springfield, IL. Filmed by the Genealogical Society of Utah, 1976, 2 rolls. FHL film #1004694-1004695. Indexed in *Illinois 1840 State Census Index,* compiled by W. David Samuelsen, et al, published by Accelerated Indexing Systems, Bountiful, UT, 1984, 294 pages. FHL book 977.3 X2j 1840. Comparisons can be made with the names found on the IL 1840 federal census. See *Illinois 1840 Federal Census Index,* edited by Ronald Vern Jackson, et al, published by Accelerated Indexing Systems, Bountiful, UT, 1977, 192 pages, FHL book 977.3 X2i 1840. The 1840 IL federal census names are also online at several sites (see online census sites below).

■ **1855 State Census of Illinois**., microfilm of original schedules at the Illinois State Archives, Springfield, IL. Several counties missing, including Carroll, Champaign, Franklin, Gallatin, Henry, Jefferson, Jo Davies, Lake, Stark, Will and Woodford. Indexed in *Name Index to Early Illinois Records, 1810-1855* by the Illinois State Archives. Census schedules filmed by the Genealogical Society of Utah, 1975, 15 rolls, as follows:

- Adams Co. - FHL film #976178
- Alexander - Clay counties, FHL film #976179.
- Clinton - Cook counties, FHL film #976180.
- Crawford - Effingham counties, FHL film #976181.
- Fayette - Hamilton counties, FHL film #976182.
- Hancock - Kane counties, FHL film #976183.
- Kankakee - LaSalle counties, FHL film #976184.
- Lawrence and Lee counties, FHL film #976185.
- Livingston - McHenry counties, FHL film, #976186.
- McLean - Massac counties, FHL film #976670.
- Menard - Ogle counties, FHL film #976671.
- Peoria - Putnam counties, FHL film #976672.
- Randolph - Sangamon counties, FHL film #976673.
- Schuyler - Wabash counties, FHL film #977062.
- Warren - Winnebago counties, FHL film #977063.

■ **1861-1862 Illinois Military Census**, microfilm of original records at the office of Secretary of State, Springfield, IL. A list, by county, of able-bodied male citizens between the ages of eighteen and forty-five in pursuance of General Orders No. 99 of the War Department and instructions of the Adjutant General of the State of Illinois. Includes Adams, Cook, Jo Daviess & Lake counties. FHL film #2209347 (Illinois military census, 1861-1862).

■ **1862-1866 Internal Revenue Assessment Lists for Illinois**, microfilm of originals at the National Archives. Includes a locality index (filmed at the beginning of each roll of film) that references counties to districts and film roll numbers. The lists are arranged by collection district and then by division. They are filmed in the order in which they are bound in the volumes. Filmed by the National Archives, series M764, 63 rolls, beginning with FHL film #1534562 (District 1, 1862-1863).

■ **1865 Illinois State Census**, microfilm of original records at the Illinois State Library,

Springfield, IL. At the time of filming, the state library was missing the 1865 census schedules for Gallatin, Mason & Monroe counties. Only Elm Grove Township is included for Tazewell County. Filmed by the Genealogical Society of Utah, 1964, 1977, 25 rolls, as follows:

- Adams, Bureau, Edwards, Ford, and Effingham counties, FHL film #972746.
- Fayette, Franklin, Grundy, Henderson, and Fulton counties, FHL film #972747.
- Jo Daviess, Pulaski, Alexander, Bond, and Boone counties, - FHL film # 972748.
- Clinton, Champaign, Clark, Cumberland, and Christian counties, FHL film #972749.
- Crawford, Carroll, DeWitt, DeKalb, Douglas, DuPage, and Brown counties, FHL film #972750.
- Coles, Calhoun, Cass, Clay, and Greene counties, FHL film #972751.
- Edgar, Jasper, Pike, Hardin, and Jefferson counties, FHL film #972752.
- Jackson, Johnson, Henry, and Hancock counties, FHL film #972753.
- Hamilton, Iroquois, Kankakee, and Knox counties, FHL film #972754.
- Jersey County, FHL film #972755.
- Kane, Kendall, and Logan counties, FHL film #972756.
- Lake, Lawrence, Lee, and Livingston counties, FHL film #972757.
- McHenry, Montgomery, Macoupin, and Ogle counties, FHL film #1012404.
- Madison and Macon counties, FHL film #972758.
- Menard, Morgan, Pope, and Richland counties, FHL film #972759.
- Cook Co. (Chicago wards 1-12), FHL film #972760.
- Cook Co. (Chicago wards 12-16; other towns), FHL film #972761.
- Randolph, Saline, Mercer, McDonough, and McLean counties, FHL film #972762.
- Marshall, Peoria, Piatt, Perry, and Putnam counties, FHL film #972763.
- Rock Island Co., FHL film #972764.
- Sangamon, St. Clair, and Tazewell (Elm Grove Township only) counties, FHL film #972765.
- Vermilion, Will, and La Salle counties, FHL film #972766.
- Marion, Massac, Moultrie, Shelby, Stephenson, Schuyler, and Stark counties, FHL film #972767.
- Scott, Union, Wayne, White, Woodford, and Washington counties, FHL film #972768.
- Williamson, Winnebago, Wabash, and Warren counties, FHL film #972769.

■ **1861-1865 Rosters of Illinois Regiments of the Civil War.** Microfilm of original *Report of the Adjutant General of the State of Illinois,* published Springfield, IL, 1867, 8 vols. Contents: Vol. 1. 1865-1866, 7th to 46th regiment; v. 2. 1861-1866, 47th to 157th regiment; v. 3. 1861-1866; 1st to 17th cavalry regiment, 29th United States colored infantry; 1st & 2nd regiments and independent batteries of artillery; also rosters of enlisted men numbered from the 7th to the 20th regiment; v. 4. 1861-1865; 21st to 47th regiments; v. 5. 1861-1866; 48th to 76th regiment; v. 6. 1861-1866; 77th to 117th regiment; v. 7. 1861- 1865; 118th to 156 infantry regiment; 1st to 3rd cavalry regiment; v. 8. 1861-1866; 4th to 17th cavalry regiment; 1st & 2nd regiments & independent batteries of artillery; colored troops; 1st army corps; recruits for regular army. The 1st to the 3rd vols. contain rosters of Civil War officers. The 3rd vol. also contains rosters of enlisted men which continues to the end of the 8th vol. Filmed for the FHL by the Library of Congress, 1989, 3 rolls, FHL film #1674241-1674243.

■ **1871-1906 Indexes to Naturalization Records, Cook County, Illinois,** microfilm of original records at the Cook County Courthouse, Chicago, Illinois. Filmed by the Genealogical Society of Utah, 1980, 2 rolls, as follows:
- Naturalization index, A-L, 1871-1906, FHL film #1023967.
- Naturalization index, M-Z, 1871-1906, FHL film #1023968.

■ **1847-1860 Illinois (State) Directories,** microfilm of originals published by various publishers. Filmed by Research Publications, Woodbridge, CT, 1980-1984, 41 microfiches, as follows:
- **1847** Illinois annual register, and Western business directory (3 fiches), FHL film #6043985.
- **1854-1855** Montague's Illinois and Missouri state directory (9 fiches), FHL film #6043986.
- **1855-1856** The Northern counties gazetteer and directory. The Chicago city directory, and business advertiser (8 fiches), FHL film #6043987.
- **1858-1859** Illinois state gazetteer and business directory... by George W. Hawes (7 fiches), FHL film #6043988
- **1860** Illinois state business directory ... by J. C. W. Bailey & Co., FHL film #6043989.

■ **1869 Illinois Central Directory,** microfilm of original published 1869, filmed by the Genealogical Society of Utah, 1975, 1 roll, FHL film #969494.

Illinois Censuses & Substitutes Online

The following databases are available online at these sites:
www.ancestry.com
- 1820 United States Federal Census
- 1830 United States Federal Census
- 1840 United States Federal Census
- 1850 United States Federal Census
- 1860 United States Federal Census
- 1870 United States Federal Census
- 1880 United States Federal Census
- 1900 United States Federal Census
- 1910 United States Federal Census
- 1920 United States Federal Census
- 1930 United States Federal Census
- Chicago Voter Registration, 1888
- Chicago Voter Registration, 1890
- Chicago Voter Registration, 1892
- Illinois Census Returns, 1810 & 1818
- Illinois Census, 1810-90
- French Colony, Louisiana, 1699 - 1732
- US Federal Census Mortality Schedules Index
- US Federal Census Mortality Schedules, 1850-1880
- US Indian Census Schedules, 1885-1940
- Illinois Census, 1820
- Vitelli Soundex of the U.S. Census

www.censusfinder.com
- Early Illinois Settlers
- 1787 Census of Kaskaskia
- 1807 Indiana Territory Census Covers all of Southern Illinois.
- 1807 Voters List
- 1810-1890 Federal Census Records at Ancestry
- 1840 Federal Census Revolutionary War Pensioners – Statewide
- 1880 Federal Census (Images)
- 1880 Federal Census Search at Family Search
- 1880 Federal Census Extraction of Southern Illinois Penitentiary
- 1883 Pensioners on the Roll – Statewide
- Illinois State Databases of Census & Genealogy Records

Online County-wide Name Lists (no. of databases): Adams (36); Alexander (2); Bond (8); Boone (0); Brown (8); Bureau (4); Calhoun (0); Carroll (25); Cass (11); Champaign (8); Christian (2); Clark (12); Clay (2); Clinton (26); Coles (34); Cook (23); Crawford (16); Cumberland (2); DeKalb (18); Dewitt (11); Douglas (1); DuPage (3); Edgar (20); Edwards (0); Effingham (1); Fayette (1); Ford (1); Franklin (54); Fulton (5); Gallatin (26); Greene (17); Grundy (6); Hamilton (22); Hancock (3); Hardin (0); Henderson (2); Henry (7); Iroquois (4); Jackson (20); Jasper (9); Jefferson (11);Jersey (4); Jo Daviess (30); Johnson (7); Kane (18); Kankakee (2); Kendall (3); Knox (21); La Salle (5); Lake (0); Lawrence (4); Lee (6); Livingston (2); Logan (5); Macon (6); Macoupin (8); Madison (14); Marion (0); Marshall (0); Mason (0); Massac (6); McDonough (9); McHenry (3); McLean (0); Menard (5); Mercer (0); Monroe (3); Montgomery (30); Morgan (17); Moultrie (27); Ogle (9); Peoria (14); Perry (23); Piatt (0); Pike (8); Pope (11); Pulaski (8); Putnam (3); Randolph (31); Richland (4); Rock Island (1); Saline (10); Sangamon (6); Schuyler (13); Scott (10); Shelby (8); St Clair (16); Stark (11); Stephenson (1); Tazewell (1); Union (20); Vermilion (11); Wabash (0); Warren (1); Washington (12); Wayne (27); White (1); Whiteside (1); Will (11); Williamson (33); Winnebago (0); and Woodford (1).

INDIANA

Censuses & Substitutes, 1783-1942

Indiana Territory was created in 1800, taken from Northwest Territory, with the bounds virtually the same as the 1790 Knox County, Northwest Territory. Unceded Indian lands had limited settlements to an area between the Wabash and Miami Rivers with most of the population near Vincennes and Jeffersonville. By 1810, the population was within four counties: Clark, Dearborn, Knox, and Harrison. Any early censuses and substitutes from these four counties cover the entire state population and are identified below. Territorial-statewide lists begin with an 1807 territorial census. Beginning in 1820 the state of Indiana began taking state censuses in various intervals, but few of these included name lists. Original returns for Blackford (1857, 1871, 1871, 1877, 1877, 1883, 1889); Henry (1919, 1931); Ripley (1919); Starke (1919); and Washington (1901) counties can be found at the Indiana State Library in Indianapolis (no FHL film). Name lists for the early counties and statewide lists are shown below:

■ **1783-1815 Knox County, Indiana, Early Land Records and Court Indexes**, published by Genealogical Services and Publications, Chicago, IL, 1973, 2 vols. Contents: v. 1. Locations entered at Vincennes, 1807-1813; Common Pleas, and county business, 1806-1810; estates; v. 2. Lists of land donations; claims; militia donations; indexes. FHL book 977.239 R2 and R2k.

■ **1787 Census, Post Vincennes, Knox County, Indiana**, in *Sycamore Leaves*, Vol. 15, No. 4 (Jun 1985).

■ *Indiana Marriages, Early to 1825: A Research Tool.* compiled, extracted & transcribed by Liahona Research, Inc.; edited by Jordan R. Dodd and Norman L. Moyes, published by Precision Indexing, Bountiful, UT, 1991, 345 pages. Lists names of brides or grooms in alphabetical order by surname, with name of spouse, date of marriage, and county where married. FHL book 977.2 V22i.

■ **1800s**, See *Index, Indiana Source Books*, compiled by Dorothy Riker, published by the Indiana Historical Society, Family History Section, 1983, 406 pages. Contains an index to marriages, wills and naturalizations which appeared in the *Hoosier Genealogist* (1961-1979) and which have been compiled into three volumes, including more than 115,000 names. FHL book 977.2 D29h index.

■ **1790-1829 Knox County, Indiana Deed Records**, microfilm of the original records at the Knox County Courthouse, Vincennes, Indiana. Original deeds recorded 1790 to 1813 were destroyed in a courthouse fire, but many of the earlier deeds were brought in and recorded again soon after the fire in 1814. Filmed by the Record Registry Corp., Indianapolis, 1936, 2 rolls, FHL film #7768 (General Index to deeds) and FHL film #7769 (Deed records).

■ **1800-1941 Indiana Deaths Index**, CD-ROM publication: *Indiana Vital Records Deaths Index, 1800 to 1941*, published by Heritage Quest, Bountiful, UT, 2001. Includes 867,132 entries covering the period of 1800-1941, along with a few entries outside that range of years. Each entry gives details on surname, given name, sex, ethnicity, age, death month, death day, death year, county, book, page, and fiche. FHL CD No. 1188.

■ **1801-1820 Pioneers.** See *Indiana Territorial Pioneer Records, 1801-1820,* compiled by Charles M. Franklin, published by Heritage House, 1983, 2 vols., 99 pages. Includes index. Contains miscellaneous records of election returns, military records, census returns, births, history, etc. Contents: v. 1. 1810-1815 -- v. 2. 1801-1820. FHL book 977.2 N4i vol. 1 & 2.

■ **1801-1877 Public Land Purchases in Indiana.** See *Indiana Land Entries,* by Margaret R. Waters, originally published Indianapolis, 1948, reprinted by The Bookmark, Knightstown, IN, 1977, 2 vols. Lists names of persons who obtained (from the federal government) an original entry of land in Indiana. Contents: v. 1, Cincinnati District, 1801-1840; v. 2, Vincennes District, 1807-1877. FHL book 977.2 R2W. and FHL film #6046718.

■ **1801-1899, Clark County, Indiana,** see *The Hoosier Journal of Ancestry, Clark County Special,* published by the Hoosier Journal, Little York, IN, 1983-1992, 2 vols., includes indexes. Contains various records of genealogical value, including township histories, marriages, probate records, census records, land records, biographies, etc., gathered from many sources in Clark County. FHL book 977.2185 B2hj vol. 1 & 2.

■ **1801-1901 Deed Records; Grantee/Grantor Index to Deeds, Clark County, Indiana,** microfilm of records located in the Clark County Recorder's Office, Jeffersonville, Indiana. Filmed by the Genealogical Society of Utah, 1985, 38 rolls, beginning with FHL film #1428648 (Grantor Index, A-R, 1801-1850).

■ **1802 Taxable Property, Knox County, Indiana,** in *Northwest Trail Tracer,* Vol. 10, No. 2 (Jun 1989) through Vol. 10, No. 4 (Dec 1989).

■ **1802, 1809 Voters, Clark County, Indiana,** microfilm of typescript located in the Jeffersonville Township Library, Jeffersonville, Indiana. Contains lists of voters compiled from the *National Genealogical Society Quarterly,* vol. 3, # 4, and from the *Hoosier Genealogist,* v. 2 (Mar/Apr 1961). Filmed by the Genealogical Society of Utah, 1985, 1 roll, FHL film #1428704.

■ **1805-1830 Deed Records, Index to Deeds, 1805-1936, Dearborn County, Indiana,** microfilm of original records in the Dearborn County courthouse, Lawrenceburg, Indiana. Filmed by the Indiana State Library, 1936, 5 rolls, beginning with FHL film #209865 (Deed index, A-B, 1805-1936).

■ **1806-1833 Marriages, Dearborn County, Indiana,** compiled by Colleen Ridlen, published Beech Grove, IN, 1989, 44 pages. Contains an index to marriages in Dearborn County, giving names of brides and grooms, name of spouse, and date of marriage. FHL book 977.211 V22r, and FHL film #6088449.

■ **1807 Indiana Territory Census,** facsimile of the original manuscript, published by the Indiana Historical Society, Indianapolis, 1980, 57 pages. Includes surname index. In 1807, Indiana Territory included Dearborn, Clark, and Knox counties, plus St. Clair and Randolph counties of Illinois. The 1807 Clark County census name list was missing, so the IHS added an 1807 voters list for Clark County, Indiana, and also for Kaskaskia (Randolph Co, IL). FHL book 977.2 X2c and FHL film #1033927. Another filming, FHL film #1428705. See also *Indiana 1807 Census Index,* compiled by Ronald Vern Jackson, et al, published by Accelerated Indexing Systems International, North Salt Lake, UT, 1986, 56 pages, FHL book 977.2 X22j.

■ **1807 Indiana Territory Census, Clark County, Indiana,** see *Index to Clark County, Indiana Territory Census, 1807,* microfilm of typescript located in the Jeffersonville Township Library, Jeffersonville, Indiana. Filmed by the Genealogical Society of Utah, 1985, 1 roll, FHL film #1428704.

■ **1807 Landowners Unpaid Taxes, Clark County, Indiana,** in *Southern Indiana Genealogical Society Quarterly,* Vol. 7, No. 4 (Oct 1986).

■ **1807 Census, Knox County, Indiana,** in *Sullivan County Historical Society Newsletter,* Vol. 8, No. 3 (May 1981) through Vol. 8, No. 6 (Nov 1981).

■ **1808 Tax Sale, Knox County, Indiana**, in *Northwest Trail Tracer*, Vol. 6, No. 2 (Jun 1985).

■ **1809-1886 Deed Records; Grantee-Grantor Index to Deeds, 1809-1888, Harrison County, Indiana**, microfilm of original records located at the Harrison County Courthouse, Corydon, Indiana. Filmed by the Genealogical Society of Utah, 1984, 28 rolls, beginning with FHL film #1404902 (Grantee Index, 1809-1863).

■ **1810-1813 Harrison County, Indiana**. See *Early records of Harrison County, Indiana*, compiled by Walter S. Beanblossom, microfilm of original manuscript, published 1975. Includes index. Contains the 1810 census and the 1813 tax list of Harrison Co., Indiana. Filmed by the Genealogical Society of Utah, 1976, 1 roll, FHL film #928263. See also, *Records of Harrison County, Indiana, from Walter Beanblossom's Collection, and Reprints From the "Ancestral News,"* compiled by Sherry Healy, for the Ancestral Trails Historical Society, Inc., Vine Grove, KY, published by McDowell Publications, Utica, KY, 150 pages; Includes surname index. Contains abstracts from 1810 census records, tax lists of 1812-1813, voter lists of 1818, mortality schedule for 1850, naturalizations of 1841-1846, and 1855-1920, citizenships for 1852, Indiana Legion (organization of companies with lists of officers and soldiers), short histories of townships, and first marriage records of Harrison County. FHL book 977.221 H2h.

■ **1811 - Indiana's First Tax List,** in *American Monthly Magazine*, Vol. 87, No. 5 (May 1953); and as "Taxpayers, 1811," in *Hoosier Genealogist*, Vol. 11, No. 3 (Jul 1971); and *Genealogist*, Vol. 10 (Feb 1972).

■ **1816 Tax Levy, Harrison County, Indiana**, in *Genealogist*, Vol. 1, No. 1 (Jan 1973).

■ *The Indiana 1820 Enumeration of Males*, compiled by Mary M. Morgan, published by the Indiana Historical Society, Family History Section, 1988, 173 pages. FHL book 977.2 X2m.

■ **1821 Tax List, Bartholomew County, Indiana**, in *Hoosier Journal of Ancestry*, Vol. 5, No. 1 (Jan 1978).

■ **1822 Poll Tax List, Lawrence County, Indiana,** in *Seedling Patch*, Vol. 3 (1983).

■ **1823-1852 Ft. Wayne Land Office Entries**, transcribed from the original tract books at the Indiana State Archives, Indianapolis. Tract books transcribed by Barbara S. Wolfe; data compiled by Helen S. Morrison, published by the State Archives, 199?, 138 pages. Contains an alphabetical listing by surname prepared by the Indiana State Archives of individual names of persons who purchased land in the areas now covered by the counties of Adams, Allen, Blackford, Cass, Clinton, DeKalb, Delaware, Grant, Howard, Huntington, Jay, Kosciusko, Lagrange, Madison, Miami, Noble, Randolph, Steuben, Tipton, Wabash, Wells and Whitley. This index serves a computerized database of 73,250 records that can be accessed at the Indiana State Archives in Indianapolis. FHL book 977.2.

■ **1824-1848 Tax Lists**, see *Indiana Tax Lists*, compiled by Jane E. Darlington, pub. 1990, 2 vols. Includes surname indexes. Arranged by county and townships, and lists name, poll, acres, section, township, and range. Contents: v. 1: Bartholomew Co., 1843, Dearborn Co., 1842, Fayette Co., 1842, Greene Co., 1843, Harrison Co., 1844, Marshall Co., 1843 (with Starke Co.), Morgan Co., 1840, Noble Co., 1847, Perry Co., 1835, and 1824-1826, 1828, 1829, 1832, 1836-1837, 1840-1843, 1845, Scott Co., 1839; v. 2: Posey Co., 1842, Putnam Co., 1845, Spencer Co., 1846, Tippecanoe Co., 1848, Switzerland Co., 1843, Vigo Co., 1824-1828, Whitley Co., 1841. FHL book 977.2 R4d v. 1 & 2.

■ **1829 Taxpayers, Fayette County, Indiana**, in *Hoosier Genealogist*, Vol. 11, No. 4 (Oct 1971).

■ **1829 Assessment Rolls of Taxable Persons & Property, Marion County, Indiana**, in *Hoosier Genealogist*, Vol. 20, No. 2 (Jun 1980).

■ **1837 Assessment List of Taxable Property, Kosciusko County, Indiana**, in *Our Missing Links*, Vol. 6, No. 1 (Spring 1982).

■ **1850-1920 Births Index**, CD-ROM publication: *Indiana Vital Records Births Index, 1850 to 1920*, published by Heritage Quest, Bountiful, UT,

2001. Includes 1,530,487 entries from 1850 to 1920, along with a few outside that range of years. Each entry details surname, child's name, father's given name, mother's given name, maiden name, sex, ethnicity, birth month, birthday, birth year, county, book, page, and fiche. FHL CD No. 1187.

■ **1850-1920 Marriage Index**, CD-ROM publication: *Indiana Vital Records Marriages Index, 1850 to 1920,* by Heritage Quest, Bountiful, UT, 2 CDs, 2001. Includes 3,042,782 entries in the time period from 1850 to 1920, along with a few entries outside that range of years. Each entry details surname, given name, father's given name, spouse's given name, spouse's surname (maiden name), sex, ethnicity, age, birth month, birth day, birth year, marriage month-day-year, county, book, page, and fiche. FHL CD No. 1185.

■ **1858-1861 Indiana (State) Directories**, microfilm of originals published by various publishers, filmed by Research Publications, Woodbridge, CT, 1980-1984, 22 fiches, as follows:
- **1858-1859** G. W. Hawes' Indiana State Gazetteer and Business Directory, (10 fiches) FHL film #6043990.
- **1860-1861** George W. Hawes' Indiana State Gazetteer and Business Directory (12 fiches), FHL film #6043991.

■ **1862-1866 Internal Revenue Assessment Lists for Indiana**, microfilm of original manuscripts located in the National Archives, Washington, DC. Lists are arranged alphabetically by surname of those being assessed for each period. Filmed by the National Archives, 1987, 42 rolls, beginning with FHL film #1491004 (District 1, division 9, special lists 1864, annual lists 1862-1864; and Divisions 9 and 11, monthly and special lists, Dec. 1862-Dec. 1866).

■ **1886-1894 Indiana Veterans Lists**. FHL title: *Enrollment of the Late Soldiers, Their Widows and Orphans of the Late Armies of the United States, Residing in the State of Indiana for the year 1886-1894,* microfilm of records located at the Indiana State Library, Indianapolis. Contains an enrollment of persons employed in the late armies of the United States, i.e., the War of 1812; the War of the United States with Mexico; the

War of 1861; and of all wars of the United States with Indian tribes. Arranged by county and by each township within a county, alphabetically by surname. By enactment of the General Assembly of the State of Indiana, each township assessor at the time of taking lists of property for taxation, was to list all persons who served in the United States armies, as well as their widows and orphans. Assessors were to return their listings to the County Clerks who in turn sent them to the Adjutant General for the State to be put on permanent file in his office. Filmed by the Genealogical Society of Utah, 1988-1990, 89 rolls, beginning with FHL film 1605057 (Adams, Bartholomew counties, 1886-).

■ **1914-1919 World War I Indiana Enrollment Cards**, microfilm of originals at the Indiana State Archives, Indianapolis, IN. Contains: statement-of-service cards, arranged in alphabetical order by surname, furnished primarily for historical and statistical purposes. Lists name, army serial number, race, residence, where inducted, date inducted, place of birth, age, organizations served in with dates of assignments and transfers, grades with date of appointment, engagements, wounds or other injuries received in action, service overseas, honorably discharged or demobilization date, percent disabled in view of occupation, and remarks. Filmed by the Genealogical Society of Utah, 1990, 35 rolls, beginning with Aarnink, Clifford F. – Baker, Ollie, FHL film #1674855.

■ **1917-1918 World War I Selective Service System Draft Registration Cards (Indiana)**, microfilm of originals at the National Archives Regional Branch in East Point, GA, part of series M1509. The draft cards are arranged alphabetically by state, then alphabetically by county or city draft board, and then alphabetically by surname of the registrants. 117 rolls cover the Indiana cards on microfilm, beginning with FHL film #1439777 (Adams County, A-Z, Allen County, A-F). **Draft Registration Cards Online:** Scanned images of the Indiana WWI draft registration cards are available at www.ancestry.com.

■ **1942 World War II Draft Registration Cards (Indiana), United States Selective Service System**, microfilm of original records at the

National Archives and Records Administration, Great Lakes Region, Chicago, Illinois. These cards represent older men, ages 45 to 65 on April 27, 1942, that were registered for the draft. They had birth dates between 28 April 1877 and 16 Feb 1897. The cards are arranged in alphabetical order by surname. Includes name, place of residence, age, place of birth, date of birth, race, weight, height, employer's name and address, name and address of person who would always know their address, color of eyes and hair. Filmed by the Genealogical Society of Utah, 2001, 174 16mm rolls, beginning with FHL film #2240128 (Aabel, Hans - Alexander, Harley J.).

■ **Indiana Biographical Index**, compiled by Lyman Platt and Jimmy Parker, microfilm of original typescript published by Genealogical Indexing Associates, Salt Lake City, 1983. This is an updated name index to biographical sketches in virtually all published Indiana county histories, which began as a WPA project in 1938, and was continued by the Indiana Historical Society in 1979. Earlier version: *Index to Persons and Firms*, which, along with all of the county histories referenced, can be found at the Indiana State Library in Indianapolis; the Allen County Public Library in Fort Wayne; or the Family History Library in Salt Lake City. Filmed by the Genealogical Society of Utah, 1984, 16 microfiches, FHL film #6331353.

Indiana Censuses & Substitutes Online

The following databases are available online at these sites:

www.ancestry.com
- 1699-1732 French Louisiana
- 1790-1890 Indiana Censuses
- 1820 United States Federal Census
- 1830 United States Federal Census
- 1840 United States Federal Census
- 1850 United States Federal Census
- 1850-1880 Mortality Schedules & Index
- 1860 United States Federal Census
- 1870 United States Federal Census
- 1880 United States Federal Census
- 1880 Clark County, Indiana Census

- 1885-1940 US Indian Census Schedules
- 1890 Federal Census Fragment
- 1900 United States Federal Census
- 1910 United States Federal Census
- 1920 United States Federal Census
- 1930 Census of Merchant Seamen
- 1930 United States Federal Census
- Vitelli Soundex of the U.S. Census

www.censusfinder.com
- 1790-1890 Indiana Census Search at Ancestry
- 1816 Post Offices & Postmasters in Indiana Territory
- 1820 Federal Census Index - Statewide
- 1830 Federal Census Index - Statewide
- 1840 Federal Census Index - Statewide
- 1880 Federal Census
- 1880 Federal Census Search at Family Search
- 1883 Pensioners on the Roll – Statewide
- Indiana State Databases of Census Records and Genealogy Databases

www.census-online.com
- 1820 Federal Census
- 1840 Federal Census – Pensioners
- Index to 1807 Territorial Census
- 1807 Voters List
- **Online County-wide Name Lists**

County (no. of databases): Adams (5); Allen (1); Bartholomew (5); Benton (18); Blackford (1); Boone (12); Brown (2); Carroll (1); Cass (4); Clark (3); Clay (31); Clinton (3); Crawford (7); Daviess (3); Dearborn (1); Decatur (12); DeKalb (41); Delaware (30); Dubois (17); Elkhart (3); Fayette (3); Floyd (1); Fountain (9); Franklin (13); Fulton (11); Gibson (10); Grant (3); Greene (2); Hamilton (5); Hancock (0); Harrison (1); Hendricks (15); Henry (10); Howard (16); Huntington (0); Jackson (1); Jasper (11); Jay (1);p Jefferson (3); Jennings (4); Johnson (6); Knox (2); Kosciusko (13); LaGrange (3); Lake (12); LaPorte (3); Lawrence (10); Madison (3); Marion (1); Marshall (14); Martin (10); Miami (8); Monroe (4); Montgomery (3); Morgan (19); Newton (18); Noble (9); Ohio (1); Orange (30); Owen (1); Parke (35); Perry (7); Pike (13); Porter (8); Posey (6); Pulaski (4); Putnam (5); Randolph (0); Ripley (1); Rush (3); Scott (18); Shelby (13); Spencer (10); St Joseph (10); Starke (0); Steuben (16); Sullivan (0); Switzerland (3); Tippecanoe (29); Tipton (1); Union (1); Vanderburgh (3); Vermillion (3); Vigo (10); Wabash (4); Warren (14); Warrick (12); Washington (7); Wayne (0); Wells (25); White (11); Whitley (2).

MICHIGAN

Censuses & Substitutes, 1703-1919

A few early censuses still exist for the Great Lakes region, taken by the French, English, and Americans. Those extant for the Michigan area, 1710-1830 were gathered together and published by the Detroit Society for Genealogical Research (see citation below). Michigan Territory also took censuses, but few of them listed the names of people. The exceptions are noted below. And, the state of Michigan conducted state censuses separate from the Federal decennial censuses, beginning with the 1837 state census, most without names, but was followed by a state census in 1845, naming all males over the age of 21). However, only St. Joseph, Lenawee, Oakland, Washtenaw and Eaton counties seem to be extant for 1845. More state censuses were taken in 1854, 1864, 1874, 1884, and 1894. Counties with surviving schedules, 1854-1894, are shown below in chronological order. A 1904 census was taken, but except for statistics, the original schedules were destroyed. All of Michigan's territorial and state censuses are listed in chronological order by county, along with any substitutes:

■ **1703-1869, Early Land Transfers, Detroit and Wayne County, Michigan**, Michigan Works Progress Administration, Vital Records Project, Michigan State Library and DAR, Louisa St. Clair Chapter, microfilm of original records (58 vols.) at the DAR Library, Washington, DC. Includes index. Filmed by the Genealogical Society of Utah, 1971, 13 rolls, beginning with FHL film #857329 (Master index to Records, vols. A, B, & C.).

■ **1710-1830**. See *Michigan Censuses, 1710-1830, Under the French, British and Americans*, edited by Donna Valley Russell, published by the Detroit Society for Genealogical Research, 1982, 291 pages. FHL book 977.4 X2r.

■ **1766-1918 Deed Records; Grantee-Grantor Index, 1700-1903, Wayne County, Michigan**, microfilm of original records in the Wayne County courthouse, Detroit, Michigan. Early deeds are written in French and English. Additional indexes are at front of some volumes. Filmed by the Genealogical Society of Utah, 1974, 210 rolls, beginning with FHL film #926443 (Grantee Index, A-D, 1700-1885).

■ **1799, 1806, 1827 Detroit Censuses**. See *Early Michigan Census Records*, compiled by Ronald Vern Jackson, et al, published by Accelerated Indexing Systems, Bountiful, UT, 1976, 11 pages. Contains the early census records of Detroit, Wayne County, Michigan, 1799, 1806, 1827. FHL book 977.433 X2p.

■ **1827 & 1834 Territorial Censuses of Washtenaw County, Michigan**, microfilm of originals at the Bentley Library at the University of Michigan in Ann Arbor, Michigan. Filmed by the Genealogical Society of Utah, 1974, 1 roll, FHL film #955813.

■ **1827 Michigan Territorial Census, Chippewa County**, in *Lines From Algoma*, Vol. 12, No. 1 (Winter 1994).

■ **1827 Detroit, Michigan Territorial Census**, microfilm of typescript (location of original not noted), filmed by the Genealogical Society of Utah, 1976, 1 roll, FHL film #928180. Possibly the same typescript, see *Michigan Territorial Census, Detroit, 1827*, compiled by B.F.H. Witherell, microfilm of original published by the Michigan State Library, 1960, 15 pages. Filmed by the Genealogical Society of Utah, 1973, FHL film 927477. See also **1827 Michigan Territorial Census, Wayne County**, in *Detroit Society for Genealogical Research Magazine*, Vol. 19, No. 2 (Winter 1955).

■ **1837 Michigan State Census, Ionia County**, in *Michigan Heritage*, Vol. 6, No. 2 (Winter 1964).

■ **1837 Michigan State Census, Kalamazoo County**, (printed abstract) compiled by Mrs. Chalmers A. (Ruth Robbins) Monteith, 46 pages. Includes index. FHL book 977.417 X2p and FHL film #925967. See also *Michigan 1837 Index Census*, compiled by W. David Samuelsen, et al, published by Accelerated Indexing, Bountiful, UT, 1984, 27 pages. Kalamazoo County only. FHL book 977.417 X22j.

■ **1837-1935 Detroit (Michigan) City Directories**, microfilm of originals published by various publishers. Filmed by Research Publications, Woodbridge, CT, 1980-1984, 46 microfiches, 72 rolls of microfilm, beginning with FHL film #6043862. This series includes city directories for 1837, 1845, 1846, 1850, and every year (or two-year span) thereafter through 1935.

■ **1845 Michigan State Census of St. Joseph, Lenawee, Washtenaw, and Eaton Counties**, (printed index), edited by Ronald Vern Jackson, et al, published by Accelerated Indexing Systems, North Salt Lake, UT, 1988, 280 pages. FHL book 977.4 X22j.

■ **1845 Michigan State Census, Washtenaw County**, in *Family History Capers*, beginning with Vol. 5, No. 2 (Oct 1981); and by townships in various issues through Vol. 11, No. 1 (Summer 1987).

■ *1845 State Census, St. Joseph County, Michigan*, (printed abstract) copied and indexed by Bette Williams, published by the author, Kalamazoo, MI, 1968, 53 pages. FHL book 977.419 X2p and FHL film #927440.

■ **1845 Michigan State Census, Eaton County**, microfilm of original records at the Michigan State Archives, Lansing, MI, filmed by the Genealogical Society of Utah, 1972, 1 roll, FHL film #915300.

■ **1845 Michigan State Census, Lenawee County**, (printed abstract), microfilm of typescript at the Library of Michigan, Lansing, MI. Produced by the DAR, Lucy Wolcott Barnum Chapter, Adrian, MI. Filmed by the Genealogical Society of Utah, 1973, 1 roll, FHL film 926729.

■ **1845 Michigan State Census, Oakland County**, see *State Census of Oakland County, Michigan For the Year 1845*, compiled by the Oakland County Genealogical Society, Birmingham, MI, 1985, 290 pages. FHL book 977.438 X2sc 1845 and FHL film #1597984.

■ **1845 Michigan State Census, St. Clair County**, see *Index to 1845 State Census of St. Clair County, Michigan: Heads of Families and Names of White Males Over Twenty-one*, compiled by the St. Clair County Family History Group, Port Huron, MI, 1990, 78 pages. Includes name and location (usually township). Names listed alphabetically. FHL book 977.441 X22i 1845 index and FHL film #1425030.

■ **1845 Michigan State Census, Washtenaw County**, microfilm of originals at the Bentley Library at the University of Michigan in Ann Arbor, Michigan. Filmed by the Genealogical Society of Utah, 1974, 1 roll, FHL film #955813.

■ **1854 Michigan State Census, Eaton County**, microfilm of original records at the Michigan State Archives, filmed by the Genealogical Society of Utah, 1972, 1 roll, FHL film #915300, part 3.

■ **1854 Michigan State Census, Emmet County**, in *Detroit Society for Genealogical Research Magazine*, Vol. 52, No. 1 (Fall 1988) through Vol. 52, No. 2 (Winter 1989).

■ *1854 & 1874 Michigan State Census, Branch County*, (printed abstract), published by the Branch County Genealogical Society, Coldwater, MI, 110 pages. From preface: "The first part of the book shows Coldwater Township [and the village of Coldwater] only for 1854. The second part of the book shows all of Branch County for 1874." FHL book 977.421 X2b and FHL film #6005282.

■ **1864 Michigan State Census, Clinton County**, microfilm of originals at the Michigan State Archives, Lansing, MI, filmed by the Genealogical Society of Utah, 1972, 1 roll, FHL film #915297.

■ **1864 Michigan State Census, Eaton County**, microfilm of original records at the Michigan State Archives, Lansing, MI. Filmed by the Genealogical Society of Utah, 1972, 1 roll, FHL film #915302.

■ **1864 Michigan State Census, Houghton County**, microfilm of original records at the Michigan State Archives, Lansing, MI. Filmed by the Genealogical Society of Utah, 1972, 1 roll, FHL film #915276.

■ **1870 Federal Census, 1884 Michigan State Census, and 1894 Michigan State Census, Isabella County, Michigan,** microfilm of originals at the Michigan State Archives. Filmed by the Genealogical Society of Utah, 1972. Includes: **1870**: Schedule 2, (persons who died during the year ending 1st June, 1870), Broomfield, Chippewa, Coe, Coldwater, Lincoln, Rolland, Sherman, Union townships, (p. 685-699); **1884**: Schedule 2, persons who died during the year ending May 31, 1884); **1884**: Schedule 4, (manufactories, mines, fisheries, products of industry during the twelve months beginning with June 1, 1883 and ending with May 31, 1884); and **1894**: Schedule 4, (manufactories, mines, fisheries, products of industry 915312.

■ **1874 Michigan State Census, Eaton County,** microfilm of original records at the Michigan State Archives, Lansing, MI. Filmed by the Genealogical Society of Utah, 1972, 1 roll, FHL film #915305.

■ **1874 Michigan State Census, Houghton County,** microfilm of original records at the Michigan State Archives, Lansing, MI. Lists of names and occupations of all males over the age of 21 with some statistics on the population, agriculture and manufacturing. Arranged by townships: L'Anse, Schoolcraft, Webster, Portage, Quincy, Adams, Baraga, Catumis, Franklin, Hancock, Huron. Filmed by the Genealogical Society of Utah, 1972, 1 roll, FHL film #915277.

■ **1884 Michigan State Census, Wayne County,** in *Detroit Society for Genealogical Research Magazine,* abstracted by townships beginning with Vol. 44 (1981) and various issues through Vol. 64 (2001).

■ **1884 Michigan State Census, Barry County,** microfilm of original manuscripts at the Michigan State Archives, Lansing. Filmed by the Genealogical Society of Utah, 1972, 2 rolls, as follows:
 • **1884** census schedules, towns of Hastings, Hope, Irving, Johnstown, Maple Grove, Orangeville, Prairieville, Assyria, Baltimore, Carlton, Castelton, Rutland, Thornapple, Woodland, Yankee Springs, Barry, and Middleville, FHL film #915281.
 • **1884** census schedules, towns of Assyria, Baltimore, Barry, Carlton, Castelton, Rutland, Thornapple, Middleville, Woodland, Yankee Springs Hastings, FHL film #915284.

■ **1884 Michigan State Census, Benzie County,** microfilm of original manuscripts at the Michigan State Archives, Lansing. Filmed by the Genealogical Society of Utah, 1972, 1 rolls, FHL film #915294.

■ **1884 Michigan State Census, Emmet County,** microfilm of original records at the Michigan State Archives, Lansing, MI. Filmed by the Genealogical Society of Utah, 1974, 1 roll, FHL film #966509.

■ **1884 Michigan State Census, Ingham County,** microfilm of original records at the Michigan State Archives, Lansing, MI. Filmed by the Genealogical Society of Utah, 1972, 1 roll, FHL film #915308.

■ **1884 Michigan State Census, Kalamazoo County,** microfilm of original records at the Michigan State Archives, Lansing, MI. Arranged alphabetically by name of township (Pavilion to Wakeshma Townships, only), then numerically by dwelling number. Filmed by the Genealogical Society of Utah, 1972, 1 roll, FHL film #915314.

■ **1884 Michigan State Census, Kent County,** microfilm of original manuscripts at the Michigan State Archives, Lansing. Filmed by the Genealogical Society of Utah, 1975, 4 rolls, as follows:
 • **1884** Grand Rapids wards 1-4 FHL film #984118.
 • **1884** Grand Rapids, wards 5-6; Byron-Cannon Townships., FHL film #984049.
 • **1884** Kent County mortality schedules, June 1883 - May 1884; Ada - Vergennes Townships, FHL film #984656.
 • **1884** Walker-Wyoming Townships, Kent County manufactories, mines, fisheries; Agriculture: townships Ada - Wyoming, FHL film #984657.

■ **1884 Michigan State Census, Kent County.** See *Index to the 1884 State Census of Kent County, Michigan*, compiled by the Western Michigan Genealogical Society, Grand Rapids, MI, 1990, 309 pages. FHL book 977.455 X22i.

■ **1884 Michigan State Census, Keweenaw County**, microfilm of original records at the Michigan State Archives, Lansing, MI. Filmed by the Genealogical Society of Utah, 1972, 1 roll, FHL film #915273.

■ **1884 Michigan State Census, Lapeer County**, microfilm of original records at the Michigan State Archives, Lansing, MI. Includes schedule 1, the listing of residents. Lists are by township followed by Lapeer City. The listing begin with Elbe Township. (Missing lists: Almont, Arcadia, Attica Burlington, Burnside, Deerfield and Dryden townships) Filmed by the Genealogical Society of Utah, 1972, 1 roll, FHL film #915318.

■ *1884 Residents of Mecosta County, Michigan*, compiled by Evelyn M. Sawyer, published 1976 by the author, 76 pages. Source is believed to be the 1884 Michigan state census. Names are listed alphabetically. Includes name, occupation, section, town/township, and postal address. FHL book 977.452 X2s.

■ **1884 Michigan State Census, Menominee County**, microfilm of the original records at the Michigan State Archives, Lansing, MI. Filmed by the Genealogical Society of Utah, 1972, 2 rolls, as follows:
- **1884** Towns of Breen, Breitung, Cedarville, Cedar River, Ingallston, Menominee, Nadeau, and Norway, FHL film #915322.
- **1884** Towns of Spalding, Stephenson, Daggett, Menominee, Breen, Breitung, Ingallston, Nadeau, and Norway, FHL film #915323.

■ **1884 Michigan State Census, Montcalm County**, microfilm of original records at the Michigan State Archives, Lansing, MI. Filmed by the Genealogical Society of Utah, 1972, 1 roll, FHL film #915326.

■ **1884 Michigan State Census, Newaygo County**, see *Index to the 1884 Newaygo County, Michigan State Census*, compiled by Evelyn M.

Sawyer, published by the author, 1997, 65 pages. FHL book 977.458 X22s 1884.

■ **1884 Michigan State Census, Ottawa County**, microfilm of original records at the Michigan State Archives, Lansing, MI. Filmed by the Genealogical Society of Utah, 1972, 2 rolls, as follows:
- **1884** Towns of Allendale – Polkton, FHL film #915331.
- **1884** Towns of Robinson – Zeeland, FHL film #915332.

See also, *The residents of the Townships of Allendale, Blendon, Georgetown, Jamestown and Zeeland of Ottawa County, Michigan From the 1884 State Census*, compiled by Evelyn M. Sawyer, published by the author, 1996, 115 pages. Includes name, age, birthplace, years as Michigan resident, township, page and family number. Names alphabetically arranges in one listing. Data was taken from 1884 Michigan State census. FHL book 977.415 X2r 1884.

■ **1884 Michigan State Census, Washtenaw County**, microfilm of originals at the Bentley Library at the University of Michigan in Ann Arbor, Michigan. Towns are intermixed. Filmed by the Genealogical Society of Utah, 1974, 2 rolls, as follows:
- **1884** Inhabitants, FHL film #955808.
- **1884** Inhabitants, agriculture, manufactories, mines, fisheries, libraries, schools, and churches, FHL film #955809.

■ **1894 Michigan State Census, Barry County**, microfilm of original manuscripts at the Michigan State Archives, Lansing. Filmed by the Genealogical Society of Utah, 1972, 2 rolls, as follows:
- **1894** census schedules, towns of Johnstown, Maple Grove, Orangeville, Prairieville, Rutland, Thornapple, Middleville, Woodland, Yankee Springs, Hastings, FHL film #915285.
- **1894** census schedules, towns of Assyria, Baltimore, Delton, Barry, Carlton, Castleton, Hastings, Hope, Irving, Maple Grove, Orangeville, Prairieville, Rutland, Thornapple, Woodland, Yankee Springs, Foster, Dickinson Co., FHL film #915286.

■ **1894 Michigan State Census, Benzie County**, microfilm of original manuscripts at the Michigan State Archives, Lansing. Filmed by the Genealogical Society of Utah, 1972, 1 rolls, FHL film #915295.

■ **1894 Michigan State Census, Bay County**, microfilm of original manuscripts at the Michigan State Archives, Lansing, MI. Filmed by the Genealogical Society of Utah, 1972, 4 rolls, as follows:
  • 1894 schedule 1, inhabitants of Bay City, wards 6-11, FHL film #915290.
  • 1894 schedule 2, persons who died during the census year; Schedule 3, statistics of agriculture; Schedule 4, manufactories, mines, and fisheries; Schedule 5 libraries and churches, FHL film #915291.
  • 1894 schedule 1, inhabitants, towns of Bangor, Beaver, Frankenlust, Fraser, Garfield, Gibson, Bentley, Hampton, Essexville, Kawkawlin, Merritt, Monitor, Mount Forest, Pinconning, Portsmouth, and Williams, FHL film #915292.
  • 1894 schedule 1, inhabitants of Bay City wards 2-5; West Bay City wards 1-6, FHL film #915293.

■ **1894 Michigan State Census, Dickinson County**, microfilm of originals at the Michigan State Archives, Lansing, MI, filmed by the Genealogical Society of Utah, 1972, 1 roll, FHL film #915299.

■ **1894 Michigan State Census, Emmet County**, microfilm of original records at the Michigan State Archives, Lansing, MI. Filmed by the Genealogical Society of Utah, 1974, 1 roll, FHL film #915306.

■ **1894 Michigan State Census, Gratiot County**, microfilm of original records at the Michigan State Archives, Lansing, MI. Arranged alphabetically by name of township (Arcadia – Newark only), then numerically by dwelling number. Filmed by the Genealogical Society of Utah, 1972, 1 roll, FHL film #915307.

■ *1894 Michigan State Census Index, Hillsdale County, Michigan,* compiled by the Southern

Michigan Genealogical Society, 1989, 208 pages. FHL book 977.429 X2hi and FHL film #6067455.

■ **1894 Michigan State Census, Ingham County**, microfilm of original records at the Michigan State Archives, Lansing, MI. Filmed by the Genealogical Society of Utah, 1972, 1 roll, FHL film #915309.

■ **1894 Michigan State Census, Iosco County**, microfilm of original records at the Michigan State Archives, Lansing, MI. Filmed by the Genealogical Society of Utah, 1972, 1 roll, FHL film #915311.

■ **1894 Michigan State Census, Kalamazoo County**, microfilm of original records at the Michigan State Archives, Lansing, MI. Filmed by the Genealogical Society of Utah, 1972, 2 rolls, as follows:
  • 1894 schedule 1, towns of Alamo-Wakeshma, FHL film #915315.
  • 1894 schedule 1, city of Kalamazoo, wards 1-5, FHL film #915316.

■ **1894 Michigan State Census, Barry County**, microfilm of original manuscripts at the Michigan State Archives, Lansing. Filmed by the Genealogical Society of Utah, 1972, 2 rolls, as follows:
  • 1894 census schedules, towns of Johnstown, Maple Grove, Orangeville, Prairieville, Rutland, Thornapple, Middleville, Woodland, Yankee Springs, Hastings, FHL film #915285.
  • 1894 census schedules, towns of Assyria, Baltimore, Delton, Barry, Carlton, Castleton, Hastings, Hope, Irving, Maple Grove, Orangeville, Prairieville, Rutland, Thornapple, Woodland, Yankee Springs, Foster, Dickinson Co., FHL film #915286.

■ **1894 Michigan State Census, Kent County**, microfilm of original manuscripts at the Michigan State Archives, Lansing. Filmed by the Genealogical Society of Utah, 1975, 4 rolls, as follows:
  • 1894 Nelson-Plainfield Townships; Gaines-Lowell Townships; and Grand Rapids, 12th

ward, FHL film #984658.
- **1894.** Grand Rapids, 11th ward, 2nd ward, and 1st ward, FHL film #984227.
- **1894** Townships of Byron – Courtland; Ada – Bowne; and Solon – Tyrone, FHL film #984228.
- **1894** Townships of Vergennes – Wyoming; and Agricultural schedules, FHL film #984229.

■ *Index to the 1894 State Census, Kent County, Michigan*, compiled by Evelyn Sawyer, published by the Western Michigan Genealogical Society, 1992, 266 pages. FHL book 977.455 X22i.

■ **1894 Michigan State Census, Keweenaw County**, microfilm of original records at the Michigan State Archives, Lansing, MI. Filmed by the Genealogical Society of Utah, 1972, 1 roll, FHL film #915273.

■ **1894 Michigan State Census, Lapeer County**, microfilm of original records at the Michigan State Archives, Lansing, MI. Filmed by the Genealogical Society of Utah, 1972, 2 rolls, as follows:
- **1894** Towns of Almont, Arcadia, Attica, Burlington, Clifford, Burnside, Deerfield, Dryden, Thornville, Elba, Goodland, Hadley, Imlay, FHL film #915319.
- **1894** Towns of Lapeer Twp., Columbiaville, Marathon, Otter Lake, Mayfield, Metamora, North Branch, Oregon, Rich, Lapeer City, wards 1-4, FHL film #915320.

■ **1894 Michigan State Census, Leelanau County**, microfilm of originals held by the Grand Traverse Genealogical Society, Traverse City, MI, Includes schedule 1 (enumeration of inhabitants). Filmed by the society, 1 roll. FHL copy is film #2223587.

■ **1894 Michigan State Census, Menominee County**, microfilm of original records at the Michigan State Archives, Lansing, MI. Filmed by the Genealogical Society of Utah, 1972, 1 roll, FHL film #915324.

■ **1894 Michigan State Census, Montcalm County**, microfilm of original records at the Michigan State Archives, Lansing, MI. Filmed by

the Genealogical Society of Utah, 1972, 1 roll, FHL film #915327.

■ *1894 Muskegon County, Michigan Census Index; Head of Household*, compiled by the Muskegon County Genealogical Society, Muskegon, MI, 1986, 101 pages. From preface: "The following index includes the names of heads of household, strays (people living in the same household with a different last name) and children over the age of 18. Parents living with children are also included." Index does not include Liber 3 (Muskegon, wards 5-8 and North Muskegon); the volume is missing. FHL book 977.457 V22m.

■ **1894 Michigan State Census, Newaygo County**, see *Index to the 1894 Newaygo County, Michigan State Census*, compiled by Evelyn M. Sawyer, published by the author, 1997, 61 pages. FHL book 977.458 X22s 1894.

■ **1894 Michigan State Census, Ottawa County**, microfilm of original records at the Michigan State Archives, Lansing, MI. Filmed by the Genealogical Society of Utah, 1972. Includes name of person conducting farm, ownership, acres of land, ditches, farm value, fences, labor costs, and estimated cost of production in 1893. FHL film #915333.

■ **1894 Michigan State Census, Washtenaw County**, microfilm of originals at the Bentley Library at the University of Michigan in Ann Arbor, Michigan. Towns are intermixed. Filmed by the Genealogical Society of Utah, 1974, 3 rolls, as follows:
- **1894** Inhabitants, FHL film #955810.
- **1894** Inhabitants, FHL film #955811.
- **1894** Inhabitants, agriculture, manufactories, mines, fisheries, libraries, and churches, FHL film #955812.

■ See also *Index of 1894 State Census for Washtenaw County, Michigan*, prepared by Sarah Casewell Angell Chapter, National Society Daughters of the American Revolution, Ann Arbor, Michigan, published by the Genealogical Society of Washtenaw County, Michigan, 1984, 224 pages. FHL book 977.435 X22i.

■ **1917-1919 Michigan Veterans Serving with Allied Forces: Census of World War I Veterans**, microfilm of original records at the Michigan State Archives in Lansing. The list is alphabetical by veteran's name. Michigan State Archives No.: MS78-92 v. 368-373. Filmed by the Genealogical Society of Utah, 1996, 5 rolls, as follows:

- WWI Veterans (A-Cole), FHL film #2056789.
- WWI Veterans (Cole-Kee), FHL film #2056790.
- WWI veterans (Kel-Pl), FHL film #2056791.
- WWI veterans (Po-Williams, F), FHL film #2056792.
- WWI veterans (Williams, G-Z), FHL film #2056793.

Michigan Censuses & Substitutes Online

The following databases are available online at these sites:

www.ancestry.com
- 1699-1732 French Louisiana Census Tables
- 1820 United States Federal Census
- 1827-1870 Michigan Censuses
- 1830 United States Federal Census
- 1840 United States Federal Census
- 1850-1880 Mortality Schedules & Index
- 1850 United States Federal Census
- 1860 United States Federal Census
- 1870 United States Federal Census
- 1880 United States Federal Census
- 1885-1940 US Indian Census Schedules
- 1890 Veterans Schedules
- 1894 Michigan State Census
- 1910 United States Federal Census
- 1920 United States Federal Census
- 1930 United States Federal Census
- Vitelli Soundex of the U.S. Census

www.censusfinder.com
- 1820 Census of the Entire Michigan Territory
- 1827-1870 Michigan Census at Ancestry
- 1830 Federal Census of Entire Michigan Territory
- 1840 Military Pensioners Census
- 1870 Federal Census Index – Statewide
- 1870 Federal Census Images – Statewide
- 1880 Federal Census (Images)
- 1880 Federal Census Search at Family Search

- 1883 Pensioners Statewide
- 1894 State Census of Veterans – Statewide
- Michigan Statewide Databases of Census & Genealogy Records

www.census-online.com
- Countywide name lists

County (no of databases): Alcona (5); Alger (3); Allegan (1); Alpena (8); Antrim (7); Arenac (6); Baraga (3); Barry (7); Bay (1); Benzie (3); Berrien (3); Branch (3); Calhoun (1); Cass (3); Charlevoix (2); Cheboygan (3); Chippewa (7); Clare (1); Clinton (5); Crawford (3); Delta (8); Dickinson (2); Eaton (11); Emmet (1); Genesee (1); Gladwin (1); Gogebic (1); Grand Traverse (5); Gratiot (3); Hillsdale (45); Houghton (6); Huron (5); Ingham (8); Ionia (5); Iosco (8); Iowa (1); Iron (1); Isabella (17); Jackson (2); Kalamazoo (4); Kalkaska (1); Kent (11); Keweenaw (23); Lake (2); Lapeer (4); Leelanau (4); Lenawee (3); Livingston (1); Luce (6); Mackinac (2); Macomb (3); Manistee (12); Manitou (1); Marquette (7); Mason (3); Mecosta (10); Menominee (3); Michilimackinac (2); Midland (7); Missaukee (23); Monroe (15); Montcalm (2); Montmorency (2); Muskegon (53); Newaygo (3); Oakland (3); Oceana (3); Ogemaw (1); Ontonagon (1); Osceola (3); Oscoda (4); Otsego (4); Ottawa (11); Presque Isle (7); Roscommon (1); Saginaw (11); Sanilac (4); Schoolcraft (2); Shiawassee (12); St Clair (7); St Joseph (31); Tuscola (6); Van Buren (5); Washtenaw (11); Wayne (8); and Wexford (2).

MINNESOTA

Censuses & Substitutes, 1836-1908

Although eastern Minnesota was part of Michigan Territory in 1830, there were no known Minnesota people included in that census. The first census which included people in present-day Minnesota was taken as part of St. Croix County, Wisconsin Territory in 1836. In the 1840 federal census, Minnesota was part of two territories, with a only few people enumerated along the Mississippi River at Ft. Snelling and Wabasha as part of Clayton County, Iowa Territory; and a few settlements east of the Mississippi as part of St. Croix County, Wisconsin Territory.

When Minnesota became a territory in 1849, a territorial census was taken for that year, followed by one in 1853 and again in 1855; the latter two are very incomplete. Surviving territorial census name lists are shown below. Just prior to statehood, the U.S. federal government funded a special Minnesota Territory census in 1857, one of only eight non-decennial federal censuses ever taken. (The others were 1864 Arizona Territory, five states/territories in 1885, and 1907 Oklahoma).

After statehood in 1858, Minnesota took state censuses for 1865, 1875, 1885, 1895, and 1905. Most of the surviving manuscripts for Minnesota's territorial/state censuses, 1849-1905, were microfilmed by the Minnesota Historical Society (MHS) in St. Paul. All of these can be viewed at the Family History Library (FHL) in Salt Lake City, however, none of the Minnesota state censuses on microfilm can be borrowed on interlibrary loan through the FHL – they must be borrowed through the MHS.

The MHS also holds the original 1850 and 1860 federal censuses for all Minnesota counties – the state copies. For these censuses, genealogists have two versions to compare on microfilm: the federal copy and the state copy. Clearly, the 1850 and 1860 state copies are different due to the addition of other schedules mixed in with the population schedules, and page numbers for the schedules do not always agree with those found on the federal set. But, fortunately, the MHS has compiled indexes to their 1850 and 1860 state copies, which are noted below. The following statewide censuses and substitutes are available to genealogists seeking Minnesota ancestors:

■ **1836 Wisconsin Territorial Census** (Including Minnesota areas west of the Mississippi). See *The First Census of the Original Counties of Dubuque and Demoine (Iowa) Taken in July, 1836*, edited by Benjamin F. Shambaugh, microfilm of original published by the Historical Department of Iowa, Des Moines, IA, 1897-1898, 93 pages. Contents: pt. 1. Dubuque County, pt. 2. Demoine County. From the original manuscript returns preserved in the office of the Secretary of State of Wisconsin. Census taken in accordance with the act of Congress erecting the territory of Wisconsin (of which these two counties at the time formed a part) comprising the present states of Iowa, Minnesota and part of North and South Dakota. Filmed by the Genealogical Society of Utah, 1978, 1 roll, FHL film #1022202. For the part of the census covering the counties east of the Mississippi River see "1837 Wisconsin Territorial Census," in *Collections of the Wisconsin State Historical Society*, v. 13, p. 247-270.

■ **1840 Federal Census of Clayton County, Iowa Territory, and St. Croix County, Wisconsin Territory**, see *Minnesota 1840 Census Index (sic)*, edited by Ronald Vern Jackson, et al, published by Accelerated Indexing Systems, Bountiful, UT, 1981, 57 pages. FHL book 977.6 X22m.

■ **1849 Census of Minnesota Territory**, (printed abstract), copy of typescript located at the Minnesota Historical Society, St. Paul, MN. FHL book 977.6 A1 No. 3 and FHL film #908224. Indexed in *Minnesota 1849 Census Index*, edited by Ronald Vern Jackson, et al, published by Accelerated Indexing Systems, Bountiful, UT, 1981, 34 pages. FHL book 977.6 X22m 1849.

■ **1849 Territorial Census of Minnesota**, name list in *Minnesota Genealogist*, Vol. 11, No. 3 (Sep 1980); and *Minnesota Genealogical Journal*, Vol. 17 (Mar 1997).

■ **1850 Federal Census, Minnesota Territory** (Federal Copy), microfilm of originals at the National Archives, Washington, DC. Minnesota Territory's census schedules (showing a population of 6,077 people) were filmed by the National Archives, 1964, 1 roll, FHL film #14834. See also *Minnesota Territorial Census, 1850*, (state copy), edited by Patricia C. Harpole and Mary D. Nagle, published by the Minnesota Historical Society, St. Paul, MN, 1972, 115 pages. Includes index. The abstracted schedules were from the state's copy of the 1850 federal census. FHL book 977.6 X2ph 1850.

■ **1853 Minnesota Territory Census**, manuscript (fragments only) at the Minnesota Historical Society, St. Paul. Not on microfilm. Check availability at MHS at **www.mnhs.org/index.htm**. Printed abstracts from what appears to be an 1853 census are: *Mendota Township, Dakota County Assessment Record and Census of Families, 1853*, compiled by Mary Bakeman, publ. MHS, St. Paul, 1995. MHS call no CS42

M553 no. 13; and *List of Inhabitants in the Town of Stillwater, 1853*, by Mary Bakeman, publ. MHS, St. Paul, 1993. MHS call no. CS42 M553 no.9; which may be the same as "List of Inhabitants, Stillwater, 1853," in *Minnesota Genealogical Journal*, Vol. 9 (Mar 1993).

■ **1855 Minnesota Territory Census**, manuscript (fragments only) at the Minnesota Historical Society, St. Paul, MN. Not on microfilm. Check availability at MHS at **www.mnhs.org/index.htm.** See *Minnesota Population Census Schedule for Chisago, Doty, and Superior Counties, Manuscript 1855*, not on microfilm. State Archives Notebooks (Barcode 192489-10). See a few printed abstracts from what appears to be names from the 1855 census: *Census of Winona Prairie and Town Proper (1855)*, compiled by Mary Bakeman, publ. MHS, St. Paul, 2001. MHS call no CS42 M553 no. 26; which may be the same as **"Census, 1855, Winona Prairie,"** in *Minnesota Genealogical Journal*, Vol. 26 (Sep 2001); and *The Lost "1855" Census*, by Mary Bakeman, publ. MHS, St. Paul, 1992. MHS call no. CS42 M553 no.8; which may be the same as **"Census, 1855,"** in *Minnesota Genealogical Journal*, Vol. 8 (Sep 1992).

■ **1857 Minnesota Territory (Federal) Census**, microfilm of original records located at the National Archives, Central Plains Region. Filmed by the National Archives, 1973, series T1175, 8 rolls, available from the FHL as follows:
- Counties of Anoka – Dodge, FHL film #944283.
- Counties of Fairbault – Freeborn, FHL film #944284.
- Counties of Goodhue – Hennepin, FHL film #944285.
- Counties of Houston – Murray, FHL film #944286.
- Counties of Nicollet – Pipestone, FHL film #944287.
- Counties of Ramsey – Sibley, FHL film #944288.
- Counties of Stearns – Waseca, FHL film #944289.
- Counties of Washington – Wright, FHL film #944290.

Note: the 1857 federal census of Minnesota Territory included seven counties (Cottonwood, Jackson, Martin, Murray, Nobles, Pipestone, and Rock) that had no population, but Democrats fabricated census schedules complete with names, ages, occupations, etc. to cover their voting fraud. Having stuffed ballot boxes with made-up names of voters, the census schedules were fraudulently created to cover the ballot fraud. For the history of this census fraud, see Robert J. Forrest, "Mythical Cities of Southwestern Minnesota," *Minnesota History*, 14 (1933), pp243-52.

■ *1857 Census Records of Jackson County, Minnesota*, compiled by Sherman Lee Pompey, microfilm of typescript published by Historical and Genealogical Pub. Co., Independence, CA, 1965, 2 pages. FHL film #1000270, item 8. (See note above).

■ *1857 Territorial Census of Olmsted County (Minnesota)*, transcribed and published by Olmsted County Genealogical Society, Rochester, MN, 1995, 342 pages. Includes index. Gives dwelling number, family number, name, age, sex, color, birthplace, voters (whether native or naturalized), occupation, page number, line number, residence, and date. FHL book 977.6155 X2o 1857.

■ **1857 Minnesota Territory (Federal) Census**, county-wide abstracts by Mary Bakeman, published by the Minnesota Historical Society, 1994-2003 for the following counties:
- **1857** Carlton, Buchanan and Pine counties, MHS call no. CS42.M553 no.12.
- **1857** Manomin county, MHS call no. CS42 M553 no.19.
- **1857** Pembina County, MHS call no. CS42 M553 no. 21-23.
- **1857** Pierce county, call no. CS42 M553 no.26.
- **1857** Anoka County, call no. CS42 .M553 No.27-29.
- **1857** Benton county, call no. CS42 M553 No.30.

■ **1860 Federal Census, Minnesota** (federal copy), microfilm of original records at the National Archives, Washington, DC. Filmed twice by the National Archives, 1950, 1967, 13 rolls, beginning with FHL film #803567 (2nd filming, Anoka, Becker, Benton, Blue Earth, Brown, Buchanan, Carver, Crow Wing, Morrison, Cass, and Itasca Counties). Indexed in *Minnesota 1860 Census Index*, edited by Ronald Vern Jackson, et al, published by Accelerated Indexing Systems, Bountiful, UT, 1980, 397 pages. FHL book 977.6 X22m 1860. See also *Index to the 1860 Federal Census Schedules for Minnesota* (state copy), microfilm of original card index at the Minnesota Historical Society, Division of Archives and Manuscripts, in St. Paul, Minnesota. From FHL catalog: "Cards are arranged by surname in a single alphabetical sequence without respect to residential location. Discrepancies may occur (pagination, name spellings, order of county subdivisions, etc.) because the index was compiled from the state copy of the 1860 federal census, not the microfilm (federal) copy. The 1860 census card index was filmed by the MHS, 31 rolls. Available from the FHL in Salt Lake City, beginning with FHL film #1373881 (Aakers, Anna - Bacon, William). Interlibrary loan of the microfilm is available from the Minnesota Historical Society only. For more information, including roll contents, see Dennis E. Meissner, *Guide to the use of the 1860 Minnesota Population Census Schedules and Index* (Minnesota Historical Society, 1978; FHL book 977.6 A1 no. 28).

■ **1862-1866 Internal Revenue Assessment Lists for Minnesota**, microfilm of originals at the National Archives, Washington, DC, series M0774. The first roll indicates location of county name lists, 3 rolls, beginning with FHL film #1602225 (District 1, division 1-6, Annual , monthly, special lists Jan-Dec 1866).

■ **1865 Minnesota State Census**, microfilm of original manuscripts by the Minnesota State Library and Records Service, 1969, 3 rolls, available at the Family History Library as follows:
  • **1865** Counties of Blue Earth, Brown, Carlton, Lake, St. Louis, Carver, Cass, Chisago, Clay, Crow Wing, Dakota, Dodge, Faribault, Fillmore, Freeborn, and Goodhue, FHL film #565714.
  • **1865** Counties of Hennepin, Houston, Insanti, Kanabec, Le Suer, McLeod, Mahnomen, Martin, Meeker, Morrison, Mower, Nicollet, Olmsted, Pine, Ramsey, Rice, FHL film #565715.
  • **1865** Counties of Scott, Sherburne, Sibley, Stearns, Steele, Todd, Wabasha, Waseca, Washington, Watonwan, Winona, Wright - FHL film #565716.

1865 film available on interlibrary loan only from the Minnesota Historical Society in St. Paul. As a guide, refer to *Inventory to a Microfilm Edition of the Minnesota State Population Census Schedules, 1865*, published 1977 by the society, 25 pages. This inventory includes four aids: a county index, an introduction, a roll list, and a roll contents list. FHL book 977.6 X23i 1865. For more information visit the MHS Web site at **www.mnhs.org/index.htm**.

■ **1865 Minnesota State Census, Chisago County**, see *Index to the 1865 Minnesota State Census for Chisago County*, by Jay W. Liedman, published by the Minnesota Historical Society, 1998. MHS microfilm call no. F612.C55 L45 1998.

■ **1865 Minnesota State Census, Carlton County**, name list in *Genealogical Society of Carlton County Quarterly*, Vol. 12, No. 1 (Oct 1989).

■ **1865 Minnesota State Census, Clay County**, name list in *Northland Newsletter*, Vol. 1, No. 3 (Jul 1969).

■ **1865 Minnesota State Census, Civil War Soldiers & Officers**, in *La Crosse Area Genealogical Quarterly*, Vol. 21, No. 1 (Feb 1999).

■ **1866 List of Civil War Soldiers**, see *Minnesota Adjutant General's Report of 1866*, Adjutant General's Office, 1866, reprinted by Park Genealogical Books, Roseville, 1997, 464 pages. Gives soldier's name, age, birthplace, rank, regiment, company, date and place mustered in, date and place mustered out, and other information. Arranged in alphabetical order by soldier's name. FHL book 977.6 M2ma.

■ *1873 Minnesota State Business Directory: Alphabetic List of Business Firms, Proprietors and Artisans, State and County Officers—With Town and County Locations*, compiled by Antona Hawkins Richardson, reprint by Paduan Press, St. Paul, MN, 2001, FHL book 977.6 E4.

■ **1875 Minnesota State Census**, microfilm of original manuscripts (all MN counties) by the State Library and Records Service, 1969, 16 rolls,. Available at the FHL in Salt Lake City, beginning with FHL film #565717 (Counties of Aitkin, Anoka, Becker, Benton, Blue Earth, and Brown).

Film available on interlibrary loan only from the Minnesota Historical Society in St. Paul. As a guide, refer to *Inventory to a Microfilm Edition of the Minnesota State Population Census Schedules, 1875*, published 1977 by the society, 39 pages. This inventory includes four aids: a county index, an introduction, a roll list, and a roll contents list. FHL book 977.6 X23i 1875. For more information visit the MHS Web site at www.mnhs.org/index.htm.

A few county-wide indexes and abstracts to the 1875 state census have been published: See *Index to the 1875 Minnesota State Census for Chisago County*, by Jay W. Liedman and Terri Bulthuis, published by the authors, Willmar, MN, 2001, 294 pages. A copy of the original 1875 state census of Chisago County is available on Family History Library microfilm number #565718. Contains a full-name index to the census and photocopies from a microfilm of the original census. FHL book 977.661 X22L and FHL film #1440586.

See also, *Index to the 1875 Minnesota State Census for Chippewa County*, by Jay W. Liedman and Terri Bulthuis, published by the authors, Willmar, MN, 2002, 157 pages. Index lists first and last name, age, place of birth, precinct and family number. Also includes photocopies from a microfilm of the census. FHL book 977.639 X22L and FHL film #6006020. See also *Second Decennial Census of the State of Minnesota, Waseca County by Township, 1875*, microfilm of originals at the Waseca County Courthouse, Waseca, MN. This is the county's duplicate set of the original 1875 census schedules. Arranged by township and gives name, age, sex, color, nativity, parents' nativity, and condition (deaf, blind, insane, etc.). Filmed by the Genealogical Society of Utah, 1983, 1 roll, FHL film #1320463.

■ **1875 Minnesota State Census, Lincoln County**, name list in *Prairieland Pioneer*, Vol. 9, No. 2 (Summer 1992) through Vol. 10, No. 4 (Winter 1993).

■ **1875 Minnesota State Census, Lyon County**, abstracts by townships, in *Prairieland Pioneer*, Vol. 3, No. 3 (Spring 1987), and various issues through Vol. 9, No. 4 (Summer 1993).

■ *1875 Census Records of Greenbush, Mille Lacs County, Minnesota*, compiled by Sherman Lee Pompey, typescript, Lists inhabitants alphabetically by surname, with age, birthplace, father's birth place, and mother's birthplace. Filmed by the Genealogical Society of Utah, 1970, 1 roll, FHL film #823651.

■ **1885 Minnesota State Census**, microfilm of originals (all MN counties) by the State Library and Records Service, St. Paul, MN, 1969, 28 rolls. Available at the FHL beginning with FHL film #56733 (Counties of Aitkin, Carlton, Kanabec, Hubbard, Cass, Anoka, Becker, Beltrami, Cook, Lake, Pipestone, and Benton (thru town of Langola). Film available on interlibrary loan only from the Minnesota Historical Society in St. Paul. As a guide, refer to *Inventory to a Microfilm Edition of the Minnesota State Population Census Schedules, 1885*, published 1977 by the society, 54 pages. This inventory includes four aids: a county index, an introduction, a roll list, and a roll contents list. FHL book 977.6 X23i 1885 And FHL film #6101555. For more information visit the MHS Web site at **www.mnhs.org/index.htm.**

■ **1885 Minnesota State Census, Lyon County**, in *Prairieland Pioneer*, Vol. 4, No. 2 (Winter 1988).

■ **1885 Minnesota State Census, McLeod County**, in *Prairieland Pioneer*, Vol. 1, No. 2 (Nov 1984).

■ **1885 Minnesota State Census, Lake Sarah Township, Murray County**, in *Prairieland Pioneer*, Vol. 4, No. 3 (Spring 1988).

■ **1885 Minnesota State Census, Surnames in Girard Township, Otter Tail County**, in *Otter Tail County Genealogical Society Newsletter*, Vol. 19, No. 1 (Mar 2001).

■ **1895 Minnesota State Census**, microfilm of originals (all MN counties) by the State Library and Records Service, St. Paul, MN, 59 rolls. Available at the FHL beginning with FHL film #565761 (Counties of Aitkin, Anoka, Becker (thru township of Green Valley). Film available on interlibrary loan only from the Minnesota Historical Society in St. Paul.

As a guide, refer to *Inventory to a Microfilm Edition of the Minnesota State Population Census Schedules, 1895*, published 1977 by the society, 71 pages. This inventory includes four aids: a county index, an introduction, a roll list, and a roll contents list. FHL book 977.6 X23i 1895. For more information visit the MHS Web site at **www.mnhs.org/index.htm.**

See also, *Index to the 1895 Minnesota State Census for Chisago County*, by Jay W. Liedman and Terri Bulthuis, published by the authors, Willmar, MN, 2000, 261 pages. FHL book 977.661 X22L 1895 and FHL film #1440404.

See also, *Index to the 1895 Minnesota State Census for Kandiyohi County*, by Jay W. Liedman and Terri Bulthuis, published by the authors, Willmar, MN, 2001, 321 pages. FHL book 977.648 X22L and FHL film #1440517.

See also *Index to the 1895 Minnesota State Census for Meeker County*, by Jay W. Liedman and Terri Bulthuis, published by the authors, Willmar, MN, 2002, 330 pages. Index lists name, age, precinct and house number. FHL book 977.649 X22L and FHL film #6005998.

■ **1895 Minnesota State Census, Menahga, Becker County**, in *Heart O'lakes Genealogical Newsletter*, Vol. 16, No. 1 (Mar 1993) and Vol. 16, No. 2 (Jun 1993).

■ **1905 Minnesota State Census**, microfilm of originals (all MN counties) by the State Library and Records Service, St. Paul, MN, 58 rolls. Available at the FHL in Salt Lake City, beginning with FHL film #928767 (Aitkin, Anoka, Becker Counties). Film available on interlibrary loan only from the Minnesota Historical Society in St. Paul.

As a guide, refer to *Inventory to a Microfilm Edition of the Minnesota State Population Census Schedules, 1905*, published 1977 by the society, 79 pages. This inventory includes four aids: a county index, an introduction, a roll list, and a roll contents list. FHL book 977.6 X23i 1905 and FHL film #6003117. For more information visit the MHS Web site at **www.mnhs.org/index.htm.**

■ **1905 Minnesota State Census, Itasca County**, see *Pines, Mines and Lakes: The Story of Itasca County, Minnesota*, by James E. Rottsolk,

published by the Itasca County Historical Society, 1960, 155 pages. Includes a transcription of the 1905 state census for the county and a list of 50-year residents living in 1958. FHL book 977.678 H2r.

■ **1905 Minnesota State Census, Chippewa County**, by townships, in *Chippewa County Clippings*, Vol. 1, No. 1 (Sep 1994) through various issues to Vol. 6, No. 4 (Dec 1999).

■ **1905 Minnesota State Census, Tyler, Lincoln County**, in *Prairieland Pioneer*, Vol. 3, No. 1 (Fall 1986) and Vol. 3, No. 2 (Winter 1986).

■ **1905 Minnesota State Census, Lyon County,** in *Prairieland Pioneer*, Vol. 1, No. 2 (Nov 1984) through Vol. 4, No. 2 (Winter 1988).

■ **1908 History**. See *Minnesota in Three Centuries, 1655 – 1908*, by Lucius Frederick Hubbard, et al, published New York, 1908, 4 vols.. Indexed in *An Every-name Index to Minnesota in Three Centuries*, compiled by Rod & Marie Nordberg for the Southern California Genealogical Society, 1990, 17 pages, FHL book 977.6 H2mi index.

Minnesota Censuses & Substitutes Online

The following databases are available at: **www.ancestry.com**
- 1699-1732 French Louisiana Census Tables
- 1835-1890 Minnesota Censuses
- 1849-1905 Minnesota Territorial & State Censuses
- 1850 United States Federal Census
- 1850-1880 Mortality Schedules & Index
- 1870 United States Federal Census
- 1880 United States Federal Census
- 1885-1940 US Indian Census Schedules
- 1890 Veterans Schedules
- 1890 US Federal Census Fragment
- 1900 United States Federal Census
- 1900-1920 Rice County, MN Census
- 1910 United States Federal Census
- 1920 United States Federal Census
- 1920 Northfield, MN Census
- 1920 Faribault, Minnesota Census,
- 1920 Winona County, Minnesota Census,
- 1930 United States Federal Census

www.censusfinder.com
- 1835-1890 Minnesota Census at Ancestry
- 1850 Federal Census Images – Statewide
- 1880 Federal Census - images
- 1880 Federal Census Search at Family Search
- Minnesota State Databases of Census & Genealogy Records

www.census-online.com
- **Countywide name lists (no of databases):** Aitkin (4); Anoka (1); Becker (25); Beltrami (0); Benton (5); Big Stone (0); Blue Earth (0); Brown (0); Carlton (1); Carver (5); Cass (0); Chippewa (0); Chisago (0); Clay (2); Clearwater (0) Cook (0); Cottonwood (0); Crow Wing (4); Dakota (4); Dodge (0); Douglas (2); Faribault (3); Fillmore (0); Freeborn (0); Goodhue (0); Grant (0); Hennepin (1); Houston (2); Hubbard (2); Isanti (0); Itasca (3); Jackson (0); Kanabec (0); Kandiyohi (0); Kittson (1); Koochiching (1); Lac Qui Parle (0); Lake (0); Lake Of The Woods (0); Le Sueur (0); Lincoln (0); Lyon (0); Mahnomen (0); Mankahta (3); Marshall (0); Martin (0); McLeod (9); Meeker (0); Mille Lacs (1); Morrison (1); Mower (0); Murray (4); Nicollet (0); Nobles (5); Norman (0); Olmsted (0); Otter Tail (0); Pembina (2); Pennington (0); Pine (0); Pipestone (0); Polk (2); Pope (1); Ramsey (2); Red Lake (0); Redwood (0); Renville (0); Rice (1); Rock (0); Roseau (1); Scott (0); Sherburne (0); Sibley (1); St Louis (1); Stearns (2); Steele (39); Stevens (0); Swift (0); Todd (0); Traverse (1); Wabasha (3); Wadena (0); Wahnata (2); Waseca (4); Washington (1); Watonwan (0); Wilkin (1); Winona (0); Wright (0); and Yellow Medicine (0).

OHIO

Censuses & Substitutes, 1787-1907

There have been no state sponsored censuses in Ohio which included the entire population. But, even without the title "census," Ohio has an abundance of tax lists and enumerations that can substitute as state censuses. For example, the State Constitution of 1802 provided for an enumeration of white male inhabitants over the age of 21 to be taken every four years for the purpose of legislative apportionment. The first of these "Quadrennial Enumerations" was taken in 1803, and continued every four years until they officially ended in 1911. Tax assessors from each county were in charge of the Quadrennial

Enumerations, and as a result, they were often mistakenly referred to as "tax lists." But the name lists were separate from tax assessment lists—they were compiled specifically for determining the number of males of voting age, and for apportionment of the state legislature. The name lists of white males over 21 often included other names of eligible males living in the same household, but more often, the extra persons were simply noted by their numbers.

Of the more than 1,800 county-wide Quadrennial Enumerations taken between 1803 and 1911, less than 100 lists have survived. Most of them are located today at one of the Ohio regional archives sites. **The Ohio Network of American History Research Centers** is divided into eight geographical areas. For information about the facilities and archival holdings of each of these Centers, make your inquiries to one of the Network sites directly. They are all located at university or historical society libraries. The best map and list of Web sites/addresses for all eight Network facilities can be found at the Bowling Green State University site at: **www.bgsu.edu/colleges/library/cac/genealogy/gene3.html.**

Most of the earliest censuses taken in the Northwest Territory and Ohio were lost. The exception was for Washington County, where Rufus Putnam's New Ohio Company kept good records beginning in 1788, and saved copies of the earliest censuses. Putnam's papers are located today at the Campus Museum of Marietta College, Marietta, Ohio.

During the first half of the 19th century, numerous tax lists were taken at the county level. These were duplicated by the local officials, with a copy sent to the state auditor's office. Most of the surviving name lists today are the original State Auditor's "duplicate" tax records, now stored at one of the Network research centers. It is also the duplicate tax lists that are more represented (compared to Quadrennial lists or census lists) with microfilm copies at the Family History Library for virtually all counties of Ohio. The series of duplicate tax lists, 1801-1814, were filmed as a series, and are included in the lists below, as well as a published statewide name index. As an example of the wealth of county-wide duplicate tax lists, from 1815 forward, the first few Ohio counties, Adams, Ashtabula, Allen, et al, are identified below. But to identify all duplicate tax lists for Ohio's 88 counties would require another chapter for Ohio. (There are at least 600 separate Ohio county tax lists on microfilm at the FHL).

Duplicate Tax Lists for all Ohio counties on microfilm can be located using the **www.familysearch.org** Website (Go to FHL Catalog — Place Search — Place: [name of county] — Part of: [Ohio] — click on "Taxation"). There have been a number of state-wide tax lists compiled and published, mostly by taking the county-wide lists for one year for all counties. Any such statewide compilations are identified below.

■ **1787-1840 Ohio**, CD-ROM publication, part of the Family Tree Maker Archives, Land and Tax Records, published by Broderbund, 1999. Contents: *Early Ohio Settlers: Purchasers of Land in Southeastern Ohio, 1800-1840 (Marietta Land Office)*, compiled by Ellen T. Berry and David A. Berry; *Early Ohio Settlers: Purchasers of Land in Southeastern Ohio, 1800-1840 (Cincinnati Land Office)*, compiled by Ellen T. Berry and David A. Berry; *Early Ohio Settlers: Purchasers of Land in East and East Central Ohio*, compiled by Ellen Thomas Berry and David A. Berry; *First Ownership of Ohio Lands*, by Albion Morris Dyer; and *Early Ohio Tax Records*, by Esther Weygandt Powell. FHL CD No. 9, pt. 651.

■ **1787-1871**. See *Virginia Military District Lands of Ohio; Indexes*, microfilm of index and original records at the State Auditor's Office in Columbus, Ohio (1958). The Index to entrymen gives name of soldier or heirs, entry number (same as the survey number), warrant number of soldier's claim, book and page number wherein found, acreage. Indexes are included in Survey books v. A [1], B, B3, C, E, F; and in most Entry books. The following information comes from the State Auditor's Office from a directory and from a booklet, *Ohio Lands: A Short History*, copyrighted in 1991. "The Virginia Military District (VMD) lands lie north of the Ohio River and between the Scioto and Little Miami Rivers. It covers all the present-day counties of Adams, Brown, Clermont, Clinton, Fayette, Highland, Madison, and Union counties; and parts of Champaign, Clark, Delaware, Franklin, Greene, Hamilton, Hardin, Logan, Marion, Pickaway, Pike, Ross, Scioto, and Warren counties. The

VMD lands were given by the State of Virginia as a reward to her Revolutionary War soldiers or their heirs. The rectangular survey system was not used in the VMD as used elsewhere in Ohio. To claim a warrant issued to a soldier, the soldier or his heirs sent the warrant to the Principal Surveyor of the Virginia District of Ohio. He in turn gave it to the Deputy Surveyor who gave a general description of the entry and then made a survey based on physical features such as certain trees, etc. The warrant then was sent to the U.S. Government and a U.S. Patent was made out. The first survey was made in 1787 and the first U.S. Patent was issued in 1796. In 1830 and 1852 the VMD warrants could be exchanged for land scrip and used to buy any public land open for sale. Virginia in 1852 ceded to the U.S. government any land not yet located in the VMD. This land was given to Ohio in 1871 and they gave it to Ohio State University. The University sold these lands into the 1940s." Filmed by the Genealogical Society of Utah, 1995, 1958, 33 rolls, beginning with FHL film #2022655 (Index to entrymen: A – Coalier).

■ **1788-1799 Northwest Territory & 1803-1817 Ohio.** See *Ohio Early Census Index*, edited by Ronald Vern Jackson et al, published by A.G.E.S., Salt Lake City, 1974, 2 vols. Contents: vol. 1: Cincinnati, 1798, 1799, 1817; vol. 2: Others, 1788, 1789, 1796, 1798, 1799. FHL book 977.1 X22jr. See also *Early Ohio Census Records*, 2nd edition, 3rd printing, published by Accelerated Indexing, Bountiful, UT, 1974, which shows censuses as those for 1800 Northwest Territory and Ohio 1803 and 1810 (Washington County only). FHL book 977.1 X2p.

■ **1788-1820 Marriages**. See *Ohio Marriages Recorded in County Courts Through 1820: An Index*, compiled by Jean Nathan, et al, published by the Ohio Genealogical Society, Mansfield, OH, 1966, 1,167 pages. FHL book 977.1 V22o.

■ **1700s-1800s**. *The Ohio Surname Index*, compiled by the Ohio Society of the Daughters of the American Revolution, under the supervision of Miss Alice Boardman, microfilm of card index, now located at the Ohio Historical Society, Columbus, OH (1984). Arranged alphabetically by surname. Some cards are out of order. Indexes individuals mentioned in various county histories and historical magazines. Film at FHL library: 64 rolls, beginning with FHL film #398201 (Aarents, William - Alkire, Ruan).

■ **1790 Northwest Territory.** See *Territorial Census Index Substitute, Ohio, 1790,* edited by Sue Powell Morgan, published by Genealogical Services, West Jordan, UT, 1998, 274 pages. Includes name, town, county, record type, date and page number. FHL book 977.1 X22m 1790.

■ *Ohio Source Records: From the Ohio Genealogical Quarterly.* Excerpted and reprinted from *The Ohio Genealogical Quarterly,* (Genealogical Publishing Co., Inc., Baltimore, 1986). with added publisher's note, contents, index, and textual notes. Contains abstracts of probate records, marriages, cemetery inscriptions, histories, family histories, tax lists, military records, etc. FHL book 977.1 D28o.

■ **1800-1803 Censuses.** See *Second Census of the United States, 1800, Population Schedules, Washington County, Territory Northwest of the River Ohio; and Population Census, 1803, Washington County, Ohio,* microfilm of originals by the National Archives, Washington, DC. Arranged in alphabetical order by township. Lists name of all free males over the age of 21. Special microfilm publication by the National Archives, 1994, series M1804, 1 roll, FHL film #2155491.

■ **1801-1814 Tax Records of Ohio,** microfilm of the original records at the Ohio Historical Society, Archives-Library Division, Columbus, Ohio. Filmed by the Genealogical Society of Utah, 1967, 14 rolls, as follows:

• **1801.** Book entries of the lands of non-residents situated between the Scioto & Little Miami Rivers commonly known by the name of the Virginia Army Lands (Virginia Military District), vol. 1, 1801, FHL film #522837.

• **1806-1807.** Tax record, vol. 2, 1806 (Adams, Athens, Franklin, Highland, Muskingum, Ross, Scioto counties), Tax record, vol. 3, 1806 (Belmont, Fairfield, Jefferson counties); Tax record, vol. 4, 1806 (Butler, Champaign, Clermont, Greene, Montgomery counties); Tax record, vol. 5, 1806 (Hamilton and Warren counties); Tax record, vol.

6, 1806 (Trumbull, Columbiana, Gallia counties; Tax record, vol. 7, 1807 (Adams, Champaign, Clermont, Green, Highland, Ross, Scioto counties), FHL film #522838.

• **1807.** Tax record, vol. 8, 1807 (Belmont, Columbiana, Jefferson counties; Tax record, vol. 9, 1807 (non- resident sixth district resident Geauga and Trumbull counties; Tax duplicates, vol. 10, 1807 (Franklin, Fairfield, Muskingum counties); Tax duplicate, vol. 11, 1807 (Butler, Warren, Hamilton, Montgomery counties), FHL film #522839.

• **1808.** Tax duplicates, vol. 12, 1808 (Fairfield and Washington counties); Tax record, vol. 13, 1808 (non residents fifth district residents Belmont, Columbiana, Jefferson counties; Tax record, vol. 14, 1808 (Adams, Greene, Hamilton, Montgomery counties), FHL film #522840.

• **1808.** Tax record, vol. 15, 1808 (Geauga, Muskingum, Trumbull counties); Tax record, vol. 16, 1808 (Athens, Franklin, Gallia, Highland counties; Tax record, vol. 17, 1808 (non residents fourth and sixth district), FHL film #522841.

• **1809.** Duplicate of land tax, vol. 18, (A - N various counties) - FHL film #522842.

• **1811.** Duplicate of land tax, vol. 19, (Adams – Hamilton), FHL film #522843.

• **1811.** Duplicate of land tax, vol. 20, (Jefferson – Warren) - FHL film #522844.

• **1812.** Duplicate of land tax, vol. 21, (Adams – Hamilton), FHL film #514124.

• **1812.** Duplicate of land tax, vol. 22, (Jefferson – Warren), FHL film #514125.

• **1813.** Duplicate of land tax, vol. 23, (Adams – Hamilton), FHL film #514126.

• **1813** Duplicate of land tax, vol. 24, (Jefferson – Warren), FHL film #514127.

• **1814.** Duplicate of land tax, vol. 25, (Adams – Franklin), FHL film #514128.

• **1814.** Duplicate of land tax, vol. 26-27, (Gallia – Warren),   FHL film #514129.

■ *Early Ohio Tax Records,* abstracts compiled by Esther Weygant Powell, Ohio State Auditor, 1971, 459 pages. FHL book 977.1 R4op. Indexed in *The Index to Early Ohio Tax Records,* compiled by Carol Willsey Bell, and friends of Esther Weygandt Powell in cooperation with the Ohio Genealogical Society, published Akron, OH, 1973, 173 pages. FHL book 977.1 R4op index and FHL film #1033949.

■ **1801-1824 Tax Lists.** See *Ohio's Virginia Military Tract: Index of 1801 Tax List,* compiled by Fay Maxwell, published by the Ohio Genealogy Center, 1991, 19 pages. From title page: "Index of the Virginia Militiamen who served in the revolution. The tract is located west of Ohio's Scioto River." Includes Hardin County 1821 & 1833 tax record, and Marion County 1824 tax record. FHL book 977.1 R4m.

■ *1802 Census of Clermont County: the Northwest Territory of the United States of America,* compiled and published by the Brown County Genealogical Society, Georgetown, OH, 1988, 9 pages. FHL book 977.1 A1 no. 323 and FHL film #6088560.

■ **1803-1827, 1831 and 1847 Quadrennial Enumerations, Adams County, Ohio,** see *Male Enumeration Lists of Adams County, Ohio,* by the Adams County Genealogical Society, West Union, OH, 2 vols., 199?. From FHL catalog: "These records may include some names from Brown County until Brown County was formed in 1819." Includes index. Contents: v. 1. 1803-1827 -- v. 2. 1831 and 1847. Library has v. 1-2 bound together. FHL book 977.186 X2m and FHL film #2055364.

■ **1804 Ohio**. See *Resident Proprietors of the Connecticut Western Reserve, 1804: An Ohio Tax List of 1804,* compiled by Nellie M. Raber, published R.D. Craig, Cincinnati, 1963, 26 pages. FHL book 977.1 A1 no. 30 and FHL film #896888. Another filming, FHL film #928353.

■ *1807 Census of Butler County, Ohio,* edited by Willard Heiss and R. Thomas Mayhill, published by Eastern Indiana Publishing Co., Knightstown, IN, 1968,. 23 pages. FHL book 977.1 A1 No. 137 and FHL film #1036243.

■ **1810 Ohio**. See *Third census of the United States, 1810, Population Schedules, Washington County, Ohio,* Includes townships of Adams, Belpre, Fearing, Grand View, Marietta, Newport, Roxburg, Salem, Warren, Waterford, Wesley, and Worcester. Lists name of head of the family and age brackets of other members of the family. Arranged in alphabetical order by township. Special microfilm publication by the National

Archives, 1994, series M1803, 1 roll, FHL film #2155490.

■ *Ohio 1810 Tax Duplicate Arranged in a State-wide Alphabetical List of Names of Taxpayers: With an Index of Names of Original Entries,* compiled by Gerald M. Petty, published by the author, Columbus, OH, 1976, 221 pages. Includes index. FHL book 977.1 R4p and FHL film #982373.

■ **1810 Tax Records of Various Ohio Counties,** microfilm of original records at the Ohio Historical Society, Archives-Library Division, Columbus, Ohio. Name lists are organized alphabetically by county. Filmed by the Genealogical Society of Utah, 1967-68, 3 rolls, beginning with FHL film #534818 (counties A-B).

■ *The 1812 Census of Ohio: A Statewide Index of Taxpayers,* published by T.L.C Genealogy, Miami Beach, FL, 1992, 221 pages. This is an alphabetical list of all resident land owners in Ohio. FHL book 977.1 R2co.

■ **1816-1838 Tax Duplicate, Adams County, Ohio,** microfilm of original records now at the Ohio Historical Society, Archives-Library Division, Columbus, Ohio. Filmed by the Genealogical Society of Utah, 1967-1968, 5 rolls, as follows:
  • **1816-1823,** FHL film #514130.
  • **1824-1829,** FHL film #514131.
  • **1830-1832,** FHL film,#514132.
  • **1833-1836,** FHL film #514133.
  • **1837-1838,** FHL film #514134.

■ **1816-1838 Duplicate Tax Records of Ashtabula County, Ohio,** microfilm of original records now at the Ohio Historical Society, Archives-Library Division, Columbus, Ohio. These records include resident and non-resident owners, delinquent tax properties, and personal property. From 1816-1825 arranged by first letter of surname and beginning in 1826 arranged by township then first letter of surname. Filmed by the Genealogical Society of Utah, 1967, 9 rolls, as follows:
  • **1816-1822,** FHL film #514136.
  • **1823-1824,** FHL film #514137.
  • **1825-1826,** FHL film #528364.

- **1827-1828**, FHL film #528365.
- **1829-1830**, FHL film #514138.
- **1831-1832**, FHL film #514139.
- **1833-1834**, FHL film #514140.
- **1835-1836**, FHL film #514141.
- **1837-1838**, FHL film #514142.

■ **1816-1838 Tax Duplicate, Athens County, Ohio,** microfilm of original records at the Ohio Historical Society, Archives-Library Division, Columbus, Ohio. Filmed by the Genealogical Society of Utah, 1967-68, 4 rolls, as follows:
- **1816-1826**, FHL film #514143.
- **1827-1830**, FHL film #514144.
- **1831-1834**, FHL film #514145.
- **1835-1838**, FHL film #514146.

■ **1816-1838 Tax Records, Belmont County, Ohio,** microfilm of original records in the Ohio Historical Society, Archives-Library Division, Columbus, Ohio. These records are duplicates that were made for the state auditors office. Filmed by the Genealogical Society of Utah, 1966, 10 rolls, as follows:
- **1816-1823**, FHL film #514147.
- **1824-1826**, FHL film #514148.
- **1827-1828**, FHL film #514149.
- **1829-1830**, FHL film #514150.
- **1831**, FHL film #830277.
- **1832**, FHL film #864973.
- **1833**, FHL film #864974.
- **1834-1835**, FHL film #864975.
- **1836-1837**, FHL film #864976.
- **1838**, FHL film #167679.

■ **1816-1838 Tax Records of Clinton County, Ohio**, microfilm of originals at the Ohio Historical Society, Archives-Library Division, Columbus, Ohio. Filmed by the Genealogical Society of Utah, 1967-1968, 4 rolls, as follows:
- **1816-1823**, FHL film #476484.
- **1824-1828**, FHL film #476485.
- **1829-1833**, FHL film #476486.
- **1834-1838**, FHL film #476487.

■ **1825 Ohio Tax List**. See *Index of the Ohio 1825 Tax Duplicate*, compiled by Gerald M. Petty, published by the author, Columbus, OH, 1981, 189 pages. FHL book 977.1 R42p and FHL film #1597666.

■ **1827 Quadrennial Enumeration, Belmont County, Ohio**, in *Genealogical Records in Belmont County, Ohio*, compiled and published by the Belmont County Chapter of the Ohio Genealogical Society, 10 vols., including local genealogy, cemeteries, newspapers, church records, vital records, and the 1827 enumeration of males over 21 years of age. FHL book 977.193 D29o, vol. 1-10.

■ **1832-1850 Duplicate Tax Records, Allen County, Ohio**, microfilm of original records now at the Center for Archival Collections, Bowling Green State University, Bowling Green, Ohio, and the Ohio Historical Society, Columbus. Includes surname indexes. Contains records of tax assessments of real estate, with description of property. Some volumes have indexes. Volume numbers for some volumes are those assigned by the Ohio Historical Society for filing purposes. Filmed by the Genealogical Society of Utah, 1967, 1974, 9 rolls, as follows:
- no dates, FHL film #954812.
- **1832-1833, 1832-1838, 1836-1839,** FHL film #954813.
- **1832-1838**, FHL film #514135.
- **1840**, FHL film #954814.
- **1841-1843**, FHL film #954815.
- **1844**, FHL film #954816.
- **1845-1846**, FHL film #954817.
- **1846-1848**, FHL film #954818.
- **1850**, FHL film #954819.

■ *1833-1994 Governor's Deeds Card Index*, microfilm of original records at the Ohio Historical Society, Archives-Library Division, Columbus, Ohio, filmed by the Genealogical Society of Utah, 1995, 4 rolls, beginning with FHL film #2022287 (Index, A – Downing).

■ **1835 Ohio Tax List**. See *Index of the Ohio 1835 Tax Duplicate*, compiled by Gerald M. Petty, published by Petty's Press, Columbus, OH, 1987, 320 pages. Includes information of name, county, township, town or village, type of tax record, and page. FHL book 977.1 R42pg.

■ **1846-1880**. See *Ashland County, Ohio Research Aid*, compiled and published by the Ashland County Chapter of the Ohio Genealogical

Society, Ashland, Ohio, 1984, 10 vols. Includes deeds records, maps, tax and chattel lists, cemetery inscriptions, and biographical sketches. FHL book 977.129 R2a vol. 1-10.

■ **1851-1900 Ohio Marriages**, see *Ohio, 1851-1900*, CD-ROM publication, part of the Family Tree Maker Family Archives, Marriage Index No. 236, published by Broderbund, 1998. Lists approximately 272,000 individuals who were married in Ohio between 1851 and 1900. FHL CD-ROM no. 9 pt. 236.

■ **1851-1907 Quadrennial Enumerations, Auglaize County, Ohio**, microfilm of original records at the Archives and Special Collections, Paul L. Dunbar Library, Wright State University, Dayton, Ohio. These records are enumerations of all the male inhabitants above the age of 21 years. Filmed by Wright State Univ., 1979, 2 rolls. FHL film #1763576-1763577.

■ **1853-1861 Ohio (State) Directories**, microfilm of originals published by various publishers, by Research Publications, Woodbridge, CT, 1980-1984, 41 microfiches, as follows:

- **1853-1854** W. W. Reilly & Co.'s Ohio State business directory by Morgan & Overend (11 fiches) FHL film #6044295.
- **1857** Williams' Ohio State register and business mirror, by C. S. Williams (5 fiches), FHL film #6044296.
- **1859-1860** George W. Hawes' Ohio State gazetteer and business directory by George W. Hawes (11 fiches), FHL film #6044297.
- **1860-1861** Geo. W. Hawes' Ohio State gazetteer, and business Directory, by George W. Hawes (14 fiches), FHL film #6044298.

■ **1907 Quadrennial Enumeration, Clinton County, Ohio**, microfilm of original records now located at the Special Collections Department, Blegen Library, University of Cincinnati, Cincinnati, Ohio. Includes townships of Adams, Chester, Clark, Green, Jefferson, Liberty, Marion, Richland, Union, Vernon, Washington, Wayne, and Wilson. Contains an enumeration of all male residents over the age of twenty one taken during the listing of property for taxation. Filmed by the Genealogical Society of Utah, 1983, 1 roll, FHL film #973424.

Ohio Censuses & Substitutes Online

The following databases are available at:
www.ancestry.com
- 1699-1732 French Louisiana Census Tables
- 1790-1890 Ohio Censuses
- 1820 United States Federal Census
- 1830 United States Federal Census
- 1840 United States Federal Census
- 1850 United States Federal Census
- 1860 Slave Schedules
- 1860 United States Federal Census
- 1860-1880 Mortality Schedules & Index
- 1870 United States Federal Census
- 1880 United States Federal Census
- 1885-1940 US Indian Census Schedules
- 1890 US Federal Census Fragment
- 1890 Veterans Schedules
- 1900 United States Federal Census
- 1910 United States Federal Census
- 1910 Miracode Index
- 1920 United States Federal Census
- 1930 United States Federal Census
- Ohio 1910 Census Miracode Index
- Vitelli Soundex of the U.S. Census

www.censusfinder.com
- 1790-1890 Ohio Census Records at Ancestry
- 1840 Census of Pensioners - Statewide
- 1880 Federal Census - images
- 1880 Federal Census Search at Family Search
- 1913-1937 Death Certificate Index – Statewide
- RootsWeb Search
- Ohio State Databases of Census & Genealogy Records

www.census-online.com
- **Countywide name lists (no. of databases):** Adams (29); Allen (8); Ashland (1); Ashtabula (11); Athens (6); Auglaize (1); Belmont (11); Brown (3); Butler (1); Carroll (0); Champaign (5); Clark (37); Clermont (7); Clinton (0); Columbiana (7); Coshocton (2); Crawford (1); Cuyahoga (14); Darke (13); Defiance (0); Delaware (0); Erie (12); Fairfield (19); Fayette (0); Franklin (1); Fulton (5); Gallia (2); Geauga (5); Greene (17); Guernsey (11); Hamilton (4); Hancock (2); Hardin (4); Harrison (1); Henry (9); Highland (0); Hocking (2); Holmes (1); Huron (4); Jackson (3); Jefferson (3); Knox (1); Lake (16); Lawrence (35); Licking (3); Logan (8); Lorain (1); Lucas (1); Madison (1); Mahoning (4); Marion (7); Medina (16); Meigs (44); Mercer (1); Miami (2); Monroe (8); Montgomery (1); Morgan (0); Morrow (4); Muskingum (98); Noble (0); Ottawa (0); Paulding (1);

Perry (6); Pickaway (0); Pike (12); Portage (0); Preble (2); Putnam (1); Richland (35); Ross (21); Sandusky (9); Scioto (15); Seneca (10); Shelby (2); Stark (1); Summit (2); Trumbull (1); Tuscarawas (4); Union (1); Van Wert (4); Vinton (4); Warren (0); Washington (3); Wayne (0); Williams (7); Wood (2); and Wyandot (0).

WISCONSIN

Censuses & Substitutes, 1830-1905

Wisconsin became a territory in 1836, taken from Michigan Territory. Its original territorial bounds included the area of present-day Minnesota east of the Mississippi River. That area was dropped in 1848 when Wisconsin became a state, leaving the area between the St. Croix River and Mississippi River without any legal system. But the situation lasted only until Minnesota Territory was created in 1849.

Soon after Wisconsin became a territory, it began taking censuses to determine its population, mainly to see if they qualified in size to petition Congress to become a state. Wisconsin's territorial censuses were taken in the years 1836, 1838, 1842, 1846 and 1847. Of the original census manuscripts, a few counties are missing from the 1846 territorial census, but the others are fairly complete.

Upon statehood in 1848, the first state constitution mandated state censuses every ten years for the purpose of apportionment of the state legislature. Accordingly, Wisconsin conducted state sponsored censuses for the years 1855, 1865, 1875, 1885, 1895, and 1905. Of these, the 1865 state census has only a handful of counties extant, while the others are mostly complete. The surviving manuscripts of all of the original territorial and state censuses taken in Wisconsin are held by the State Historical Society of Wisconsin – Archives Division, in Madison, Wisconsin.

By an amendment to the state constitution in 1910, Wisconsin began using the federal decennial censuses to determine state population and apportionment of the state legislature.

Therefore, the 1905 state census was the last one taken in Wisconsin.

All of the censuses 1836-1895 are head of households censuses, and they vary in content with added information, e.g., no. of males and females, no. of persons of foreign birth, deaf, dumb, blind, insane, etc. In the 1885 and 1895 state censuses, a special added list was prepared, giving the names of living war veterans.

Adding to the superb array of territorial and state censuses available, Wisconsin also has the original state copies of its 1850, 1860, and 1870 federal censuses. These original schedules have not been microfilmed, but the Historical Society has prepared every-name indexes to each of their state copies. As a means of comparing the two sets, the starting FHL film numbers for the 1850, 1860, and 1870 federal censuses are noted below, followed by any state-wide indexes; and the indexes to Wisconsin's state copies.

The only Wisconsin census to list the names of all family members was the 1905 state census. As the culmination of all Wisconsin state censuses, it is in every way a detailed and useful genealogical tool, showing relationships, parent's birthplace, etc. An every-name index to the 1905 state census was prepared by the State Historical Society, a card index organized by county. The microfilmed card index is an excellent starting point for genealogical research in Wisconsin, particularly for the great numbers of immigrants from the 1880s to the early 1900s who settled in Wisconsin. Thus, the climax to this listing of state censuses is the identification of all 1905 census schedules and the county-wide name indexes available on microfilm.

Wisconsin's territorial, state, and federal censuses (and a few census substitutes) are listed in chronological order below.

■ **1830-1850 Censuses, Iowa County, Wisconsin,** see *Iowa County Heritage,* printed abstracts of censuses from the 1830 Michigan Territory census; the 1836, 1838, 1840, 1842, and 1847 Wisconsin Territory censuses; and the Wisconsin federal census of 1850. Published in 4 vols., 1967 (publisher not noted). FHL book 977.5 B4f vol. 1-4. (Vols. 1 & 2 relate to Iowa County, WI; Vol. 3 relates to Grant Co., WI; & Vol. 4 relates to Jo Daviess County, IL). From introduction: "When organized as a county, under the territorial government of Michigan, in 1829, Iowa county contained within its jurisdiction the present counties of Dane, Green, Grant, LaFayette, and a part of Rock, thus embracing almost one-half of Wisconsin which lies south of the Wisconsin River." Filmed by the Genealogical Society of Utah, 1987, FHL film #1320510, containing the following items from Vols. 1 & 2:

- **1830** federal census of Iowa County, Michigan Territory.
- **1836** territorial census of Iowa County, Wisconsin Territory.
- **1838** territorial census of Iowa county, Wisconsin Territory (incomplete).
- **1840** federal census of Iowa County, Wisconsin Territory
- **1842** territorial census of Iowa County, Wisconsin Territory.
- **1847** territorial census of Iowa and LaFayette counties, Wisconsin Territory
- **1850** federal census of Iowa County, Wisconsin.

■ **1836 Wisconsin Territorial Census**, microfilm of original records at the State Historical Society of Wisconsin – Archives Division, Madison, WI. This is a head of households census similar in format to the 1830 federal census. Originals filmed by the Genealogical Society of Utah, 1980, 1 roll, FHL film #1293919. The name list was published in *Collections of the Wisconsin State Historical Society*, vol. 13, (1895), p. 247-270; reprinted as "The Territorial Census For 1836," by Reuben Gold Thwaites, editor. The article was also filmed by the Genealogical Society of Utah, 1980, 1 roll, FHL film #1293922. Indexed in *Wisconsin 1836 Census Index*, edited by Ronald Vern Jackson and Gary Ronald Teeples, published by Accelerated Indexing, Bountiful, UT, 1976, 24 pages. FHL book 977.5 X2 1836.

■ **1838 Wisconsin Territorial Census**, microfilm of original records at the State Historical Society of Wisconsin – Archives Division, Madison, WI. Head of household census similar in format to the 1836 territorial census. Originals filmed by the Genealogical Society of Utah, 1980, 1 roll, FHL film #1293919. Indexed in *Wisconsin 1838 Census Index*, edited by Ronald Vern Jackson, et al, Accelerated Indexing Systems, Bountiful, UT, 1984, 27 pages. FHL book 977.5 X22j 1838.

■ **1842 Wisconsin Territorial Census**, microfilm of original records at the State Historical Society of Wisconsin – Archives Division, Madison, WI. This is a head of households census similar in content to the 1838 territorial census. Filmed by the Genealogical Society of Utah, 1980, 1 roll, FHL film #1293919. Indexed in *Wisconsin 1842 Census Index*, edited by Ronald Vern Jackson, et al, published by Accelerated Indexing Systems, Bountiful, UT, 1984, 110 pages. FHL book 977.5 X22j 1842.

■ **1846 Wisconsin Territorial Census**, microfilm of original records at the State Historical Society of Wisconsin – Archives Division, Madison, WI. Includes name of head of family; number of males and females by color, those of foreign birth, deaf, dumb, blind, or insane. Incomplete schedules for the counties of Crawford and Fond du lac; and Grand Rapids in Portage County. No schedules at all for Chippewa, LaPointe, or Richland counties. Filmed by the Genealogical Society of Utah, 1980, 1 roll, FHL film #1293920.

■ **1847 Wisconsin Territorial Census**, microfilm of original records at the State Historical Society of Wisconsin – Archives Division, Madison, WI. This was a head of households census with a format similar to the 1846 territorial census, complete for all counties except Sheboygan county is missing. Filmed by the Genealogical Society of Utah, 1980, 2 rolls, as follows:

- **1847** territorial census, Brown to Sheboygan Co. (Sheboygan missing), FHL film #1293921.
- **1847** territorial census, Walworth to Winnebago Co., FHL film #1293922.

■ **1850 Wisconsin Federal Census (Federal Copy)**, microfilm of original records at the National Archives, Washington, DC. The census schedules include the names of all members of a family, age, sex, and place of birth. Since Wisconsin has the state copies of the same federal census schedules, a comparison can made between the federal and state copies. The federal set was filmed by the National Archives, 1964, 16 rolls, beginning with FHL film #34508 (Adams, Brown, Calumet, Chippewa, and Columbia Counties).

■ **Every-name Index to the 1850 Federal Census of Wisconsin (State Copy)**, microfilm of original card index at the State Historical Society of Wisconsin – Archives Division, Madison, WI. The index is to the state copy, and volumes and page numbers given in the census index do not always match the federal copy of the census. The alphabetized list of names is for the entire state, regardless of county of residence. Filmed by the University of Wisconsin Film Laboratory, 1971, 36 rolls, beginning with FHL film #933599 (Aaby – Autthouse).

■ **1855 Wisconsin State Census**, microfilm of original records at the Wisconsin State Historical Society – Archives Division Madison, WI. This is a head of households census similar in format to the 1847 census layout. Complete for all counties except Kewaunee County is missing. Filmed by the Genealogical Society of Utah, 1979, 4 rolls, as follows:
- **1855** state census, Adams - Dane, Douglas, Dunn counties, vols. 1-3, FHL film #1032686.
- **1855** state census, Dodge, Fond du Lac - LaPointe counties, vols. 4-9, FHL film #1032687.
- **1855** state census, Manitowoc - Rock counties, vols. 10-14, FHL film #1032688.
- **1855** state census, St. Croix – Winnebago counties, vols. 15-18, FHL film #1032689.

■ **1855 Wisconsin State Census Index**, see *Wisconsin 1855 census Index*, edited by Ronald Vern Jackson, et al, published by Accelerated Indexing, Bountiful, UT, 1984, 417 pages. FHL book 977.5 X22w 1855.

■ **1857-1859 Wisconsin (State) Directories**, microfilm of originals published by various publishers. Filmed by Research Publications, Woodbridge, CT, 1980-1984, 17 microfiches, as follows:
- **1857-1858,** The Wisconsin State directory, by Smith, Du Moulin & Co. (7 fiches), FHL film #6044651.
- **1858,** Strickland's North-Western almanac and business directory by Strickland & Co. (2 fiches), FHL film #6044652.
- **1858-1859,** The Wisconsin State directory by Strickland & Co. (8 fiches), FHL film #6044653.

■ **1860 Wisconsin Federal Census (Federal Copy)**, microfilm of original records in the National Archives, Washington, DC. The 1860 census was filmed twice. The second filming is listed first and is usually easier to read. However, since some of the records were faded or lost between the first and second filming, search the first filming whenever the material on the second filming is too light or missing. FHL film copies on 49 rolls, beginning with FHL film #805399 (2nd filming, Adams and Bad Ax Counties). The 1860 federal census for Wisconsin is indexed at HeritageQuest Online (head of households), Ancestry.com (every-name), and a few other Web sites. See the listing for online censuses at the end of this Wisconsin bibliography.

■ **Every-name Index to the 1860 Federal Census of Wisconsin (State Copy),** microfilm of original index at the State Historical Society of Wisconsin – Archives Division, Madison, WI. The index is to the state copy, and volumes and page numbers given in the index do not always match the federal copy of the census. The alphabetized list of names is for the entire state, regardless of county of residence. Filmed by the University of Wisconsin Film Laboratory, 1971, 95 rolls, beginning with FHL film #933635 (Aaby – Ambrosch).

■ **1861-1865 Index to Compiled Service Records of Volunteer Union Soldiers Who Served in Organizations From the State of Wisconsin**, microfilm of original records in the National Archives, Washington, DC. The FHL only has the index to compiled service records. To obtain information from the service record itself, contact the National Archives. Filmed by the National Archives, 1964, series M0559, 33 rolls, beginning with FHL film #882486 (Index, A-Bak, 1861-1865). A searchable name index to 6.3 million Union and Confederate Civil War soldiers and sailors for all states is now online at the National Park Service Web site at **www.civilwar.nps.gov/cwss/.**

■ **1865 Wisconsin State Census.** The state's original set was destroyed, but there are duplicate copies that exist for six counties, indexed in *1865 Wisconsin State Census: The Six*

Surviving Counties, Dunn, Green, Jackson, Kewaunee, Ozaukee, Sheboygan, transcription and index, compiled by Barry Christopher Noonan, published by the author, Madison, WI, 1993, 353 pages. Copy at the State Historical Society library, call no. F580 N66 1993. The original manuscripts of the six surviving counties are available on microfilm, as follows:

- **1865 Wisconsin State Census, Dunn County**, microfilm of original records now located at the Stout Area Research Center at Menomonie, Wisconsin. Head of households census. Filmed by the Genealogical Society of Utah, 1981, 1 roll, FHL film #1298908.

- **1865 Wisconsin State Census, Green County, Wisconsin**, microfilm of original records at the State Historical Society of Wisconsin at Madison, WI. Head of households census. Filmed by the Genealogical Society of Utah, 1981, 1 roll, FHL film #1306084.

- **1865 Wisconsin State Census, Jackson County, Wisconsin**, microfilm of original records at the State Historical Society of Wisconsin at Madison, WI. Head of households census. Filmed by the Genealogical Society of Utah, 1981, 1 roll, FHL film #1306084.

- **1865 Wisconsin State Census, Kewaunee County, Wisconsin**, microfilm of originals at the State Historical Society of Wisconsin, Madison, WI. Head of households census. Filmed by the State Historical Society, 2003, 1 roll, FHL film #2311106.

- **1865 Wisconsin State Census, Ozaukee County, Wisconsin**, microfilm of originals at the State Historical Society of Wisconsin, Madison, WI. Head of households census. Filmed by the State Historical Society, 2003, 1 roll, FHL film #2311107.

- **1865 Wisconsin State Census, Sheboygan County, Wisconsin**, microfilm of original records at the Sheboygan County courthouse, Sheboygan, Wisconsin. Heads of household census. Includes towns of Abbott (Sherman), Greenbush, Herman, Holland, Lima, Lyndon, Mitchell, Mosel, Plymouth, Rhine, Russell, Scott, Sheboygan, Sheboygan Falls, Wilson, village of Sheboygan Falls, and city of Sheboygan. Filmed by the Genealogical Society of Utah, 1983, 1 roll, FHL film #1392915. See also *Copy of the Sheboygan County Census, 1865, State of Wisconsin: Enumeration of the Inhabitants in Sheboygan County* , copied by the Sheboygan County Genealogical Society, Sheboygan Falls, WI, 1985, 123 pages. FHL book 977.569 X2c.

■ **1870 Wisconsin Federal Census (Federal Copy)**, microfilm of original records at the National Archives, Washington, DC. The 1870 census was filmed twice. The second filming is listed first and is usually easier to read. However, since some of the records were faded or lost between the first and second filming, search the first filming whenever the material on the second filming is too light to read. FHL film copies on 60 rolls, beginning with FHL film #553202 (Adams, Ashland, Barron, Bayfield, and Brown Counties). Heads of households Indexed in *Wisconsin 1870 U.S. Federal Census Index*, CD-ROM publication by Heritage Quest, Bountiful, UT, 2001. FHL CD #1179. 1870 images are available at **www.ancestry.com.**

■ **Every-name Index to the 1870 Federal Census of Wisconsin (State Copy),** microfilm of original card index at the State Historical Society of Wisconsin – Archives Division, Madison, WI. The index is to the state copy, and volumes and page numbers given do not always match the federal copy of the census. The alphabetized list of names is for the entire state, regardless of county of residence. Filmed by the University of Wisconsin Film Laboratory, 1971, 135 rolls, beginning with FHL film #933730 (Aaby – Allen, Myron).

■ **1875 Wisconsin State Census**, microfilm of original records at the State Historical Society of Wisconsin – Archives Division, Madison, WI. Head of household census similar to the 1855 state census format. Filmed by the Genealogical Society of Utah, 1979, 6 rolls, as follows:

- **1875** state census, Adams - Calumet (part) counties, vol. 1, FHL film #1032689.
- **1875** state census, Calumet (cont.) – Eau Claire counties, vol. 1-3, FHL film #1032690.
- **1875** state census, Fond du Lac – Juneau counties, vol. 4-5, FHL film #1032691.
- **1875** state census, Kenosha – Milwaukee counties, vol. 6-, FHL film #1032692.
- **1875** state census, Monroe – Sheboygan counties, vol. 8-10, FHL film #1032693.
- **1875** state census, Sheboygan – Wood counties, vol. 10-12, FHL film #1032694.

■ **1880 Wisconsin Soldiers and Sailors**, see *Wisconsin Soldiers and Sailors Reunion: Containing the Post Office Address, Occupation* *and Name of Every Wisconsin Soldier and Sailor Now Living ... Also the Name of Every Wisconsin Soldier Who Perished in the War ... Also, a Complete Roster of Wisconsin's Armed Military Organizations*, contributed by J. A. Kellogg, et al, original published Fond du Lac, WI by Star Steam Job and Book Printing House, 1880, 309 pages. Reprinted by University Publications of America, Bethesda, MD, 1993, filmed by the Genealogical Society of Utah, 4 microfiches, FHL film #6118307.

■ **1885 Wisconsin State Census**, microfilm of original records at the State Historical Society of Wisconsin – Archives Division, Madison, WI. Head of households census, schedules complete for all Wisconsin counties. Also includes county by county "Enumeration of Soldiers and Sailors of the Late War" (Civil War). Filmed by the Genealogical Society of Utah, 1979, 10 rolls, as follows:

- **1885** state census schedules, Adams – Clark counties, FHL film #1032695.
- **1885** state census schedules, Columbia – Dunn counties, FHL film #1032696.
- **1885** state census schedules, Dunn – Green Lake counties, FHL film #1032697.
- **1885** state census schedules, Iowa – Lincoln counties, FHL film #1032698.
- **1885** state census schedules, Manitowoc, Marathon, Marinette, Marquette, Monroe, Milwaukee County, & Milwaukee City, wards 1- FHL film #1032699.
- **1885** state census schedules, Milwaukee City, wards 4-13; Oconto – Portage counties, FHL film #1032700.
- **1885** state census schedules, Portage, Price, Pepin, Pierce, Racine, Richland, Rock, St. Croix, and Sauk counties, FHL film #1032701.
- **1885** state census schedules, Sauk – Walworth counties, FHL film #1032702.
- **1885** state census schedules, Waukesha - Wood counties; and Enumeration of Soldiers & Sailors, Adams - Dunn counties, FHL film #1032703.
- **1885** Enumeration of Soldiers & Sailors, Eau Claire – Wood counties, FHL film #1032704.

■ **1885 Wisconsin State Census Statistics and Lists of Civil War Veterans**. (official printed report). Full book title: *Tabular Statements of the Census Enumeration, and the Agricultural,* *Mineral and Manufacturing Interests of the State: Also Alphabetical List of the Soldiers and Sailors of the Late War Residing in the State, June 20, 1885*, published for the Wisconsin Secretary of State by Democrat Printing Company, State Printers, Madison, WI, 1886, 791 pages. FHL book 977.5   X2w and FHL film #962237.

■ **1895 Wisconsin State Census**, microfilm of original records at the State Historical Society of Wisconsin – Archives Division, Madison, WI. Head of households census, complete for all Wisconsin counties. Also includes a separate name list of living veterans for each county. Filmed by the Genealogical Society of Utah, 1979, 12 rolls, as follows:

- **1895** state census schedules, Adams – Columbia counties, FHL film #1032705.
- **1895** state census schedules Columbia - Dunn counties, FHL film #1032706.
- **1895** state census schedules Dunn – Green Lake counties, FHL film #1032707.
- **1895** state census schedules, Iowa – La Crosse counties, FHL film #1032708.
- **1895** state census schedules Lafayette – Monroe counties, FHL film #1032709.
- **1895** state census schedules, Milwaukee County, Milwaukee City, wards 1-9, FHL film #1032710.
- **1895** state census schedules Milwaukee City, wards 10-18, Milwaukee County, FHL film #1032711.
- **1895** state census schedules, Milwaukee County & Oconto - Racine counties, FHL Film [1032712]
- **1895** state census schedules, Racine – Taylor counties, FHL film #1032713.
- **1895** state census schedules Taylor – Waupaca counties, FHL film #1032714.
- **1895** state census schedules, Waushara - Wood counties; and Enumeration of Soldiers & sailors, Adams - Jefferson counties, FHL film #1032715.
- **1895** Enumeration of Soldiers & sailors, Jefferson – Wood counties, FHL film #1032716.

■ *1895 Wisconsin Soldiers in Soldier Homes*, compiled by Bev Hetzel, published by the author, West Bend, WI, 19[--], 24 pages. Names, with annotations, are in alphabetical order. The list was taken from a 1895 census report & from a two-volume set on the Civil War. FHL book 977.5 M2he.

■ **1905 Wisconsin State Census**, microfilm of original records at the State Historical Society of Wisconsin – Archives Division, Madison, WI. Contents: Name of each individual; relationship to head of household; color/race; sex; age at last birthday; marital status; place of birth, by state or country; place of birth of parents; occupation, if 14 years or older; number of months unemployed; and whether a home or farm was owned outright, mortgaged, or rented. Filmed by the State Historical Society, 1952, 36 rolls, as follows:

- **1905** state census schedules, Adams, Ashland, Barron counties, FHL film #1020439.
- **1905** state census schedules, Bayfield and Brown counties, FHL film #1020440.
- **1905** state census schedules, Buffalo, Burnett, Calumet counties, FHL film #1020441.
- **1905** state census schedules, Chippewa and Clark counties, FHL film #1020442.
- **1905** state census schedules, Columbia and Crawford counties, FHL film #1020443.
- **1905** state census schedules, Dane County, FHL film #1020444.
- **1905** state census schedules, Dodge and Door counties, FHL film #1020445.
- **1905** state census schedules, Douglas and Dunn counties, FHL film #1020446.
- **1905** state census schedules, Eau Claire and Florence counties, FHL film #1020447.
- **1905** state census schedules, Fond du Lac and Forest counties, FHL film #1020448.
- **1905** state census schedules, Grant and Green counties, FHL film #1020449.
- **1905** state census schedules, Green Lake, Iowa, Iron, & Jackson counties, FHL film #1020450.
- **1905** state census schedules, Jefferson and Juneau counties, FHL film #1020451.
- **1905** state census schedules, Kenosha, Kewaunee, La Crosse counties, FHL film #1020452.
- **1905** state census schedules, Lafayette, Langlade, Lincoln counties, FHL film #1020453.
- **1905** state census schedules, Manitowoc County, FHL film #1020454 .
- **1905** state census schedules, Marathon County, FHL film #1020455.
- **1905** state census schedules, Marinette, Marquette, Monroe counties, FHL film #1020978.
- **1905** state census schedules, Milwaukee County; and city of Milwaukee, Ward 1, FHL film #1020991.

- **1905** state census schedules, city of Milwaukee, wards 2-8, FHL film #1020992.
- **1905** state census schedules, city of Milwaukee, wards 8-11, FHL film #1020993.
- **1905** state census schedules, city of Milwaukee, wards 11-14, FHL film #1020994.
- **1905** state census schedules, city of Milwaukee, wards 15-19, FHL film#1020995.
- **1905** state census schedules, City of Milwaukee wards, 19-23, FHL film #1020996.
- **1905** state census schedules, Oconto, Oneida, Outagamie counties, FHL film #1020979.
- **1905** state census schedules, Ozaukee, Pepin, Pierce, Polk counties, FHL film #1020980.
- **1905** state census schedules, Portage and Price counties, FHL film #1020981.
- **1905** state census schedules, Racine and Richland counties, FHL film #1020982.
- **1905** state census schedules, Rock and Rusk counties, FHL film #1020983.
- **1905** state census schedules, St. Croix, Sauk, Sawyer counties, FHL film #1020984.
- **1905** state census schedules, Shawano and Sheboygan counties, FHL film #1020985.
- **1905** state census schedules, Taylor, Trempealeau, Vernon, Vilas counties, FHL film #1020986.
- **1905** state census schedules, Walworth, Washburn, Washington counties, FHL film #1020987.
- **1905** state census schedules, Waukesha and Waupaca counties, FHL film #1020988.
- **1905** state census schedules, Waushara and Winnebago counties, FHL film #1020989.
- **1905** state census schedules, Wood County, FHL film #1020990.

■ **1905 Wisconsin State Census Index**, microfilm of original card indexes (by county) at the State Historical Society of Wisconsin, Archives Division, Madison, WI. Surname, first name indexes in alphabetical order for each county. All county-wide indexes filmed by the Genealogical Society of Utah, 1978-1985, 444 rolls, 16mm film. Name of county, no. of rolls, and FHL film numbers, as follows:

- **Adams County**, 2 rolls: FHL film#1266809 & 1266816.
- **Ashland County**, 5 rolls: FHL film #1379406-1379410.
- **Barron County**, 6 rolls: FHL film #1275513-1275518.
- **Bayfield County**, 3 rolls, FHL film #1275792-1275794.

- **Brown County**, 10 rolls, FHL film #1308729-1308738.
- **Buffalo County**, 4 rolls, FHL film #1205863-1205864; and 1205884 – 1205885.
- **Burnett County**, 2 rolls, FHL film #1266822-1266823.
- **Calumet County**, 4 rolls, FHL film #1205801-1205804.
- **Chippewa County**, 6 rolls FHL film #1308739-1308744.
- **Clark County**, 6 rolls, FHL film #1308912-1308915; and 1308930-1308931.
- **Columbia County**, 6 rolls, FHL film #1266834-1266836; and 1266853-1266855.
- **Crawford County**, 3 rolls, FHL film #1266817-1266819.
- **Dane County**, 14 rolls, FHL film #1205164-1205177.
- **Dodge County**, 9 rolls, FHL film #1266825-1266833.
- **Door County**, 4 rolls, FHL film #1292223-1292226.
- **Douglas County**, 8 rolls, FHL film #1292204 – 1292211.
- **Dunn County**, 5 rolls, FHL film #1308703-1308707.
- **Eau Claire County**, 7 rolls, FHL film #1308716-1308722.
- **Florence County**, 1 roll, FHL film #1292411.
- **Fond du Lac County**, 10 rolls, FHL film #1275547-1275553; 1275657- 1275658; and 1275721.
- **Forest County**, 1 roll, FHL film #1266875.
- **Green County**, 5 rolls, FHL film #1266655-1266659.
- **Green Lake County**, 3 rolls, FHL film #1275544 – 1275546.
- **Iowa County**, 4 rolls, FHL film #1275509-1275512.
- **Iron County**, 1 roll, FHL film #1266824.
- **Jackson County**, 4 rolls, FHL film #1205885-1205888.
- **Jefferson County**, 7 rolls, FHL film #1205789-1205795.
- **Juneau County**, 5 rolls, FHL film #1292531-1292535.
- **Kenosha County**, 6 rolls, FHL film #1275787-1275792.
- **Kewaunee County**, 4 rolls, FHL film #1292212-1292215.
- **La Crosse County**, 8 rolls, FHL film #1308708-1308715.
- **Lafayette County**, 4 rolls, FHL film #1275795-1275796; and 1275826-1275827.
- **Langlade County**, 3 rolls, FHL film #1292227-1292229.
- **Lincoln County**, 4 rolls, FHL film #1292230-1292233.
- **Manitowoc County**, 7 rolls, FHL film #1275931-1275935; 1275979-1275980.
- **Marathon County**, 10 rolls, FHL film #1275518-1275522; 1275531-1275532; and 1275541-1275543.
- **Marinette County**, 7 rolls, FHL film #1205854-1205860.
- **Marquette County**, 2 rolls, FHL film #1266957-1266958.
- **Menominee County**, no FHL film.
- **Milwaukee County**, 69 rolls, FHL film #1378977-1378979; 1381572-1381580; 1379186-1379193; 1379227- 1379229; 1379237; 1379239; 1381616-1379336; and 1379372- 1379374.
- **Monroe County**, 7 rolls, FHL film #1266803-1266809.
- **Oconto County**, 5 rolls, FHL film #1205796-1205800.
- **Oneida County**, 2 rolls, FHL film #1292218-1292219.
- **Outagamie County**, 10 rolls, FHL film #1292521-1292530.
- **Ozaukee County**, 4 rolls, FHL film #1205860-1205863.
- **Pepin County**, 2 rolls, FHL film #1292216-1292217.
- **Pierce County**, 5 rolls, FHL film #1292536; 1292514-1292517.
- **Polk County**, 4 rolls, FHL film #1205999-1206000; 1266802- 1266803.
- **Portage County**, 6 rolls, FHL film #1308723-1308728.
- **Price County**, 3 rolls, FHL film #1292220-1292222.
- **Racine County**, 10 rolls, FHL film #1275980; 1266902-1266904; and 1266951-1266956
- **Richland County**, 4 rolls, FHL film #1292234-1292235; 1292250-1292251.
- **Rock County**, 10 rolls, FHL film #1292317; 1292382-1292390.
- **Rusk County**, 2 rolls, FHL film #1266859-1266860.
- **Sauk County**, 6 rolls, FHL film #1266876-1266881.
- **Sawyer County**, 1 roll, FHL film #1266821
- **Shawano County**, 7 rolls, FHL film #1275721-1275722; and 1275783- 1275787.
- **Sheboygan County**, 11rolls, FHL film #1308691-1308694; and 1308696-1308702.
- **St. Croix County**, 6 rolls, FHL film #1292518-1292520; and 1308575-1308577.
- **Taylor County**, 2 rolls, FHL film #1266856-1266857.
- **Trempealeau County**, 5 rolls, FHL film # 1276463-1276465; and 1308910-1308911.

- **Vernon County**, 6 rolls, FHL film #1292252-1292257.
- **Vilas County**, 1 roll, FHL film #1266858
- **Walworth County**, 6 rolls, FHL film #1276457-1276462.
- **Washburn County**, 1 roll, FHL film #1266820.
- **Washington County**, 5 rolls, FHL film #1205888-1205892.
- **Waukesha County**, 7 rolls, FHL film #1308844-1308849; and 1276456.
- **Waupaca County**, 7 rolls, FHL film #1266959-1266964; and 1266654.
- **Waushara County**, 4 rolls, FHL film #1292407-1292410.
- **Winnebago County**, 12 rolls, FHL film #1275827-1275828; 1275891-275899; and 1275930.
- **Wood County**, 6 rolls, FHL film #1266660-1266661; 1002396; and 1266945-1266947.

Wisconsin Censuses & Substitutes Online

■ **Wisconsin Online Name Index**. Sponsored by the State Historical Society of Wisconsin.. Go to **www.wisconsinhistory.org/wni/**. Search through more than 100,000 obituaries, personal sketches, and other short biographies of Wisconsin people.

■ **Wisconsin Genealogical Research Service:** Sponsored by the State Historical Society of Wisconsin. Searchable databases online at: **www.wisconsinhistory.org/genealogy/ogrs/**
- Wisconsin Birth Records (1850-1907)
- Wisconsin Marriage Records (1836-1907)
- Wisconsin Death Records (1850-1907)
- Wisconsin Civil War Service Records

■ **Wisconsin Censuses Online.** The following databases are available online at:
Ancestry.com
- 1820-1890 Wisconsin Censuses
- 1699-1732 French Louisiana Census Tables
- 1840 United States Federal Census
- 1850 United States Federal Census
- 1850-1880 Mortality Schedules & Index
- 1860 Slave Schedules
- 1860 United States Federal Census

- 1870 United States Federal Census
- 1870 WI Census, Winnebago County, Oshkosh
- 1880 United States Federal Census
- 1885-1940 US Indian Census Schedules
- 1890 Veterans Schedules
- 1895 Wisconsin State Census
- 1900 United States Federal Census
- 1900 Marinette County, WI
- 1905 Wisconsin State Census
- 1910 United States Federal Census
- 1920 United States Federal Census
- 1930 United States Federal Census
- Vitelli Soundex of the U.S. Census
- Wisconsin Census, 1820-90

www.censusfinder.com
- 1820-1890 Wisconsin Census Records at Ancestry
- 1830 Census Index of Iowa County in Michigan Territory - Present day Wisconsin
- 1836 Territorial Census Index of Wisconsin
- 1880 Federal Census
- 1880 Federal Census Search at Family Search
- RootsWeb Search
- Wisconsin Civil War Soldiers Database
- Wisconsin State Databases of Census & Genealogy Records

www.census-online.com
- **Countywide name lists (no. of databases):** Adams (1); Ashland (2); Barron (13); Bayfield (3); Brown (10); Buffalo (1); Burnett (1); Calumet (24); Chippewa (8); Clark (6); Columbia (0); Crawford (2); Dane (2); Dodge (2); Door (14); Douglas (1); Dunn (9); Eau Claire (0); Florence (0); Fond du Lac (32); Forest (0); Grant (0); Green (3); Green Lake (4); Iowa (2); Iron (0); Jackson (1); Jefferson (2); Juneau (156); Kenosha (2); Kewaunee (1); La Crosse (1); Lafayette (0); Langlade (0); Lincoln (4); Manitowoc (28); Marathon (32); Marinette (0); Marquette (61); Menominee (0); Milwaukee (4); Monroe (44); Oconto (4); Oneida (1); Outagamie (0); Ozaukee (14); Pepin (2); Pierce (57); Polk (5); Portage (18); Price (2); Racine (1); Richland (18); Rock (8); Rusk (0); Sauk (2); Sawyer (0); Shawano (4); Sheboygan (29); St Croix (4); Taylor (8); Trempealeau (1); Vernon (1); Vilas (0); Walworth (0); Washburn (1); Washington (6); Waukesha (1); Waupaca (6); Waushara (0); Winnebago (39); and Wood (0).

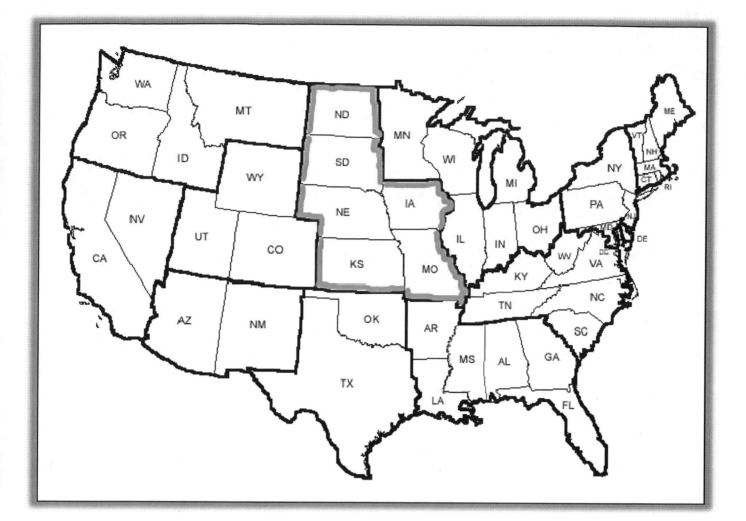

Chapter 6E – The Central Plains

Iowa, Kansas, Missouri, Nebraska; and Dakota Territory, North Dakota, and South Dakota

Historical Timeline for the Central Plains

1673 Mississippi River. French explorers Jolliet and Marquette left their base in Quebec, and made their way to the Illinois River, which they descended to discover the Mississippi River. They then descended the Mississippi passing by the present-day states of Illinois, Iowa, Missouri, Kentucky, Tennessee, and Arkansas, but returned to the Great Lakes area without ever reaching the mouth of the Mississippi.

1682 Louisiana. French explorers Cavalier and LaSalle erected a cross near the confluence of the Mississippi River and the Gulf of Mexico, after floating down the river from the Great Lakes area. They claimed the entire Mississippi basin for Louis XIV of France, for whom Louisiana was named. For the next 80 years, Louisiana was part of "New France," an area mostly exploited for its natural resources, rather than a place for settlement.

1738 Dakota Country. Pierre Gaultier de la

Vérendrye, a French explorer, visited Mandan villages near the Missouri River. This was the first known white expedition into what is now North Dakota.

1750. Ste. Genevieve was founded by French traders, the first permanent white settlement in present-day Missouri.

1762 Louisiana. Towards the end of the French and Indian War, France transferred to Spain their claim to Louisiana. In Europe, the war was known as the "Seven Years War."

1763. Treaty of Paris ending the Seven Years War officially settled cross claims for lands in North America. The British claims to present-day Canada and all lands east of the Mississippi were confirmed, along with the Spanish claims west of the Mississippi. France, the loser of the war, was essentially removed from its North American claims, except for New Orleans and a few forts along the St. Lawrence River.

1764. St. Louis was founded by Pierre Laclede Liguest. No one bothered to tell him that France no longer owned the area.

1783 United States of America. The treaty of Paris of 1783 first recognized the United States as an independent republic, with borders from the Atlantic Ocean to the Mississippi River. The treaty also reaffirmed the claims of Britain to present-day Canada; and Spain's claim to all lands west of the Mississippi River, including Louisiana.

1792 Dakota Country. Jacques D'Englise opened trade on the Missouri River between Mandan villages and Spanish interests from St. Louis.

1797 Dakota - Red River Country. Chaboillez, a French trader of the Red River Settlement opened a post at Pembina.

1800 Louisiana. After defeating the Spanish in battle, Napoleon acquired title of Louisiana from Spain. At the treaty of San Ildefonso, the Spanish acknowledged that it was too costly to explore this new country and could not see the rewards being worth the investment. They traded Louisiana to Napoleon for a couple of small duchies in Italy.

1803 Louisiana Purchase. The United States purchased Louisiana from France. Sent by President Jefferson to attempt the purchase of New Orleans only, the American negotiators (James Madison and Robert Livingston) were surprised when Napoleon offered the entire tract to them. The Louisiana Purchase was generally described as the "drainage of the Mississippi and Missouri River basins." Adding the area doubled the size of the United States.

1804 Louisiana District and Orleans Territory. Congress divides the Louisiana Purchase into two districts: Orleans Territory, mostly the same as the present state of Louisiana, and Louisiana District, the remainder of the tract. Louisiana District had virtually no inhabitants, except for an outpost at St. Louis, and was soon attached to Indiana Territory for administration. Also in 1804, Lewis and Clark's Corps of Discovery began its trek from St. Louis to the Pacific Ocean.

1805. Louisiana Territory established; the seat of government was St. Louis. Also in this year, Lt. Zebulon Pike of the U.S. Army and a small party investigates the Mississippi River above St. Louis, with specific orders to note especially the rivers, prairies, islands, mines, quarries, timber, and any Indian villages and settlements they encountered.

1812. Louisiana Territory renamed **Missouri Territory**, after Orleans Territory becomes the state of Louisiana. The first general assembly of the Territory of Missouri met (Oct. 1); the five original counties were organized:

Cape Girardeau, New Madrid, St. Charles, St. Louis, and Ste. Genevieve.

1818. The 49th parallel was agreed to as the boundary between the U.S. and Great Britain in a treaty whereby the United States acquired possession of the upper Red River drainage.

1819. Arkansas Territory created, reducing the size of Missouri Territory. The area included all of present-day Arkansas and most of Oklahoma.

1820. The "Missouri Compromise" allowed Missouri to enter the Union as a slave state and Maine as a free state, thus keeping the balance of slave and free states equal in Congress. Although Missouri was allowed to enter as a slave state, the remaining portion of the Louisiana Purchase area north of the 36° 30′ line was to be forever free of slavery.

1821. Missouri admitted as a state with St. Louis as the capital. Also in this year, William Becknell, a Missouri trader, was the first to follow the route that was to become known as the Santa Fe Trail.

1823 Nebraska Country. Bellevue becomes the first permanent settlement in present-day Nebraska.

1826 Missouri. State capital moved from St. Louis to Jefferson City.

1829 Sublette's Trace. William Sublette's pack-train, en route west by way of Independence, Missouri for the first time traveled out the Santa Fe Trail some distance before turning northwest toward the Kansas River. This trace later became the established Oregon-California trail route.

1830 Oregon Trail. Jedediah Smith, David Jackson, and William Sublette set out from St. Louis. They followed a route up the Missouri River to the Platte River. Instead of following the

Missouri north as Lewis and Clark did, they went west on the Platte River. These were the first travelers on what was to become the Oregon Trail. By the 1840s the southern starting point of the trail went west from Independence MO to Kansas City, northwest to Ft. Kearney (Nebraska) and then turned west again, heading to the mouth of the Columbia River at the Pacific Ocean.

1832. The steamboat *Yellowstone* began the first annual fur-trading voyages up the Missouri River, reaching Fort Union, now present North Dakota.

1833 Black Hawk Cession. After the Black Hawk War of 1832, the Sauk tribe of present-day Iowa was forced to cede land on the west side of the Mississippi River to the United States, which was open for legal white settlement after 1 June 1833.

1834. Michigan Territory organized - extended as far west as the Missouri River.

1836 Wisconsin Territory created - extended as far west as the Missouri River.

1837 Platte Purchase. President Martin Van Buren issued a proclamation which completed the annexation of the Platte Purchase area to Missouri, establishing the northwestern border of the state.

1838. Iowa Territory created, encompassing all lands north of the present state of Missouri between the Mississippi and Missouri Rivers.

1841. First emigrant wagon train for the Pacific. The Bidwell-Bartleson party's journey west was from Independence, Missouri, via "Sublette's Trace" (or, the now developing Oregon-California trail).

1842 Nebraska Country. The word "Nebraska" first began to appear in publications in 1842 after

John C. Fremont explored the Platte Valley and Nebraska areas.

1843. First settlement at present site of Kansas City, Kansas.

1846. Iowa becomes the 29th state.

1849 Gold Rush. With the discovery of gold in California, the Missouri towns of St. Louis, Independence, Westport, and St. Joseph became points of departure for emigrants bound for California, making Missouri the "Gateway to the West."

1849. Minnesota Territory established, including all land north of the present state of Iowa between the Mississippi and Missouri Rivers.

1854. (May 30). **Kansas-Nebraska Act** passes U.S. Congress — territories of Kansas and of Nebraska established. The act also allowed people in the territories of Kansas and Nebraska to decide for themselves whether or not to allow slavery within their borders. The Act served to repeal the Missouri Compromise of 1820 which had prohibited slavery north of latitude 36°30′.

1858-1861 Unorganized Dakota. When Minnesota was admitted as a state in 1858 with its present boundaries, Dakota was orphaned. The area from the western Minnesota line to the Missouri River was enumerated in the 1860 federal census as "Unorganized Dakota."

1860 Nebraska Territory. Population rose from 6,269 in 1854 to 28,841 in 1860. Having surpassed the minimum population requirement, Nebraska Territory immediately began petitioning Congress to become a state.

1860 Pony Express established. The two-thousand-mile Pony Express ran from St. Joseph, Missouri, to Sacramento, California.

1861. Kansas admitted to the Union as the 34th state, with Topeka the state capital.

1861. Dakota Territory was officially organized by the Federal government and William Jayne was appointed the first governor.

1867. Nebraska joined the Union as the 37th state, with Omaha as the capital until a year later, when Lincoln was chosen.

1889 South Dakota and **North Dakota** admitted as states with their present boundaries. Although Dakota Territory had petitioned Congress to be a single state, that would have caused two Democratic senators to be added, which would have upset the balance. By splitting Dakota Territory into two states, two Republican senators and two Democratic senators were added to Congress, maintaining the balance of power.

1918 Iowa. Governor Harding issued a proclamation which forbid the use of any language but English in public gatherings of two or more people. This was nicknamed the "Babel Proclamation."

1941 South Dakota. Mt. Rushmore monument finished.

1946 Missouri. Winston Churchill, former Prime Minister of England, delivered his "Iron Curtain" speech at Fulton's Westminster College.

1961 North Dakota. Roger Maris from Fargo broke Babe Ruth's single season home run record.

1965 St. Louis, Missouri. The Gateway Arch (Jefferson National Expansion Memorial) designed by Eero Saarinen was completed. Located on the original settlement site of St. Louis, it symbolizes the role of St. Louis in the development of the western frontier.

1974. Gerald Ford, born in Omaha, Nebraska, becomes President of the United States.

1996 Kansas. Bob Dole, from Russell, Kansas, ran for President of the United States. He lost.

IOWA

State Censuses & Substitutes, 1836-1925

The land known as Iowa was opened for white settlement after the Black Hawk War of 1832. In 1834, the area was added to Michigan Territory, in 1836 to Wisconsin Territory. Iowa became a territory in 1838, and a state in 1846. Territorial censuses include Iowa areas taken by Wisconsin in 1836, and Iowa Territory in 1838. The state of Iowa conducted statewide censuses in 1847, 1849, 1854, 1856, 1859, 1862, 1865, 1867, 1869, 1873, 1875, 1885, 1895, 1905, 1915, and 1925. Censuses taken 1836-1854 were head of household name lists. Those from 1856 forward included every member of a family All extant state census schedules were microfilmed by the Genealogical Society of Utah and are identified below. In addition, several county-wide name lists from the Iowa state censuses have been extracted; a selected list of them are noted below.

■ **Index to the Iowa Records Section.** *A Reference Guide to the DAR Volumes*, contains an alphabetical listing by county of Iowa cemetery, marriage, death and probate records produced by the DAR and the WPA which are housed at the State Historical Society of Iowa, Iowa City, Iowa. This guidebook leads a researcher to the wealth of indexed materials for all Iowa counties. FHL book 977.7 V22in.

■ *Iowa Census Statistics, 1836-1880.* An invaluable book relating to Iowa territorial, state, and federal censuses, 1836-1880, was published by the Iowa Secretary of State in 1880 with the title *Census of Iowa for 1880, And the Same Compared With the Findings of Each of the Other States: And Also With all Former Enumerations of the Territory Now Embraced Within the Limits of the State of Iowa, With Other Historical and Statistical Data*, by John A. T. Hull, Secretary of State, printed by order of the General assembly. Microfilm of originals published by F.M. Mills, Des Moines, 1883, 744 pages. Contains historical and statistical data about the state of Iowa and its counties, but does not enumerate the population by name or household. Population totals from various enumerations of each county, as well as totals for towns and villages are given. Filmed by the Genealogical Society of Utah, 1997, 10 microfiche, FHL film #6126432. Also filmed by W.C. Cox Co., Tucson, AZ, 1974, FHL film #1000024.

■ **1836 Wisconsin Territory Census.** See *The First Census of the Original Counties of Dubuque and Demoine (Iowa) Taken in July, 1836*, edited by Benjamin F. Shambaugh, microfilm of original published by the Historical Department of Iowa, Des Moines, 1897-1898. 2 parts in 1 vol., 93 pages. Contents: part 1: Dubuque County; part 2: Demoine County. From the original manuscript returns preserved in the office of the Secretary of State of Wisconsin. Census taken in accordance with the act of Congress erecting the territory of Wisconsin (of which these two counties at the time formed a part) comprising the present states of Iowa, Minnesota and part of North and South Dakota. Includes names of heads of households with number of males and females by age brackets. Filmed by the Genealogical Society of Utah, 1978, 1 roll, FHL film #1022202, another filming, #989450. See also *Iowa 1836 Territorial Census Index*, edited by Ronald Vern Jackson, et al, published by Accelerated Indexing Systems, Bountiful, UT, 1976, 35 pages. FHL book 977.7 X22j.

■ **1838 Iowa Territory Census.** See *Iowa 1838 Territorial Census Index*, edited by Ronald Vern

Jackson, et al, published by Accelerated Indexing Systems, Bountiful, UT, 1984. FHL book 977.7 X22ji 1838. See also Marie Haefner, "The Census of 1838," in *The Palimpsest*, Vol. 19 (May 1938) pp 185-192.

■ **1840 Federal Census, Iowa Territory.** In 1840, Iowa Territory included lands between the Mississippi and Missouri Rivers, from its present boundary with Missouri to the western part of present Minnesota, and North and South Dakota. This head of household federal census is included with the state census reports because it predates all Iowa State censuses and is fairly complete for the modern area of Iowa. An extract was done as *The 1840 Iowa Census*, compiled by Rowene Obert, Helen Blumhagen, Wilma Adkins, published Salt Lake City, UT 1968. Includes index. Includes the 18 original counties and several precincts which comprised the entire area of Iowa Territory. FHL book 977.7 X2p 1840 and FHL film #844885.

■ **1841-1849 Iowa Territory Censuses.** A compilation of name lists was published as *Iowa Census Records, 1841-1849*, edited by Ronald Vern Jackson, et al, published by Accelerated Indexing Systems, Salt Lake City, UT, 1979, 1981, FHL book 977.7 X22i 1841-1849.

■ **1846 Iowa State Census.** Microfilm of originals at the State Historical Society of Iowa, Des Moines, Iowa. FHL title: *1846 Census of Louisa, Polk, and Wapello counties, Iowa*. Includes a 4-page typescript of the Polk County census that was done by the Iowa Writers Project of the Works Progress Administration in 1940 and retyped in 1970. Names heads of households. Filmed by the Genealogical Society of Utah, 1978, 1 roll, FHL film #1022202.

■ **1846 Directory.** See *A glimpse of Iowa in 1846*, by John B. Newhall; published by Thurston and Tizzard, 2 fiches, FHL film #6043998.

■ **1847 Iowa State Census.** Microfilm of originals at the State Historical Society of Iowa, Des Moines, Iowa. FHL title: *Census of Clinton, Davis, Louisa, Marion, Scott, Van Buren, and Wapello counties, Iowa, 1847*. Includes a 9-page typescript of Davis County census transcribed by Joe and Madeline Huff in 1975 and an 8-page photocopy of typescript of Louisa County census transcribed by Madeline Huff in 1974. Names heads of households and total numbers in the family. Filmed by the Genealogical Society of Utah, 1978, 1 roll, FHL film #1022202.

■ **1847 Iowa State Census, Clinton County, Iowa,** name list in *The American Genealogist*, Vol. 43, No. 1 (Jan 1967); and *Hawkeye Heritage*, Vol. 10, No. 3 (Jul 1975).

■ **1847 Iowa State Census, Davis County, Iowa,** in *The American Genealogist*, Vol. 42, No. 4 (Oct 1966); and in *Hawkeye Heritage*, Vol. 11, No. 1 (Jan 1976).

■ **1847 Iowa State Census, Marion County,** in *Hawkeye Heritage*, Vol. 3, No. 2 (Apr 1968).

■ **1847 Iowa State Census, Van Buren County,** in *Hawkeye Heritage*, Vol. 1, No. 1 (Winter 1966); and in *Van Buren Iowa Quill*, beginning with Vol. 2, No. 1 (Winter 1967).

■ **1849 Iowa State Census.** Microfilm of typescript copies of the extant population schedules at the State Historical Society of Iowa,, Des Moines, Iowa. FHL title: *Census of Benton, Boone, Clinton, Jackson, Louisa, Madison, Poweshiek, Scott, Van Buren and Washington counties, Iowa. 1849*. Heads of households. Includes photocopies of typescript material transcribed by Madeline and Joe Huff, Lida Lisle Greene, Mary A. Fullbright, and Robert Fisher. The typescript of Washington County was filmed with the Madison County record. FHL film #1022202.

■ **1849 Iowa State Census, Boone County**, name list in *Hawkeye Heritage*, Vol. 1, No. 2 (Spring 1966).

■ **1851 Iowa State Census.** Microfilm of the extant population schedules at the State Historical Society of Iowa, Des Moines, Iowa. FHL title: *Census of Cedar, Clinton, Decatur, Guthrie, Iowa, Jackson, Jasper, Jefferson, Johnson, Madison, Mahaska, Page, Pottawattamie, Poweshiek, Scott, and Washington Counties, Iowa, 1851.* Heads of households. Filmed by the Genealogical Society of Utah, 1978, FHL film #1022203.

■ **1851-1859 Iowa Territory Censuses.** A compilation of name lists published as *Iowa Census Records, 1851-1859*, edited by Ronald Vern Jackson, et al, published by Accelerated Indexing Systems, North Salt Lake, UT, 1981, FHL book 977.7 X2i 1851-1859.

■ **1852 Iowa State Census.** Microfilm of extant population schedules at the State Historical Society of Iowa, Des Moines, Iowa. FHL title: *1852 Census of Various Counties in Iowa.* Heads of households. Filmed by the Genealogical Society of Utah, 1978, 2 rolls, as follows:
  • Appanoose - Lucas Counties, FHL film #1022204.
  • Madison - Wayne counties, FHL film #1022205.
Indexed in *Iowa 1852*, edited by Ronald Vern Jackson, published by Accelerated Indexing Systems, 1988, 610 pages. FHL book 977.7 X22io.

■ *1854 Census of Various Counties in Iowa,* microfilm of extant population schedules at the State Historical Society of Iowa, Des Moines, Iowa. Heads of households. Filmed by the Genealogical Society of Utah, 1978, 3 rolls, as follows:
  • Adams - Lee Counties, FHL film #1022206.
  • Linn - Winneshiek Counties, FHL film #1022207.
  • Duplicate film of Page, Polk, Pottawattamie, and Poweshiek Counties, FHL film #1022210.

■ **1854 Iowa State Census, Clarke County, Iowa**, full name list in *Hawkeye Heritage*, Vol. 3, No. 4 (Oct 1968), and index of surnames in *Clarke County Roots & Branches*, Vol. 6, No. 3 (Sep 1997).

■ **1854, 1856, 1860 Census Indexes, Wayne County, Iowa,** microfilm of original records in Corydon, Iowa. Filmed by the Genealogical Society of Utah, 1990, 1 roll, FHL film #1673539.

■ **1856 State Census of Iowa,** microfilm of extant population schedules at the State Historical Society of Iowa, Des Moines. The first modern census for Iowa, the 1856 identifies all members of family listed by name, age, nativity, occupation, length of time in Iowa, etc., plus agriculture, domestic and general manufactures. Filmed by the Genealogical Society of Utah, 1977, 26 rolls, beginning with FHL film #1021290 (Adair-Audubon counties). Locate film numbers for all 26 rolls at the **www.familysearch.org** site. Go to FHL Library / Catalog / place search: "Iowa" / Iowa – Census – 1856.

■ **1856 Iowa State Census, Adair County, Iowa,** name list published serially in the *Adair County Anquestors*, beginning with Vol. 9, No. 1 (Dec 1996).

■ **1856 Iowa State Census, Calhoun County, Iowa,** name list published in *Hawkeye Heritage*, Vol. 5, No. 4 (Oct 1970).

■ **1856 Iowa State Census, Clarke County, Iowa,** name list in *Clarke County Roots & Branches*, beginning with Vol. 5, No. 4 (Dec 1996).

■ **1856 Iowa State Census, Davis County, Iowa,** name list in *Davis County Genealogical Society Newsletter*, beginning with Vol. 5, No. 3 (Fall 1987).

■ **1856 Iowa State Census, Franklin County, Iowa,** name list in the *Franklin Record*, beginning with the April 1988 issue; and in *Hawkeye Heritage*, Vol. 22, No. 3 (1987).

■ **1856 Iowa State Census, Greene County, Iowa**, name list in *Greene Gleanings*, beginning with the February 1993 issue.

■ **1856 Iowa State Census, Hardin County, Iowa,** name list in *Hawkeye Heritage,* Vol. 3, No. 3 (Jul 1968).

■ **1856 Iowa State Census, Jones County, Iowa,** in *News 'N' Notes*, beginning with Vol. 3, No. 1 (Jan 1992).

■ **1856 Iowa State Census, Kossuth County,** name list in *Hawkeye Heritage,* Vol. 3, No. 1 (Jan 1968).

■ **1856 Iowa State Census, Allen Township, Polk County,** name list in *Pioneer Trails*, Vol. 7, No. 4 (Dec 1987).

■ **1856 Iowa State Census, Sac County, Iowa**, in *Sacoge News*, beginning with Vol. 7, No. 1 (Jan 1986).

■ **1856 Iowa State Census, Story County, Iowa,** in *Hawkeye Heritage,* Vol. 13, No. 4 (Fall 1978).

■ **1856 Iowa State Census, Wayne County, Iowa,** compiled by Wayne County Genealogical Society, Corydon, Iowa. Published by the Iowa Genealogical Society, 1985, FHL book 977.788 X2c 1856.

■ **1856 State Census, Webster County, Iowa,** microfilm of typescript transcribed by Hamilton Heritage, 97 pages. Filmed by the Genealogical Society of Utah, 1990, 1 roll, FHL film #1672462.

■ **1856 Iowa State Census of Woodbury County,** compiled in 1994 by Peggy Powell and MaryAnn Haafke for the Woodbury County Genealogical Society, Sioux City, Iowa. FHL book 977.741 X29p.

■ **1859 Iowa State Census, Carroll and Sac Counties,** microfilm of the extant population schedules at the State Historical Society of Iowa, Des Moines, Iowa. Includes names lists for Carroll and Sac counties only. Filmed by the Genealogical Society of Utah, 1978, 1 roll, FHL film #1022208.

■ **1862 Iowa State Census (Statistics)**. FHL title: *Census Returns of the Different Counties of the State of Iowa for the Year 1862: Showing in Detail the Population, Agricultural Statistics, Domestic and General Manufactures, &c.*, Iowa Census Board, 1863. Filmed by W. C. Cox Co., Tucson, AZ, 1974, 1 roll, FHL film #1000025.

■ **1862-1866 Internal Revenue Assessment Lists for Iowa,** microfilm of originals in the National Archives in Washington, D. C. See beginning of film for list of the counties and what districts they are in. Filmed by the National Archives, Washington, D.C., Series M0766, 16 rolls, beginning with FHL film #1534648 (Assessment Lists, District 1, division 1-11, annual 1862).

■ **1867 Iowa State Census (Statistics)**. FHL title: *The Census of Iowa, as Returned in the Year 1867,* Iowa Census Board, 1867. Filmed by W. C. Cox Co., Tucson, AZ, 1974, 1 roll, FHL film #1000025.

■ **1867 Iowa State Census, Newton, Jasper County, Iowa,** name list in *Jasper County Gleaner*, Vol. 8, No. 1 (Jan 1986).

■ **1869 Iowa State Census (Statistics)**. FHL title: *The Census of Iowa as Returned in the Year 1869.* Filmed by W. C. Cox Co., Tucson, AZ, 1974, 1 roll, FHL film #1000025.

■ **1875 Biographies.** As part of *A. T. Andreas' Illustrated Historical Atlas of the State of Iowa, 1875,* by A. T. Andreas, published by Lakeside

Press, Chicago, 1875. This is the standard history of Iowa. Includes biographical sketches of Iowa's earliest settlers, and statistics from the 1875 state census of Iowa, fully indexed. Filmed by the Genealogical Society of Utah, 1975, 1 roll, FHL film #980875; 3 additional filmings: #908275, #966235, and #981935.

■ **1875 Iowa State Census, Webster County**, name list in *Webster County Genie Gleaners*, Vol. 12, No. 3 (Jul 2000).

■ **1885 Iowa State Census**, microfilm of originals at the State Historical Society of Iowa, Des Moines, Iowa. Some townships are missing, but every county is represented with full census schedules of the population. The census schedules provide detailed information for all members of a family, relationship to head of house, an exact property location, whether a street address in a town or an indication of a Range-Township-Section of a farm; age, birthplace by county for a person born in Iowa, or the state/country of birth; nativity of parents, whether first papers filed for aliens; and more, such as occupation and military information. Filmed by the Genealogical Society of Utah, 1977, 95 rolls, beginning with FHL film #1021316 (Adair County). Locate film numbers for all 95 rolls at the **www.familysearch.org** site. Go to FHL Library / Catalog / place search: "Iowa" / Iowa – Census – 1885.

■ **1885 Iowa State Census, Wapello County, Iowa,** in *Southern Genealogists Exchange Quarterly*, Vol. 22, No. 100 (Winter 1981).

■ **1885 Iowa State Census, Wayne County, Iowa; Index to 1885 Wayne County, Iowa State Census,** compiled by Wayne County Genealogical Society, Corydon, Iowa, published by the Iowa Genealogical Society, Des Moines, Iowa, 1998, 90 pages. FHL book 977.788 X22w 1885, and FHL film #795989.

■ **1885 Iowa State Census, Webster County, Iowa,** compiled by Webster County Genealogical Society, Fort Dodge, IA, published by the Iowa Genealogical Society, 1990. FHL book 977.751 X2w and FHL film #6104038.

■ **1892 Farm Directory.** See *Farmers of Iowa: A List of Farmers of Each County With Post Office*, microfilm of original published 1892 (publisher not noted). Filmed by the Genealogical Society of Utah, 1978, FHL film #1024846.

■ **1895 Iowa State Census,** microfilm of originals at the State Historical Society of Iowa, Des Moines, Iowa. Complete for all counties. The census schedules provide detailed information about persons, similar to the 1885 but adding special questions for military service in the Civil War and the Spanish American War, including the exact company and regiment of service. Also, the 1895 asks for "Religious Belief." Filmed by the Genealogical Society of Utah, 1977. 121 rolls, beginning with FHL film #1021706 (Adair County). Locate film numbers for all 121 rolls at the **www.familysearch.org** site. Go to FHL Library/Catalog/place search: "Iowa"/ Iowa – Census – 1895.

■ **1895 Iowa State Census Index, Wayne County, Iowa,** compiled by Wayne County Genealogical Society, Corydon, Iowa, published by the Iowa Genealogical Society, 1999, 189 pages. Names are in alphabetical order. FHL book 977.788 X22w 1895, and FHL film #6004945.

■ **1895 Iowa State Census, Webster County, Iowa,** name list in *Webster County Genie Gleaners*, beginning with Vol. 2, No. 3 (Oct 1990). Complete name list published in 6 vols. by the Iowa Genealogical Society, 1991. FHL has bound 6 vols. into 3 vols., FHL book 977.751 X2w vol. 1-3 and FHL film #2055294.

■ **1901-1919 Iowa State Directories,** microfilm of originals published by various publishers. Published by Research Publications, Inc., Woodbridge, CT, 1980-1984, 9 rolls at FHL, as follows:

- **1901-1902** Polk's Iowa state gazetteer and business directory, FHL film #1759801.
- **1903-1904** Polk's Iowa state gazetteer and business directory, FHL film #1759802.
- **1905-1906** Polk's Iowa state gazetteer and business directory, FHL film #1759803.
- **1908-1909** Polk's Iowa state gazetteer and business directory, FHL film #1759804.
- **1910-1911** Polk's Iowa state gazetteer and business directory, FHL film #1759805.
- **1912-1913** Polk's Iowa state gazetteer and business directory, FHL film #1759806.
- **1914-1915** Polk's Iowa state gazetteer and business directory, FHL film #1759807.
- **1916-1917** Polk's Iowa state gazetteer and business directory, FHL film #1759807.
- **1918-1919** Polk's Iowa state gazetteer and business directory, FHL film #1759808.

■ **1905 Iowa State Census Schedules**, microfilm copy of original records located at the State Historical Society of Iowa, Des Moines, Iowa. Includes name of each member of a family, age, nativity, time in US, time in Iowa, nativity of parents, and extensive military information, including branch of service, company, regiment, and war. Filmed by the Genealogical Society of Utah, 1985, 454 rolls, beginning with FHL film #1430251 (Adair County). Locate film numbers for all 454 rolls at the **www.familysearch.org** site. Go to FHL Library / Catalog / place search: "Iowa"/Iowa – Census – 1905.

■ **1905 Iowa State Census Register,** microfilm of originals at the State Historical Society of Iowa, Des Moines. Taken from the full census schedules, the *Census Register* is a series of cards, organized by township within each county, showing a page number, surname, first name, post office, township, and town or city. The Register provides a quicker look-up of names in the full census schedules. Filmed by the

Genealogical Society of Utah, 1978, 43 rolls, beginning with FHL film #1026366 (Adair and Adams counties). Locate film numbers for all 43 rolls at the **www.familysearch.org** site. Go to FHL Library/Catalog/place search: "Iowa"/Iowa – Census – 1905.

■ **1915 Iowa State Census,** microfilm copy of extant census records located at the State Historical Society of Iowa, Des Moines, Iowa. The 1915 census name lists were prepared on cards, and organized alphabetically within each county. Cards that were illegible or that contained only a first name appear at the beginning of each county under the heading "miscellaneous." There are a number of duplicate filmings of various counties included in the set. The 1915 census gives a name for each member of a family, relationship to head, age, occupation, total earnings, birthplace, if foreign born, if naturalized, years in Iowa and U.S., marital status, etc. Filmed by the Genealogical Society of Utah, 1985-1986, 1989, 583 rolls, beginning with FHL film #1379445 (Adair County, Abbott, A. – Fredricks, J.). Locate film numbers for all 583 rolls at the **www.familysearch.org** site. Go to FHL Library / Catalog / Place search: "Iowa" / Iowa – Census – 1915.

■ **1925 Iowa State Census,** microfilm of original census records at the State Historical Society of Iowa, Des Moines, Iowa. This census is unique as it recorded the names of the parents of all persons enumerated This is the only known census ever taken in the United States to give the *father's name* and *mother's maiden name*, whether a county, territorial, state, or federal census. As a result, an Iowa 1925 census listing may give a genealogist up to four generations of the ancestry for a single person. (Say a head of house had a spouse, children, a parent, or perhaps a grandparent living with the family in 1925 – in such cases, the census would show the names of children, parents, grandparents, and great-grandparents, dating back to 1800 or earlier). The 1925 census also lists nativity, place of parents marriage, religion, birthplaces, military service, and much more. Filmed by the State Historical Society of Iowa, 1976, 434 rolls, beginning with FHL film #1429191 (Adair County). Locate film numbers for all 434 rolls at the **www.familysearch.org** site. Go to FHL Library / Catalog / place search: "Iowa"/Iowa – Census – 1925.

■ **1925 Iowa State Census Index,** (For residents of selected cities), microfilm of original records at the State Historical Society of Iowa, Des Moines, Iowa. Arranged by city, then alphabetically by surname. Index lists name, address, book/line (from schedules), county of residence, for the following cities:

- **Boone** (Boone Co.),
- **Cedar Falls** (Black Hawk Co.),
- **Centerville** (Appanoose Co.),
- **Cedar Rapids** (Linn Co.),
- **Clinton** (Clinton Co.),
- **Council Bluffs** (Pottawattamie Co.),
- **Dubuque** (Dubuque Co.),
- **Ottumwa** (Wapello Co.),
- **Sioux City** (Woodbury Co.),
- **Waterloo** (Black Hawk Co.),
- **Davenport** (Scott Co.), and
- **Des Moines** (Polk Co.).

Filmed by the State Historical Society of Iowa, Des Moines, Iowa, 1980, 29 rolls, beginning with FHL film #1430705 (Boone, Cedar Falls, Centerville, & Cedar Rapids, pt. 1).

■ **1925 Iowa State Census, Webster County, Iowa,** compiled by Webster County Genealogical Society, researched and typed by Marion Martin Pliner, published by the Iowa Genealogical Society, Des Moines, Iowa, 1994. Contains an index arranged in alphabetical order by surname of persons in each household, and book number of original census. FHL book 977.751 X22w 1925, and FHL film #2055296.

Iowa Censuses & Substitutes Online

The following databases are available online at these sites:

www.ancestry.com
- 1699-1722 French Louisiana Census Tables
- 1836-1925 Iowa State Census Collection: 1836, 1838, 1847, 1849, 1854, 1856, 1859, 1873, 1875, 1885, 1895, 1905, 1915, 1925.
- 1838-1870 Iowa Census Indexes (AIS)
- 1840 United States Federal Census
- 1840 Revolutionary War Pensioner Census
- 1850-1880 Mortality Schedules & Index
- 1850 United States Federal Census
- 1860 United States Federal Census
- 1870 United States Federal Census
- 1860 United States Federal Census
- 1880 United States Federal Census
- 1920 United States Federal Census
- 1885 Iowa State Census
- 1885-1940 US Indian Census Schedules
- 1910 United States Federal Census
- 1920 United States Federal Census
- 1930 United States Federal Census
- 1930 Census of Merchant Seamen
- Vitelli Soundex of the US Census

www.censusfinder.com
- 1838-1870 Federal Census of Iowa at Ancestry
- 1840 Federal Census of Pensioners
- 1882 Iowa State Gazetteer
- 1880 Federal Census - Norwegians
- 1880 Federal Census (images)
- 1880 Federal Census Search at Family Search
- 1883 Pensioners on the Roll – Statewide

www.census-online.com
- 1840 Federal Census
- **Online county-wide name lists** (no. of databases) Adair (6); Adams (1); Allamakee (31); Appanoose (4); Audubon (2); Benton (13); Black Hawk (1); Boone (1); Bremer (4); Buchanan (4); Buena Vista (18); Butler (14); Calhoun (16); Carroll (1); Cass (0); Cedar (16); Cerro Gordo (2); Cherokee (1); Chickasaw (0); Clarke (3); Clay (0); Clayton (13); Clinton (83); Crawford (6); Dallas (4); Davis (0); Decatur (0); Delaware (1); Des Moines (0); Dickinson (0); Dubuque (22); Emmet (0); Fayette (10); Floyd

(0); Franklin (0); Fremont (18); Greene (0); Grundy (2); Guthrie (2); Hamilton (0); Hancock (4); Hardin (4); Harrison (4); Henry (1); Howard (0); Humboldt (0); Ida (3); Iowa (2); Jackson (2); Jasper (12); Jefferson (0); Johnson (0); Jones (94); Keokuk (2); Kossuth (0); Lee (2); Linn (9); Louisa (5); Lucas (0); Lyon (0); Madison (30); Mahaska (1); Marion (1); Marshall (2); Mills (25); Mitchell (0); Monona (1); Monroe (19); Montgomery (0); Muscatine (5); O'Brien (3); Osceola (0); Page (7); Palo Alto (14); Plymouth (2); Pocahontas (0); Polk (2); Pottawattamie (11); Poweshiek (0); Ringgold (1); Sac (1); Scott (16); Shelby (1); Sioux (0); Story (5); Tama (1); Taylor (1); Union (0); Van Buren (7); Wapello (0); Warren (4); Washington (4); Wayne (2); Webster (0); Winnebago (0); Winneshiek (0); Woodbury (1); Worth (0); and Wright (0).

■ **1836-1925 Iowa State Census Extraction Forms Online.** For free downloadable census extraction forms, visit the **http://censustools.com/** website to find forms created as Excel spreadsheets. Presently, there are forms for the 1836 Iowa Territory Census; and the 1856, 1885, 1895, 1905, 1915, and 1925 state censuses.

KANSAS

State Censuses & Substitutes, 1854-1925

Kansas Territory and Nebraska Territory were both created 30 May 1854 as part of the "Kansas-Nebraska Act," which was landmark legislation relating to the issue of "slave" versus "free" states prior to the Civil War. Originally, there was a plan to create one Nebraska Territory from the sprawling area ranging from the Indian Territory to the Canadian border, and west of the Missouri River to the Continental Divide. Splitting the huge tract into two territories was an attempt to keep the balance of free versus slave state representation maintained in Congress since the Missouri Compromise of 1820.

As soon as they reached the population minimum for becoming a state, both Nebraska and Kansas territories were allowed to choose whether they would become a free or slave state by popular vote of its registered voters. Nebraska was clearly in the "free state" camp, its area west of the free state of Iowa, and well north of the area where the slavery issue was rampant. But Kansas was just west of the slave state of Missouri, and whether it would vote free or slave was immediately in question.

Although most of the earliest Kansas settlers were only interested in farming the fertile land of the prairie, the political climate of the time created a battleground over the slavery issue. Thousands of people came into Kansas for the purpose of voting (and fighting) for or against slavery, which led to the label of "Bleeding Kansas" for the new territory.

In 1855, Kansas Territory began taking annual censuses, mainly as a means of counting voters and to determine their political views on the slavery issue. In fact, some of these censuses were separated by voters who were "Free State," "Pro-Slavery," or "Doubtful." Territorial censuses were taken in 1855, 1856, 1857, 1858, and 1859.

For genealogists searching for Kansas ancestors, the territorial censuses must be viewed with the historical background of a divided territory, in which thousands of non-Kansas people invaded the area to vote. Over half of the voters were not registered in Kansas. One community census total was shown to have 20 registered voters out of the 600 who voted. But any census name list that survives is worthwhile, because it identifies actual people, whether locals or invaders, and comparing name lists from surrounding states for the same time period may reveal which political side your ancestor favored.

From 1854 to 1859, Kansas Territory had two territorial governments, one "Free State," the other "Pro-Slavery." A new territorial government was formed in 1859 which immediately petitioned Congress to become a state, and as a free state. Southern interests in Congress prevented the Kansas petition from enactment, and Kansas did not enter the Union as a free state until after the secession of the southern states from Congress.

From 1855-1861, Kansas Territory included a substantial portion of present-day Colorado, and the first censuses taken in that area were those taken by Kansas.

Kansas became a state in 1861. Soon after, the Kansas legislature passed a law requiring a state census every ten years for the purpose of determining population totals by county, and apportionment of its state legislature. The first state census was in 1865, continuing in 1875, 1885, 1895, 1905, 1915, and 1925. The law requiring decennial state census was repealed in 1933, and thereafter, Kansas began using the federal decennial censuses for population totals and apportionment of both state and federal offices.

Except for a few missing counties for the early census years, all of the original territorial and state census manuscripts survive for the period 1855-1925. The originals are all located today at the Kansas State Historical Society (KSHS) in Topcka. All have been microfilmed and are available on interlibrary loan from the KSHS. (For information on how to order any item, visit their Internet site designed just for interlibrary loan questions at **www.kshs.org/library/illpoli.htm.**

In addition, the Family History Library in Salt Lake City has most (but not all) of the Kansas state census microfilm available on interlibrary loan to its Family History Centers. KSHS reel numbers and FHL film numbers are identified for each state census resource below. A well organized review of the Kansas state censuses for genealogists can be found at the KSHS website at **www.kshs.org/genealogists/census/ kansas/index.htm**.

Added to the bibliography of statewide censuses below are a few statewide name lists, which can act as census substitutes. Several countywide census extracts and indexes are also included, and online databases are identified: See the *Guide To Microfilm Collections of the Kansas State Historical Society*, compiled and edited by David A. Haury. Published by the society, 1991, 428 pages. Contains sections on newspapers, directories, census records, plat books and atlases, and manuscripts. FHL book 978.163/T1 A3h.

■ *Kansas Biographical Index: Town, Community & Organization Histories: More Than 35,000 Citations From 258 Volumes of Kansas Town, Community and Organization Histories*, compiled by Patricia Douglass Smith and Stanley Clifford Smith, published by the authors, Garden City, KS, 2001, 1st Edition, 328 pages. 2nd Edition: "69,000 Citations From 183 Volumes." Index lists name of person, county or community name, number of source (refers to bibliography at beginning of book) and page number in original source. FHL book 978.1 D32sp (1st ed.) and 978.1 D32sm (2nd ed.).

■ *The 1854-1856 Voters of the Territory of Kansas: Includes the Eighteen Original Districts and Voting Qualifications*, compiled by Debra Graden, published 1999, publisher not noted, 630 pages. Lists voters alphabetically by surname. FHL book 978.1 N4g.

■ **1855 Kansas Territorial Census**, microfilm of originals at the Kansas State Historical Society, Topeka, KS. The 1855 census, called by the governor, lists the inhabitants of Kansas Territory by election districts. There is a map at the beginning of the microfilm showing the location of the election districts. KSHS film #K-1 shows election districts, filmed in the following order: 1-4; 7-8; 5-6; 9-13; 15; 14; and 16-17. Reel KS-1 contains a name index to the entire state. Filmed by the society, 1951. FHL's copy is film #570188. Printed extract and index privately published as *The Census of the Territory of Kansas, February, 1855: With Index and Map of Kansas Election Districts in 1854*, edited by

Willard C. Heiss, published by The Bookmark, Knightstown, IN, 1997, 38 pages. FHL book 978. X2p 1855 and FHL film #896835.

■ **1855 Kansas Territorial Census,** name index serialized in *Kansas Records and Reviews,* beginning with Vol. 1, (Apr 1994); and in *Bluestem Root Diggers Genealogical Quarterly,* starting with Vol. 6, No. 3 (Jul 1996).

■ **1855 and 1865 Kansas Censuses, Leavenworth County, Kansas,** by the Leavenworth County Genealogical Society, Leavenworth, Kansas, 1996, 38 pages. Each section is arranged in alphabetical order by the person's surname. The 1855 census was compiled from voter records and gives name and birthplace. The 1865 census is divided into townships and gives name and page number. FHL book 978.138 X22sp.

■ **1856 Name Lists.** See *An Index to the Report of the Special Committee Appointed to Investigate the Troubles in Kansas, 1856,* compiled by Robert A. Hodge, published by the author, Fredericksburg, Virginia, 1984, 2 vols. 396 pages. The Kansas-Nebraska Act of 1854 provided for the organization of the Kansas Territory in preparation for statehood. This act required the citizens of the territory to vote on the issue of slavery. Due to disagreement as to what constituted authorized voters, the House of Representatives of the U. S. Congress appointed a special committee to investigate the issue. The bulk of the report consisted of testimonies, lists of names from the census records, poll books and voting registers. This is an index to that report. Contents: v. 1. A-L -- v. 2. M-Z. FHL book 978.1 X3h, v.1 & 2, also on 6 microfiche, FHL film #6111324.

■ **1856, 1857, and 1858 Kansas Territorial Censuses,** microfilm of original records at the Kansas State Historical Society in Topeka, KS. The 1856, 1857, and 1858 census name lists were

filmed together on one roll (KSHS reel no. K-1; FHL film #1405337). Contents: **1856:** 4th district, Kansas Territory (includes part of Douglas, Johnson and Franklin counties). District No. 4 was divided by "Free State", "Pro-Slavery", or "Doubtful." **1857:** Counties of Allen (part of 18th district), 4th district (copy of 1856 list), Anderson, Atchison (3rd district), Bourbon, Dorn, McGee, Brown, Calhoun, Davis, Doniphan, Douglas, Jefferson, Johnson, Leavenworth, Linn, Lykins, Marshall, Nemaha, Pottawatomie, and Riley. Also the census of Shawnees, native or adopted. **1858:** Johnson and Marshall counties only. These census records represent only a partial listing of voters. Indexed as *Kansas 1856-1858,* edited by Ronald Vern Jackson, et al, published by Accelerated Indexing Systems, North Salt Lake, UT, 1987, 318 pages. FHL book 978.1 X2k 1856-1858.

■ **1856 Kansas Territorial Census, Geary County,** name list in *Kansas Kin,* Vol. 18, No. 1 (Feb 1980).

■ **1856 Kansas Territorial Census, Pottawatomie County,** name list in *Kansas Kin,* Vol. 18, No. 1 (Feb 1980).

■ **1856 Kansas Territorial Census, Riley County,** name list in *Kansas Kin,* Vol. 18, No. 1 (Feb 1980).

■ *1857 Census of Doniphan County, Territory of Kansas,* typescript, compiled and published by Northwest Missouri Genealogical Society, St. Joseph, Missouri, 1982, 11 pages. FHL book 978.135 X28e.

■ **1857 Kansas Territorial Census, Bourbon County,** name list in *Relatively Seeking,* Vol. 9, No. 1 (Spring 1988).

■ **1857 Kansas Territorial Census, Calhoun County,** name list in *Topeka Genealogical Society Quarterly,* Vol. 3, No. 1 (Jan 1973).

■ **1857 Kansas Territorial Census, Davis County (now Geary County)**, name list in *Kansas Kin*, Vol. 17, No. 2 (May 1979).

■ **1857 Kansas Territorial Census, Douglas County**, name list in *Pioneer*, Vol. 6, No. 1 (Summer 1982).

■ **1857 Kansas Territorial Census, Jefferson County**, name list in *Yesteryears*, Vol. 5, No. 2 (Oct 1984).

■ **1857 Kansas Territorial Census, Marshall County**, name list in *Kansas Kin*, Vol. 17, No. 2 (May 1979).

■ **1857 Kansas Territorial Census, McGee County**, name list in *Relatively Seeking*, Vol. 9, No. 1 (Spring 1988).

■ **1857 Kansas Territorial Census, Nemaha County**, name list in *Nemaha County Genealogical Society Newsletter*, Vol. 2, No. 3 (Feb 1995).

■ **1857 Kansas Territorial Census, Neosho County**, name list in *Relatively Seeking*, Vol. 9, No. 1 (Spring 1988).

■ **1857 Kansas Territorial Census, Pottawatomie County**, name list in *Kansas Kin*, Vol. 17, No. 2 (May 1979).

■ **1858 Kansas Territorial Census, Marshall County**, name list in *Kansas Kin*, Vol. 20, No. 3 (Aug 1982).

■ **1859 Kansas Territorial Census** microfilm of original records at the Kansas State Historical Society in Topeka, Kansas. The census lists voters by county, giving names of voters, dates of settlement, heads of families not voters, number of minors, number of colored persons, total, and remarks (often gives occupation). Filmed by the KSHS, 1972, reel No. K-1, FHL film #1654575. Note: although the KSHS website states that the

1856-1859 censuses were indexed and a book is available, that may not be the case – since the only known printed index was for the 1856-1858 censuses (the Jackson index above). But, just in case, it is suggested that a researcher in Topeka ask for the cited index to see if it really includes 1859 or not.

■ *1859 Census of Coffey County, Kansas*, compiled by Wanda Houck Christy, published by Coffey County Genealogical Society, Burlington, KS, 1985, FHL book 978.1 A1 no. 144.

■ *1859 Woodson County, Kansas Census*, copied from original records by Wanda Christy, published by the Coffey County Genealogical Society, Burlington, KS, 1985, 8 pages. 978.1 A1 no. 54.

■ **1859 Kansas Territorial Census, Pottawatomie County**, name list in *Kansas Kin*, Vol. 18, No. 4 (Nov 1980).

■ **1859 Kansas Territorial Census, Shawnee County**, name list in *Hedge Post*, Vol. 25, No. 3 (Dec 1999).

■ **1859 Kansas Territorial Census, Wabaunsee County**, in *Kansas Kin*, Vol. 19, No. 2 (May 1981).

■ **1859 Kansas Territorial Census, Washington County**, name list in *Kansas Kin*, Vol. 18, No. 3 (Aug 1980).

■ **1859 Kansas Territorial Census, Wyandot County**, see "Members of Wyandot families, 1859," in *Kansas State Historical Society Collections*, Vol. 15 (1919).

■ **1860 Kansas Territory Federal Census – Territory's Original Copy**, microfilm of original records at the Kansas State Historical Society, Topeka, KS. This federal census included here with the state censuses because it is the original territorial set of the 1860 federal census, filmed separately from the federal copy. It is also fairly complete, taken just prior to statehood, and includes the area of old Arapahoe County, now Colorado. A name index to the 1860 Kansas Territory Census was compiled by the WPA in the late 1930s and the index was microfilmed by the KSHS. (No copy at FHL). For an alpha list of names on each microfilm roll and the reel numbers, go to: **www.kshs.org/genealogists/ census/kansas/census1860ks.htm**.

See also, *Kansas Territorial Settlers of 1860 who were born in Tennessee, Virginia, North Carolina and South Carolina: A Compilation With Historical Annotations and Editorial Comment*, by Clara Hamlett Robertson, published by Genealogical Publishing Co., Inc. Baltimore, 1976, 187 pages. Taken from the WPA index of the eleven-volume hand-written census books in the Kansas State Historical Society Archives together with maps of Kansas and eastern Colorado showing the area included in the Kansas Territory, 1854-1861. FHL book 978.1 H2ro.

■ **Index to the 1860 Kansas Territory Census (Federal Copy).** See *Kansas 1860 Territorial Census Index*, edited by Ronald Vern Jackson and Gary Ronald Teeples, published by Accelerated Indexing Systems, Bountiful, UT, 1978, 153 pages. Indexes names to pages from the federal copy and may not agree with indexed pages in the KS territorial set.

■ **1861-1865 Kansas Military Records.** See *Index to Compiled Service Records of Volunteer Union Soldiers Who Served in Organizations From the State of Kansas*, Adjutant General's Office, indexed by surname of soldier. Filmed by the National Archives, Washington, DC, 1964, 10 rolls, as follows:
- A-Br, FHL film #881837.
- Bu-C, FHL film #881838.
- D-F, FHL film #881839.
- G-Hom, FHL film #881840.
- Hon-Le, FHL film #881841.
- Lg-Mi, FHL film #881842.
- Mo-Ral, FHL film #881843.
- Ram-Sk, FHL film #881844.
- Sl-U, FHL film #881845.
- V-Z, FHL film #881846.

■ **1862-1866 Internal Revenue Lists for Kansas**, microfilm of originals at the National Archives, Central Plains Region, Kansas City, MO. Filmed by the National Archives, 1985, 3 rolls, as follows:
- Annual lists 1863-1864; Monthly lists Sept. 1862-Dec. 1864; and Special lists Aug.-Dec. 1864, FHL film #1578484.
- Annual lists 1865; Monthly lists 1865; Special lists 1865, FHL film #1578485.
- Annual lists 1866; Monthly lists 1866, FHL film #1578486.

■ **1865 Kansas State Census**, microfilm of originals at the Kansas State Historical Society, Topeka, KS. Filmed by the KSHS, 1951, 8 rolls, (FHL set has 9 rolls) as follows:
- Allen, Anderson, and Atchison Counties, KSHS reel K-1, FHL film #570189.
- Bourbon, Brown, Butler, Chase, Clay and Coffey Counties, KSHS reel K-2; FHL film #570190.
- Davies, Dickinson, Doniphan and Douglas Counties, KSHS reel K-3; FHL film #570191 (excludes Douglas).
- Douglas County, FHL film #570192.
- Franklin, Greenwood, Jackson, Jefferson, and Johnson Counties, KSHS reel K-4; FHL film #570193.
- Leavenworth County, KSHS reel K-5; FHL film #570194.
- Linn, Lyon, Marion, Marshall, Miami and Morris Counties, KSHS reel K-6; FHL film #570195.
- Nemaha, Neosho, Osage, Ottawa, Pottawatomie, Riley, Saline, Shawnee, Wabaunsee, Woodson, and Wyandotte Counties, KSHS reel K-7; FHL film #570196.
- Social Statistics (no names listed), KSHS reel K-8; FHL film #570197.

■ **1865 Kansas State Census Index**, (entire state) available on microfilm at the Kansas State Historical Society, Topeka, KS. (No copy at FHL). The KSHS microfilm index circulates through interlibrary loan. Filmed by the KSHS, 37 rolls, beginning with KS-1, No Name - Babcock, Eli). Locate film numbers for all 37 rolls at the KSHS website: **www.kshs.org/genealogists/ census/kansas/census1865ks.htm#microfilm**.

■ **1865 Kansas State Census, Bourbon County**, name list in *Four States Genealogist*, Vol. 2, No. 2 (Jan 1970).

■ **1865 Kansas State Census, Butler County**, extract and index in *Midwest Genealogical Register*, Vol. 19, No. 3 (Oct 1984).

■ **1865 Kansas State Census, Franklin County**, surname index in *Franklin County Kansas Genealogical Society Quarterly*, Vol. 3, No. 2 (Feb 1995).

■ **1865 Kansas State Census**, countywide extracts and/or indexes, available at the KSHS:
  • **Leavenworth County** (call no. K 929.4 Pam vol. 1, no. 2).
  • **Osage County** (call no. K 929.4 - Os1 1865).
  • **Ottawa County** (call no. K 929.4 - Sa3c 1865).
  • **Pottawatomie County** (call no. K 929.4 - P85 1865).
  • **Riley County** (call no. 929.4 -R45 1855-1880).
  • **Saline County** (call no. K 929.4 - Sa3c 1865).
  • **Wabaunsee County** (call no. K 929.4 - W11 1865).

■ **1865 Kansas State Census**, Countywide extracts and/or indexes, available at the FHL:
  • **Atchison County**, FHL book 978.136 X2o 1865.
  • **Dickinson County**, FHL book 978.1 A1 no. 67.
  • **Greenwood County**, FHL book 978.1 A1 no. 202.
  • **Leavenworth County**, FHL book 978.138 X22sp (includes 1855)
  • **Ottawa County**, FHL book 978.1 A1 No. 186.
  • **Pottawatomie County**, FHL book 978.132 X2p.
  • **Riley County**, FHL book 978.1 A1 No. 151.
  • **Saline County**, FHL book 978.1 A1 No. 186.
  • **Wabaunsee County**, FHL book 978.1 A1 No. 109.

■ *1872 Census of Ford County, Kansas*, microfilm of typescript copy, taken from "Early Ford County" by Ida Ellen Rath. Includes list from coroner's records of Ford County (1883-1938). Arranged alphabetically by surname. Filmed by the Genealogical Society of Utah, 1983, 1 roll, FHL film #1035609).

■ **1875 Kansas State Census**, microfilm of originals at the Kansas State Historical Society, Topeka, KS. The 1875 census lists all members of household by name, including age, sex, race or color, state or country of birth, and where from to Kansas (state or country). Filmed by the KSHS, 21 rolls, 1951, beginning with KSHS reel 1875 K-1 (Allen, Anderson, Atchison and Barber Counties). Locate film numbers for all 21 reels at the KSHS website: **www.kshs.org/genealogists/ census/kansas/census1875ks.htm#microfilm**. The FHL set contains 23 rolls, beginning with FHL film #570198 (Allen – Barber counties). Locate film numbers for all 23 rolls at the **www.familysearch.org** site. Go to FHL Library / Catalog / place search: "Kansas" / Kansas – Census – 1875.

■ **1875 Kansas State Census Index**, (entire state) available on microfilm at the Kansas State Historical Society, Topeka, KS. (No copy at FHL). The KSHS microfilm index circulates through interlibrary loan. List the year and reel number when placing an interlibrary loan request. Filmed by the KSHS, 157 rolls, beginning with reel #KS-1 (Child – Alexander, E. M.). Locate film numbers for all 157 rolls at the KSHS website: **www.kshs.org/genealogists/census/kansas/ census1875ks.htm#microfilm**.

■ **1875 Kansas State Census, Barton County**, name list in *Barton County Genealogical Society Quarterly*, beginning with Vol. 10, No. 2 (Spring 1990).

■ **1875 Kansas State Census, Franklin County**, surname index in *Franklin County Kansas Genealogical Society Quarterly*, Vol. 3, No. 3 (Aug 1995).

■ **1875 Kansas State Census**, countywide extracts and/or indexes, available at the KSHS:
- **Crawford County** (call no. K 929.4 -C85 1875)
- **Dickinson County** (call no. K 929.4 -D56 1875)
- **Harvey County** (call no. K 929.4 Pam vol. 1, no. 1)
- **Jefferson County** (call no. K 929.4 -J35 1875)
- **Montgomery County**, Cherry Township (call no. K 929.4 -M76 1870-1900)
- **Pawnee County** (call no. K 929.4 - P28 1875)
- **Phillips County** (call no. K 929.4 - P54 1875)
- **Riley County** (call no. K 929.4 – R45 1855-1880)
- **Saline County** (city of Salina only) (call no. K 929.4 -Sa3 Sa33 1875)
- **Sedgwick County** (call no. K 929.4 -Se2 1875)
- **Sumner County** (call no. K 929.4 - Su6 1875)
- **Wilson County** (call no. 929.4 - W69 1875).

■ **1875 Kansas State Census**, countywide extracts and/or indexes, available at the FHL:
- **Atchison County**, see FHL book 978.136 X2o 1865.
- **Douglas County**, see FHL book 978.165 X2d 1875.
- **Jefferson County**, see FHL book 978.137 X22ei 1875
- **Riley County**, FHL book 978.128 X2d.
- **Sedgwick County**, FHL book 978.186 X2c 1875.
- **Wilson County**, FHL book 978.1925 X2i.

■ **1880 Kansas Federal Census, Brown County, Kansas.** Microfilm of original records at the Brown County Courthouse in Hiawatha, Kansas. This is the "1880 Short Form," Brown county's original copy of the federal census. (This is the only known 1880 original county list surviving for all of Kansas). FHL title, *Lists of Persons in Brown County, Kansas.* Divided by township and arranged within each township in alphabetical order by first letter of surname. Gives name, color, sex and age. Filmed by the Genealogical Society of Utah, 1993, 1 roll, FHL film #1871055. Compare this name list with the federal copy of the 1880 census from Brown County, Kansas, filmed by the National Archives (FHL film #1254374).

■ **1883 History**. See *History of the State of Kansas: Containing a Full Account of its Growth From an Uninhabited Territory to a Wealthy and Important State, of its Early Settlement, A Supplementary History and Description of its Counties, Cities, Towns and Villages, Their Advantages, Industries and Commerce, to Which Are Added Biographical Sketches and Portraits of Prominent Men and Early Settlers*, by A. T. Andreas, original published Chicago, 1883, reprint published by Walsworth Pub. Co., Marceline, MO, 1976, 2 vols., Includes index. FHL book 978.1 H2hi 1976 and FHL film #982248.

■ **1885 Kansas State Census**, microfilm of originals at the Kansas State Historical Society, Topeka, KS. The 1885 census lists all members of a household by name, including age, sex, race or color, and state or country of birth. Also listed: where from to Kansas (state or country) and military record (condition of discharge, state of enlistment, letter or name of company or command, number of regiment or other organization to which attached, arm of the service, and name of military prison if confined in one). Filmed by the society, 1969-1970, 146 rolls beginning with KSHS reel K-1 (Allen Co. – Humboldt city and twp.; Iola Twp.). Locate film numbers for all 146 reels at the KSHS website: **www.kshs.org/genealogists/census/kansas/ census1885ks.htm#microfilm**. The FHL set contains 151 rolls, beginning with FHL film #975699 (Allen Co. - Humboldt city and twp.; Iola Twp.). Locate film numbers for all 151 rolls at the **www.familysearch.org** site. Go to FHL Library / Catalog / place search: "Kansas" / Kansas – Census – 1885.

■ **1885 Kansas State Census Index (City of Topeka)**, available on micro film at the Kansas State Historical Society, Topeka, KS. (No copy at FHL). The KSHS microfilm index circulates through interlibrary loan. List the year and reel number when placing an interlibrary loan request. Filmed by the KSHS, 7 rolls, beginning with reel #KS-1 (Abarr, Mary - Collisi, Wm.). Locate film numbers for all 7 rolls at the **www.familysearch.org** site. Go to FHL Library /

Catalog / place search: "Kansas" / Kansas –
Census – 1885.

■ **1885 List of Soldiers**. See *Kansas Settlers of
the Grand Army of the Republic, 1885: A
Compiled List of Union soldiers Listed in the
State Census of 1885 from Dickinson, Ellsworth,
Lincoln, McPherson, Ottawa and Saline
Counties*, compiled by Robert A. VanDyne,
published by Smoky Valley Genealogical Society,
Salina, KS, 198?, 82 pages. Gives name, age,
birthplace, regiment and company, and other
notes. Includes index. FHL book 978.15 M2v.

■ **1885 Kansas State Census, Butler County**,
name list published serially in *Midwest
Genealogical Register*, beginning with Vol. 18, No.
2 (Jul 1983).

■ **1885 Kansas State Census, Cherokee County**,
complete name index published in *Relatively
Seeking*, Vol. 11, No. 1 (Spring 2000).

■ **1885 Kansas State Census, Franklin County**,
name lists by townships, in *Franklin County
Kansas Genealogical Society Quarterly*, beginning
with Vol. 7, No. 1 (1999).

■ **1885 Kansas State Census**, countywide extracts
and/or indexes, available at the KSHS:
- **Crawford County** (call no. K 929.4 - C85 1885).
- **Dickinson County** (call no. K 929.4 -D56 1885)
- **Jefferson County** (call no. K 929.4 -J35 1885)
- **Leavenworth County** (call no. K 929.4 -L48 1885)
- **Montgomery County**, Cherry Township (call no. K 929.4 -M76 1870-1900)
- **Montgomery County**, W. Cherry Township (call no. K 929.4 -M76 1880-1900)
- **Riley County** (call no. K 929.4 - R45 1885)
- **Wilson County** (call no. K 929.4 - W69 1885)

■ **1885 Kansas State Census**, countywide extracts
and/or indexes, available at the FHL:
- **Leavenworth County**, FHL book 978.138 X22s.
- **Riley County**, FHL book 978.128 X2dk.
- **Wilson County**, FHL book 978.1925 X22i.

■ **1895 Kansas State Census**, microfilm of
originals at the Kansas State Historical Society,
Topeka, KS. The 1895 census lists all members of
household by name, including age, sex, race or
color, and state or country of birth. Also listed:
where from to Kansas (state or country) and
military record (condition of discharge, state of
enlistment, letter or name of company or
command, number of regiment or other
organization to which attached, arm of the
service, and name of military prison if confined
in one). Filmed by the society, 1953-1958, KSHS
set contains 169 rolls, beginning with #1895-K-1
(Allen County, townships, A-Z). Locate film
numbers for all 169 reels at the KSHS website:
**www.kshs.org/genealogists/census/kansas/
census1895ks.htm#microfilm.**
The FHL set contains 202 rolls, beginning with
FHL film #570221 (Allen County, townships, C-
S). Locate film numbers for all 202 rolls at the
www.familysearch.org site. Go to FHL Library /
Catalog / place search: "Kansas" / Kansas –
Census – 1895.

■ **1895 Kansas State Census Index**, microfilm
available at the Kansas State Historical Society,
Topeka, KS. Indexes for Clay and Ness counties
and the cities of Topeka and Fort Scott, and
Soldier and Topeka townships in Shawnee
county are available on microfilm. This microfilm
circulates through interlibrary loan from KSHS:
- 1895 Index - Clay & Ness Counties (KS-1-7).
- 1895 Index - City of Fort Scott (KS-8-11).
- 1895 Index - City of Topeka, Topeka Township & Soldier Township, all in Shawnee County
An online index to the KS 1895 State Census
shown under Kansas Censuses & Substitutes
Online below.

■ **1895 Kansas State Census**, countywide extracts
and/or indexes, available at the KSHS:
- **Atchison County, City of Atchison** call no. K 929.4 -At2 1895)
- **Clay County** (call no. K 929.4 - C57 1895)
- **Crawford County, City of Pittsburg** (card index)
- **Montgomery County, Cherry Township** (call no. K 929.4 -M76 1870-1900)

- **Montgomery County, West Cherry Township** (call no. K 929.4 -M76 1880-1900)
- **Phillips County, Prairie View Township** (call no. 978.1 -P54 P884, pgs. 371-382)
- **Reno County, City of Hutchinson** (card index)
- **Riley County** (call no. K 929.4 - R45 1895)
- **Thomas County** (card index)
- **Trego County** (card index)
- **Wilson County** (call no. K 929.4 - W69 1895).

■ **1895 Kansas State Census**, countywide extracts and/or indexes, available at the FHL:
- **Jefferson County**, FHL book 978.137 X22i 1895.
- **Clay County**, FHL book 978.1275 X2b 1895.
- **Riley County**, FHL book 978.128 X22k 1895.
- **Wilson County**, FHL book 978.1925 X22i.

■ **1895 Kansas State Census, Cherokee County**, name list in *Prospectors, Diggers, and Doers*, beginning with Vol. 5 (1983).

■ **1895 Kansas State Census, Barton County**, name list in *Barton County Genealogical Society Quarterly*, beginning with Vol. 2, No. 2 (1982).

■ **1895 Kansas State Census, Morton County**, in *Genealogical Council of Kansas Newsletter*, beginning with Vol. 21, No. 1 (Jul 1995).

■ **1895 Kansas State Census, Sedgwick County**, see "Residents age 21+ years, 1895," in *Midwest Genealogical Register*, Vol. 6, No. 1 (Jun 1971).

■ **1905 Kansas State Census**, microfilm of originals at the Kansas State Historical Society, Topeka, KS. The 1905 census lists all members of household by name, including age, sex, race or color, and state or country of birth. Also listed: where from to Kansas (state or country) and military record (condition of discharge, state of enlistment, letter or name of company or command, number of regiment or other organization to which attached, arm of the service, and name of military prison if confined in one). Filmed by the society, 181 rolls,

beginning with #1905-K-1 (Allen County cities of Bassett, Elsmore, Gas City, Humboldt & Iola, pt. 1). (The FHL does not have this series of microfilm). Locate film numbers for all 181 reels at the KSHS website: **www.kshs.org/genealogists/census/kansas/ census1905ks.htm#microfilm.**

■ **1905 Kansas State Census Index**, (For residents of selected cities), microfilm of originals at the Kansas State Historical Society, Topeka, KS. Arranged by city, then alphabetically by surname. Index lists full name, county of residence, and page on the census schedules where the person was shown. Index for the following cities:
- **Ft. Scott** (Bourbon Co.), KS-1-4.
- **Pittsburg** (Crawford Co.), KS-41-45.
- **Lawrence** (Douglas Co.), KS-29-33.
- **Ottawa** (Franklin Co.), KS-39-41.
- **Leavenworth** (Leavenworth Co.), KS-33-39.
- **Hutchinson** (Reno Co.), KS-4-7.
- **Salina** (Salina Co.), KS-45-47.
- **Topeka** (city), **Topeka Township**, and **Soldier Township** (Shawnee Co.), KS-48-60.
- **Wichita** (Sedgwick Co.), KS-60-69.
- **Kansas City, Argentine** and **Rosedale** (Wyandotte Co.), KS-7-29.

This microfilm circulates through interlibrary loan from KSHS. (No FHL film). When ordering, list the year and reel number when placing an interlibrary loan request (e.g., "1905-KS-7") Locate cities and alpha breakdown for each surname per roll at the KSHS website: **www.kshs.org/genealogists/census/kansas/ census1905ks.htm#microfilm.**

■ **1905 Kansas State Census, Wilson County**, index of names in *Heritage Genealogical Society Quarterly*, Vol. 16, No. 2 (Sep 1986) through Vol. 17, No. 1 (Jul 1987).

■ **1905 Kansas State Census**, countywide extracts and/or indexes, available at the KSHS:
- **Riley County** (call no. K 929.4 - R45 1905)
- **Wilson County** (call no. K 929.4 - W69 1905)

■ **1905 Kansas State Census**, countywide extracts and/or indexes, available at the FHL:
- **Riley County**, FHL book 978.128.

■ **1915 Kansas State Census**, microfilm of originals at the Kansas State Historical Society, Topeka, KS. (No FHL film). The 1915 census lists all members of household by name, including age, sex, race or color, and state or country of birth. Also listed: where from to Kansas (state or country) and military record (condition of discharge, state of enlistment, letter or name of company or command, number of regiment or other organization to which attached, arm of the service, and name of military prison if confined in one). Filmed by the society, 271 rolls, beginning with #1915-K-1 (Allen County cities of Bassett, Carlyle, Elsmore, Gas City, Geneva, Humboldt & Iola, pt. 1). Locate film numbers for all 271 reels at the KSHS website: **www.kshs.org/genealogists/census/kansas/census1915ks.htm#microfilm.**

■ **1915 Kansas State Census Index**, (For residents of selected cities), microfilm of originals at the Kansas State Historical Society, Topeka, KS. (No FHL film). This microfilm circulates through interlibrary loan from KSHS. List the year and reel number when placing an interlibrary loan request.
- **Fort Scott** (Bourbon County), 1915-KS-69, KS-1, and KS-2
- **Pittsburg** (Crawford County), 1915-KS-36-40.
- **Leavenworth** (Leavenworth County), 1915-KS-30-36.
- **Topeka Township** (excludes city of Topeka), and **Soldier Township** (Shawnee County), 1915-KS-41-42.
- **Wichita** (Sedgwick County), 1915 - KS-42-57.
- **Kansas City** & **Rosedale** (Wyandotte County), 1915-KS-3-30.

■ **1915 Kansas State Census**, countywide extracts and/or indexes, available at the KSHS:
- **Atchison**, **Lawrence**, and **Topeka** street address index.
- **Benton City** (Butler County), call no. K 369.133

K133m Ser.2 v.164 p.1)
- **Kiowa County** card index.
- **Riley County** (call no. K 929.4 - R45 1915 vol. 1-4)

■ *1915 Kansas State Census Abstract, Riley County*, compiled by Stella Frey, Golda Sitz, and Peggy Ward, editing assistance by Mary Cottom, published by the Riley County Genealogical, Society, Manhattan, KS, 1990, 459 pages. FHL book 978.128 X2f 1915.

■ **1918 Registration Affidavits of Aliens (Kansas)**, microfilm of originals at the National Archives Branch in Kansas City, Missouri. Alphabetical name lists are by county. Filmed by the Genealogical Society of Utah, 1991, 20 rolls, beginning with FHL film #1769240 (Registration affidavits of alien enemy 1918, Allen County-Atchison County). Locate film numbers for all 20 rolls at the **www.familysearch.org** site. Go to FHL Library / Catalog / place search: "Kansas" / Kansas – Naturalization and citizenship / Registration affidavits of aliens, 1918. Affidavits indexed in *Registration of Axis Aliens in Kansas: January, 1918 through June, 1918*, indexed and published by Kansas Statistical Publications Company, Overland Park, KS, 1992, 76 pages. All males not naturalized who were subjects of the German Empire, Alsace-Lorraine in France, and Schleswig-Holstein in Denmark were required to register with the Department of Justice. A number of their spouses were also listed. See FHL book 978.1 P4r.

■ **1925 Kansas State Census**, microfilm of originals at the Kansas State Historical Society, Topeka, KS. (The FHL does not have this series of microfilm). The 1925 census lists all members of household by name, including age, sex, race or color, marital status, state or country of birth, and relationship to head of household. Also listed: where from to Kansas (state or country), military record (condition of discharge, state of enlistment, letter or name of company or command, number of regiment or other organization to which attached, arm of the service, and name of military prison if confined in one), and citizenship (year of immigration to the U.S. and year of naturalization if naturalized). Filmed by the society, 177 rolls, beginning with KSHS reel #1925-K-1 (Allen County: Bassett, Elsmore, Gas City, Humboldt, Iola, LaHarpe, Mildred, Moran, Carlyle & Cottage Grove Twp.). Locate film numbers for all 271 reels at the KSHS website: **www.kshs.org/genealogists/census/kansas/census1925ks.htm#microfilm.**

■ **1925 Kansas State Census Index, Shawnee County,** microfilm of originals at the Kansas State Historical Society, Topeka, KS. (No FHL film). This microfilm circulates through interlibrary loan from KSHS. List the year and reel number when placing an interlibrary loan request.
   • **Topeka Township** (excluding city of Topeka) & **Soldier Township** (Shawnee County), 1925-K-57, K - 1, & K – 2.

■ **1925 Kansas State Census, Shawnee County,** see "County Home Residents, 1925 state census," in *Topeka Genealogical Society Quarterly*, Vol. 29, No. 4 (Oct 1999).

Kansas Censuses & Substitutes Online

■ **1895 Kansas State Census Index (Online).** Visit the KSHS 1895 state census site to find an online index at **www.kshs.org/genealogists/census/kansas/census1895ks.htm#indexes.** From the KSHS website: "Counties completely indexed as of November 2005: Allen, Atchison, Barber, Barton, Chase, Clark, Edwards, Ellis, Gove, Greeley, Greenwood, Harper, Haskell, Hodgeman, Jackson, Jefferson, Kearny, Kiowa, Labette, Lane, Lincoln, Marion, Mitchell, Montgomery, Morton, Osage, Pratt, Rawlins, Republic, Rush, Russell, Scott, Sedgwick (including the city of Wichita), Thomas, Trego, Wabaunsee, Wallace, Wichita, and Woodson."

"Counties that are partially indexed: Anderson, Butler, Gray, Lyon, Norton, Phillips, Reno, Shawnee, and Sumner. The city of Topeka (Shawnee County) is in process; a complete Topeka index is available only on microfilm. To search the online index, enter a surname and/or a county, township or city, and click 'search'. First names may also be entered; however, many individuals were listed only by their initials."

The website note doesn't mention it, but the index includes a "Soundex" search as well, and you only need to enter a surname to start a search, making this a very useful resource.

Personal note: Because of this wonderful online index, I discovered Ira and Elizabeth Dollarhyde living in the city of Greensburg, Kiowa County, Kansas in 1895. I had them in the 1880 federal census in Indiana, and I found them in the 1900 federal census of Washington State – but without an 1890 federal census, I had lost them for that time period. Thank you, Kansas State Historical Society!

■ **Kansas Censuses & Substitutes Online.** The following databases are available online at these sites:
www.ancestry.com
   • 1850-90 Federal Census Indexes (AIS)
   • 1850-1880 Mortality Schedules & Index
   • 1855 KS Territory Census (2)
   • 1856 KS Territory Census
   • 1857 KS Territory Census
   • 1858 KS Territory Census
   • 1859 KS Territory Census
   • 1865 KS State Census
   • 1865, 1875, 1885, 1905, 1915 KS State Census, Riley County
   • 1875 KS State Census
   • 1880 Federal Census
   • 1885 KS State Census
   • 1885-1940 Indian Census Schedules
   • 1895 KS State Census
   • 1900 Federal Census
   • 1905 KS State Census
   • 1910 Federal Census
   • 1915 KS State Census
   • 1920 Federal Census
   • 1930 Federal Census

www.censusfinder.com

- 1878-1894 Students at School For The Blind
- 1880 Federal Census – Images.
- 1880 Federal Census Search at Family Search
- 1883 Pensioners Roll for all Kansas Counties
- 1895 Kansas State Census Statewide Index
- 1917-1918 Draft Cards in Kansas state
- 1917-1918 Statewide Index of Alien Enemy Registrants
- 1941 Veterinarians List - Kansas Statewide
- Kansas Statewide Databases of Census & Genealogy Records

www.census-online.com

Federal Census

- 1880, 1885, 1900 Censuses - Surname "Cook"

State Census

- 1895 State Census - Searchable Index

Territorial Census

- 1855 Territory of Kansas Census
- **Links to online name lists by county (no. of databases):** Allen (2); Anderson (34); Atchison (5); Barber (2); Barton (7); Bourbon (2); Breckenridge (6); Brown (3); Butler (7); Chase (8); Chautauqua (6); Cherokee (3); Cheyenne (1); Clark (2); Clay (4); Cloud (7); Coffey (14); Comanche (7); Cowley (3); Crawford (4); Decatur (4); Dickinson (12); Doniphan (3); Douglas (2); Edwards (3); Elk (3); Ellis (4); Ellsworth (4); Finney (1); Ford (7); Franklin (4); Geary (1); Godfrey (2); Gove (0); Graham (2); Grant (3); Gray (1); Greeley (3); Greenwood (7); Hamilton (3); Harper (5); Harvey (2); Haskell (0); Hodgeman (3); Howard (1); Jackson (2); Jefferson (3); Jewell (5); Johnson (2); Kearny (2); Kingman (2); Kiowa (1); Labette (2); Lane (1); Leavenworth (6); Lincoln (6); Linn (2); Logan (3); Lyon (4); Madison (3); Marion (6); Marshall (13); McPherson (2); Meade (2); Miami (9); Mitchell (2); Montgomery (3); Morris (3); Morton (1); Nemaha (11); Neosho (11); Ness (2); Norton (1); Osage (9); Osborne (2); Ottawa (2); Pawnee (2); Phillips (4); Pottawatomie (5); Pratt (2); Rawlins (2); Reno (2); Republic (1); Rice (2); Riley (2); Rooks (2); Rush (2); Russell (2); Saline (4); Scott (1); Sedgwick (11); Sequoyah (1); Seward (1); Shawnee (3); Sheridan (1); Sherman (1); Smith (2); St. John (1); Stafford (2); Stanton (0); Stevens (1); Sumner (5); Thomas (1); Trego (3); Wabaunsee (2); Wallace (1); Washington (2); Wichita (1); Wilson (9); Woodson (2); and Wyandotte (3).

■ **Kansas State Census Extraction Forms Online.** For free downloadable census extraction forms, visit the **http://censustools.com/** website to find forms created as Excel spreadsheets. Presently, there are forms for the Kansas State Censuses for 1865, 1875, 1885, 1895, 1905, 1915, and 1925.

MISSOURI

Censuses & Substitutes, 1762-1921

The great basin of the Mississippi River was first claimed by France in 1682. Named Louisiana after Louis XIV, the settled areas consisted of a few trading posts along the Mississippi River for the next 120 years. The earliest French settlements in Louisiana were Natchez (1716); New Orleans (1718); Baton Rouge (1719); Ste. Genevieve (1750); and St. Louis (1764), the latter two in modern Missouri. The French managed their colonies closely, taking frequent censuses of potential taxpayers, and some of the name lists still exist for that era.

France transferred title of Louisiana to Spain in 1762, resulting from its defeats in the French and Indian War, but the Spanish never had much of a presence in Louisiana. They attempted to administer the area from their bases in the Caribbean and Mexico. For the 38 years of Spanish rule, the leftover French traders/settlers remained in Louisiana, while the Spanish rulers mostly ignored Louisiana as being too big and too expensive to explore or settle. However, as with all of its colonies, the Spanish bureaucracy was fond of listing names of potential taxpayers. Several tax lists from the Spanish era still exist, located in the Madrid and Seville archives.

After defeating the Spanish in battle in 1800, Napoleon gained title to Louisiana for France again, but with rebellions going on in the French West Indies, Napoleon found it difficult to administer the area. For the next three years, the

French presence in Louisiana amounted to a squad of about 20 troops billeted at Baton Rouge.

The United States purchased Louisiana from Napoleon in 1803. The following year, Congress created two districts in the area, Orleans Territory (which was mostly the same as the present-day state of Louisiana; and Louisiana District, the rest of the tract. In 1805, Louisiana District became Louisiana Territory, with the seat of government at St. Louis.

When the state of Louisiana was admitted to the Union in 1812, the original Louisiana Territory was renamed Missouri Territory. The first general assembly of the Territory of Missouri met in October 1812, reaffirming the five original districts created from 1805-1811, which were renamed "counties" in 1812. The five original districts/counties were Cape Girardeau, New Madrid, St. Charles, St. Louis, and Ste. Genevieve. A handful of censuses were taken for Missouri Territory, 1812-1819, but except for a couple of lists for St. Charles county in 1817 and 1819, only statistical summaries have survived. The 1820 federal census taken for Missouri Territory was also lost.

The events leading up to Missouri's statehood included the "Missouri Compromise of 1820," landmark legislation relating to free versus slave states, allowing Missouri to become a slave state and Maine to become a free state. Maine and Missouri were admitted to the Union in 1820 and 1821, respectively.

The state of Missouri took several state censuses, but few have survived. An inventory of county repositories by the Missouri State Archives reveals a few county copies of state censuses survive for 1844, 1845, 1846, 1852, 1856, 1864, and 1868. For the 1876 Missouri State Census, a total of 24 county name lists survive. The state census original manuscripts are spread across the state, usually located at a county clerk's office in a county courthouse. Most (but not all) have been microfilmed by the Genealogical Society of Utah for the Family History Library (FHL) in Salt Lake City.

More common than censuses, however, are the countywide tax lists from the 1820s to the 1890s, which exist for all 114 Missouri counties (and the independent city of St. Louis). At least 50 counties have tax lists that have been extracted, abstracted, or indexed; published as microfilm reproductions, articles in periodicals, or books. Unpublished extant tax lists can be found using the Missouri State Archives' *Local Records Inventory Database*, where a search can made for every county of Missouri for county records, including censuses; tax lists; birth, marriage, and death records; and miscellaneous court records residing in local repositories. A selection of these unpublished lists are included here, but the bibliography is primarily for identifying published lists.

The published tax lists were mostly microfilmed by the Genealogical Society of Utah. And, a number of censuses and tax lists have been extracted by various individuals and genealogical societies, and these are noted in the bibliography that follows. Along with the countywide tax lists, the statewide census substitutes such as tax and military lists may provide genealogists with the best chance of finding an ancestor's name listed, confirming a place of residence, and perhaps leading to more resources available at a particular county repository, such as deed indexes, probates, naturalizations, etc. Published censuses and substitutes for Missouri are identified below, organized in chronological order:

■ **1535-1839.** See *Missouri Genealogical Records & Abstracts*, by Sherida K. Eddlemon; surname index by Marlene Towle, published by Heritage Books, Bowie, MD, 1990, 7 vols. Includes records from over 40 Missouri counties: marriage records, Spanish censuses, tax lists, estrays, cemetery listings, slave bills of sale, land records including French and Spanish land grants, military records, mortality schedules, court records, marriage records, etc. Contents: vol. 1: 1766-1839; vol. 2: 1752-1839; vol. 3: 1787-1839; vol. 4: 1741-1839; vol. 5: 1755-1839; vol. 6: 1621-1839; vol. 7: 1535-1839. FHL book 977.8 R4e, v.1-7.

■ **1762-1800.** See *The Spanish Regime in Missouri: A Collection of Papers and Documents Relating to Upper Louisiana Principally Within the Present limits of Missouri During the Dominion of Spain, From the Archives of the Indies at Seville*, edited and with an introduction and notes, biographical and explanatory by Louis Houck, originally published by R. R. Donnelley & Sons, Chicago, 1909, 2 vols., filmed for the FHL by the Library of Congress, Photoduplication Service, 1990, 1 roll, FHL film #1723770.

■ **1781-1797.** See *Anglo-Americans in Spanish Archives: Lists of Anglo-American Settlers in the Spanish Colonies of America; A finding Aid*, by Lawrence H. Feldman, published by Genealogical Publishing Co., Inc., Baltimore, 1991, 349 pages. From source materials available in Spanish archives, the author has abstracted from original census documents genealogical data about individuals and families who settled in Spanish lands within the present-day states of Florida, Alabama, Mississippi, Louisiana, and Missouri in the US and parts of Central America. Includes bibliographical references and an index of personal names. FHL book 973 X2fe.

■ *Index to French and Spanish Land Grants, Recorded in Registers of Land Titles in Missouri: Books A, B, C, D, E*, copied from an index prepared by the staff at the Missouri State Archives by Betty Harvey Williams, Warrensburg, MO, 1977, 25 pages, FHL book 977.8 R22if.

■ **1815-1922 Court Records; 1815-1900 Index to Court Records, Cape Girardeau County, Missouri**, microfilm of original records at the Cape Girardeau County courthouse, Jackson, Missouri. From 1812 to 1830, Cape Girardeau covered an area of 22 modern Missouri counties. Filmed by the Genealogical Society of Utah, 1973, 8 rolls, beginning with FHL film #925694 (Index to court records, v. 1-2, 1815-1900).

■ **1817-1819.** See *Enumeration of the County of St. Charles, Missouri Territory for the years 1817 and 1819: With Some Selected Marriage and Cemetery Records And a Full Surname Index*, transcribed by Melvin B. Goe, Sr., published by McDowell Publications, Utica, KY, 1980, 63 pages. FHL book 977.839 X2g.

■ *1818-1883 Missouri pioneers, New Madrid County*, compiled by Audrey L. Woodruff, published by Boyd Publications, Milledgeville, GA, 1995, 32 pages. From 1812 to 1830, New Madrid County covered an area of 23 modern Missouri counties. Includes abstracts of administrative [probate] records, Book A, 1832-1846, the 1860 mortality schedule for New Madrid County, an 1818 list of delinquent taxes for part of New Madrid County, and an 1883 list of military pensioners. Book A includes early wills and administrative bonds for intestate estates. Includes index of surnames. FHL book 977.8985 P2w.

■ *Missouri Taxpayers, 1819-1826,* compiled by Lois Stanley, George F. Wilson, and Maryhelen Wilson, published by the Southern Historical Press, Greenville, SC, 1990, 133 pages. Extracted from county tax lists in Missouri, the names are in alphabetical order by county. Includes about 14,000 names. FHL book 977.8 R4s.

■ *Ten Thousand Missouri Taxpayers*, compiled by Sherida K. Eddlemon, published by Heritage Books, Bowie, MD, 1996, 239 pages. FHL book 977.8 R48k.

■ **1819-1931.** See *Missouri Ancestors*, a compilation of various county records, published by Stan and Jackie Parks, Burkburnett, TX, 1980,

9 vols. Contents: vol. 1: Crawford County, index to probate records 1851-1920 and Pleasant Hill Baptist Cemetery records /compiled by Rosalea Hopper;- vol. 2: Washington County deed book "A" 1821-1834 and Horine Cemetery, Richwoods, Missouri, Masonic Cemetery, Blackwell, Missouri; vol. 3: Jefferson County 1930 election poll book, DeSoto, Missouri, and Jefferson County cemeteries; vol. 4: General election pollbook, DeSoto, Missouri 1928, and Jefferson County cemeteries; vol. 5: Potosi City Cemetery, Potosi, Missouri; vol. 6: Jefferson County original land entries; vol. 7: Wayne County cemeteries; vol. 8: Madison County deed books "A" & "B", 1819-1830; and vol. 9: Jefferson County 1931 election poll book, DeSoto, Missouri, and Herculaneum Cemetery. FHL book 977.862 P22h v. 1-9.

■ **1820-1853.** See *Missouri Pioneers of Boone County*, compiled by InfoTech Publications, published by Boyd Publishers., Milledgeville, GA, 1992, 1995, 82 pages. Includes surname index. Contains information from original land patents, an 1821 tax list, marriages for 1820-1849, and the 1853 steward's book from the Columbia Circuit of the Methodist Episcopal Church, Missouri Conference. FHL book 977.829 V29m.

■ **1821-1928 Court records, Gasconade County, Missouri**, microfilm of original records at the Gasconade County courthouse, Hermann, MO. Filmed by the Genealogical Society of Utah, 1973, 6 rolls, beginning with FHL film #944573 (Index, v. A-B 1821-1856).

■ *1822-1891 Missouri Pioneers of Clay County, Missouri*, compiled and published by InfoTech Publications, Bowling Green, MO, 1992, 92 pages. Includes surname index. Contains various information about early residents of Clay County taken from "Missouri Pioneers," "Missouri Miscellany," and "Genealogical Notes from the Liberty Tribune." These records include an 1822 tax list; an account of Company C in Doniphan's expedition in the Mexican War; a list of Liberty

Tribune subscribers; excerpts from Liberty Tribune articles about voter registration after the Civil War; an 1895 list of men age 70 and older; an 1883-1884 death register; a history of the Cumberland Presbyterian Church; a 1901 list of Confederate dead of Clay County; a list of former Confederates of Camp McCarthy; and abstracts of wills and administrations, Books A, B C, and D. FHL book 977.816 H2m.

■ **1824-1831 Tax Books, St. Louis County, Missouri**, microfilm of the original records, filmed by the St. Louis Microfilm Dept., 1964, FHL film #1005418. See also *Tax List of City Tenants, 1947-1950*, FHL film #1005423.

■ **1827-1892 Miscellaneous Court Records, Marion County, Missouri**, originals in the courthouse, Palmyra, MO. Includes petitions, censuses, JP, and Bonds. No FHL microfilm, inventoried by the Missouri State Archives at **www.sos.mo.gov/CountyInventory/index.asp**.

■ *1830 Assessor's Book, Callaway County, Missouri: A Transcription From the Original as Recorded by James Baker, 1830 Assessor*, transcribed and published by The Kingdom of Callaway Historical Society, Fulton, MO, 1985, 85 pages. Includes index. FHL book 977.8335 R4a.

■ **1833-1843 Tax Lists**, see *Greene County, Missouri Tax Assessors' List, 1833, 1834, 1835 & 1843*, compiled by members of the Ozarks Genealogical Society, Springfield, MO, published by the society, 1988, 151 pages. During this period, Greene County comprised what is now all of the counties of; Barry, Barton, Christian, Dade, Greene, Jasper, Lawrence, McDonald, Newton, Stone and Webster, and portions of Cedar, Dallas, Douglas, Laclede, Polk, Taney, Vernon and Wright. FHL book 977.878 R4g.

■ *1836 Tax List of St. Charles County, Missouri*, photocopies of original records at the county courthouse in St. Charles, MO. Compiled by the St. Charles County Genealogical Society, published by the society, 1996, 40 pages. FHL book 977.839 R4e 1836.

■ *1837 Tax List of St. Charles County, Missouri,* photocopies of original records at the county courthouse in St. Charles, MO. Compiled by the St. Charles County Genealogical Society, published by the society, 1998, 50 pages. FHL book 977.839 R4s 1837. See also *Non-Resident Tax Lists, St. Charles Co., MO, 1836-1845,* FHL book 977.839 R4n.

■ *1837 Tax List, Polk County, Missouri,* photocopies of originals at the Polk County Courthouse, Bolivar, MO, compiled by Linda Crawford, published by the Polk County Genealogical Society, Bolivar, MO, 1999, 25 pages, with added index. In 1827, Polk County included all of what is now Dallas County, the northwest corner of Webster County, the south half of Hickory County, the east half of Cedar County, the northeast corner of Dade County and the southeast corner of St. Clair County. FHL book 977.877 R4p.

■ **1838 Personal Property Tax Record, St. Charles City, St. Charles County, Missouri,** originals at the St. Charles City Clerk's office. No FHL microfilm – inventoried by the Missouri State Archives at **www.sos.mo.gov/ CountyInventory/index.asp.**

■ **1839-1849.** See *Platte County, Missouri Records 1839 - 1849: 1840 Federal Census; Sale of Sixteenth Section; 1842 Land Records and Tax Lists of 1839, 1847 and 1849,* transcribed by Betty Runner Murray, published by the Platte County Historical Society, Platte City, MO, 1993, 297 pages. Includes full name index. FHL book 977.8135 N2p.

■ **1840, 1842, 1846 Tax Lists, Buchanan County, Missouri,** microfilm of original records in the Buchanan County courthouse, St. Joseph,

Missouri. Filmed by the Genealogical Society of Utah, 1976, 1 roll, FHL film #1004389.

■ **1841-1863.** See *Polk County, Missouri Tax Assessment Books,* transcribed and compiled by Maxine Dunaway, published by the author, Springfield, MO, 1986, 2 Vols. (FHL bound 7 vols. in 2). Contents: Vol. 1. 1841, 1844, 1848, 1854, 1861, 1865; Vol. 2: 1863. Includes full name indexes of additional names. FHL book 977.877 R48d v.1-2, and FHL film #1597842.

■ **1844 Missouri State Census, Callaway County, Missouri,** microfilm of original records at the Callaway County courthouse, Fulton, MO. Filmed (with 1876 census) by the Genealogical Society of Utah, 1976, 2 rolls, FHL film #1006456.

■ *1844-1956 Genealogical Data, Callaway County, Missouri: Reported in a Chronological Index to Selected Articles,* compiled by Kenneth E. Weant, published by the author, Arlington, TX, 1996, 14 vols. Much of the information in the early volumes was taken from newspaper records, but later volumes include census and other records. Indexes included in each volume. Contents: Vol. 1: Deaths from the Fulton telegraph & gazette newspapers; 4 August 1848 to December 1886; Vol. 2: Deaths from the Fulton telegraph & gazette newspapers; January 1887 to December 1911; Vol. 3: Deaths from the Fulton telegraph & gazette newspapers; January 1911 to December 1926; Vol. 4: Deaths from Auxvasse review; 3 January 1889 to 26 December 1912: Vol. 5: Veterans, War of 1812 to World War II; Vol. 7-8: Deaths from the Fulton Missouri telegraph, 5 January 1927-25 October 1956; Vol. 9: Marriages [from various papers], 1 January 1870-31 December 1899; Vol. 10: Marriages [from various papers], 1 January 1900-28 December 1922; Vol. 11: 1844 Missouri special census, miscellaneous vital records, July 1883-June 1888; Vol. 12: 1876 Missouri special farm census; Vol. 13: Chronological index to selected articles from misc. Mokane, Missouri newspapers, 3 August 1900 to 24 December 1924; Vol. 14: Deaths reported in and chronological index to selected articles from the Mokane Missourian, 14 January to 30 December 1948. The FHL library has bound some volumes together. Vol. 7-8 are one volume, v. 11-12 are one volume, and v. 13-14 are one volume. Library has v. 1-5, 7-14. FHL book 977.8335 B32w v. 1-14.

■ **1844-1865 Tax Records, Osage County, Missouri**, microfilm of original records in the Osage County courthouse, Linn, Missouri. Contains an 1844 tax list, 1844 land list, and 1865 tax book. Filmed by the Genealogical Society of Utah, 1976, 1 roll, FHL film #1006457.

■ *1845 Assessors Book, Henry County, Missouri*, compiled by Betty Harvey Williams, published by the author, 1977, 46 pages. FHL book 977.8462 R4w.

■ **1845 Interment Record, McDaniel Cemetery, and 1853 School Enumerations, Clinton County, Missouri**, originals at Clinton County repositories, no FHL film, inventoried by the MO State Archives at **www.sos.mo.gov/ CountyInventory/index.asp**.

■ *1845 List of Taxable Lands in Mississippi County, Missouri*, indexed by Shirley Robinson Bryant for Mississippi County Genealogical Society, published by the society, 1986, 27 pages. FHL book 977.8983 R4b.

■ *1846 Tax List, Moniteau County, Missouri*, submitted to the FHL by Peter Schlup, published (?), 47 pages. FHL film #977.852 R4s.

■ **1846 Missouri State Census, St. Joseph, Buchanan County**, name list in *Northwest Missouri Genealogical Society Journal*, Vol. 16, No. 1 (Apr 1996).

■ **1850 Federal Census, Monroe County, Missouri (county's original copy),** original at the County Clerk's Office, Paris, MO. No FHL microfilm, inventoried by the Missouri State Archives at **www.sos.mo.gov/ CountyInventory/index.asp**.

■ **1850, 1860, and 1870 Federal Censuses, Perry County, Missouri (county's original copies),** originals at the County Clerk's Office, Perryville, MO. No FHL microfilm, inventoried by the Missouri State Archives at **www.sos.mo.gov/ CountyInventory/index.asp**.

■ *1852 Missouri State Census, St. Charles County, Missouri,* extracted from originals at the St. Charles city clerk's office and the county clerk's office, by Mary Ethel Buschmeyer, Eunice Webbink, and Vera Haeussermann, published by Lineage Press, Bridgeton, MO, 1985, 63 pages. FHL book 977.839 X2st.

■ **1818-1950 Tax Lists, City of St. Louis, Missouri,** microfilm of original records, as follows:
  • **1818, 1820, 1822-1827, 1829, 1831-1835, 1837-1838** Tax Records, FHL film #980602.
  • **1838, 1840, 1843, 1844** Tax records, FHL film #980603.
  • **1844-1846** Tax records, FHL film #980604.
  • **1846-1849** Tax records, FHL film #980605.
  • **1849-1850** Tax records, FHL film #980606.
  • **1850-1852** Tax records, FHL film #981624.
  • **1852-1853, 1863, 1849** Tax records, FHL film #981625.
  • **1828-1829, 1836-1837, 1843** Tax records, FHL film #981626.
  • **1844, 1847-1848, 1850, 1898** Index to securities and contracts, **1900** Office plats; abstract of certified, special tax bills; and **1944** real estate tax book, FHL film #981627.
  • **1824-1827, 1829, 1831** Tax records, FHL film #981628.
  • **1859-1862** Collector's account; City revenue **1851-1870;** and Record of real estate sales **1859,** FHL film #981656.

- **1849-1851** Collector's account; Real estate assessments and collections **1860-1863**; Personal property and poll tax **1862-1866**, FHL film #981657.
- **1853** Account books of collection of taxes, real & personal property, Comptrollers Office, FHL film #981642.
- **1853-1904** Index card to special tax books, FHL #1001239, #1001238, and #1001240.
- **1864-1865** Individual Tax Bills Paid to St. Louis Assessor, FHL film #1005420.
- **1864-1866** Merchant, Real Estate, and Personal Tax Bills, Carondelet. FHL film # 981656.
- **1867-1869** Special Tax,; and **1863-1864** Delinquent tax claims, FHL film #981654.
- **1869-1881** St. Louis Comptrollers Office, 72 rolls, beginning with FHL film # 981637.
- **1861-1922** Special tax bills, FHL film #981653.

■ **1856-1862 Tax books, Osage County, Missouri**, microfilm of original records at the Osage County courthouse. Filmed by the Genealogical Society of Utah, 1972, 1 roll, FHL film #913752.

■ *1861 Tax Assessor's Book, Gentry County, Missouri*, extracted from the original book at the Gentry County courthouse, Albany, MO, by the Northwest Missouri Genealogical Society, St. Joseph, MO, 1982, 82 pages. FHL book 977.8145 R4g.

■ **1861-1865. Index to Soldiers & Sailors of the Civil War.** A searchable name index to 6.3 million Union and Confederate Civil War soldiers is now available online at the National Park Service Web site. A search can be done by surname, first name, state, or unit. Missouri supplied 265,994 men to the war; 70,691 Confederate, and 195,303 Union. To search for one go to the NPS Web site at **www.civilwar.nps.gov/cwss/**.

■ *1862 Rebel List of Polk County, Missouri*, transcribed and arranged by Maxine Dunaway, Springfield, MO, 1984, 73 pages. Transcribed from the back of an old tax assessment book in

Polk County, Missouri. FHL 977.877 R4d and FHL film # 6088808.

■ *1862 Tax Assessor's Book, Worth County, Missouri*, extracted from the originals at the Worth County Courthouse, Grant City, Missouri, by John A. Ostertag, published by the Northwest Missouri Genealogical Society, St. Joseph, MO, 1982, 57 pages. FHL book 977.8143 R4w.

■ **1862-1866 Internal Revenue Assessment Lists for the State of Missouri**, microfilm of originals at the National Archives, Washington, DC. Names are in alphabetical order by first letters of surnames only. Names are grouped by the divisions of each tax district. Typically, each roll of film contains several divisions. Filmed by the National Archives, series M0776, 1984, 22 rolls, District 1 (St. Louis), FHL film #1695299. For a list of districts, counties, and film numbers for all 22 rolls, go to the **www.familysearch.org** site, FHL library / Catalog / Place search: "Missouri" / Missouri – Taxation.

■ *1864 Missouri State Census, Gasconade County, Missouri*, photocopies of original documents at the Gasconade County courthouse, Hermann, MO, reproduced and indexed by Robert E. Parkin, published by Genealogical Research and Productions, 1980, 64 pages. FHL book 977.861 X2e and FHL film #6075652.

■ *1868 Tax Assessment Book, Benton County, Missouri*, compiled by Betty Harvey Williams, published by the author, Warrensburg, MO, 1977, 90 pages. Includes surname index. Includes delinquent tax book for the county, Dec. 1869. Names are listed in alphabetical order by first letter of the surname. FHL book 977.8493 R4w.

■ **1868-1885 Land Assessments, Christian County, Missouri**, microfilm of original records at the Christian County Courthouse, Ozark, MO. Filmed by the Genealogical Society of Utah, 1973,

4 rolls, beginning with FHL film #931911 (Assessments, 1868, 1870, 1872-1873).

■ **1868 Missouri State Census, Cape Girardeau County, Missouri**, microfilm of original records at the Cape Girardeau County courthouse, Jackson, Missouri. Filmed (with 1876 census) by the Genealogical Society of Utah, 1976, 1 roll, FHL film #1006668.

■ *1868 Missouri State Census, St. Charles County, Missouri*, transcribed from originals at the County Clerk of St. Charles County by Carrol Geerling, published by Lineage Press, Bridgeton, MO, 1988, 212 pages. FHL book 977.839 X2g.

■ **1869 Census of Carondelet** (now part of St. Louis, Missouri), microfilm of originals by Carondelet city assessor, Filmed by the City of St. Louis, 1963, FHL film #981654.

■ **1870 Federal Census, Monroe County, Missouri (county's original copy),** original at the County Clerk's Office, Paris, MO. No FHL microfilm. Inventoried by the Missouri State Archives at **www.sos.mo.gov/CountyInventory/ index.asp.**

■ **1875-1885 Tax Lists.** See *Howell County, Missouri, Personal Property Tax Books, 1875 & 1885 and West Plains, Missouri, School Records, 1884-1887,* compiled by Jacqueline Hogan Williams and Betty Harvey Williams, published by the authors, Warrensburg, MO, 1973, 61 pages. Includes index. FHL book 977.885 R4w.

■ **1876 Missouri State Census, Benton County, Missouri**, microfilm of original records at the Benton County courthouse, Warsaw, MO. Filmed by the Genealogical Society of Utah, 1973, 1 roll, FHL film #945728. Indexed in *1876 Benton County, Missouri State Census*, compiled by Jacqueline Hogan Williams and Betty Harvey Williams, published by the authors,

Warrensburg, MO, 1969, 119 pages, FHL book 977.849 X2p.

■ **1876 Missouri State Census, Butler County, Missouri**, photocopies of original documents at the Butler County Courthouse, Poplar Bluff, MO, compiled by Thelma S. McManus and Robert E. Parkin, published by Genealogical Research & Publications, 1981, 80 pages. Includes index. FHL book 977.893 X2e. See also "1876 Missouri State Census Index, Butler County," in *Area Footprints*, Vol. 10, No. 3-4

■ **1876 Missouri State Census, Callaway County, Missouri**, microfilm of original records at the Callaway County courthouse, Fulton, MO. Filmed (with 1844 census) by the Genealogical Society of Utah, 1976, 2 rolls, FHL film #1006456.

■ **1876 Missouri State Census, Cass County, Missouri**, originals at the County Clerk's Office, Cass County Courthouse, Harrisonville, MO. No FHL microfilm – inventoried by the Missouri State Archives at **www.sos.mo.gov/CountyInventory/index.asp.**

■ **1876 Missouri State Census, Cape Girardeau County, Missouri**, microfilm of originals at the Cape Girardeau County courthouse, Jackson, Missouri. Filmed (with 1868 census) by the Genealogical Society of Utah, 1976, 2 rolls, FHL film #100666-1000667. Extracted and indexed in Quinton Keller and Jo Ann Keller, *Census of Cape Girardeau County, Missouri Taken in 1876*, published St. Louis, 1974. (book not at FHL).

■ **1876 Missouri State Census of Christian County**, microfilm of original records at the Christian County courthouse, Ozark, MO. Filmed by the Genealogical Society of Utah, 1973, 1 roll, FHL film #931909.

■ *An Index to 1876 census of Greene County, Missouri*, compiled by the Greene County Archives and Records Center, Springfield, MO,

1992, 202 pages. FHL book 977.878 X22es.

■ **1876 Missouri State Census, Daviess County, Missouri**, originals at the County Clerk's Office, Gallatin, MO. No FHL microfilm, inventoried by the Missouri State Archives at **www.sos.mo.gov/CountyInventory/index.asp**.

■ **1876 Missouri State Census, Holt County, Missouri**, microfilm of original records in the Holt County courthouse, Oregon, Missouri. Arranged by township and range numbers. Filmed by the Genealogical Society of Utah, 1976, 1 roll, FHL film #1005363.

■ **1876 Missouri State Census, Howard County, Missouri**, microfilm of originals at the County Clerk's office, Fayette, Missouri. Filmed by the Genealogical Society of Utah, 1974, 1 roll, FHL film #963407.

■ *1876 Census of the County of Iron, State of Missouri*, from originals at the Iron County Courthouse, Ironton, MO. Information transcribed by Millie and Edward Preissle, published by the authors, Houston, MO, 198?, 194 pages. Includes index. FHL book 977.8883 X2c and FHL film #1320670.

■ **1876 Missouri State Census, McDonald County, Missouri**, microfilm of original records at the Recorder of Deeds, McDonald County courthouse, Pineville, MO. Filmed by the Genealogical Society of Utah, 1984, 1 roll, FHL film #930080. Another filming, #1016634. The name list extracted, see "1876 Missouri State Census, McDonald County," in *Newton County Roots*, Vol. 4, No. 3 (Sep 1992).

■ **1876 Missouri State Census, Moniteau County, Missouri, by Township**. Microfilm of original manuscript at a private residence in California, Missouri. Filmed by the Missouri State Archives, 1983, 1 roll FHL film #1759291.

■ *1876 Census, Montgomery County, Missouri*, extracted and published by Mid-Missouri Genealogical Society, Jefferson City, Missouri, 1996, 191 pages. Includes index. FHL book 977.8382 X2c.

■ **1876 Missouri State Census, Perry County, Missouri**, originals at the Perry County Clerk's Office, Perryville, MO. No FHL microfilm, inventoried by the Missouri State Archives at **www.sos.mo.gov/CountyInventory/index.asp**. See also, *County of Perry, State of Missouri, 1876*, compiled by Bill Bow for the Perry County Historical Society, Perryville, Missouri, 1989, 56 pages. Includes 1876 census; and some 1875-1876 articles from the Weekly Perryville Union. FHL book 977.8694 X2c.

■ *1876 Missouri State Census, Phelps County, Missouri*, originals at the Phelps County Clerk's office, Rolla, MO. Copy transcribed by John E.C. Simmons, published by the author, St. John, MO, 1987, 3 pages, 238 columns. FHL book 977.8594 X2s. See also, "1876 Missouri State Census, Phelps County," in *Phelps County Genealogical Society Quarterly*, Vol. 4, No. 2 (Apr 1988) through Vol. 5, No. 3 (Jul 1989).

■ **1876 Missouri State Census, Reynolds County**, originals at the County Clerk's office, Centerville, Missouri. Filmed by the Genealogical Society of Utah, 1977, as "Census Record, 1876," FHL film #1016081.

■ **1876 Missouri State Census, Scott County**, originals at the County Clerk's office, Benton, Missouri. No FHL microfilm, inventoried by the Missouri State Archives at **www.sos.mo.gov/CountyInventory/index.asp**.

■ *1876 Missouri State Census of St. Charles County, Missouri*, transcribed and indexed by Carrol Geerling, published by Lineage Press, Bridgeton, MO, 1988, 333 pages.

■ **1876 Missouri State Census, St. Francois County, Missouri**, microfilm of original records at the St. Francois County Clerk's office, Farmington, Missouri. filmed by the Genealogical Society of Utah, 1976, 1 roll, FHL film #1006662.

■ *1876 Census, County of Texas, State of Missouri: Books One and Two*, transcribed by Edward and Millie Preissle, published by Texas County Missouri Genealogical Society, Houston, MO, 1983, 180 pages. Includes surname index. Includes Boone, Carroll, Current, Date, Jackson, Lynch, Ozark, Ribidoux, Sherrill, and Upton townships. Parts of Clinton, Morris, Pierce, and Piney townships are also included. FHL book 977.884 X2c; FHL film #1597827; and microfiche # 6005969.

■ **1876 Missouri State Census, Webster County, Missouri**, originals at the County Clerk's office, Marshfield, MO. No FHL microfilm, inventoried by the Missouri State Archives at **www.sos.mo.gov/CountyInventory/index.asp**.

■ **1876 Missouri State Census, Worth County, Missouri**, originals at the County Clerk's office, Grant City, Missouri. Includes Fletchall, Union, and Smith Townships. No FHL microfilm, inventoried by the Missouri State Archives at **www.sos.mo.gov/CountyInventory/index.asp**.

■ **1880 Short Form, Gentry County, Missouri**. State archives title: "1880 Census Record Book by Township," original at the Gentry County Clerk's Office, Albany, Missouri. This is Gentry County's original copy of the 1880 federal Census. Arranged in alphabetical order for each township. No FHL microfilm, inventoried by the Missouri State Archives at **www.sos.mo.gov/CountyInventory/index.asp**.

■ **1880 Short Form, Holt County, Missouri**, county's copy of the 1880 federal census, originals at the County Clerk's office, Oregon, MO. Includes Benton Township, east of Bluff

Road, excluding Mound City. No FHL microfilm, inventoried by the Missouri State Archives at **www.sos.mo.gov/CountyInventory/index.asp**.

■ **1880 Short Form, Perry County, Missouri**, county's copy of the 1880 federal census, originals at the County Clerk's office, Perryville, MO. No FHL microfilm, inventoried by the Missouri State Archives at **www.sos.mo.gov/CountyInventory/index.asp**.

■ **1880 Short Form, Schuyler County, Missouri**, original county copy of the 1880 federal census at the Schuyler County Recorder of Deeds, Lancaster, Missouri. Filmed by the Genealogical Society of Utah in 1977 with title, "Census of Schuyler County, Missouri, 1880," FHL film #1012039.

■ **1881 Land Assessment Book, Reynolds County**, Missouri, microfilm of originals at the Reynolds County courthouse. Filmed by the Genealogical Society of Utah, 1977, 1 roll, FHL #1016081.

■ **1888 History**. See *Barry County, Missouri Tax Payers & Soldiers, Biographical Index to Goodspeeds, 1888*, compiled by Pioneer Enterprises, Billings, MO, 1967, 34 pages. FHL book 977.8 A1 no. 3 and FHL film #824280.

■ *1890 Boone County, Missouri Tax Records, A Census Substitute: With Complete Index*, published by the Genealogical Society of Central Missouri, Columbia, MO, 1999, 254 pages. FHL book 977.829 R4b.

■ *Poll Tax Book For the Year 1900, Boone County, Missouri*, compiled and published by the Genealogical Society of Central, Missouri, 199?, 26 pages. FHL book 977.829 R48p.

■ *1890 Real Estate Tax Book Index, St. Charles County, Missouri*, compiled by Colleen Heitmann Schaeper, published by St. Charles County Genealogical Society, St. Charles, MO,

1999, 50 pages. FHL book 977.839 R42s 1890. See also *1890 School Tax Book Index, St. Charles County, Missouri*, compiled by Maryalee Roellig, published by St. Charles County Genealogical Society, St. Charles, Missouri, 1999, 73 pages, FHL book 977.839 R42r.

■ **1887-1901**. See *Buchanan County, Missouri Taxpayers List*, compiled by Debra Graden, published by Grey Ink, Leavenworth, KS, 2001, 4 vols. Compiled from portions of the Hoye city directories. Contains names, townships, and post offices of taxpayers. Contents: Vol. 1: Taxpayers from St. Joseph, Missouri, 1887-1890; Vol. 2: Taxpayers from Buchanan County, Missouri (excluding St. Joseph, Missouri), 1902-1906; Vol. 3: Taxpayers from Buchanan County, Missouri (excluding St. Joseph, Missouri) 1891-1895 [and] 1896-1901, FHL book 977.8132 R4g, vol. 1-4.

■ *1890 St. Joseph, Missouri City Directory: Includes County Taxpayers*, compiled by Debra Graden, originally published by Hoye City Directory Co., 1890, reprinted by Grey Ink, Leavenworth, KS, 1999, 514 pages. Contains an introduction, street directory, abbreviations, and the names of citizens and businesses located in the city of St. Joseph, Missouri. Also includes names of county taxpayers for the same year. FHL book 977.8132/S1 E4g.

■ *The 1890 Tax List of Phelps County, Missouri*, compiled and typed by Dennis A. Peterman, published by the author, Rolla, MO, 1988, 208 pages. FHL book 977.8594 R4p.

■ *1890 Texas County, Missouri Tax Payer's List*, transcribed by the Texas County Clerk's Office, published by the Texas County, Missouri Genealogical and Historical Society, Houston, TX, 39 pages. FHL book 977.884 R4t.

■ *1890 Tax Book, Worth County, Missouri, Including Real and Personal Property*, compiled by Mrs. William K. Ray, published by Missouri State Genealogical Association, Columbia, MO, 198?, 51 pages. Contains towns: Allen Township, Denver, Smith Township, Allenville (later Allendale), Fletchall Township, Grant City and Iona City, Greene Township, Oxford, Union Township, Isadora and Sheridan. FHL book 977.8143 R4r.

■ *1892 Tax book, Wright County, Missouri*, photocopy of original records at the Wright County Courthouse, Hartville, Missouri, compiled by Gloria Bogart Carter, published by the author, Springfield, MO, 1990, 220 pages. Names are in alphabetical order by township. FHL book 977.8825 R4t and FHL film #1697982.

■ **1893-1955 Circuit Court Records, Wayne County, Missouri**, microfilm of original records at the Wayne County Courthouse, Greenville, Missouri. Indexes are at front of each volume. Much of the material is related to tax judgments, listing names of people. Filmed by the Genealogical Society of Utah, 1973, 1996, 11 rolls, beginning with FHL film #927307 (Miscellaneous Records, vol. 1, 1900-1914).

■ **1895-1908 Tax List**. See *Early Merchants of Stone County, Missouri, 1895-1908: Taken From the Merchants' License Tax Book Which is Retained by the County Court House, located in Galena, Missouri*, compiled by Elizabeth B. Langley, published 1967, 20 pages. FHL book 977.8 A1 no. 4 and FHL film # 844972.

■ **1921 History**. See *Centennial History of Missouri (The Center State): One Hundred Years in the Union, 1820-1921*, by Walter Barlow Stevens, published by S.J. Clarke Pub. Co., St. Louis, 1921, 7 vols., FHL book 977.8 H2s. Biographies in Vols. 3 and 6, which were indexed in *Biographical Index to the Centennial History of Missouri*, compiled and published by Mrs. Leister E. Presley, Searcy, AR, 19??, 21 pages. FHL book 977.8 H2s index. See also *Biographical Index to the Centennial history of*

Missouri: Volumes III, IV, V, and VI, by Elizabeth B. Langley, Billings, Missouri, 1968, 22 pages. FHL book 977.8 H2s index.

Missouri Censuses & Substitutes Online

■ **Missouri State Archives Online Resources.** Go to **www.sos.mo.gov/archives/resources/ordb.asp** for access to these online databases:

- **Archives Online Catalog**. Search collections by title, author, subject, or keyword. Covers virtually all collections on microfilm.
- **Birth & Death Records Database**. An abstract of the birth, stillbirth, and death records recorded before 1909 and that are available on microfilm at the Missouri State Archives. Images of the actual birth and death certificates are going online over time.
- **Civil War Provost Marshal Index Database**. Name index to soldiers with any military actions, court martial, etc.
- **Coroner's Inquest Database**. The database search engine allows searches by county, name of deceased, cause of death, and/or year of death (or range of years).
- **Local Records Inventory Database.** A search can made for every county of Missouri for county records, including censuses; tax lists; birth, marriage, and death records; and miscellaneous court records residing in local repositories.

■ Missouri **Censuses & Substitutes Online**. The following databases are available online at these sites:

www.ancestry.com
- 1699-1732 French Colony Census Tables
- 1830-70 Census Indexes (AIS)
- 1830 Federal Census
- 1840 Federal Census
- 1840 Revolutionary War Pensioners
- 1850 Federal Census
- 1850 Slave Schedules
- 1850-1880 Mortality Schedules & Index
- 1860 Federal Census
- 1860 Slave Schedules
- 1870 Federal Census
- 1880 Federal Census

- 1885-1940 Indian Census Schedules
- 1880 Federal Census, Howell County
- 1890 Veterans Schedules
- 1900 Federal Census
- 1910 Federal Census
- 1920 Federal Census
- 1920 Federal Census, Franklin County
- 1920 Federal Census, Holt County
- 1880 Federal Census, Howell County
- 1930 Federal Census
- 1930 Census of Merchant Seamen

www.censusfinder.com
- 1830-1870 Missouri Census Records at Ancestry
- 1830-1850 Statewide Federal Census Images
- 1850-1860 Slave Schedules
- 1840 Census of Military Pensioners
- 1880 Federal Census - Images
- 1880 Federal Census Search at Family Search
- 1883 Missouri Pensioners - Statewide
- 1883-1890 Missouri Birth and Death Records Search Engine - Statewide
- RootsWeb Search
- Missouri State Databases of Census & Genealogy Records

www.census-online.com
- **Countywide census databases (No. of databases):** Adair (6); Andrew (2); Atchison (4); Audrain (3); Barry (4); Barton (1); Bates (3); Benton (15); Bollinger (4); Boone (9); Buchanan (27); Butler (79); Caldwell (3); Callaway (27); Camden (2); Cape Girardeau (5); Carroll (10); Carter (15); Cass (2); Cedar (7); Chariton (16); Christian (7); Clark (4); Clay (4); Clinton (3); Cole (7); Cooper (10); Crawford (4); Dade (5); Dallas (3); Daviess (5); DeKalb (2); Dent (1); Douglas (4); Dunklin (4); Franklin (4); Gasconade (5); Gentry (2); Greene (4); Grundy (12); Harrison (2); Henry (30); Hickory (3); Holt (9); Howard (22); Howell (15); Iron (2); Jackson (4); Jasper (10); Jefferson (4); Johnson (13); Knox (5); Laclede (2); Lafayette (4); Lawrence (11); Lewis (28); Lincoln (5); Linn (6); Livingston (3); Macon (7); Madison (18); Maries (1); Marion (4); McDonald (6); Mercer (2); Miller (12); Mississippi (7); Moniteau (10); Monroe (3); Montgomery (12); Morgan (7); New Madrid (9); Newton (15); Nodaway (9); Oregon (4); Osage (2); Ozark (2); Pemiscot (2); Perry (11); Pettis (10); Phelps (2); Pike (5); Platte (4); Polk (5); Pulaski (22); Putnam (2); Ralls (5); Randolph (53); Ray (10); Reynolds (6); Ripley (7); Rives (1); Saline (10); Schuyler (11); Scotland (7); Scott (8); Shannon (3);

Shelby (4); St Charles (4); St Clair (2); St Francois (5); St Genevieve (14); St Louis (5); St Louis City (8); Stoddard (4); Stone (9); Sullivan (7); Taney (7); Texas (4); Van Buren (1); Vernon (1); Warren (3); Washington (14); Wayne (11); Webster (1); Worth (13); and Wright (9).

NEBRASKA

Censuses & Substitutes, 1854-1976

As part of the Louisiana Purchase of 1803, the area of Nebraska became part of Louisiana Territory in 1805; which was renamed Missouri Territory in 1812. After Missouri became a state in 1821, the remaining northern portion of the Louisiana Purchase area was designated as "Unorganized Territory." The first permanent white settlement in Nebraska was in 1823 at Bellevue, a few miles south of present Omaha.

Nebraska became a territory in 1854 as part of the "Kansas-Nebraska Act," the landmark legislation relating to free versus slave states prior to the Civil War. Both Kansas and Nebraska were expected to vote on the slavery issue, and both territories immediately began taking annual censuses to determine their numbers of registered voters. The first Nebraska Territory censuses were taken in 1854, 1855, and 1856, which were head of households name lists covering the eastern half of present-day Nebraska (the only part with population).

The surviving census schedules for Nebraska Territory are fairly complete, with the originals located at the Nebraska State Historical Society Archives (NSHS) in Lincoln, Nebraska.

From 1854 until 1861, Nebraska Territory spanned from its border with Kansas Territory to the Canadian border; and from the Missouri River to the Continental Divide. Although sparsely populated during that period, Nebraska Territory included a large part of the present states of Colorado, Wyoming, Montana, North Dakota, and South Dakota.

The 1860 federal census taken in Nebraska Territory included mining camps in present-day Colorado (Boulder, Altoona, and a few other northeastern Colorado towns), which were added at the end of the enumeration lists for Nebraska towns, identified on the census schedules as *Unorganized West of 101° 30'*.

The last census prior to statehood was taken in 1865. After statehood in 1867, the Nebraska legislature called for annual censuses, including lists of births and deaths to be gathered by the county tax assessors. Of these, references to state censuses can be found only for 1869, 1874, 1875, 1876, 1877, 1878, 1879, 1882, 1883, and 1884. Very few of these censuses have survived, but a few countywide lists have been extracted and are shown below.

The Nebraska state census act was repealed in 1885, but in that year, the Federal Government offered any state or territory an option for an assisted state census, providing federal money to help pay for them. Nebraska was one of only five states or territories that took up the offer. The 1885 state census of Nebraska was completed using the same forms that had been used in the 1880 federal census. The 1885 proved to be the last state census in Nebraska.

The Web site for NSHS makes this statement about its territorial and state censuses: "The Society holds county census records for a few counties for miscellaneous years from 1854 to 1898. For a listing of these records, as well as a more detailed description of all Nebraska census records, please request Reference Leaflet number two. (Leaflet No. 2 is online at **www.nebraskahistory.org/lib-arch/services/ refrence/la_pubs/census2.htm**). "The staff will check census records for mail requests only when the exact name of the family (first and last name of head of household) is given along with the location of residence if known (county and either precinct or nearby town). Census records are not available through interlibrary loan from the Society."

The NSHS refers genealogists to the Nebraska RootsWeb site for lists of published censuses for Nebraska. Although the state's original copies are available for "look ups" and photocopies of original pages can be made, there is no record that any of them have been microfilmed. The Family History Library in Salt Lake City has virtually no Nebraska census records other than the 1885 and federal censuses. And, there are very few countywide census extracts, abstracts, or indexes available, except for those done by the Nebraska Genealogical Society (NGS) back in the 1930s and 1940s. The NGS published full abstracts of the Nebraska territorial and state censuses, from 1854 to 1869. All of the published censuses are now available online, where a search for any Nebraska location is possible.

The territorial and state censuses, and census substitutes are identified below:

■ **1854-1869 Nebraska Territory and State Censuses**. Extant lists were extracted and published in *Nebraska & Midwest Genealogical Records* (N&MGR), a publication of the Nebraska Genealogical Society, 1922-1944. The RootsWeb site for Nebraska has put all of the census articles from the N&MGR online at: **www.rootsweb.com/ ~neresour/OLLibrary/Journals/NMGR/ censindx.html.** The 1854, 1855, and 1856 territorial censuses are fairly complete for all counties. The 1865 has name lists for Cuming and Otoe counties only; and the 1869 state census has lists for Butler and Stanton counties only. Direct links to the name lists are organized as follows:

- 1854 District 1 (including Pawnee & Richardson County, and parts of current Gage, Johnson, Nemaha counties).
- 1854 District 2 (primarily Nemaha & Otoe counties).
- 1854 District 3 (Cass County).
- 1854 District 4 (Douglas & Sarpy counties).
- 1854 District 5 (Dodge County plus).
- 1854 District 6 (Burt & Washington counties).
- 1855 Cass Co.

- 1855 Dodge Co.
- 1855 Douglas Co.
- 1855 Nemaha Co.
- 1855 Otoe Co.
- 1855 Pawnee Co.
- 1855 Richardson Co.
- 1855 Washington Co.
- 1856 Burt Co.
- 1856 Cass Co.
- 1856 Clay Co (area that is now Lancaster & Gage Co).
- 1856 Colfax Co (see Platte Co).
- 1856 Cuming.
- 1856 Dakota Co (includes Dixon Co).
- 1856 Dixon Co (see Dakota Co).
- 1856 Dodge Co.
- 1856 Douglas Co (Southern district - now Sarpy Co).
- 1856 Douglas Co Northern District.
- 1856 Gage Co (see Clay Co).
- 1856 Johnson Co (see Nemaha Co).
- 1856 Lancaster Co.
- 1856 Lancaster Co (also see Clay Co).
- 1856 Nemaha Co.
- 1856 Otoe Co.
- 1856 Pawnee Co.
- 1856 Platte Co.
- 1856 Richardson Co.
- 1856 Sarpy Co (see Douglas Co., Southern District).
- 1856 Washington Co.
- 1865 Cuming Co.
- 1865 Otoe Co.
- 1869 Butler Co.
- 1869 Stanton Co.

■ **1854 Nebraska Territory Census**, name list in *Roots and Leaves*, Jan 1978 issue.

■ **1854 Nebraska Territory Census, Nemaha County**, name list in *Genealogist's Post*, Vol. 4, No. 11 (Nov 1967) through Vol. 5, No. 2 (Feb 1968).

■ *1854, 1855, 1856 Nebraska Territory Censuses*, extracted by E. Evelyn Cox, published by the author, Ellensburg, WA, 1977. FHL book 978.2 X2p 1854-1856, and FHL film #1036024, and microfiche #6051283.

■ **1855 Nebraska Territory Census, Dodge County**, name list in *Roots and Leaves*, Vol. 17, No. 3 (Fall 1994).

■ **1855 Nebraska State Census, Washington County**, name list in *Roots and Leaves*, Vol. 3, No. 3 (Fall 1980).

■ **1856 Nebraska Territory Census, Burt County**, name list in *Roots and Leaves*, Vol. 3, No. 3 (Fall 1980).

■ **1856 Nebraska Territory Census, Dodge County**, name list in *Roots and Leaves*, Vol. 17, No. 4 (Winter 1994).

■ **1856 Nebraska Territory Census, Pawnee County**, name list in *Genealogist's Post*, Vol. 4, No. 6 (Jun 1967).

■ **1856 Nebraska Territory Census, Sarpy County**, name list in *Remains to be Found*, March 1986 issue.

■ **1856 Nebraska Territory Census, Washington County**, name list in *Roots and Leaves*, Vol. 4, No. 1 (Spring 1981).

■ **1859 Nebraska Territory Census, Saunders County, Salt Creek**, name list in *Nebraska Ancestree*, Vol. 2, No. 1 (Summer 1979).

■ **1865 Nebraska Territory Census, Cuming County**, name list and annotations in *Roots and Leaves*, Vol. 3, No. 1 (Spring 1980).

■ **1866-1921 Omaha and Douglas County Directories**, microfilm of originals at various libraries and societies, filmed by Research Publications, Woodbridge, CT, 1980-1984, 25 rolls, beginning with FHL film 1377220 (1866 Collins' Omaha Directory). Locate film number and years for all 25 rolls at the **www.familysearch.org** Web site. Go to FHL library / Catalog / Place search: "Nebraska" /

click on "View Related Places" / Nebraska – Douglas / Nebraska, Douglas – Directories / Omaha (Nebraska) city directories.

■ **1872 Tax List, Antelope County, Nebraska**, in *Nebraska Ancestree*, Vol. 9, No. 3 (Winter 1987), and Vol. 11, No. 1 (Summer 1988).

■ **1875-1877 Tax Receipts, Dawson County, Nebraska**, in *Dawson County Genealogical Newsletter*, Vol. 12, No. 2 (Summer 1998) and Vol. 12, No. 3 (Fall 1998).

■ *1876 Tax List, Dodge County, Nebraska*, compiled and published by the Eastern Nebraska Genealogical Society, Fremont, NE, 2000, 26 pages. Includes surname index. Contains name of property owner, taxation number, description of property, amount of tax liability. Includes Dodge County tax books, nos. 6, 8 and 10. FHL book 978.2235 R4d.

■ *1876 Nebraska State Census, Sarpy County, with Mortality Schedule; and 1885 State Census*, compiled and published by the Eastern Nebraska Genealogical Society, Fremont, NE, 1989, 63 pages. Contains an abstract of the 1885 and 1876 Sarpy County census, arranged in alphabetical order by surname, showing name of head of household, names of other persons in the household, ages, places of birth, other information, township where living, and frame number on microfilm of original census. Index by surname is to the mortality schedules which are not included in this book. FHL book 978.2256 X22s.

■ **1879 Tax Assessors Book, Center Township, Buffalo County, Nebraska**, in *Buffalo Chip*, Vol. 14, No. 1 (Spring 1991).

■ **1881 Tax Assessors Book of Personal and Real Estate, Buffalo County, Nebraska**, in *Buffalo Chip*, Vol. 17, No. 2-3 (Summer 1994).

■ **1881 Personal Tax List, Greeley County, Nebraska**, in *Nebraska Ancestree*, Vol. 11, No. 1 (Summer 1988).

■ **1882 Personal Property Tax List, Shelton Precinct, Buffalo County, Nebraska**, in *Buffalo Chip*, Vol.. 8, No. 1 (Winter 1985) and Vol. 8, No. 2-4 (Spring 1985).

■ **1882-1885 Poll Tax, Dawson County, Nebraska**, in *Nebraska Ancestree*, Vol. 20, No. 1 (Summer 1987) and Vol. 20, No. 2 (Fall 1997).

■ **1882 History.** See *History of the State of Nebraska: Containing a Full Account of its Early Settlements; Also an Extended Description of its Counties, Cities, Towns and Villages. and Biographical Sketches*, by A. T. Andreas, published by Western Historical Co., Chicago, 1882, 2 vols., 1,506 pages. This is the standard history of Nebraska. In the "Military History" section are complete rosters of those persons serving in Nebraska units during the Civil War and Indian campaigns on the Plains, 1861-1869. These rosters list names, dates of service, Nebraska residence, and remarks about their service. Contents: Part 1: Early history of Nebraska to Dundy County; Part 2: Fillmore County to York County. FHL book 978.2 H2h and FHL film #1000178. Indexed in *Index to History of the State of Nebraska: Published in Chicago by the Western Historical Company, A.T. Andreas, Proprietor, 1882, and Commonly Known as Andreas' History of Nebraska*, compiled by Raymond E. Dale, originally published by the Nebraska State Historical Society, 1963, 500 pages. Filmed by the Genealogical Society of Utah, FHL film #1689292.

■ **1883-1935 Lincoln City and Lancaster County Directories**, microfilm of original records located in various libraries and societies, filmed by Research Publications, Inc., Woodbridge, CT, 199?, 15 rolls, beginning with FHL film #2156801 (1883-1884 Wolfe's Lincoln city directory). To locate all rolls and directory years, visit the www.familysearch.org website (Go to: Library / FHL catalog / Place search: "Nebraska" / click on "View Related Places" for a county list / Lancaster County / Nebraska, Lancaster / Nebraska, Lancaster – Directories.

■ **1885 Nebraska State/Federal Census**, microfilm of originals located at the National Archives Branch, Kansas City, MO. The 1885 census was taken on the same forms used for the 1880 federal census – however, first names were rarely shown, but given as initials only, followed by the surname. The law authorizing the 1885 census required that a copy of the enumeration be kept in Nebraska, another sent to Washington, DC. Only the federal copy exists, which is missing Blaine and Chase counties. Filmed by the National Archives, 1961, 56 rolls, beginning with FHL film #499529 (Adams County, vol. 1). To locate film numbers for all 56 rolls, use the **www.familysearch.org** site. Go to FHL Library / Catalog / place search: "Nebraska"/Nebraska – Census – 1885.

■ *1885 Lincoln County, Nebraska State Census*, transcribed and published by Gloria Pressnall, aided by members of the North Platte Genealogical Society, 1987, 150 pages. Includes index and reprints of 1885 maps of North Platte and Lincoln County. FHL book 978.282 X2p. Also on 3 microfiche, FHL film #6050983.

■ *1885 Washington County, Nebraska State Census*, compiled and published by the Eastern Nebraska Genealogical Society, Fremont, NE, 1989, 97 pages. Contains an abstract of the Washington County, Nebraska 1885 census arranged in alphabetical order by surname. FHL book 978.2245 X28w.

■ **1886-1891 Directories.** The Nebraska State Historical Society has an 1886 and an 1890-91 *Nebraska Gazetteer and Business Directory* that lists farmers and businessmen by towns and

counties. Both provide name, occupation, post office address, and county of residence. The 1886 Gazetteer is indexed. The Society has Nebraska gazetteers for other years that list businessmen, but not farmers, by towns and counties only. These were published irregularly between 1879-1917. Microfilm copies of the gazetteers are available through interlibrary loan. None of these directories is available at the FHL in Salt Lake City. For information about borrowing materials on microfilm from the NSHS, visit their Web site relating to interlibrary loans at:
http://www.nebraskahistory.org/lib-arch/services/refrence/loans.htm.

■ *1886 Douglas County, Nebraska Voter Registration List,* published by the Greater Omaha Genealogical Society, 1981, 84 pages. Includes index. FHL book 978.2254 N4d.

■ *1887 Abstract of Tax List, Box Butte County, Nebraska,* compiled by Janella Guthrie, published by the Northwest Genealogical Society, Alliance, NE, 1980, 49 pages.

■ **1888 Tax List, Fillmore County, Nebraska**, in *Nebraska Ancestree*, Vol. 7, No. 2 (Fall 1984).

■ **1889 Tax List, Personal Property, Brown County, Nebraska**, (by Precinct), in *Nebraska Ancestree*, Vol. 5, No. 2 (Fall 1982) through Vol. 8, No. 2 (Fall 1984), and Vol. 23, No. 3 (Spring 2001).

■ *1889-1906 Scotts Bluff County, Nebraska, Index of Head of Family Names, Personal Property Assessment; Incomplete: Castle Rock Precinct, Ford Precinct, Gering Precinct, Highland Precinct, Kiowa Precinct, Mitchell Precinct, Rose Precinct, Roubedeau / Robidoux Precinct, Tabor Precinct, and Winter Creek Precinct,* compiled and published by the Rebecca Winters Genealogical Society, Scottsbluff, NE, 1998, various pagings. FHL book 978.298 R4.

■ **1892-1896 Poll & Personal Taxes, Buffalo County, Nebraska**, typed by Wilma Holderness Burgland; printed by Lynnda Wohleb Shaffer, published by the Fort Kearny Genealogical Society, Fort Kearny, NE, 1985, 141 pages. From introduction: "In this book, you will find the names of the heads of the household that were levied a personal or poll tax during 1892-96 in Buffalo County, Nebraska. We have not indicated whether the tax was for personal or poll in this index. We felt it more important to just get the list of the names of people living in the area." See FHL book 978.245 R4p.

■ **1906-1916 York City/County Directories**, microfilm of original records located in various libraries and societies, filmed by Primary Source Microfilm, Woodbridge, CT, 199?, 1 roll, containing R.L. Polk & Co.'s York City directory, including a list of taxpayers in York County, 1906-1907; FHL film #2310390 Item 1; R.L. Polk & Co.'s York City directory, 1908, and list of taxpayers in York County, FHL film #2310390 Item 2; R.L. Polk & Co.'s York City directory, 1911 FHL film #2310390 Item 3 ; R.L. Polk & Co.'s York City directory, 1913-1914, FHL film #310390 Item 4; and R.. Polk & Co.'s York City directory, 1915-1916 and taxpayers in York County, FHL film #10390, Item 5.

■ *1976 Bicentennial Album of Pawnee County: Containing Plats of the Precincts, Directory, Pictures, Histories, Cattle Brands, etc.,* compiled by Brand Irons Pictorial County Albums, McPherson, KS, 1976, 406 pages. Includes biographical sketches of many Pawnee County families. FHL book 978.2284 H2b.

Nebraska Censuses & Substitutes Online

■ **Online 1885 Nebraska State Census (RootsWeb & Ancestry).** A textual extract of the 1885 census is online at the Nebraska roots web site, organized by county at: **www.rootsweb.com/~usgenweb/ne/state/1885cens.htm.**

An every-name index to the 1885 Nebraska State census is also included at the **www.ancestry.com** site.

■ **Nebraska Censuses & Substitutes Online.** The following databases are available online at these sites:

www.ancestry.com
- 1699-1732 French Colony Census Tables
- 1850-1880 Mortality Schedules & Index
- 1854-1870 Census Indexes (AIS)
- 1860 Federal Census
- 1870 Federal Census
- 1880 Federal Census
- 1885 Nebraska State Census
- 1885-1940 Indian Census Schedules
- 1890 Veterans Schedules
- 1900 Federal Census
- 1910 Federal Census
- 1920 Federal Census
- 1930 Federal Census
- 1930 Census of Merchant Seamen

www.censusfinder.com
- 1854, 1855, 1856, 1865 & 1869 Territorial & State Census Transcriptions
- 1854-1870 Nebraska Census at Ancestry
- 1860 Territorial Census Index, Surnames A-F
- 1860 Territorial Census Index, Surnames G-N
- 1860 Territorial Census Index, Surnames O-Z
- 1880 Federal Census of Norwegians
- 1880 Federal Census - Images
- 1880 Federal Census Search at Family Search
- 1893 Roster of Nebraska Veterans
- 1940 Who's Who in Nebraska
- Nebraska State Databases of Census and Genealogy Records

www.census-online.com
- **Countywide census databases (No. of databases):** Adams (1); Antelope (0); Arthur (0); Banner (0); Blackbird (2); Blaine (1); Boone (0); Box Butte (0); Boyd (0); Brown (0); Buffalo (4); Burt (2); Butler (1); Calhoun (1); Cass (2); Cedar (4); Chase (0); Cherry (0); Cheyenne (0); Clay (3); Colfax (2); Cuming (6); Custer (1); Dakota (1); Dawes (1); Dawson (5); Deuel (0); Dixon (1); Dodge (1); Douglas (2); Dundy (0); Fillmore (2); Fort Laramie (2); Franklin (4); Frontier (2); Furnas (0); Gage (0); Garden (0); Garfield (0); Gosper (0); Grant (0); Greeley (0); Hall (3); Hamilton (2); Harlan (0); Hayes (0); Hitchcock (0); Holt (0); Hooker (0); Howard (0); Izard (1); Jefferson (0); Johnson (1); Kearney (2); Keith (0); Keya Paha (0); Kimball (0); Knox (1); Lancaster (1); Leau Qui Court (1); Lincoln (0); Logan (0); Loup (0); Madison (0); McPherson (4); Merrick (1); Morrill (1); Nance (0); Nemaha (2); Nuckolls (3); Otoe (7); Pawnee (1); Perkins (1); Phelps (0); Pierce (4); Platte (3); Polk (2); Red Willow (0); Richardson (7); Rock (0); Saline (0); Sarpy (0); Saunders (0); Scotts Bluff (0); Seward (0); Sheridan (0); Sherman (1); Shorter (2); Sioux (0); Stanton (0); Thayer (0); Thomas (0); Thurston (0); Valley (0); Washington (1); Wayne (3); Webster (0); Wheeler (0); Winnebago (2); and York (3).

DAKOTA TERRITORY

Area Censuses, 1832-1885

The French trading posts which came to be known as the Red River Settlements, were mainly north of present North Dakota in what is now Manitoba, but there were a number of French traders who came down the Red River into the Dakotas to establish trade with the Indians, some as early as 1738. The northern Dakota area was not American territory until 1818, when the U.S. and Britain agreed on the 49th parallel as the international boundary from the Lake of Woods to the Continental Divide.

There are several extant censuses available at the Provincial Archives of Manitoba relating to the Red River Settlement. The people identified therein may be some of those who traveled back and forth into the *Dacotah* country. So, the earliest censuses identifying Dakota people may be in Canada.

The first U.S. census taken in the Dakota country was the 1836 Wisconsin Territory census, which included the Pembina settlement on the Red River (south of the Canadian border). In the 1850 federal census, the populated Dakota country areas east of the Missouri River were part of Pembina County, Minnesota Territory. The same area was included in the 1857 Minnesota census.

When Minnesota became a state in 1858, the Dakota area was orphaned, and remained without jurisdiction for three years. The area from the Minnesota line to the Missouri River was enumerated as "Unorganized Dakota" in the 1860 federal census, while Dakota areas west of the Missouri River were part of Nebraska Territory. Most of the population of Unorganized Dakota in 1860 was located at the Red River/Pembina settlements. (Of these, well over half of the residents show a birth place as "Canada"). For convenience, the 1860 federal census for Unorganized Dakota enumerated a few inhabitants of the western frontier, even though the outposts were actually part of Nebraska Territory. Ft. Union, on the Missouri River; and Ft. Alexander on the Yellowstone River, were both included with Unorganized Dakota. Ft. Alexander was located in present-day Rosebud County, Montana; while Ft. Union was located almost exactly on the present-day North Dakota/Montana line. Other outposts enumerated in the Unorganized Dakota census were the Missouri River outposts at Ft. Clark, Ft. William, and Ft. Stevenson; the Orphan's Village on the Red River; and the Old Trading House on the Niobrara River. The entire population of Unorganized Dakota was less than 5,000 people, but, virtually everyone was enumerated in the 1860 federal census.

Dakota Territory was created in 1861, with nearly the same boundaries as the area of the two present states of North Dakota and South Dakota. The territory took only one territorial census, a special enumeration taken in 1885 with federal assistance. The original manuscripts for the 1885 Dakota Territory census schedules were divided, the northern counties kept at the State Historical Society of North Dakota (SHSND) in Bismarck; the southern counties at the South Dakota State Historical Society in Pierre.

An index to the North Dakota portion of the 1885 Dakota Territory census is now available on the Internet. Because the censuses were divided, published 1885 abstracts and indexes are shown under their respective states.

■ **1832-1870 Red River Censuses**. See *Red River Settlement and Province of Manitoba: A Typed Card Index to the Nominal Census Returns, 1832-1870*, microfilm of original records in possession of the Provincial Archives of Manitoba, Winnipeg, Canada. The original Red River Settlement censuses were taken by the Hudson's Bay Company. The Red River Settlement was located in the Red and Assiniboine Rivers area of Manitoba. Early French trappers, traders, and settlers were known to move up and down the Red River between present-day Manitoba and North Dakota. They were the founders of Pembina in present-day North Dakota. This is a combined index to the nominal (head of household) census returns for 1832, 1833, 1838, 1840, 1843, 1846-47, 1849, 1856 (incomplete) and every-name 1870, for the Lower Settlement, Grant Town and Indian villages. Filmed by the Genealogical Society of Utah, 1985, 3 rolls, beginning with FHL film #1420272. See also *Surname Index to the 1870 Census of Manitoba and Red River*, compiled by Eric Jonasson, published by Wheatfield Press, Winnipeg, 1981, 27 pages, FHL book 971.27 X22j 1870. **Note:** The 1870 Manitoba and Red River census names all members of a family, relationship to head, age, sex, occupation, religion, whether Métis (French & Indian blood), or other race; and identifies the full name of a father and full maiden name of a mother for each person. It is one of the most detailed censuses ever done in North America. This may be the place to find an elusive Dakota ancestor.

■ **1836 Wisconsin Territory Census**. See *The First Census of the Original Counties of Dubuque and Demoine (Iowa) Taken in July, 1836*, edited by Benjamin F. Shambaugh, published by the Historical Department of Iowa, 1897-1898, 93 pages. Includes Pembina settlements in present-day North Dakota. From the original manuscript returns preserved in the office of the Secretary of State of Wisconsin. Census taken in accordance with the act of Congress erecting the territory of Wisconsin (of which these two counties at the time formed a part) comprising the present states of Iowa, Minnesota and part of North and South Dakota. Filmed by the Genealogical Society of Utah, 1978, 1 roll, FHL film #1022202. Another filming, #989450.

■ **1838 Iowa Territory Census**, see *Iowa 1838 Territorial Census Index*, edited by Ronald Vern Jackson, et al, published by Accelerated Indexing Systems, Bountiful, UT, 1984. FHL book 977.7 X22ji 1838. Includes the Pembina settlements in present-day North Dakota. See also Marie Haefner, "The Census of 1838," in *The Palimpsest*, Vol. 19 (May 1938) pp 185-192.

■ **1840 Federal Census, Iowa Territory**. In 1840, Iowa Territory included lands between the Mississippi and Missouri Rivers, from its present boundary with Missouri to the western part of present Minnesota, and North and South Dakota. An extract was done as *The 1840 Iowa Census*, compiled by Rowene Obert, Helen Blumhagen, Wilma Adkins, published Salt Lake City, UT 1968. Includes index. Includes the 18 original counties and several precincts which comprised the entire area of Iowa Territory. FHL book 977.7 X2p 1840 and FHL film #844885.

■ **1850 Federal Census, Minnesota Territory (State Copy)**. See *Dakota Census Index; 1850 Pembina District*, edited by Ronald Vern Jackson, published by Accelerated Indexing Systems, Bountiful, UT, 1982, 61 pages. The names from Pembina County were extracted from the state copy of the Minnesota Territory 1850 census, located at the Minnesota State Historical Society in St. Paul. FHL book 978 X22d 1850. See also *Minnesota Territorial Census, 1850*, edited by Patricia C. Harpole and Mary D.

Nagle, published by the Minnesota Historical Society, 1972, 115 pages. FHL book 977.6 X2ph 1850. The federal copy of the 1850 MN Territory census schedules can be found on FHL film #14834.

■ **1857 Federal Census, Minnesota Territory**, microfilm of original records located at the National Archives, Central Plains Region. Filmed by the National Archives, 1973, series T1175, 8 rolls, available from the FHL, including Pembina County (present North Dakota) on FHL film #944287.

■ **1857 Federal Census Abstracts, Minnesota Territory**, county-wide abstracts by Mary Bakeman, published by the Minnesota Historical Society, 1994-2003 for all counties, including 1857 Pembina County, MHS call no. CS42 .M553 no. 21-23.

■ **"1861 Dakota Inhabitants, A-D,"** in *Wymondak Messenger*, (Summer 1989).

■ **"1861 Dakota Inhabitants, D-M,"** in *Wymondak Messenger*, (Fall 1989).

■ **"1861 Dakota Inhabitants, M-Z,"** in *Wymondak Messenger*, (Winter 1990).

■ **1861-1865 Military Records**. See *Index to Compiled Service Records of Volunteer Union soldiers Who Served in Organizations From the Territory of Dakota*, microfilm of the original records in the National Archives, Washington, DC, series M0536, 1 roll, NARA film #M536-1, FHL film #881616.

■ **1882 Tax List, Burleigh County, Dakota Territory**, in *Bismarck-Mandan Historical and Genealogical Society*, Vol. 10, No. 1 (Mar 1981) through Vol. 12, No. 4 (Dec 1983); and Vol. 14, No. 4 (Dec 1985) through Vol. 15, No. 3 (Sep 1986).

■ **1882 Census, Pennington County, Dakota Territory**, in *Black Hills Nuggets*, Vol. 15, No. 4 (Nov 1982).

■ **1883 Directory**. See *The Leading Business Men of Dakota Cities: Accompanying the Map of Dakota Territory, Name and Address*, microfilm of original published by Warner & Foote, Minneapolis, MN, 1883, 105 pages. Filmed for the FHL by the Library of Congress, 1984, 1 roll, FHL film #1464014.

■ **1885 Special Census, Marshall County, Dakota Territory**, in *South Dakota Genealogical Society Quarterly*, Vol. 11, No. 1 (Jul 1992).

■ **1885 Ex-soldiers Census, Walworth County, Dakota Territory**, in *South Dakota Genealogical Society Quarterly*, Vol. 13, No. 9 (Jan 1995).

NORTH DAKOTA

Censuses & Substitutes, 1885-1925

After admission to the Union in 1889, the state of North Dakota took three state sponsored-censuses, in 1905, 1915 and 1925. Only statistical summaries of the 1905 state census survive, but the full census schedules for the 1915 and 1925 censuses are extant. (Although authorized for 1935, the legislature decided to stop taking censuses during the early 1930s, deeming it too expensive due to the economic conditions). The original state censuses for 1915 and 1925 are located at the State Historical Society of North Dakota in Bismarck. There are no complete indexes, but both censuses were microfilmed by the society and are available on inter-library loan. Copies of the microfilm can be also used at the Family History Library in Salt Lake City, but as part of the agreement to acquire the film, they are not allowed to circulate on interlibrary loan through the FHL. The North Dakota censuses

begin with the Dakota Territorial census of 1885, which was divided into northern and southern counties. The original manuscripts for the 1885 census for the North Dakota counties are located at the State Historical Society of North Dakota in Bismarck.

■ **1885 Territorial Census, Dakota Territory (North Dakota Counties)**, microfilm of original records located at the State Archives and Historical Research Library of the State Historical Society of North Dakota, filmed by the society, 12 rolls, available on interlibrary loan. (Film not available at the FHL). 50 of the 56 northern counties that existed in 1885 are extant. See also *Dakota Territorial Census of 1885: From the Original Records on File at Bismarck, N.D.*, in *North Dakota Historical Quarterly*, Vol. 4 (1913), pages 338-448. Information includes name, sex, age, relationship to head of family, occupation, birthplace, father's birth-place, and mother's birthplace. Census returns for the North Dakota counties of Allred, Bowman, Buford, Dunn, McIntosh, McKenzie, Mercer, Mountraille, Oliver, Renville, Stanton, Towner, Villard, Wallace, Ward, Wells and Wynn. (Note that this is only 17 of the 50 ND counties that have survived). See also *North Dakota 1885 Census Index*, edited by Ronald Vern Jackson, published by Accelerated Indexing Systems, Bountiful, UT, 1982, 61 pages, FHL book 978.4 X22j 1885. It is not clear whether this index was prepared from the 50 original counties at the SHSND archives, or from the 12 counties identified in the NDHSQ extract.

■ **1885 Dakota Territory Census (North Dakota Counties)**, published indexes by county. A division of work between the North Dakota Institute for Regional Studies, North Dakota State University, Fargo, North Dakota, (NDIRS), and the Bismarck-Mandan Historical and Genealogical Society, Bismarck, (B-MHGS). These countywide indexes were used to input the electronic database now online. The individual books produced are all available at the FHL in Salt Lake City:

- Barnes County, by NDIRS, FHL book 978.432 X22s and FHL film #2055549.
- Benson County, by B-MHGS, FHL book 978.439 X22b, and FHL film #1425174.
- Billings County, by B-MHGS, FHL book 978.494 X22b.
- Burleigh County, by B-MHGS, FHL book 978.494 X22b and FHL film #2055286.
- Cass County, by NDIRS, FHL book 978.432 X22s.
- Dickey County, by B-MHGS, FHL book 978.454 X22b.
- Emmons County, by B-MHGS, FHL book 978.447 X22b.
- Fargo (city), by NDIRS, FHL book 978.413/F1 X22s.
- Griggs County (with Steele Co.), by NDIRS, FHL book 978.433 X22s.
- Kidder County, by B-MHGS, FHL book 978.457 X22b.
- La Moure County, by B-MHGS, FHL book 978.453 X22b.
- Logan County, by B-MHGS, FHL book 978.456 X22b.
- McLean County, by B-MHGS, FHL book 978.475 X22b.
- Morton County, by B-MHGS, FHL book 978.485 X22b.
- Nelson County (with Ramsey Co.), by NDIRS, FHL book 978.435 X22b.
- Ramsey County (with Nelson Co.), by NDIRS, FHL book 978.435 X22b.
- Richland County, by NDIRS, FHL book 978.412 X22s.
- Rolette County, by B-MHGS, FHL book 978.4592 X22b.
- Stark County, by B-MHGS, FHL book 978.4844 X22b.
- Steele County (with Griggs Co.), by NDIRS, FHL book 978.433.X22s.
- Traill County, by NDIRS, FHL book 978.414 X22b.

■ **1915 North Dakota State Census Schedules**, microfilm of original records at the State Historical Society of North Dakota, Bismarck. Filmed by the society, 19??. FHL has 25 rolls, no circulation to family history centers. Contents:

- Adams County, FHL film #1731408.
- Benson County, FHL film #1731409.
- Bottineau, Bowman, & Burke counties, FHL film #1731410.
- Burleigh & Cass (part), FHL film #1731411.
- Cass (part) & Cavalier (part), FHL film #1731412.
- Cavalier (part), Dickey, & Divide (part), FHL film #1731413.
- Divide (part), Dunn & Emmons counties, FHL film #1731414.
- Foster, Golden Valley counties; & Grand Forks City (part), FHL film #1731415.
- Grand Forks City (part), Griggs County, Hettinger County (part), FHL film #1731416.
- Hettinger (part), Kidder & La Moure counties, FHL film #1731417.
- Logan, McHenry counties, & McIntosh (school dist. #1), FHL film #1731418.
- McIntosh (school dist. #2), McKenzie & McLean county (part), FHL film #1731419.
- McLean County (part), Mercer & Morton County (part), FHL film #1731420.
- Morton County (part) & Mountrail County (part), FHL film #1731421.
- Mountrail County (part), Nelson & Oliver County, FHL film #1731422.
- Pembina, Pierce, & Ramsey County (part), FHL film #1731423.
- Ramsey County (part), Ransom & Renville County (part), FHL film #1731424.
- Renville County (part), Richland & Rolette County (part), FHL film #1731425.
- Rolette County (part), Sargent & Sheridan counties, FHL film #1731426.
- Sioux, Slope, & Stark counties, FHL film #1731427.
- Steele & Stutsman County (part), FHL film #1731428.
- Stutsman County (part), Towner, & Traill County (part), FHL film #1731429.
- Traill County (part), Walsh & Ward County (part), FHL film #1731430.
- Ward County (H-W) Wells County (part), FHL film #1731431.
- Wells County (part), & Williams County, FHL film #1731432.

■ **1915 North Dakota State Census, Bottineau County, Blaine Twp.**, in *North Central North Dakota Genealogical Record*, No. 84 (Sep 2000).

■ **1915 North Dakota State Census, Burke County**, in *North Central North Dakota Genealogical Record*, Vol. 1, (Nov 1983).

■ **1915 North Dakota State Census, Mountrail County**, in *North Central North Dakota Genealogical Record*, No. 82, (Mar 2000); and Mar 2001.

■ **1917-1918 Civilian Draft Registrations**, see *North Dakota, World War I Selective Service System Draft Registration Cards, 1917-1918*, microfilm of original records at the National Archives in East Point, Georgia. The draft cards are arranged alphabetically by state, then alphabetically by county or city, and then alphabetically by surname of registrants. Filmed by the National Archives, 1987-1988, 30 rolls, beginning with FHL film #1819402 (Adams Co., A-Z; Barnes Co., A-S).

■ **1917-1918 North Dakota Military List**. See *Roster of the Men and Women Who Served in the Army or Naval Service Including the Marine Corps, or the United States or its Allies From the State of North Dakota in the World War, 1917-1918*, prepared and published under the direction of Brigadier General G. Angus Fraser, Legislative Assembly of North Dakota, printed by Bismarck Tribune Co., Bismarck, ND, 1931, 4 vols. Contents: vol. 1: Asberg to Flagg; vol. 2: Flagg to Lark; vol. 3: Larkee to Rice; and vol. 4: Rich to Zygmond. FHL book 978.4 M23a v. 1-4, and FHL film #982257 (vols. 1-2) and 982258 (vols. 3-4).

■ **1925 North Dakota State Census Schedules**, microfilm of original records filmed by the State Historical Society in Bismarck, North Dakota. FHL has 16 rolls, no circulation to family history centers. Contents:
- Adams, Barnes, Benson, Billings counties, FHL film #1731393.
- Bottineau, Bowman, Burke, Burleigh counties, FHL film #1731394 (another copy, FHL film #1433999).
- Bismarck (city), Cass County & Fargo (city), FHL film #1731395.
- Fargo (city), Cass, Cavalier, Dickey & Divide counties, FHL film #1731396.
- Divide, Dunn, Eddy, Emmons, Foster & Golden Valley counties, FHL film #1731397.
- Grand Forks, Grant & Griggs counties, FHL film #1731398.
- Hettinger, Kidder, La Moure, Logan & McHenry counties, FHL film #1731399.
- McHenry, McIntosh, McKenzie & McLean counties, FHL film #1731400.
- Mercer, Morton, Mountrail & Nelson counties, FHL film #1731401.
- Oliver, Pembina, Pierce & Ramsey counties, FHL film #1731402.
- Ransom, Renville, Richland & Rolette counties, FHL film #1731403.
- Sargent, Sheridan, Sioux, Slope, Stark & Steele counties, FHL film #1731404.
- Stutsman, Towner & Traill counties, FHL film #1731405.
- Walsh & Ward counties, FHL film #1731406.
- Wells & Williams counties, Fort Berthold (McLean County) & Devil's Lake Sioux Reservation. Includes list of townships with population in each county, FHL film #1731407.

North Dakota Censuses & Substitutes Online

■ **Online Index – 1885 Dakota Territory Census (North Dakota Counties)**. This is a searchable index sponsored by the Institute for Regional Studies, North Dakota State University, Fargo, ND. Schedules have survived for fifty of the fifty-six counties which existed in the northern half of Dakota Territory. All fifty counties are now indexed and contained in this database. The missing county schedules include Boreham, DeSmet, Flannery, Hettinger, Sheridan, and Stevens. Go to the following website: **www.lib.ndsu.nodak.edu/ndirs/databases/census.php.**

■ **North Dakota Censuses & Substitutes Online**. The following databases are available online at these sites:

www.ancestry.com

- 1850-1880 Mortality Schedules &Index
- 1870-1890 Census Indexes (AIS)
- 1885-1940 Indian Census Schedules
- 1890 Veterans Schedules
- 1889-1892 Grand Forks, North Dakota Directories
- 1900 Federal Census
- 1910 Federal Census
- 1915 North Dakota State Census
- 1920 Federal Census
- 1925 North Dakota State Census
- 1930 Federal Census
- American Soldiers of World War I
- 1994 Phone and Address Directory
- 2000 Phone and Address Directory

www.censusfinder.com

- North Dakota Statewide Census Records Online:
- 1870-1890 North Dakota Census Records at Ancestry
- 1860 Federal Census Images of Entire Dakota Territory (Unorganized Dakota)
- 1880 Norwegians in Dakota Territory
- 1880 Federal Census Records – Images
- 1880 Federal Census Records Search at Family Search
- 1885 Dakota Territory Census Records
- North Dakota State Databases of Census & Genealogy Records

www.census-online.com

Countywide census databases (No. of databases):
Adams (0); Barnes (5); Benson (1); Billings (2); Bottineau (1); Bowman (0); Burke (0); Burleigh (2); Cass (4); Cavalier (4); Dickey (25); Divide (0); Dunn (0); Eddy (1); Emmons (6); Foster (2); Golden Valley (0); Grand Forks (2); Grant (0); Griggs (1); Hettinger (0); Kidder (2); La Moure (2); Logan (1); McHenry (1); McIntosh (1); McKenzie (1); McLean (1); Mercer (3); Morton (7); Mountrail (1); Nelson (3); Oliver (1); Pembina (4); Pierce (1); Ramsey (2); Ransom (2); Renville (1); Richland (4); Rolette (1); Sargent (1); Sheridan (0); Sioux (1); Slope (8); Stark (3); Steele (2); Stutsman (2); Towner (3); Traill (2); Walsh (4); Ward (1); Wells (1); and Williams (1).

SOUTH DAKOTA

Censuses & Substitutes, 1885-1945

Censuses for the state of South Dakota begin with the Dakota Territory census of 1885, which was divided by northern and southern counties, the originals for the southern portion located at the South Dakota State Historical Society (SDSHS) in Pierre.

South Dakota became a state in 1889. In 1895, the state began taking state censuses, which continued every ten years until the last one in 1945. The 1895 state census was taken with a format similar to the 1885 Dakota Territory census. Unfortunately, only six counties for the census of 1895 have survived.

All subsequent state censuses are virtually complete, the originals located at the SDSHS. The 1905, 1915, 1925, 1935, and 1945 censuses were all tabulations compiled on 3" x 5" index cards, one card per person giving a full name and detailed personal information for each. (Those from 1915 forward give the maiden name of a wife, if the person were married). The ingenious South Dakotans made use of college and high school students to take their censuses, using sortable index cards for each person enumerated. The cards were then arranged in alphabetical order by surname for the entire state, which is how the censuses are still organized and stored today at the SDSHS archives. (One wonders if the person in charge of the South Dakota state censuses was a *genealogist*).

The surviving South Dakota census schedules for 1885 and 1895 were microfilmed by the SDSHS in 1971, and copies are available at the Family History Library in Salt Lake City. The state censuses 1905-1945 were microfilmed 2002-

2004 by the Genealogical Society of Utah for the Family History Library. South Dakota censuses and substitutes are identified below:

■ **1885 Dakota Territory Census**, microfilm of original records (for southern Dakota Territory counties) at the South Dakota State Historical Society in Pierre, South Dakota. Most of the 1895 Census has been lost or destroyed. The only known county schedules are for Beadle, Brule, Charles Mix, Edmunds, Fall River, Faulk, Hand, Hanson, Hutchinson, Hyde, Lake, Lincoln, Marshall, McPherson, Moody, Roberts, Sanborn, Spink, Stanley, and Turner counties. Filmed by the SDSHS in 1971, 2 rolls at the FHL, as follows:
- Beadle, Butte, Charles Mix, Edmunds, Fall River, Faulk, Hand, Hanson, Hutchinson and Hyde Counties, FHL film #1405268.
- Lake, Lincoln, Marshall, McPherson, Moody, Roberts, Sanborn, Spink, Stanley and Turner Counties, FHL film #1405269.

The above surviving schedules were indexed in *South Dakota 1885 Census Index*, compiled by Ronald Vern Jackson, Scott D. Rosenkilde, and W. David Samuelsen, published by Accelerated Indexing Systems, 1984, 296 pages. FHL book 978.3 X22j.

■ **1890 Federal Census, Population Schedules, Jefferson Township, Union County, South Dakota**, microfilm of original records in the National Archives at Washington, D.C. Most of the 1890 population schedules were so badly damaged by fire in the Commerce Department Building in January 1921 that they were disposed of. Only a few schedules are extant. Included on the microfilm are the surviving names from Jefferson Township, Union County, South Dakota on FHL film # 926499.

■ **1895 South Dakota State Census**, microfilm of originals located at the South Dakota State Historical Society in Pierre, South Dakota, filmed by the society, 1971, 1 roll. FHL title: *Partial South Dakota 1895 Census Population Schedules*. Most of the 1895 schedules were destroyed. Surviving

counties: Beadle, Brule, Pratt, Presho, Campbell and Charles Mix counties. See FHL film #1405183.

■ **1905 South Dakota State Census**, microfilm of original records at the South Dakota State Historical Society in Pierre, South Dakota. Consists of cards containing statistical data for all individuals enumerated in the state. The cards are arranged alphabetically by surname. The last name on each roll is repeated as the first name on the next roll. Information given includes the individual's name, address, age, sex, color, nationality, occupation, ability to read and write, whether blind, deaf and dumb, idiotic or insane, place of birth, years in South Dakota, years in United States, birthplace of father and birthplace of mother. Filmed by the Genealogical Society of Utah, 2002, 125 rolls, beginning with FHL film #2139869 (Aaberg, Albert – Aldous, William).

■ **1915 South Dakota State Census**, microfilm of original records at the South Dakota Historical Society in Pierre. Consists of cards containing statistical data for all individuals enumerated in the state. The cards are arranged in alphabetical order. The cards for the last name on each roll are filmed again at the beginning of the next roll. Each person's card includes: county; post office where person received mail; township name; if in a city, city name; ward; age; occupation; owner or renter of residence; place of birth; ancestry; years living in SD; years living in US; birthplace of father and birthplace of mother; extent of education and whether a graduate; military service, including wars fought, state of service, company, regiment; marital status; maiden name of wife; year married; church affiliation; sex; ethnicity (color); and marital status; whether the person could read and write; whether blind, deaf, idiotic, or insane; naturalized, if foreign born; and the name of the Enumerator. Filmed by the Genealogical Society of Utah, 2002, 182 rolls, beginning with FHL film #2283045 (Aaberg, Agnes - Akre, Emma).

■ **1925 South Dakota State Census**, microfilm of original records at the South Dakota State Historical Society in Pierre. Consists of cards containing statistical data for all individuals enumerated in the state. The cards are arranged alphabetically by surname. The last name on each roll is repeated as the first name on the next roll. Each card contains: name of person, county, post office where person received mail; town or township name (if in a town, ward number); person's age, occupation, whether owner or renter, place of birth, years living in SD, years living in US; if foreign born, whether naturalized; birthplace of father and birthplace of mother; extent of education; military service, including wars fought, state, company, regiment, and division; marital status, maiden name of wife, year married, church affiliation; sex, ethnicity (color); Misc. (read, write, blind, deaf, idiotic, insane); and the name of the Enumerator. Filmed by the Genealogical Society of Utah, 2003, 213 rolls, beginning with FHL film #2368063 (Aabelson, Magnus - Afrank, Mollie).

■ **1935 South Dakota State Census**, microfilm of original records at the South Dakota State Historical Society in Pierre. Consists of cards containing statistical data for all individuals enumerated in the state. The cards are arranged alphabetically by surname. The last name on each roll is repeated as the first name on the next roll. Each card contains: name of person, county, post office where person received mail; town or township name (if in a town, ward number); person's age, occupation, whether owner or renter, place of birth, years living in SD, years living in US; if foreign born, whether naturalized; birthplace of father and birthplace of mother; extent of education; military service, including wars fought, state, company, regiment, and division; marital status, maiden name of wife, year married, church affiliation; sex, ethnicity (color); Misc. (read, write, blind, deaf, idiotic,

insane); and the name of the Enumerator. Filmed by the Genealogical Society of Utah, 2003, 733 rolls, beginning with FHL film #2369161 (Aaberg, Adoph – Adolph, Ina).

■ **1945 South Dakota State Census**, microfilm of original records located at the South Dakota State Historical Society, Pierre, SD. Consists of cards containing statistical data for all individuals enumerated in the state. The cards are arranged alphabetically by surname. The last name on each roll is repeated as the first name on the next roll. Each card contains: name of person, county, post office where person received mail; town or township name (if in a town, ward number); person's age, occupation, whether owner or renter, place of birth, years living in SD, years living in US; if foreign born, whether naturalized; birthplace of father and birthplace of mother; extent of education; military service, including wars fought, state, company, regiment, and division; marital status, maiden name of wife, year married, church affiliation; sex, ethnicity (color); Misc. (read, write, blind, deaf, idiotic, insane); and the name of the Enumerator. The 1945 census cards were microfilmed by the Genealogical Society of Utah, completed in late 2004, 193 rolls, beginning with FHL film #2370848.

South Dakota Censuses & Substitutes Online

■ **South Dakota Censuses & Substitutes Online**. The following databases are available online at these sites:
www.ancestry.com
- 1850-1880 Mortality Schedules &Index
- 1870-1890 Census Indexes (AIS)
- 1885 Territorial Census
- 1885-1940 Indian Census Schedules
- 1890 Veterans Schedules
- 1895 South Dakota State Census

- 1900 Federal Census
- 1910 Federal Census
- 1920 Federal Census
- 1930 Federal Census

www.censusfinder.com

- South Dakota Statewide Census Records Online:
- 1870-1890 South Dakota Census (AIS) Records at Ancestry
- 1860 Federal Census Images of Entire Dakota Territory (Unorganized Dakota)
- 1880 Norwegians in Dakota Territory
- 1880 Federal Census Records – Images
- 1880 Federal Census Records Search at Family Search
- 1885 Dakota Territory Census Records
- South Dakota State Databases of Census & Genealogy Records

www.census-online.com

Countywide census databases (No. of databases):
Aurora (3); Beadle (2); Bennett (0); Bon Homme (3); (0); Campbell (2); Charles Mix (1); Clark (2); Clay (2); Codington (1); Corson (0); Custer (0); Davison (1); Day (1); Deuel (3); Dewey (0); Douglas (1); Edmunds (1); Fall River (1); Faulk (2); Grant (1); Gregory (0); Haakon (0); Hamlin (0); Hand (0); Hanson (0); Harding (0); Hughes (7); Hutchinson (0); Hyde (0); Jackson (0); Jayne (1); Jerauld (0); Jones (0); Kingsbury (0); Lake (0); Lawrence (0); Lincoln (1); Lyman (1); Marshall (4); McCook (0); McPherson (2); Meade (0); Mellette (3); Miner (0); Minnehaha (1); Moody (0); Pennington (0); Perkins (0); Potter (0); Roberts (0); Sanborn (0); Shannon (1); Spink (0); Stanley (1); Sully (1); Todd (1); Tripp (0); Turner (0); Union (0); Walworth (3); Yankton (1); and Ziebach (0).